MORE THAN CONQUERORS

Copyright © 1992 The Moody Bible
Institute of Chicago

Library of Congress Cataloging-in-
Publication Data

More than conquerors: portraits of
believers from all walks of life/
  John D. Woodbridge, general
editor.
  360pp. 68 ch.
  Includes bibliographical references
and index.
  ISBN 0-8024-9054-9
  1. Christian biography.
I. Woodbridge, John D., 1941-
BR1700.2.M655 1992
209'.2'2--dc20
[B]   92-13318
                  CIP

Designed and produced for
Moody Press by
Three's Company,
12 Flitcroft Street,
London WC2H 8DJ

Editor: Tim Dowley

Designer: Peter Wyart

Worldwide co-edition organized
and produced by
Angus Hudson Ltd,
Mill Hill,
London NW7 3SA

Printed in England by BPCC Hazells
Ltd

Moody Press, a ministry of the
Moody Bible Institute, is designed for
education, evangelization, and edification. If we may assist you in knowing more about Christ and the
Christian life, please write us without
obligation: Moody Press, c/o MLM,
Chicago, Illinois 60610, U.S.A.
1 2 3 4 5 95 94 93 92

MORE THAN
Conquerors

Contents

Preachers

Sport & Entertainment

Reformers

Student Work

Thinkers

Industry & Commerce

Index

Authors

Batson, Beatrice
Professor, Wheaton, Illinois.
Fyodor Dostoievski

Bebbington, David
Lecturer in History, Stirling,
Scotland.
William Wilberforce

Bendroth, Margaret
Professor, Cambridge,
Massachusetts.
Amy Carmichael,
Jeremiah Lanphier,
Harriet Beecher Stowe

Boyd, Jonathan
Historian, Baltimore,
Maryland.
Eric Liddell

Bright, William (Bill)
Evangelist and Christian
Leader, Orlando, Florida.
Joon Gon Kim

Chesebrough, David
Professor, Bloomington,
Illinois.
"Stonewall" Jackson

Cooper, Dale
Chaplain, Grand Rapids,
Michigan.
Brother Roger of Taizé

Coutts, John
Writer, Gravesend, Kent,
England.
Thomas Barnardo,
William Booth

Dallimore, Arnold
Pastor and writer, Cottam,
Ontario, Canada.
C. H. Spurgeon

Davey, Cyril
Pastor and writer, Bristol,
England.
Sadhu Sundar Singh

Davis, Willard
Pastor and historian,
Washington, D.C.
Abraham Lincoln

Dorsett, Lyle
Professor, Wheaton, Illinois.
George MacDonald

Durham, Ken
Writer, Colorado Springs,
Colorado.
R. G. LeTourneau

Erickson, Nancy
Professor, Due West, South
Carolina.
Mary Slessor

Estep, W. R.
Professor, Fort Worth, Texas.
Lottie Moon

Fisher, David
Writer, Wheaton, Illinois.
Henry F. Schaefer III

Flood, Robert
Writer, Olympia Fields,
Illinois.
J. C. Penney

Fuller, Harold
Missionary and writer,
Ontario, Canada.
Byang Kato

Gilliver, William
Writer and publisher, Sydney,
Australia.
Paul White

Glass, William
Professor, Beloit, Wisconsin.
John Wanamaker

Griffin, William
Writer and publisher, New
Orleans, Louisiana.
C. S. Lewis

Gunther, Peter
Writer and publisher,
Colorado Springs, Colorado.
Ken Taylor

Hannah, John
Professor, Dallas, Texas.
Billy Sunday

Hart, Daryl
Professor, Wheaton, Illinois.
J. Gresham Machen

Hogan, Samuel
Professor and pastor, South
Hamilton, Massachusetts.
John Jasper

Howard, David
Missionary and writer,
Singapore.
Jim Elliot

Jasper, Tony
Writer, London, England.
Cliff Richard

Jenkins, Jerry
Writer, Zion, Illinois.
Tom Landry,
Bobby Richardson

Johnson, Gwynne
Writer, Dallas, Texas.
Audrey Johnson

Johnson, Lin
Writer, Des Plains, Illinois.
Henrietta Mears

Keylock, Leslie R.
Professor and writer, Chicago,
Illinois.
Cyrus McCormick

Lanning, Raymond
Pastor, Coopersville,
Michigan.
Martyn Lloyd-Jones

Lawton, Kim
Writer and reporter,
Washington, D.C.
Elizabeth Dole

McKnight, Scot
Professor, Deerfield, Illinois.
Sir William Ramsay

Metzger, Will
Writer and student worker,
Newark, Delaware.
J. I. Packer

Nettles, Thomas
Professor, Deerfield, Illinois.
Robert E. Lee

Noll, Mark
Professor, Wheaton, Illinois.
Woodrow Wilson

O'Day, Joseph
Writer and editor, Chicago,
Illinois.
Charles Malik,
C. Stacey Woods

Pierard, Richard
Professor, Terre Haute,
Indiana.
John R. Mott,
Martin Niemöller

Pollock, John
Writer, South Molton, Devon,
England.
Lord Shaftesbury,
C. T. Studd,
J. Hudson Taylor

Ramey, Robert F.
Writer and editor, Chicago,
Illinois.
Billy Graham

Rhoton, Elaine
Writer, Mosbach, Germany.
Brother Andrew,
George Verwer

de Rosset, Rosalie
Professor, Chicago, Illinois.
A. W. Tozer

Sanford, David
Writer, Portland, Oregon.
Luis Palau

Senter, Mark
Professor, Deerfield, Illinois.
Torrey Johnson,
Dawson Trotman

Shelley, Bruce L.
Professor, Denver, Colorado.
Charles Fuller

Sidey, Ken
Writer and reporter, Carol
Stream, Illinois.
Bill Bright

Simms, Rupert
Professor, Chicago, Illinois.
George Washington Carver,
E. V. Hill

Stanislaw, Richard
Professor and college
administrator, Upland,
Indiana.
Fanny Crosby

Stewart, David
Pastor and writer, Auckland,
New Zealand.
Robert A. Laidlaw

Strom, Kay Marshal
Writer, Santa Barbara,
California.
Eugenia Price

Tucker, Ruth
Professor and writer, Grand
Rapids, Michigan.
John Sung,
Corrie Ten Boom

Vaughn, Ellen Santilli
Writer, Washington, D.C.
Chuck Colson

Vincent, James
Writer and editor, Chicago,
Illinois.
D. L. Moody

Woodbridge, John D.
Professor, Deerfield, Illinois.
Karen Johnson

Wyrtzen, David
Pastor and writer, Midlothian,
Texas.
Jack Wyrtzen

Introduction

The people of Rome in the first century of the Christian era had access to remarkable pageantry. Parades and festivals welcomed home triumphant generals who had won resounding victories in neighboring or distant imperial provinces. With drumbeats and pomp the parades undoubtedly inspired awe in many onlookers who craned their necks to get a glance at the city's latest hero. These conquering commanders were about the task of exacting submission to Roman will. The Roman military was then, and remained, a powerful force to be reckoned with.

The Apostle Paul apparently knew that the Christians at Rome to whom he addressed his epistle (what became the book of Romans) were quite familiar with the resplendent glory of the Roman Empire. After all, their church was located in the capital of that empire.

And yet Paul boldly proclaimed to these Christians: "We are more than conquerors through him who loved us." (Romans 8:37). What did he mean? How could persecuted Christians of the struggling, new church at Rome be "more than conquerors"? What could make them greater conquerors than Roman commanders who had just returned home with booty and trophies, all primed to receive the laurels and adulation of enthusiastic crowds for their exploits?

Christian triumph

Paul had earlier explained what the nature of a Christian triumph is. Christians are always victorious in the sense that they cannot be separated from the love of God. In fact, nothing or no one can separate those who are in Christ from that love.

The Apostle Paul listed specific foes that the believer through Christ vanquishes: tribulation, distress, persecution, famine, nakedness, peril, the sword, slaughter. No small list of defeated enemies. For twentieth-century Western Christians living in relative comfort, this list may not seem particularly applicable to their lives. They have never fallen victim to famine or to the sword. For Christians who have suffered persecution and loss, whether in the first century or the twentieth, it constitutes a list of very real enemies. For Roman Christians, Paul's words represented a message of comfort. Not many years after they received Paul's letter, some of

Titus' Arch, Rome, commemorates the Emperor's military triumph.

these same Christians apparently were set ablaze on wooden stakes while Nero, a cruel and treacherous Roman Emperor, drove his chariot among them leering and grimacing, without any sign of pity.

According to Paul, then, any Christian, found in Christ, is "more than a conqueror." The Christian may be put to death; or may die exhausted and worn out; or may be overlooked and despised; or may have experienced any of a thousand types of misery the human condition can amply dish out. And yet, even a jut-chinned Roman Emperor, clothed in purple and crushing garlands under foot, could never match the ultimate triumph of such a one as Jesus Christ. What a divine irony the apostle lays before us in this passage!

More than conquerors?

It is in this Pauline sense that we have described people in this book as "more than conquerors." By no secular standards would a number of these individuals qualify to be called "conquerors" if we mean by this expression "becoming number one," winning fame, sporting wealth, or wielding power. Indeed, some of the missionaries and evangelists described in this book were despised by those to whom they were presenting the gospel; they often found themselves financially destitute, and politically powerless. By contrast, others in this volume enjoyed worldwide prominence and wealth and traveled among the elite of this world. But from the perch of popularity and power, they stood out as witnesses for Christ, overcoming the temptations that often beset those to whom much has been given.

The Romans carry the menorah from Jerusalem in their triumphal procession.

The men and women and one teenager, then, whose stories grace this volume, step forth from various ranks of society: missionaries, a former slave, presidents of the United States, British politicians, preachers and evangelists, business persons, world-renowned writers, sports figures and entertainers, teachers, scientists, musicians, "reformers," pastors, and others. Timewise, they have lived in the nineteenth and twentieth centuries. Geographically speaking, they come from the four corners of the world (although a goodly proportion are North American and British). They belong to churches ranging from Anglican and Orthodox, to Baptist and Independent. Their ethnic and cultural backgrounds differ widely. However different they may be, these are people whose lives have here been brought together to celebrate their common commitment to the Lord Jesus Christ.

Role models

From reading their stories we may learn much about how to live the Christian life better. We humans are quite impressed by the role modeling of other persons we see around about us— for good or for ill. As Christians we are not immune from negative modeling. The values we see endorsed or flaunted by athletes, musicians and stars of popular culture, or by politicians and teachers may affect us in ways that wear down our own ethical and moral commitments, as well as reroute our life aspirations. On the other hand, we can be greatly encouraged to renew our faith commitments by carefully examining positive modeling.

To whom may we turn for better modeling if we are disappointed with the values often propagated in the culture at large? Obviously, the Christian's foremost model is Jesus Christ Himself. The author of the

Epistle to the Hebrews gives us the good counsel to keep our eyes fixed upon Him: "... let us throw off everything that hinders and the sin that so easily entangles, and let us run with perseverance the race marked out for us." (Hebrews 12:1b–2). The same author also provides us with a set of role models to reflect upon in his list of men and women of faith: Abel, Noah, Abraham, Moses, Rahab, David, and others. These biblical characters, despite their many weaknesses, triumphed over enormous adversities through their faith (Hebrews 11).

Godly living

Throughout the history of the church, believers have looked to the lives of other Christians for examples of "authentic" godly living. The Christians of the early church have often been cited as believers who were willing to follow their Lord, even to martyrdom. In his very insightful book *Pia desideria* (1675), the German Phillip Spener encouraged his readers to church renewal by reminding them that the same power of the Holy Spirit that gave determination and resolution to the early church was as readily available to Christians of his own day:

Histories of the church testify that the early Christian Church was in such a blessed state that as a rule Christians could be identified by their godly life, which distinguished them from other people.... The condition of the early Christian church puts our hot-and-cold condition to shame. At the same time it demonstrates that what we are seeking is not impossible, as many imagine.... It is the same Holy Spirit who is bestowed on us by God who once effected all things in the early Christians, and he is neither less active today to accomplish the work of sanctification in us. If this does not happen, the sole reason must be that we do not allow, but rather hinder, the Holy Spirit's work.*

By reviewing the achievements of the early Christians through the Holy Spirit's power, Spener hoped to inspire contemporary Christians to rely on the Holy Spirit as well.

Looking to the lives of other Christians for role modeling can be, therefore, very inspiring and instructive. But we must be careful that we do not turn these Christians into "superstars" who never succumbed to temptations and who never experienced failure of any kind. Every Christian encounters difficulties and heartaches in this pilgrimage called life. Even the early church had its own fair share of adherents who became apostates, or who were unable to resist the allure of egoism, materialism, or sexual impurity.

"Warts and all"

In this particular book we are focusing on more recent Christians. We have asked our authors to write about their subjects in a realistic manner, that is, "warts and all." The writers were requested to describe the person in terms of the individual's spirituality as honestly as possible. If we are to benefit from the way other Christians have lived, it is of paramount importance that we have accurate assessments of the ways in which these people faced the kinds of adversities and temptations we ourselves confront. Little is gained by sheltering us from their weaknesses. We felt it was essential to achieve a realism, whilst not pandering to revelations of a sensational nature.

The verbal portraits drawn by our authors, then, are more than traditional biographies. When possible, the writers have attempted to discover what was the nature of the faith that made these people think and act the way they did or do. What principles did they follow? How did they overcome bouts of discouragement, genuine setbacks, or nagging temptations? How did they handle the surprising burden that financial success or popularity often bring to a person's life? Studying the stories recounted in this book may help us to understand the Christian life better.

A rich mix

The process of choosing which persons should be included in these pages was a complex one. Dr. Tim Dowley, of Three's Company, London, England, drew up an initial list of potential subjects. At a planning meeting held at Moody Press, Dr. Dowley and his associates, members of the staff at Moody Press, and the editor modified the list by either adding to or subtracting names from it. Participants at the meeting aimed to select men and women from various walks of life and from different nationalities. As the project developed, other names were added or subtracted at the suggestion of colleagues. Moreover, a mix of individuals was sought: on the one hand, those who are more familiar to the Christian public, and on the other, those who are relatively unknown to others.

Those of us working on the project quickly became aware of the fact that there are stories of literally thousands of people whose lives deserve to be told just as much as the stories of those written about in this volume. We encountered the staggering but wonderful reality that during the period from 1800 to the present day, there have been millions of Christians throughout the world who have loved and served the Lord faithfully and have been "more than conquerors." See in this way, the arbitrary character of our own selection process became all the more apparent to us. Moreover, we became aware that a number of the individuals whose names were suggested did not share all of the same evangelical convictions that many of us hold dear.

A special word of thanks should be given to the accomplished authors from several lands who so graciously agreed to contribute essays to this volume. Whatever merits this book might possess belong to them. Also, special thanks should be expressed to Kristine Boyd, the general editor's secretary. Her enthusiasm for this project and her tireless efforts in tackling the myriad details associated with its realization are greatly appreciated.

Common traits

One remaining question needs to be addressed. Do any common traits characterize the lives of the Christians discussed in this book? In one sense each of us as readers will probably recognize a list of traits slightly different from the lists others would propose. But a potential list might run like this.

A number of these individuals seem to have struggled in their Christian walk until they gave up trying to orchestrate their own lives. After they "let go" and trusted God to do with their lives whatever He wanted, they discovered greater peace and their ministries blossomed more fully. Many experienced rounds of truly enervating self-doubt and despair before seeing the Lord work in power in their particular difficult circumstances. A great number took on challenges that from a human point of view were simply impossible. Their confidence in the Lord's power and grace was so strong that they brushed off criticisms of naysayers. Most of these individuals viewed prayer as an indispensable source of spiritual power for their ministries. Many of them loved the Word of God. They relied upon it as a lamp to their feet and a light to their path. A number who were raised in Christian homes did not commit themselves to the Lord until they were adults; Abraham Lincoln did not do so until the very end of his life. Many of these individuals were genuinely humble; they did not seek to impress others with their accomplishments but freely and sincerely gave away any glory to the Lord. Perhaps the most common characteristic running through their lives is the seriousness of their commitment to the Lord Jesus whom they loved. These were not "Sunday" Christians who paraded their Christianity as a matter of social convention. Most of them were deadly serious; they wanted to love the Lord their God with all their hearts, souls, and minds, and their neighbors as themselves.

As the editor of this book, on occasion I have been deeply moved by reading the essays that the authors sent to my desk. To get to know those whose stories fill this book, even through the veiled medium of words, is like meeting new friends who have much to teach us about the Lord they knew, or know, very well. Many of their stories deserve to be told again and again, for their Christian role modeling, even if described from the "warts and all" perspective, has been exemplary. We would do well to consider much of it worthy of imitation.

John D. Woodbridge

---

*Theodore Tappert (ed.), Philadelphia: Fortress Press, 1980.

Politics & Public Life

ABRAHAM LINCOLN

Savior of a Nation

N ever before in the nation's history had there been so *unusual a time!* A man had been elected president though not even appearing on the ballot in ten states! Even before arriving in Washington, every mail delivery brought more death threats and ominous warnings. Close friends advised that he resign before taking the oath of office! A plot to assassinate the president-elect had been uncovered forcing the last leg of his trip to Washington to be in the dead of night, without family, under heavy guard, and incognito!

Never before had a President elect faced so *unusual a task!* Six states had already seceded from the Union before the inauguration! A secessionist government had been established, large quantities of munitions were on their way to Confederate forts, a siege on the City of Washington had been plotted! Disunity reigned ... hatred and distrust abounded... the North against the South, friend against friend, and brother against brother!

But, never before had so *unusual a man* been elected President of the United States!

The ugliest man in the world
A tall, gaunt, strange-looking man stood looking in a mirror. With arms and legs totally out of proportion to his torso, a face that resembled a rutabaga, shrivelled skin, hair that was absolutely rebellious and ears that seemed to "flap in the wind," he at last exclaimed aloud to himself, "It's true, Abe Lincoln, you are the ugliest man in the world. If I ever see a man uglier than you, I'm going to shoot him on the spot!"

Who was this grotesque individual destined to become the sixteenth president of the United States? After a span of one hundred and twenty-five years since his death, and in the wake of more than ten thousand books describing his life and times, many Americans still ask that very question, and still seek to fathom the complexities that comprised this "man who belongs to the ages."

Nominated only narrowly on

the fourth ballot by a seriously divided Republican Party, and elected with less than a 40 percent popular vote by his countrymen, in 1861 he became the president of a nation hopelessly torn by bitter disunity.

Log-cabin childhood

A personal trek to greatness from the depths of insignificance, and the overcoming of tremendous obstacles along the way to success is a familiar tale in America. But one would be hard-pressed to discover a rise to greatness from a more wretched origin than is chronicled in the life of Abe Lincoln. Recent research has shown that his father, Thomas Lincoln, was not the improvident, irresponsible and indolent parent to young Abe that early biographers have suggested. Nevertheless, the dirt-floor, one-room cabin long associated with Lincoln is not apocryphal, and well depicts the stark poverty, dearth of cultural refinement, and sheer difficulty of life that surrounded Lincoln as a young boy.

And yet, little Abe Lincoln was well blessed and enriched by a religious heritage that would shape his life and prepare him for one of the most monumental tasks of all history. Nancy Lincoln created a religious atmosphere in that cabin home, and spent Sunday afternoons often with Abe upon her knee reading to him from the family Bible,

President Abraham Lincoln (1809–65).

THE LIFE OF

Abraham Lincoln

1809	Born in Hardin County, Kentucky
1818	Death of mother
1831	Defeated for Illinois State Legislature
1834	Elected to State Legislature
1835	Death of fiancée, Anne Rutledge
1842	Marries Mary Todd
1843	Defeated for United States Congress
1846	Elected to U.S. Congress
1848	Defeated for Reelection to U.S. Congress
1855	Defeated for U.S. Senate
1856	Defeated for U.S. Vice Presidential nomination
1858	Defeated for U.S. Senate
1860	Becomes President of the United States
1863	Signs Emancipation Proclamation Delivers Gettysburg Address
1864	Elected to second presidential term
1865	Assassinated in Ford Theater, Washington, D.C., on April 14

and especially impressing upon him the Ten Commandments. Her last words to him when he was but nine years of age were, "Abe, I'm going to leave you now and I shall not return. I want you to be kind to your father and live as I have taught you. Love your heavenly Father and keep His commandments." Sarah Bush, who was to become Abe's stepmother, only served to reinforce the religious impact of his mother. She took Abe and his sister, Sarah, to the Pigeon Creek Hard Shell Baptist Church every Sunday. Sunday after Sunday young Abraham sat motionless and listened intently to the long, fiery orations of simple but devout prairie preachers as they expounded on predestination, the fear of the Lord, and the new birth.

It appears Tom Lincoln would have been content for Abe to have gained a "real 'eddication of readin', writin', and cipherin'," but the young man had an insatiable appetite for something far greater. Having learned to read and write in a one room "blab" school, a nine-mile walk from home, he began eagerly to devour every printed page that fell into his hand. He read and reread *Aesop's Fables*, *Robinson Crusoe*, *Pilgrim's Progress*, a short history of the United States, Weema's *Life of George Washington*, and, of course, the King James Version of the Bible.

"I'll hit it hard"

In part it was the thirst for knowledge that led Lincoln away from the prairie homestead, now moved to Illinois, and caused him as a flatbed hand to set sail for New Orleans. There Lincoln witnessed a scene that was to shape his heart and mind for a lifetime. In May 1831, for the first time, he encountered the horrors of a slave auction. He stood in silence while his heart bled and his resolve became forever fixed. William Herndon, his lifelong law partner, said, "Slavery ran the iron into him then and there, and bidding his companions follow him Lincoln said, 'By God, boys, let's get away from this. If I ever get a chance to hit that thing, I'll hit it hard.'"

Defeated in his first endeavor to seek a seat in the Illinois State Legislature in 1832, he won with an overwhelming plurality in 1834 the first of what would result in four successive terms. Persistence in his self-styled law study resulted in his

being formally admitted to the Illinois Bar on March 1, 1837. Soon after he moved to the new capital of Illinois, Springfield, on an invitation to become a law partner there. A few months later, he and several other lawyers attended a camp meeting on the outskirts of Springfield. A Bible preacher by the name of Rev. Dr. Peter Akers preached a sermon that night on the subject, "The Dominion of Jesus Christ."

The point of the sermon was that the dominion of Christ could not come in America until slavery would eventually be destroyed by civil war. "I am not a prophet, nor the son of a prophet," the preacher declared, "but I am a student of the prophets. As I read prophecy, American slavery will come to an end in some near decade. I think in the sixties...." After a graphic description of the war that was to come, he brought his sermon to a climactic end by exclaiming, "Who can tell but that the man who shall lead us through the strife may be standing in this presence!" Only a few feet away from him stood Lincoln, absorbed in every word. "Those words were from beyond the speaker..." Abe Lincoln quietly remarked, "The doctor has persuaded me that slavery will go down with the crash of a civil war." The next morning he said, "I am utterly unable to shake from myself the conviction that I shall be involved in that tragedy." Many were the epic moments in the shaping of Lincoln's life: this was certainly one of them.

Successful lawyer

Along with the growth of his reputation and influence as a politician, his law practice now escalated. His sense of truth and justice contributed a great deal to his effectiveness. His very appearance in a court of law came to cause judges and juries to presume that right was on his side!

In 1846 he was elected to the United States Congress, after a hard-fought campaign against Peter Cartright, the famed Methodist circuit rider. While the campaign was under way, Cartright's supporters proclaimed Lincoln to be an infidel. Lincoln waited until he had won the election before replying to the charge. In a handbill which was undiscovered until 1942, Lincoln responded, "That I am not a member of any Christian church is true; but I have never denied the truth of the Scriptures; and I have never spoken with intentional disrespect of religion in general...."

Returning to Springfield, a retired member of Congress after just one term, Lincoln's law practice now reached new heights of success. The Illinois Central Railroad retained him on a permanent basis, and Erasmus Corning of Albany, New York, president of the New York Central Railroad, also sought his services on a permanent basis. Corning introduced their first meeting with the statement: "I understand that in Illinois, you never lose a case." For all practical purposes, it appeared that Lincoln had withdrawn permanently from the political scene.

Fortunately for the nation, his time was but drawing near. In 1854 the slavery issue began to polarize the nation as nothing had ever done before, and God's purposes in Lincoln's life were about to unfold dramatically.

Portrait of Abraham Lincoln by Charles Wesley Jarvis, 1861.

Catapulted to fame

The Republican Party rather suddenly emerged, and Abe Lincoln found himself catapulted to national reputation as the most logical combatant to the famed pro-slavery senator, Stephen Arnold Douglas from Illinois. The Whigs strongly considered Lincoln for a Senate seat in 1854, and the first Republican national convention gave him respectable but unsuccessful support for the Vice Presidential nomination in 1856. But now, with Douglas's senatorial seat expiring in 1858, Lincoln seemed the natural opponent and was given the Republican Party nomination. In his acceptance speech he set the tone for what was to follow with the memorable and famous words: "A house divided against itself cannot stand. I believe the government cannot endure half slave and half free. I do not expect the Union to be dissolved... but I do expect it will cease to be divided."

The eyes of the nation were now turned upon the series of seven Lincoln–Douglas debates. On the surface, Lincoln was thought to have been no match for the distinguished Douglas, and in the early debates the press generally confirmed the presupposition. Yet, even the press changed its stance as the public was more and more impressed with the integrity, logic, and eloquence of Lincoln. One Easterner inquired, "Who is this man who is replying to Douglas from your State? Do you realize that no greater speeches have been made in the history of our country?... That his knowledge is profound, his logic unanswerable, his style inimitable?" Although Mr. Lincoln amassed a majority of votes on election day, under the apportionment law then in effect, it was Douglas who was declared the winner.

Lincoln experienced one of his bitterest moments. "It hurts too bad to laugh," he admitted, "and I am too big to cry." Recovering from his disappointment, Lincoln wrote to Dr. A. G. Henry, "I am glad I made the late race. It gave me a hearing on the great and durable question of the age which I would have had in no other way; and though I now sink out of view and shall be forgotten, I believe I have made some marks which shall tell for the cause of civil liberty long after I am gone."

"Mary, we've won!"
But by no means was he to "sink out of view." On the contrary, letters of congratulation and encouragement poured in from all over the nation, as well as invitations to speak! In only twelve months he addressed twenty-three major audiences and traveled four thousand miles. Party leaders instantly spoke of him as a potential pres-

idential candidate, and indeed when the heat died down from the 1860 Republican National Convention, Abraham Lincoln emerged as the winner of the party's presidential nomination!

"Mary, we've won!" had been the jubilant shout of Abe Lincoln to his wife on election night, November 6, 1860. But in the weeks that preceded his inauguration he was to discover that no man had ever assumed the Presidency of the United States surrounded by issues

> *"You may burn my body to ashes and scatter them to the winds of heaven. You may drag my soul down to the regions of darkness and despair. But you will never get me to support a measure which I believe is wrong."*

of the seriousness and gravity that confronted him!

Within six weeks following the election, there was dancing and fireworks in the streets of Charleston, South Carolina. South Carolina had seceded and declared a new "Declaration of Independence." Six other states would quickly follow, and two days before Lincoln left for Washington, Jefferson Davis was elected president of a newly formed nation!

For three months Lincoln was forced to sit idly by while the outgoing Buchanan administration, torn by disloyalty, did nothing to arrest the dissolving of the Union. Amid scores of threats on his life, countless

sleepless, distressed nights, the loss of forty pounds, and with the conviction that he would not return alive, the president-elect bade a tearful farewell to Springfield. On only two occasions did his voice become choked and tears fill his eyes as he spoke publicly; and this was one of them! "I now leave not knowing when or whether I may return, with a task before me greater than that which rested upon Washington. Without the assistance of the Divine Being who ever attended him, I cannot succeed. With that assistance, I cannot fail." For a most unusual task God had prepared a most unusual man. John Hay expressed the sentiments of many when he said, "I believe the hand of God placed him where he is."

The same John Hay, Lincoln's personal secretary, perhaps unwittingly expressed the distinctive qualities of leadership God had cultivated in Lincoln when he said of him, "There is no man in the country so wise, so gentle, and so firm." Lincoln was indeed firm: "You may burn my body to ashes and scatter them to the winds of heaven. You may drag my soul down to the regions of darkness and despair. But you will never get me to support a measure which I believe is wrong."

Save the Union!
Such firmness was revealed in less than forty-eight hours in the presidential chair! Lincoln traced America's democratic birthright right back to the Declaration of Independence and the founding fathers. He saw the Declaration as the cord

Abraham Lincoln with Pinkerton and John C.McClerland at Antietam.

hood friend, and his world had been devastated three years later by the death of his beloved sister, Sarah. In 1835, the death of his fiancée, Anne Rutledge, had been almost too much for him to bear. In his despair he said, "There is nothing to live for now," and for years visiting her grave seven miles outside New Salem, Illinois, was a Lincoln ritual.

The sadness that lifelong marked the features of Lincoln, and the melancholia that was characteristic of his personality, were thus only reinforced by the domestic sorrow that struck the Lincoln home at the height of his professional success, in 1850. Abraham and Mary's second son, Eddie, died after an illness of fifty-two days. They were inconsolable in their grief.

Beneath the firm, determined exterior was to be found now a tender, sensitive, gentle spirit, which was touched by the heartache of a nation in grave emotional crisis. He openly wept over the loss of both Union and Rebel lives, which, by the end of the War, were to number more than six hundred thousand. He frequently paced the floors by night, and was discovered one morning having spent the night with head in hands, grieving and praying for the nation he loved. Reading aloud Oliver Wendell Holmes's poem, "Lexington," to his friend Noah Brooks, "he came to the lines: 'Green be the grass where her martyrs are lying! Shroudless and tombless they sunk to their rest.' His voice quavered, he choked, and handing the volume back to Brooks he whispered, 'You read it; I can't.'"

Lincoln's profound wisdom, shown on an almost daily basis,

that bound the states in an indissoluble union. Secession was simply not an option to him, even in the face of contrary views, such as those held by influential Northerners: Harold Greeley, in a two-column article, bitterly attacked the president for his procrastination on the slavery issue. Lincoln responded firmly. "My paramount object in this struggle is to save the Union, and is not either to save nor to destroy slavery."

"Malice toward none" was very much more to Lincoln than

a poetic phrase incorporated in an address. It demonstrated the very sensitivity required to lead a broken, bleeding nation... a compassion born of a life of personal sorrow.

More tears

At the age of nine he had known the emptiness that comes to a sobbing child when his mother lies cold in death. He never forgot her, and often referred to her as his "angel mother." At sixteen he had been shattered by the insanity of a close boy-was evidenced in the stand he had taken regarding slavery. "If slavery is not wrong, nothing is wrong," he repeated on several occasions. Regardless of this, his presidential oath demanded that his first responsibility be to preserve the Union.

Freedom

He felt that in preserving the nation, slavery would be contained and would ultimately die a natural death. He reasoned that an ill-timed proclamation would alienate the border states, change the focus of the war, cause additional unrest in the North, and ultimately jeopardize the Union. But when the right time arrived, Lincoln solemnly announced to his Cabinet, "I made a solemn vow before God, that if General Lee was driven back from Pennsylvania, I would crown the result by the declaration of freedom to the slaves." This action caused deep bitterness in the South and much criticism in the North, yet it seemed to rally the Union, brought new hope to the Negro, and deterred European governments from aligning themselves with the Confederacy!

A crude cultural heritage and a meager formal education give no explanation for the wisdom evidenced in this one man. Within the context of his spiritual life was to be found the real secret of his wisdom, for "the fear of the Lord is the beginning of wisdom."

Even a cursory study of the life of Abraham Lincoln demonstrates that, even though he was not a conventional church member, he was a devout, God-fearing man. His biographies provide numerous accounts of his respect for deity, knowledge of and reverence for Scripture, and of his devotion to prayer. When the Civil War reached its darkest hour, he called for a "national day of fasting and prayer," and, after Gettysburg, it was he who proclaimed "a day of thanksgiving" which became an annual national event.

Most honest lawyer

That his childhood religious training, with its emphasis on the Ten Commandments, had a profound effect upon the life and character of the president is indisputable. He bore the title, "most honest lawyer east of China." On many occasions as a young lawyer he would remind an opponent of the points of his own argument. When in 1860 he took the oath of office, upholding the oath became for him a matter of personal integrity. When asked about his honesty, on a number of occasions he reminisced to his mother's voice, "Thou shalt not steal.... Thou shalt not bear false witness," and to her last words, "Love your heavenly Father, and keep His commandments."

But deep in Lincoln's heart, try as he might to keep God's Law, was his awareness of the reality that he fell far short of the glory of God. He knew it even as a boy as can be seen by the scribbling in his arithmetic book: "Abe Lincoln, his hand and pen, he will be good, but God knows when!" This little verse is witness to the guilt and self-condemnation that surrounded him the greater part of his life and especially during the war years. It is evidenced in his statement to a group of Baltimore clergymen: "I wish I were more pious."

For this one who was called the "most religious of all our presidents," for Abe Lincoln who had tried so valiantly to keep God's law, there was something his closest associates viewed as lacking. His personal bodyguard expressed it well when he said, "The misery that dripped from Lincoln as he walked was caused by his lack of personal faith." For all of his knowledge of Scripture and his association with the great ministers of his day, he failed, for the better part of his life, to comprehend that the salvation of the Lord is "not by works which we have done," and that it is "by grace ye are saved through faith, and that not of yourselves," effort and piousness notwithstanding.

Consecrated to Christ

It appears that the grace of God was to be understood by Lincoln and a personal relationship with the Savior established only after yet another private tragedy would compound his public sorrow. Tragedy was to make its presence known in the White House with the sudden death of little Willie, the Lincoln's youngest child, and the apple of the president's eye. In the hour of his inconsolable grief, Willie's nurse shared with the president her very personal relationship with Jesus Christ and encouraged him to know the Savior. Lincoln, by his own testimony, did not immediately respond, but some time later he related to a friend his new found peace. He said, "When I left Springfield, I asked the people to pray for me; I was not a Christian. When I buried my son—the severest trial of my life—I was not a Christian. But when I went to Gettysburg, and saw the graves of thousands of our soldiers, I then and there consecrated myself to Christ." With deep emotion he told his friends that he had at last found the peace for which he longed.

In the days that followed, Abe Lincoln worshiped regularly at New York Avenue Presbyterian Church, not only on Sunday, but at the Wednesday evening prayer service as well! Dr. Phineas Gurley, the godly pastor of the church, became the president's personal confidant, and relates the fact that. Lincoln had discussed with him his desire to make public his confession of faith and to unite in membership. Some months later, his second inaugural address was like the Gettysburg Address, a classic that reads like a sermon, with two complete verses of Scripture and fourteen references to God! But, within weeks the nation would mourn its tragic loss, and Abe Lincoln would dwell in the presence of the Christ whom he had now come to love and know so personally!

Palm Sunday 1865 was marked by rejoicing in the city streets of the North. General Robert E. Lee had surrendered at Appomattox, and to all intents and purposes the Civil War was over. The president gave thanks to God, and without a triumphal word, directed the attention of the nation to the task of reconstructing the South and to the healing of our Southern "brothers and sisters."

Five days later, on Good Friday, church bells began to peal in Washington, then in Philadelphia, then in New York City and across the nation; the president was dead! Even before he was buried, the president's name would be linked with Washington's. "Washington the father of the nation.... Lincoln the savior of the nation!"

Humble, self-effacing Abe Lincoln would have been very uncomfortable with the epithet of "savior" being attached in any manner to his name. Yet, the Union had been preserved, and God had used a most unusual man to accomplish His eternal purposes.

Further Reading

Basler, Roy P. *The Collected Works of Abraham Lincoln.* 7 vols. New Brunswick, N.J.: Rutgers U., 1953.

Owen, Frederick G. *Abraham Lincoln: the Man and His Faith.* Wheaton, Ill.: Tyndale, 1981.

Randall, J. G. *Lincoln The President: Last Full Measure.* New York: Dodd, Mead, 1955.

Sandburg, Carl. *Abraham Lincoln: The Prairie Years.* 2 vols. New York: Harcourt, Brace, 1926.

_____. *Abraham Lincoln: The War Years.* 4 vols. New York: Harcourt, Brace, 1939.

Like a stone wall

"Stonewall" Jackson is regarded as one of the outstanding tacticians in military history. His victories on the battlefield, as well as in his life in general, are an account of continually overcoming superior odds.

Because of a limited education in his early years, Jackson's dreams of entering West Point Military Academy seemed impossible. However, after he barely passed the entrance exams, he eventually graduated seventeenth in a class of fifty-nine cadets at the Point. He fought with distinction in the Mexican War, and during the 1850s he taught at Virginia Military Institute.

Standing firm

In 1861 Jackson joined the Confederate Army. At the first Battle of Bull Run (Manassas), he won his famous nickname when his brigade stood firm— "like a stone wall"—before a Union attack. Following Bull Run, Jackson rendered significant military leadership in battles where Confederate forces were greatly outnumbered.

In the Valley Campaign, Second Bull Run, Antietam, Fredericksburg, and Chancellorsville, Jackson defeated Federal troops whose combined strength was several times his own. Only in the Peninsular Campaign, due to physical exhaustion, was Jackson's performance ineffective. At Chancellorsville, after another brilliant victory, Jackson was wounded by gunfire from his own men, who mistook him for the enemy. When he died a few days later, chances of a Confederate victory died with him.

"Stonewall" Jackson

The General who Looked to God

Thomas Jonathan Jackson's interest in the Christian faith began in his early years. As a teenager, he would sometimes walk three miles on a Sunday to hear a sermon, and during those years he was regarded by many as a promising biblical scholar. In his early twenties, while participating in the Mexican War, he began a more serious spiritual pursuit. He made a careful study of the Roman Catholic faith, and although there was much that impressed him, as exemplified by Mexico's devout parishioners, he knew that a more simple faith was what he wanted.

There is no record of an abrupt or startling transformation in Jackson's life. Although the change was slow, almost imperceptible, it was decisive. In 1848, on Sunday April 29, Jackson publicly declared his faith by baptism at St. John's Episcopal Church in New York City, while he was stationed at Fort Hamilton, New York. Still unsure about which denomination he favored, he wanted it understood that he was not join-

> "Captain, my religious belief teaches me to feel as safe in battle as in bed. God has fixed the time for my death. I do not concern myself about that, but to always be ready, no matter when it may overtake me."

ing the Episcopal Church, he was committing his life to the "known will of God." It was a commitment he struggled to keep for the rest of his life.

Deacon Jackson

In 1851 Jackson began a ten-year term as an instructor at the Virginia Military Institute in Lexington. He was not a popular teacher at VMI. Most students regarded him as overly pious, rigid, and inflexible. He became the object of cadet pranks and derisive poetry. He joined the Presbyterian Church of the community after being assured by the pastor that he did not have to accept all points of Presbyterian theology. The sincerity and intensity of Jackson's spiritual devotion caused his fellow church members to feel that they were backsliders. He became a deacon in the church, and for the rest of his life he was often referred to as "Deacon Jackson." He also adopted a strict code of personal conduct. Dancing, theater-going, card playing, smoking, and drinking were eliminated from his life.

ous times throughout his life, Jackson owned slaves. Unlike some owners, however, he believed that blacks were human beings who had a right to be treated with kindness and respect. For Jackson, slaves were children of God with souls to be saved. In the autumn of 1855, Jackson began a Sunday school class for local blacks, most of whom were slaves. Initially, he taught the class himself. Later, while fighting with the Confederate Army, he sent back funds to assure the continuance of the class.

As safe in battle as in bed

In 1861 when Virginia seceded from the Union, Jackson resigned his commission in the United States Army in order to fight for the Confederacy. Though certain friends and a few family members urged him not to desert the Union, Jackson was convinced that the South's cause was God's cause. His military exploits on behalf of that cause are well known. The part played by his faith in his battlefield experiences and in his military life is less known.

Thomas "Stonewall" Jackson, from a contemporary print.

On August 4, 1853, he married Elinor Judkin. It was a beautiful relationship and Elinor was instrumental in cracking the shy and aloof wall her husband had built around his life. In October of the following year, Jackson's newly found joy turned to devastation when Elinor died in childbirth. His shield of faith had its first real test. Jackson reconsecrated himself to Christ. His belief in the providence of God assured him that there was a purpose in his loss and that lessons could be gained from his bereavement. He asserted that he could

suffer any misfortune if he were sure it was the will of God. More attention and time were given to matters of faith and duties in the church. Slowly but surely, the clouds began to part. In 1857 a new joy came to his life when he married Mary Anna Morrison. Both of his wives were daughters of Presbyterian ministers. Morning family prayers, with servants in attendance, were a daily feature in the Jackson household.

Jackson was not opposed to slavery. He believed the institution, for some unknown reason, was established by God. At vari-

Early on in the war, after Jackson had demonstrated extraordinary courage in battle, another officer asked him how he could remain so calm while shells and bullets rained about his head. Jackson, with a serious look, replied, "Captain, my religious belief teaches me to feel as safe in battle as in bed. God has fixed the time for my death. I do not concern myself about that, but to always be ready, no matter when it may overtake me." Then he added, "Captain, that is the way all men should live, and then all would be equally brave."

THE LIFE OF
"Stonewall" Jackson

1824	Born in Clarksburg, Virginia (now West Virginia)
1846	Graduates from West Point Begins participation in Mexican War
1849	Makes public profession of faith through baptism
1851	Becomes a professor at Virginia Military Institute Joins Presbyterian Church
1853	Marries Elinor Judkin
1857	Marries Mary Anna Morrison after death of first wife
1861	Joins the Confederate Army First Battle of Bull Run
1862	Leadership in Peninsular Campaign, Valley Campaign, Second Bull Run, Antietam, Fredericksburg, and other battles
1863	Fatally wounded in the Battle of Chancellorsville

"Stonewall" Jackson.

Jackson was a strong believer in the providence of God. God ordained war. God brought about battlefield victories and administered defeats. Therefore, when Jackson was victorious in battle, he always gave credit to God. Following the Second Battle of Bull Run, when someone suggested that victory had been achieved as a result of brave fighting, Jackson replied, "No, it has been won by nothing but the blessing and protection of Providence." After he had won yet another victory, he confided to a friend, "Without God's blessing I look for no success, and for every success my prayer is, that all glory may be given unto Him to whom it is properly due." He fought hard against the "sin of ambition."

Speaking to Heaven's King

Prayer played an essential role in Jackson's life and career. All who were associated with him knew that Jackson prayed passionately before making major decisions, and on the eve of battle he would arise several times during the night to ask for God's blessings and guidance. After hearing Jackson pray, one minister said, "He did not pray to men, but to God. He seemed to realize that he was speaking to Heaven's King."

Jackson regarded the ministry as life's highest calling. During the war years he would often invite pastors and chaplains of nearby churches to his tent to debates and discussions on biblical and theological matters. The general could more than hold his own in such conversations, and they seemed to exhilarate him. Jackson was also instrumental in establishing a chaplain's association to work with his troops. When selecting chaplains, he declared, "I would like to see no questions asked... as to what denomination a chaplain belongs, but let the question be, 'Does he preach the Gospel?'"

Jackson's seriousness about matters of faith, his emphasis upon religious observances, his opposition to Sunday mail, his often stern demeanor, and his abstinence from various "joys" of life, caused some of his soldiers

Opposite: The death of Jackson at the Battle of Chancellorsville, May 1863.

to regard him as an extremist. Some coined an alternative nickname, "Old Blue Light," but all of his troops respected their general too much to ever laugh at him.

As Jackson's faith sustained him in life, so it upheld him as he approached death. Wounded by gunfire from his own men on May 2, 1863, he lingered for a few days. His left arm needed amputation. As his condition became worse, Jackson made the following remark, "I see from the number of physicians that you think my condition dangerous, but I thank God, if it is His will, that I am ready to go." On May 10 he uttered his final words: "Let us cross over the river, and rest under the shade of the trees." It was Sunday— for many years it had been his desire to die on a Sunday.

Further Reading

Dabney, Robert Lewis. *Life and Campaigns of Lieutenant General Thomas J. Jackson.* New York: Blelock and Company, 1866.

Freeman, Douglas Southall. *Lee's Lieutenants.* 3 volumes. New York: Charles Scribner's Sons, 1942–44.

Tate, Allen. *Stonewall Jackson.* Ann Arbor: University of Michigan Press, 1957.

Vandiver, Frank Everson. *Mighty Stonewall.* New York: McGraw-Hill, 1957.

Robert E. Lee

THE WORLD'S GREAT SOLDIER

Military genius

Robert E. Lee was universally acclaimed as the greatest military genius of his century and a rival to those of any age. As impressive as his aptitude for war was his gentle, noble, and manly spirit.

As the son of the great Revolutionary "Light Horse Harry" Lee, Robert E. Lee enjoyed uncanny bellic astuteness. His native skills were honed through his superior performance at West Point, his indefatigable commitment to detail and duty as an army engineer, his invaluable service as engineer, scout, and soldier in the Mexican War, and his ingenious management of sparse resources and personnel against overwhelming numbers and material in the Civil War.

Independence

Though Lee opposed both slavery and secession, he could not go to war against his family, friends, and native state. He was convinced that the war was fought for the protection of constitutional independence, both individual and political, and was joined only as a protection against an unjust aggression.

After the surrender he urged all Southerners to submit without bitterness to God's designs and the authority of the United States. His presidency of Washington College in Lexington, Virginia, raised the college to an admirable level of scholarship and helped inculcate Christian character in the students.

Lee was sustained by a deep and unflinching sense of the goodness of God's mysterious providence, a commitment to the daily study of the Bible as the Word of God, and a personal submission to the doctrines of God's grace in the Gospel.

Opposite: General Robert E. Lee; portrait by Edward Caledon Bruce, 1864–65.

"Duty is the sublimest word in the English language," wrote Robert E. Lee to his son Custis. Renowned as the General of the Confederate Army in the War Between the States, Robert Edward Lee is a premier example of noble character produced by the grace of God through great trial and sorrow.

Robert E. Lee's own notable sense of duty came early, for his father died while Robert was a boy. The brilliant and energetic performance of Lee's father, Richard Henry Lee, in the Revolutionary War gained him a popularity that seated him in the Virginia House of Delegates in 1785 and in the governor's chair for three one-year terms. His funeral oration for George Washington in 1799 included the now famous characterization "First in war, first in peace, and first in the hearts of his countrymen." Nevertheless, he ran through the fortune of two wives, including that of Robert E. Lee's mother, his second wife, Ann Hill Carter. His debts and depression, combined with the injuries he had received from a melée in Baltimore, drove him to the West Indies in 1814, when Robert was still six years old. His family never saw him again, because he returned to America only in time to die, on March 24, 1818, in the home of Nathanael Green in Georgia.

Richard Lee's death may have released the Lees from his debts, but it also left Robert responsible for managing the house, the servants, marketing, and horse and carriage. Childhood diversions vanished as Robert cared for his invalid mother and found ways to make her laugh through her profound sadness. When her son finally left for West Point in June, 1825, Ann Lee confided in her sister-in-law, "You know what I have lost. He is son, daughter, and everything to me!"

Southern aristocrat

His pre-West Point education included significant work in classic literature ("Homer & Longinus, Tacitus & Cicero" as well as "all the minor classics") and advanced mathematics. Just as valuable, however, were the lengthy periods spent in company with his mother and her social contacts. The best graces of Southern aristocracy became his.

No less central was Robert Lee's regular attendance at Christ Church, Alexandria, which still maintained George Washington's pew and used Washington's Bible for public Scripture reading. The sermons and catechizing from Bishop

Meade instilled biblical truth into Lee's discerning mind. His appreciation of the impact of Meade's influence is seen in a letter of May 16, 1861. Lee had attended the church convention in which Meade preached his fiftieth-anniversary sermon. "It was most impressive," Lee had written, "and more than once, I felt tears coursing down my cheeks.... It was full of humility and self-reproach." Meade's own estimation of Lee was very laudatory: "It is a great relief to me that in the Providence of God so important a station has been assigned to you, as I believe that by natural and acquired endowments and by the grace of God you are better qualified for the same than any other of our citizens of Virginia."

General Robert E. Lee on his famous horse "Traveler".

In God's hands

For many years, this sense of providence and utter dependence on God had grown in Lee. In 1857, sensing some danger from Indians in Texas he wrote, "I know in whose powerful hands I am, and on Him I rely, and feel that in all our life we are upheld and sustained by Divine Providence, and that providence requires us to use the means He has put under our control." Later in a letter to his son Rooney he declared, "May Almighty God have you in His holy keeping. To His Merciful Providence I commit you, and will rely upon Him, and the Efficacy of the prayers that will be daily and hourly offered up by those who love you." He was not slow in seeing calamities as a demonstration of the "justice of His afflictions" and even the "scourge of God . . . to repress the sins of our people."

Using "the beautiful funeral service" in the Episcopal prayer book, Lee officiated at the funerals of two children who died

THE LIFE OF
Robert Edward Lee

1807	Born in Stratford, Virginia, January 19
1825–29	Attends West Point military academy
1846–48	Serves during Mexican War
1852–55	Superintendent of West Point
1855–61	Serves as Lieutenant Colonel of cavalry on the Texas Frontier
1859	Commands troops sent to suppress John Brown's raid at Harper's Ferry
1861	Resigns his commission in the United States Army Joins Confederate Army and takes command of the Army of Northern Virginia
1865	Appointed General-in-Chief of the armies of the Confederate States in February
1865	Surrenders to Grant at Appomattox Courthouse, Virginia on April 9
1870	Dies October 12

Robert E Lee.

in Texas. He empathized with the anguish of the parents, yet fully believed "It was done in mercy to both—mercy to the child, mercy to the parents. The former has been saved from sin and misery here, and the latter have been given a touching appeal and powerful inducement to prepare for hereafter. May it prove effectual, and may they require no further severe admonition."

Lee loved the Bible. He led his family in daily devotions and read it every day when away. After the war he served as President of the Rockbridge County Bible Society to assist in "extending the inestimable knowledge of the priceless truths of the Bible."

The universal balm

Robert Lee's moral character was beyond reproach. Not only did he abstain from personal vices but he also practiced and encouraged the love of one's enemies. He advised Rooney that he "always be distinguished for [his] avoidance of the 'universal balm,' *whiskey*, and every immorality"—words from a man who carried a gift bottle of "fine old whiskey" all the way through the Mexican War and, in the end, returned it to its donor to demonstrate that he could "get on without liquor." On hearing that Rooney was smoking, Lee admonished him with the following words: "it was dangerous to meddle with" and he had "much better employment for [his] mouth." He should reserve it for legitimate pleasure and not "poison and corrupt it with stale vapors or tarnish your beard with their stench." Alexander Stephens, having known of Lee only by his reputation as the consummate soldier, assumed that he shared all the vices of his companions and was surprised that "he used no stimulants, was free even from the use of tobacco, and that he was absolutely stainless in his private life."

Lee viewed slavery as a "moral and political evil in any country" and was resolved to aid its abolition with his prayers and all "justifiable means in our power." He shared the views of some Southerners, however, that Providence would accomplish God's purposes slowly. The abolitionist must recognize that "he has neither the right nor the power of operating except by moral means and suasion; and if he means well to the slave, he must not create angry feelings in the master." He viewed this as neither a happy or defensible situation but as analogous to the progress of Christian faith in the world. "The doctrines and miracles of our Saviour have required nearly two thousand years to convert but a small part of the human race, and even among Christian nations what gross errors still exist!"

No bitter spirit

The grace of a non-embittered spirit testified to the genuineness of Lee's Christian character. In the years that followed the war Lee lived as a paroled prisoner of war. This was accomplished under the terms of surrender, written by U. S. Grant. In spite of guarantees in those terms, Lee was indicted for treason in June 1865. He expressed no desire "to avoid trial" and was "ready to meet any charges," but did desire that the provisions of the surrender be attended to. Through the intervention of Grant, the charges were dropped. although Lee's application for reinstatement as an American citizen, including an oath of loyalty, was ignored.

The notarized document, including a pledge to "abide by and faithfully support all laws and proclamations which have been made during the existing rebellion with reference to the emancipation of slaves," was found in an old file drawer in Washington in the mid 1970s. It was at this time that the United States House of Representatives voted unanimously to restore the citizenship of Robert E. Lee. In spite of personal recriminations in his own time, Lee never stopped admonishing all in the South "to unite in the restoration of the country and the reestablishment of peace and harmony." In pursuit of those goals, he personally intended to learn from the experience "under the guidance of an ever-merciful God."

Nor did Lee harbor bitterness. When Lee was indicted, a minister friend of his expressed bitterness and indignation within a small group gathered in Lee's home. Lee diverted the subject to other topics by responding, "Well, it matters little what they may do to me. I am old and have but a short time to live anyhow." Later he followed the minister to the door and said, "Doctor, there is a good old book which I read, and you preach from, which says, 'Love your enemies, bless them that curse you, do good to them that hate you, and pray for them which despitefully use you.' Do you think your remarks were quite in the spirit of that teaching?" After some apology came from the minister, Lee added, "I have fought against the people of the North because I believed they were seeking to wrest from the South dearest rights. But I have never cherished toward them bitter or vindictive feelings, and

> *"I am nothing but a poor sinner, trusting in Christ alone for salvation, and need all of the prayers they can offer for me."*

have never seen the day when I did not pray for them."

Perhaps Lee's humble, forgiving spirit arose out of the profound sense he had of his own sin. Though viewing an infant in "purity and innocence, unpolluted by sin, and uncontaminated by the vices of the world," when he felt his own sin he would say, "Man's nature is So Selfish So weak. Every feeling every passion urging him to folly, excess & sin that I am disgusted with myself & Sometimes with all the world." When told by a Confederate chaplain of the fervent prayers which had been offered on his behalf, he responded with a flushed face and tears in his eyes, "Please thank them for that, sir.... And I can only say that I am nothing but a poor sinner, trusting in Christ alone for salvation, and need all of the prayers they can offer for me."

Looking unto Jesus

His concern for gospel salvation extended to others, and he was elated by the great revival that swept the Army of Northern Virginia with fifteen thousand conversions in the last two years of the war. As president of Washington College, Lee rejoiced when the preaching of John A. Broadus "gave our young men the very marrow of the Gospel, and with a simple earnestness that must have reached their hearts and done them good." To a supporter of

the college he confided, "I shall fail in the leading object that brought me here, unless these young men become real Christians." And at a Concert of Prayer for Colleges, Lee told one of the speakers, "Our great want is a revival that shall bring these young men to Christ."

J. W. Jones, a leading Baptist pastor in Virginia, who had closely observed the general, gave a fitting assessment of the Christian, Robert E. Lee:

If I have ever come in contact with a sincere, devout Christian —one who, seeing himself to be a sinner, trusted alone in the merits of Christ—who humbly tried to walk the path of duty, "looking unto Jesus the author and finisher of our faith," and whose piety was constantly exemplified in his daily life, that man was the world's great soldier, and model man, Robert Edward Lee.

Further Reading

Anderson, Nancy Scott and Anderson, Dwight. *The Generals: Ulysses S. Grant and Robert E. Lee.* New York: Alfred A. Knopf, 1988.

Freeman, Douglas Southall. *R. E. Lee: A Biography.* 4 vols. New York: 1934–35.

Jones, J. William. *Christ in the Camp; or, Religion in the Confederate Army.* B. F. Johnson & Co., 1887. Reprint. Harrisonburg, Va.: Sprinkle Publications, 1986.

_____. *Life and Letters of General Robert E. Lee.* Harrisonburg, Va.: Sprinkle Publications, 1986.

Woodrow Wilson

Fighting for a Just Peace

W hen the presidential party arrived at Pueblo, Colorado, on September 25, 1919, it was obvious that the president, who was showing every one of his sixty-two years, was in difficulty. It had been a gruelling trip—more than three weeks of constant speechmaking, long train rides, tumultuous crowds, and political passion at its height. He was campaigning for what he thought was the last chance of the civilized world to replace violent nationalism with virtuous diplomacy. Already this president had gained eminence as an educator and as a statesman. Within the year massive throngs in war-torn Europe had hailed him as the savior of the world order. But in Pueblo, this master of oratory stumbled during his speech. Still, he made it to the conclusion: "The American people always rise to... the truth of justice and of liberty and of peace.... That truth... is going to lead us, and through us the world, out into pastures of quietness and peace such as the world never dreamed of before."

Debilitating stroke

That night he suffered a debilitating stroke. The tour had to end. Invalided and isolated, he could not prevent his political enemies from keeping America out of the League of Nations. Soon the president was out of office, an embittered, physically shattered man. Even worse, his hopes for America's leadership for peace in the world were not fulfilled. In spite of his herculean efforts, an even more destructive war would break out in Europe within twenty years. The president was Woodrow Wilson, a serious-minded and dedicated Christian. Was he, even in failure, more than a conqueror?

A southern boyhood

Thomas Woodrow Wilson (he dropped "Tommy" as a young man) was born in Staunton, Virginia, nearly five years before the start of the Civil War. Throughout his life, he remained deeply attached to the South and to many of its values. Even more profound, however, was the legacy of his family. Wilson's father was a minister in the Southern Presbyterian church, a man marked by a sense of insecurity, but also by his wide learning and a great capacity for loving his family. Joseph Ruggles Wilson achieved considerable distinction in the ministry, as moderator of the Southern Presbyterian Church in 1879, as its long-time Stated Clerk, and as a much-respected minister and a professor in a number of Southern states. But above all other concerns, he was devoted to his family, and most of all to his son.

Only occasionally with the aid of tutors, Joseph Wilson and his wife, Janet Woodrow Wilson, oversaw the education of that son themselves. Early on they recognized his ability with words and so encouraged him to write, debate, and orate. Even more, they grounded him in the Christian faith. The boy was a constant, and soon enthusiastic, church attender. He was trained in habits of personal Bible reading, which lasted his entire life. He was required to keep Sunday as a sabbath separate to God, a duty which he came to regard as a great privilege. (Years later as a new president looking for a Washington physician, he

THE LIFE OF

Woodrow Wilson

1856	Born in Staunton, Virginia, on December 29
1879	Graduates from the College of New Jersey (now Princeton University)
1883–85	Graduate studies at The Johns Hopkins University
1885	Marries Ellen Louise Axson
1890–1902	Professor of political science at Princeton University
1902–10	President of Princeton
1910	Governor of the state of New Jersey
1912	Becomes President of the United States
1914	Death of Ellen Axson Wilson
1915	Marries Edith Bolling Galt
1916	Reelected president of the United States
1917	Leads the United States into World War I in April
1918	World War I ends in November
1918–19	Negotiates Treaty of Versailles to end the war Creates the League of Nations
1919	Suffers a debilitating stroke in Pueblo, Colorado, on September 25
1920	Leaves the presidency to retire in Washington, D.C.
1924	Dies in Washington, D.C.

chided Dr. Cary T. Grayson, later to become a trusted friend, for telling him he was too sick to go to church on Sunday.) From his childhood, Woodrow Wilson also absorbed from his parents the religious approach which he held towards life in the world.

Unique balance

That approach centered on the concept of covenant. God had made certain rules for people to live by, and he had made them definite promises. The promises to individuals made by God included the offer of salvation to those who trusted in him, and for all peoples, a guarantee of peace and social harmony to those who pursued justice. The covenant represented a unique balance for Wilson: it called for the most strenuous exertions from all individuals, but it also accorded greatest respect to the organic bonds between church and society. As a history teacher, this covenantal framework made Wilson unusually partial to the Reformer, John Calvin (who, as he told his students, was "the greatest reforming Christian *statesman*"). As world leader, it was this teaching that allowed Wilson to think that the efforts of righteous individuals could transform the community of nations.

The extraordinary energy that drove Wilson in his work as an academic, a writer and speaker, politician and statesman, has sometimes been ascribed simply to factors of his personality. It is true that he had extraordinary high ambitions for himself. On his thirty-third birthday he penned a private question to himself: "Why may not the present age write, through me, its political *autobiography*?" But the secret of his energy was more than personal, it was also directly religious. He believed that God ruled over the world, and that individuals could become servants of God's will in the world. That conviction, even more than his admittedly driven personality, fueled the achievements of this singular life.

Wilson took several years to find himself after leaving home for college. At the Presbyterian Davidson College he suffered from various ailments, but then blossomed at Princeton, which was still a college dominated by Presbyterian interests. There he played baseball and cheered on the football team, but gave his concentrated energies to debate, study, and friendships. He did not enjoy success as a young lawyer in Atlanta. Yet it was during his brief stint there— while more interested in books

and his biography of George Washington, was criticised as superficial by his academic peers. His essays and books in political science, on the other hand, were well received by both academics and the general public alike. These works were marked by a passionate interest in bringing the ideals of equity, progress, and fair-mindedness to contemporary politics.

President of Princeton

When Wilson was elected as the president of Princeton in 1902, he turned to the public tasks of his new office with enthusiasm. Whilst he still continued to teach regularly throughout his time as president, he gave himself increasingly to visionary plans for the university and to ever broader statements on public issues. The energy that made him so successful as a lecturer and public speaker did have a negative side. With those who failed to support his proposals he could seem as high-handed as others thought him high-minded.

Especially after a stroke in 1906 (he had probably suffered another, slighter stroke in 1896), his personality hardened. Always a goal-directed person, he seemed to become even more driven. The result was a series of clashes with colleagues who had egos and visions as large as his own. When the trustees and certain factions of the faculty disagreed with Wilson's plans to democratize student life and keep graduate education liberal rather than professional, bitter disputes broke out. Because of this bitterness, Wilson was ready when leaders of New Jersey's Democratic party asked him to run for governor in 1910.

than in gaining clients—that Wilson met Ellen Louise Axson, the wife to whom he would be devoted until her death early in his tenure as president.

It was not until his return to academic life that Wilson's considerable abilities and vaulting ambition found their natural outlet. He greatly enjoyed his studies at Johns Hopkins in Baltimore, then the leading center of graduate studies in the United States. On the basis of his outstanding work at Johns

Hopkins, Wilson entered into a rapidly rising academic career, the culmination of which was his appointment to teach at Princeton in 1890. As a teacher Wilson was a rousing success. While not approachable in a friendly way, he was always considerate to students. And he was a spellbinding lecturer.

Wilson was also enjoying new prominence as a writer. In spite of the fact that his historical writing, such as an illustrated history of the United States,

The was the opportunity for him to enter the wider stage, for which he had been preparing during his entire life.

Wilson was elected governor of New Jersey as a result of the efforts of a top-down political machine. But he soon proved to be his own man, with a great desire for reform. The reputation which he had gained in New Jersey propelled him to the nomination for president in 1912. When Republican support was divided between William Howard Taft and Theodore Roosevelt, Woodrow Wilson edged into the White House. As a "progressive" president with a congressional majority, he successfully secured a range of reforming legislation, which included the checking of the power of corporate trusts; the creation of the Federal Reserve System which would protect banking; a reduction of tariffs to encourage trade; mandating an eight-hour work day for railway workers; and the establishment of the first national child-labor standards. On the basis of this record, and for his part in keeping the United States out of the 1914 European war, Wilson was reelected to a second term in 1916. He worked to keep the United States out of the war. But when Germany's actions on the high seas made national sentiment increasingly hostile, Wilson reluctantly led the country into war.

Fourteen Points

In keeping with his high ideals, however, Wilson hoped the war could promote higher standards of international justice. In early 1918, while battles still raged in Europe, Woodrow Wilson made his famous Fourteen Points proposal to try

President Woodrow Wilson.

to settle the peace. The Points called upon nations to renounce secret agreements and to allow subjected peoples to settle their own destinies democratically. Wilson's Fourteen Points also called, most momentously, for the establishment of a League of Nations.

After the war ended in November 1918, Wilson himself went to Paris as head of the American peace delegation. In Britain and on the Continent he was hailed by tremendous crowds. In contrast to those who had brought about the carnage of the war, Wilson was seen as a leader of principle who put the interests of the people above selfish factions. Treaty negotiations were brutal. Exhausted by the wrangling, Wilson gave way on many of his Fourteen Points. But he convinced the peace conference to accept the League of Nations, in the hope that this would prevent another general war.

Disillusioned

Back at home, however, Republicans had regained control of the Senate in 1918, and they were not as persuaded as Wilson that the League was in the best interests of the United States. Led by Senator Henry Cabot Lodge of Massachusetts, the Senators asked for amendments to the treaty before giving their consent. To Wilson, such opposition was even more reprehensible than opposition to his academic ideas at Princeton. In response, he resolved to tour the country and convince the Senate, through a great outpouring of public support, that it should confirm the treaty without amendments. Yet Wilson had been grievously weakened by the stress of the war and the tension of the peace table, the result of which was his collapse in Pueblo. The United States would not join the League. Woodrow Wilson went to his grave still confident in his ideals, but also embittered about the failure of his policy.

Christians are left with many profound questions when they review the career of Woodrow Wilson. Beyond doubt, he was a larger-than-life leader, and had extraordinary abilities. This conclusion survives the frank admission of Wilson's blind spots, for he was not perfect. For example, he was not prepared to extend equality to African Americans, nor was he prepared to credit his opponents with worthy motives. Yet, even his enemies recognized Wilson's desire to move both domestic politics and international affairs to a higher moral plane.

Christian statesman?
A more serious question concerns the nature of Wilson's Christian vision. Throughout his life, Wilson experienced a number of intimate Christian experiences. He underwent a sobering conversion in the winter of 1872–73. Later, whilst teaching at Wesleyan, he was so moved by hearing the preaching of D. L. Moody that he set aside the written prayers, with which he regularly began class, to pray spontaneously "in his own words" for the students. Whilst recovering from the first of his strokes, he wrote that he saw Christianity not as ethics or "a philosophy of altruism," but as, primarily, "love, clear-sighted, loyal, personal," as shown in Christ who "came, not to save himself, assuredly, but to save the world." While resident in the White House, Woodrow Wilson insisted on faithful church attendance, and he also engaged in exercises of personal faith, including hymn singing with his family.

Yet, on balance, Wilson's faith was more moral than evangelical, more a source of ethics than a message of grace. And one of its chief purposes was to support his belief in the progress of humanity. Thus, when Wilson delivered a well-received public address on the Bible in 1911, he stressed its political character: Scripture was "the 'Magna Carta' of the human soul." His genuine affection for the Bible was mixed with a great deal of questionable commentary about the supposedly exalted character of America. Wilson ended this speech by saying, "I ask of every man and woman in this audience that from this night on they will realize that part of the destiny of America lies in their daily perusal of this great book of revelations—that if they would see America free and pure they will make their own spirits free and pure by this baptism of the Holy Scripture."

The secret of Woodrow Wilson as a Christian statesman, but also his limitations, is found in this quotation. Wilson was perhaps too prone to equate American ideals with the ideals of Scripture. He was perhaps blind to Scripture's own teaching about human sinfulness and the need for grace (and not just statesmanship) to make a better world. He was perhaps also too confident that the exertions of only a few humans could transform human nature to prevent war from taking place again.

But if these were limits to Wilson's vision, they were matched by extraordinary strengths. Wilson did not regard politics as a scramble for gain, or international diplomacy as merely a way of securing the best deal for his own nation.

Rather, he saw that people were made by God to enjoy His goodness and His grace. They were made by God to be free. They were made to reflect the dignity of their Creator. God had made it possible, he felt, for politics and diplomacy to encourage both human dignity and social harmony. Whatever flaws may be discovered in Wilson's vision, these higher ideals command our respect. In a century which suffered and was bloodied by schemes of empire-building and eager resorts to war, such ideals stand as a sign of contradiction. They are ideals grounded in the Christian education Woodrow Wilson received as a child and in the Christian faith which he nourished throughout his life. They were ideals rooted in the covenant promises of God.

Link, Arthur S. *Wilson.* 5 vols. to date. Princeton: Princeton U., 1947–.

_____. "Woodrow Wilson and His Presbyterian Inheritance" and "The Higher Realism of Woodrow Wilson." In *The Higher Realism of Woodrow Wilson.* Nashville: Vanderbilt U., 1971.

Mulder, John M. *Woodrow Wilson: The Years of Preparation.* Princeton: Princeton U., 1978.

Born on January 14, 1892, into a pastor's family in Lippstadt, Westphalia, young Martin Niemöller acquired a deep sense of piety, which was characterized by a simple, childlike devotion to Jesus. The "church" for him was the entire Christian way of life, and he never demonstrated much interest in theology or intellectual exercises. Through his father's involvement in the "social question"—the concern of Protestants for the victims of the industrial age—he was sensitized to this dimension of the Christian faith.

After high school graduation in 1910, Niemöller entered naval cadet training, was commissioned, and in World War I was assigned to submarine duty. By 1918 Niemöller commanded his own U-boat. A decorated officer, he emerged from the war with a strong sense of patriotism, heroic devotion to duty, and political conservatism. Like many of his generation, he saw no future in the liberal democracy of the postwar Weimar Republic and so he resigned his commission. On Easter Sunday 1919 he married Else Bremer, sister of his best friend and fellow officer. She was to bear him seven children. (In 1961 she was

killed in an auto accident, and he married Sybil von Sell ten years later.)

Niemöller dabbled briefly with farming, and then began to study for the ministry at the University of Münster while working at odd jobs to support a

growing family. In 1924, he graduated, was ordained, and took an administrative position in the Münster office of the Inner Mission. He served with the social service agency for seven years and then accepted a pastorate at St. Anne's Church in Berlin-Dahlem. It was to be the only parish he ever served.

Martin Niemöller: German Pastor
Hitler's Personal Prisoner

An extraordinarily controversial personality, Martin Niemöller began his career in the Imperial Germany Navy and was a submarine commander in World War I. After the defeat he studied theology and was ordained in the Prussian Protestant church. He served seven years with the Inner Mission, the church's main social service agency, and then in 1931 accepted a call to a church in the fashionable Berlin suburb of Dahlem.

Welcomes Hitler
At this time a strong conservative and German nationalist, he welcomed Hitler's appointment as chancellor as the beginning of a national renewal. Soon, however, he became embroiled in

a conflict with the "German Christians" who were attempting to take power in the church and restructure it along Nazi lines.

Confessing Church
Niemöller played a major role in the formation of the Confessing Church, which sought to counter these actions. Following increasing pressure and police harassment, he was arrested in 1937 and placed in a concentration camp as "Hitler's personal prisoner." After the war he worked for the rehabilitation of the German church and traveled around the world promoting ecumenical church unity and pacifism, but his political shift to the left alienated many of his former admirers.

Fervent nationalist
At this time he was a fervent nationalist and wished to renew the alliance between the church and the German nation which allegedly had been broken by the "red" republic. As early as 1924, badly deceived by the sham piety (the "positive Christianity") expressed by Hitler and the National Socialists, Niemöller had voted for the National Socialist Party, and welcomed the Führer's accession to power in 1933 as Germany's hour of liberation from the stranglehold of the atheistic Marxists.

However, he soon realized how serious a challenge to the integrity of the church was being made by pro-Nazi "German Christians," a heretical group whose members rejected the uniqueness of Scripture as the witness to God and argued that He also spoke through nature, creation, and in human beings themselves. From this premise they concluded that race, nation, and German culture were "orders of creation" and that Jews were the enemy of Christianity and humankind. They boldly sought to take control of the Protestant church and restructure it in accordance with what they felt was the will of the Führer. The efforts of Martin Niemöller and his allies to block their state-sanctioned moves marked the start of the "Church Struggle" (*Kirchenkampf*).

Young reformers

Niemöller and several friends in Berlin formed the "Young Reformation Movement," which immediately went on the offensive against the "German Christians" and insisted firmly on the freedom of the church from all political pressures. A major issue in 1933 was the attempt to apply to the church the notorious "Aryan paragraph" which required the dismissal of all pastors of "Jewish ancestry." The controversy led Niemöller to see that anti-Judaism was more than just a matter of church freedom; it was really a question of theology.

To counter the church authorities' intention to remove all pastors who had at least one grandparent who was Jewish ("non-Aryan" as the Nazis put it) or who were married to a woman in this category, on September 21, 1933, Niemöller formed the "Pastors' Emergency League." The group pledged its allegiance solely to the Bible and the Reformation confessions as the correct interpretation of Scripture, and declared that the Aryan Paragraph violated this confessional stance. By January 1934 over one-third of the Protestant pastors had joined the League. At a meeting in

Niemöller's home on October 20, an eight-member Council of Brethren was formed to coordinate its efforts.

The German Christians' moves to nazify the church structure and implement their corrupt theology (moves which

Pastor Martin Niemöller in 1939.

included purging Scripture of its "Jewish elements") led to such unrest and disorder in the church and embarrassing criticism of Germany in the foreign press that they soon fell out of favor with the Nazi regime. Niemöller professed continuing loyalty to Hitler, which resulted in tensions with those with

more insight, such as Dietrich Bonhoeffer.

Meeting Hitler

The Pastors' Emergency League categorically rejected the order by the Nazi sycophant, "Reich Bishop" Ludwig Müller, that banned criticism of the church leadership (an order known as the "Muzzling Decree" of January 4, 1934), and a delegation of dissenting pastors secured an audience with Hitler in order to explain what the controversy was about. It would be the only time Niemöller ever met the Führer. When he told Hitler that the struggle was being carried on not only out of concern for the church but also for the German people and state, the Führer retorted that the clergy should leave the care of the Third Reich to him and the pastors involve themselves with getting people to heaven and looking after the church. Niemöller responded that the church has a responsibility for the people, which was laid upon it by God, and "neither you nor anyone else can take that away from us."

From this point on the Nazi authorities tightened the screws on him. He was under constant Gestapo surveillance and attempts were made to suspend him from his pulpit. At the same time, he encouraged lay people to become involved in the

THE LIFE OF

Martin Niemöller

1892	Born in Lippstadt, Germany
1918	Commands U-Boat UC67
1919–24	Studies theology, Münster University
1924	Ordination in the Prussian Church
1924–31	Manages Inner Mission, Münster
1933	Hitler named chancellor Formation of Pastors' Emergency League
1934	Meets with Hitler Barmen Theological Declaration
1937	Arrest and imprisonment
1938	Trial and acquittal Sent to Sachsenhausen
1941	Transferred to Dachau
1945	Liberation
1952	Joins World Peace Committee
1961	Elected to World Council of Churches presidium
1984	Dies in Wiesbaden, Germany

Martin Niemöller and his wife Elisabeth in 1961.

resistance and worked to create a new church structure through the calling of "free synods" which reinforced the doctrines of the traditional confessions against the innovations of the German Christians. These synods were the core of the "Confessing Church," which functioned as a party within the existing Protestant church rather than as a separate organization. Although the Church Struggle was basically a conflict over church organization, the doctrinal issues arising from its role in a tyrannical, pagan regime could not be avoided.

At the landmark "Confessing" Synod of Barmen in May 1934, in which Niemöller participated, a theological statement was adopted decisively rejecting the "false gospel" that God had revealed himself through the German nation, German race

and blood, or Adolf Hitler. Niemöller affirmed that the churches and congregations that accepted the Barmen Declaration were the legitimate Protestant church and he worked to win the endorsement for his claim from Christians outside Germany.

Concentration camp

As his attacks on the nazification of the church and racial

doctrines intensified and he publicly identified and prayed for Confessing Church colleagues who had been arrested, his position became more precarious. On July 1, 1937, his home in Dahlem was raided by the secret police and he was placed in Berlin's Moabit prison. When brought to trial the following February he was all but acquitted, and the angry Hitler ordered that he should be held in solitary confinement in Sachsenhausen concentration camp as "my personal prisoner." In spite of intense international pressure the Führer refused to release him, but fear of foreign opinion spared him from almost certain execution. When World War II broke out Niemöller, still a German nationalist, volunteered for naval service, but his request was rejected. In July 1941 he was moved to the Dachau camp where the conditions of his confinement were somewhat better, and he was liberated by American soldiers in 1945.

Guilt
In the immediate postwar years, controversy swirled around Niemöller because of his patriotic past, his insistence that even German Protestants should accept some of responsibility for the evils of Nazism, and his opposition to the policies of the authorities of the Allied occupation. He was to play a key role in drafting the "Stuttgart Declaration of Guilt" (October 18, 1945), in which several church leaders criticized themselves "for not witnessing more courageously, for not praying more faithfully, for not believing more joyously, and for not loving more ardently." He saw this acknowledgment as necessary for the renewal of the church.

Niemöller also identified the sufferings of German Jews and Communists with the sacrifice of Jesus, which was reflected in a famous statement which he repeated in his speeches:
They came for the Communists, and I didn't object For I wasn't a Communist; They came for the Socialists, and I didn't object For I wasn't a Socialist; They came for the labor leaders, and I didn't object For I wasn't a labor leader; They came for the Jews, and I didn't object For I wasn't a Jew; Then they came for me And there was no one left to object

During the next three decades he was prominent in German and international church circles. He was the foreign representative of the German Protestant church until 1956, president of the regional church of Hesse-Nassau, 1947–64, and a member of the presidium of the World Council of Churches, 1961–68. A member of the left-wing World Peace Committee, he traveled incessantly, promoting international conciliation. His strong criticism of West German rearmament, anti-Communism, and South African apartheid, his fervent advocacy of pacifism and of nuclear disarmament, his favorable attitude toward Soviet Russia, and his fostering of Christian-Jewish understanding made him a controversial figure. He remained active even in retirement, and he died peacefully in Wiesbaden on March 5, 1984.

Further Reading

Bentley, James. *Martin Niemöller.* New York: Free Press, 1984.

Locke, Hubert, ed. *Exile in the Fatherland: Martin Niemöller's Letters from Moabit Prison.* 1986.

Niemöller, Martin. *From U-Boat to Pulpit.* London: W. Hodge, 1936.

_____. *Dachau Sermons.* New York: Harper and Brothers, 1936.

Charles Malik

SAVING THE UNIVERSITY

Charles Habib Malik evidenced a rare mixture of deep spirituality and disciplined intellect. He was steeped in learning yet held tenaciously to the truth of the historic Christian creeds and the doctrines of the Bible. He made a personal habit of reading fourteen chapters of the Bible every day, not just in his native language (Arabic) or in English but in several languages, including Greek and French. In this way he read through the whole of the Bible every few months. "I live in and on the Bible for long hours every day," he said. "The Bible is the source of every good thought and impulse I have. In the Bible God Himself, the Creator of everything from nothing, speaks to me and to the world directly, about Himself, about ourselves, and about His will for the course of events and for the consummation of history."

Malik exalted the Person of Jesus Christ as of paramount importance on world history: "The greatest revolution ever was Jesus Christ himself; not his ideas, not his teachings, not his moral principles, but he himself; for nothing is greater, more revolutionary and more unbelievable than the Gospel of the Crucified, Resurrected and Glorified God who is to come again to judge the living and the dead."

As a statesman, Malik was nearly without peer. He is the only person to have presided over five major organs of the United Nations: he was president of the U.N. General Assembly, president of the U.N. Security Council, chairman of the U.N. Commission on Human Rights (succeeding Eleanor Roosevelt), chairman of the Third Committee of the General Assembly, and president of the Economic and Social Council.

> *"Save the university, and you save Western civilization and therewith the world."*

Human rights

As president of the Economic and Social Council and a member of the U.N. Commission on Human Rights, he helped develop the Universal Declaration of Human Rights. Several articles of that declaration are of special importance to Christians. The document recognizes the family as "the natural and fundamental group unit of society," entitled to protection by the state. It affirms for each person "freedom of thought, conscience and religion" and the freedom, "in public or private, to manifest his religion or belief in teaching, practice, worship and observance." It declared that education should fully develop the human personality and that parents "have the prior right to choose the kind of education that shall be given to their children."

The amazing thing about Malik is that his search for spiritual and religious truth was as intense as his search for truth about the external world. He believed that so-called "religious" truth was every bit as valid as "scientific" truth. Each had its rightful place, and neither had the right to deny the other:

A Christian can only bless and rejoice in all truth, provided each truth is put in its rightful place... and provided no attested truth or fact or being is arbitrarily denied its rightful place in the scheme of things. For the moment a truth arrogates to itself a place that is not its own or denies other truths, it becomes untruth. When a scientist affirms the truth of his science and denies the truth of religion or morality or great art, then, while his scientific truth, so far as it goes, stands, he himself as a person becomes untrue in the sense that he had denied some truth.

Charles Habib Malik's life had a twofold goal: evangelism and education. He believed that the chief concern of Christians should encompass both the spiritual salvation of people and the intellectual pursuit of the truth. Malik strongly believed that evangelism is always the most important task to be undertaken by moral man. "But how to order the mind on sound Christian principles at the very heart of where it is formed and informed, namely," he affirmed, "in the universities, is one of the two greatest themes that can be considered.... The problem is not only to win souls but to save minds. If you win the whole world and lose the mind of the world, you will soon discover you have not won the world. Indeed it may turn out that you have actually lost the world."

As a consequence, his interest in universities was immense: "Save the university," he stated, "and you save Western civilization and therewith the world."

The perils of anti-intellectualism
In Malik's view, however, the church is ill-equipped to meet the vital challenge of saving minds. The typical evangelical does not understand the influence and power that Christian

Human Rights

From time to time in the course of Christian history, movements have arisen whose effect has been to stifle the human mind and spirit. At such time God has raised up men and women of extraordinary intellect and ability—coupled with unbending commitment to Jesus Christ—to sound the need for highly educated Christians in the vital arenas of influence and power. Such a man for the second half of the twentieth century was Charles Habib Malik.

Human rights
Arguably one of the greatest statesmen of our century, Charles Malik was a fierce defender of human rights and a strong advocate of education as critical for the advancement and propagation of the gospel throughout the world. He was the recipient of more than fifty honorary doctoral degrees from leading universities and colleges in America, Canada, and Europe.

Decorated
Because of his service in the interest of international peace and human rights, he was decorated by twelve countries and was awarded the highest order of Lebanon for distinguished service. Over a period of two decades, he held five different offices in the United Nations, including chairman of the U.N. Human Rights Commission.

Charles Malik in New York when President of the 13th session of the United Nations Assembly, 1958.

THE LIFE OF

Charles Habib Malik

1906	Born, Bterram, Al-Koura, Lebanon
1927	Receives B.A., American University, Beirut
1937	Receives M.A., Ph.D., Harvard University
1941	Marries Eva Badr
1945	Signs United Nations Charter
1945–54	Member, Lebanese delegation to the U.N.
1946–49	Member, U.N. Economic and Social Council
1947–54	Member, U.N. Commission on Human Rights
1949	President, U.N. Economic and Social Council
1951–52	Chairman, U.N. Commission on Human Rights
1953–54	President, U.N. Security Council
1956–58	Minister of Foreign Affairs, Lebanon
1957–60	Member, Lebanese Parliament
1958–59	President, 13th Session, U.N. General Assembly
1961–62	Professor, American University, Washington, D.C.
1962–76	Professor, American University, Beirut
1966–72	Vice President, United Bible Societies
1967–71	President, World Council of Christian Education
1987	Dies on December 28

thought could wield in the world should it once again become dominant. The greatest danger besetting American Evangelical Christianity, Malik felt, is the danger of anti-intellectualism.

Too many Christians have retreated from the influential sphere of secular scholarship and given it up to anti-Christian thought without a fight. This has been extremely damaging to the witness of the church. "Who among the Evangelicals can stand up to the great secular or naturalistic or atheistic scholars on their own terms of scholarship and research?" he challenged. "Who among the Evangelical scholars is quoted as a normative source by the greatest secular authorities on history or philosophy or psychology or sociology or politics?" No longer does the world look to the church for answers to its most pressing problems. The church has become societally irrelevant.

Malik passionately wanted to see dedicated Christians committed to recapturing the Western university for Christ. Jesus Christ made the creation of the university possible.

But today the university is the fountainhead of both truth and deviation from the truth. According to Malik, the great institutions of learning have forsaken Christ and denied religious truth: "There is something almost universally absent in all the humanities." He also lamented that atheism is the besetting danger often accompanying scientific pursuit.

Malik's vision

It was Charles Malik's passionate vision to see "an institution that will produce as many Nobel Prize winners as saints, an institution in which, while producing in every field the finest works of thought and learning in the world, Jesus Christ will at the same time find Himself perfectly at home in it—in every dormitory and lecture hall and library and laboratory." But the problem, he believed, "is for the church to realize that no greater service can it render both itself and the cause of the gospel, with which it is entrusted, than to try to recapture the universities for Christ on whom they were all originally founded.... More potently than by any other means, change the university and you change the world."

Charles Malik, who himself overcame anti-Christian bias in politics and higher education, challenges us to enter the political arena and to recapture the universities for Christ.

Further Reading

Charles Malik, ed. *God and Man in Contemporary Christian Thought*. Syracuse: Syracuse U., 1970.

Charles Malik. *Wonder of Being*. Waco, Texas: Word, 1974.

Charles Malik. *The Two Tasks*. Birmingham, Ala.: Cornerstone, 1980.

Charles Malik. *A Christian Critique of the University*. Downers Grove, Ill.: InterVarsity, 1982.

Elizabeth Hanford Dole

For Such a Time as This

When, in late 1990, Elizabeth Hanford Dole announced she was leaving her post as Labor Secretary in George Bush's Cabinet to become president of the American Red Cross, political pundits in Washington speculated that the reason was financial. As Labor Secretary, she earned $98,000 a year. The salary at the American Red Cross was listed at $200,000. Yet, on her first day at the American Red Cross, Mrs. Dole announced that she would not be accepting a salary during her first year as a show of solidarity with the organization's volunteers. "The best way I can let volunteers know of their importance is to be one of them, to earn the patch on my sleeve," she said.

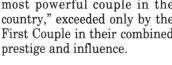

It was not the first time Elizabeth Hanford Dole had confounded the expectations of those around her. As a young woman, Mrs. Dole disconcerted her parents by her decision to study political science rather than home economics. Later, as she moved on to Harvard Law School and up the various echelons of federal government bureaucracy, she joined the ranks of the pioneer women who proved that it was possible to be successful in realms previously dominated by white males. But perhaps her biggest surprise came during a 1987 speech in Washington, D.C.

It had been a time of unprecedented personal visibility and accolade for Elizabeth Dole. Her husband, U.S. Senator Robert Dole (R-Kansas), was running for president, and she had resigned her ground-breaking post as Secretary of Transportation to campaign for him. There was talk of a Dole–Dole presidential ticket, but the joke around Washington was that no one knew which Dole should have the top billing. Together, they were dubbed "the second most powerful couple in the country," exceeded only by the First Couple in their combined prestige and influence.

Prayer breakfast

Yet, during an address before world leaders, business executives, and politicians gathered for the National Prayer Breakfast, Mrs. Dole spoke not of achieving political power or surviving at the top, but rather of an enduring faith in Jesus Christ. She transfixed her audience with a personal account of the spiritual journey which, she said, had led her to conclude that worldly success was empty at best. "Life is not just a few years to spend on self-indulgence and career advancement," she said. "It is a privilege, a responsibility, a stewardship to be lived according to a much higher calling—God's calling."

Confirmation

Under the hot glare of television lights, reporters, bureaucrats, and Washington's social elite jostled for space in the crowded Senate Commerce Committee hearing room on January 16, 1983. The occasion? The confirmation hearing of Elizabeth Hanford Dole, Ronald Reagan's first female Cabinet nominee. During her nearly twenty years of government service, Mrs. Dole's warm personality and keen political savvy had propelled her to immense grassroots popularity. Adding to the intrigue of the hearing was the fact that U.S. Sen. Robert Dole (R-Kansas) would be the one to present his wife to his Senate colleagues. The Senator's introduction was peppered with his characteristic wry sense of humor. Observing that he could identify with American patriot Nathan Hale, the senator asserted to the committee, "I regret that I have but one wife to give for my country's infrastructure."

Senator Dole's remark may have been made in jest, but over the years, many in the nation have no doubt shared the regret that there is only one Elizabeth Hanford Dole. For indeed, from her various government appointments to her presidential Cabinet positions to her post as president of the American Red Cross, Elizabeth Hanford Dole has devoted virtually all of her adult life to public service. Yet for her, public service is defined more in terms of ministry than politics. And she is always quick to explain that her ethic of service was formed at an early age, rooted in a religious faith that has stood the test of time. She admits that once she got caught in the power grind that can be Washington, D.C., but she also acknowledges that her perspective is now a very different one.

Eternal heirlooms

Elizabeth Hanford Dole was born on July 20, 1936 in Salisbury, North Carolina, a Southern community where, she says, "religion exerts a powerful hold." Dole speaks often of the impact that had on her own life. "In a world where so little seems permanent, we draw from eternal truths, expressed in customs handed on like fine family silver from one generation to the next," she writes in her autobiography, *The Doles: Unlimited Partners*.

Christianity exerted a powerful hold on the Hanford family, as it did on Salisbury itself. Dole describes discovering after her father's death in 1981 that for years he had secretly kept rents low for widowed and disadvantaged residents of buildings that he owned. "It was Dad's expression of a practical faith that regarded every man as his brother's keeper," she says. She further describes her mother's pride in the family's blood relation to Francis Asbury, the early American Methodist evangelist.

THE LIFE OF
Elizabeth Hanford Dole

1936	Birth in Salisbury, North Carolina
1958	Graduates from Duke University, North Carolina
1965	Obtains Law degree from Harvard University, Massachusetts
1966	Holds first government position
1971	Appointed deputy director at the Nixon White House Office of Consumer Affairs
1975	Marries Senator Robert Dole (R-Kansas)
1980	First female appointee in the Reagan Administration
1983	Secretary of Transportation—first woman in Reagan Cabinet
1989	Secretary of Labor in the Bush Administration
1991	First female president of the American Red Cross since founder Clara Barton

---

Among her warmest remembrances are times with her grandmother, "Mom Cathey," whom she calls "more than a role model" in the formation of her own religious beliefs. "Through her example, I was encouraged to have a vital, living faith," Dole says. She recalls Sunday afternoons in Mom Cathey's living room, eating cookies and listening to Bible stories with various cousins. Her grandmother was a "continuous reader of the Bible," she remembers. "In her eyes, we were each pilgrims on the road to grace, yet it was a joyous faith that she practiced. It had none of the smug or solemn piety that can sometimes frighten a child," Dole says. "Laughter came as naturally to her lips as prayer."

No blueprint

Elizabeth Dole's pattern of achievement was also set at an early age. Throughout her childhood, she was active in both church and civic functions and excelled at school. She recalls that her first political position was president of the third-grade bird club. She also experienced an early taste of the societal obstacles she would later face. Her bid to become Boyden High School president failed—despite her campaign manager drawing analogies to the newly-crowned Queen Elizabeth II of England. Apparently, Dole recalls, Boyden High School was not quite ready for a female leader, even if Britain was.

In the 1950s, most young women made preparation for their future by grooming themselves to be good wives and mothers. Yet, Dole found herself being drawn in a different direction. She was innately fascinated by government and politics, and so, to the chagrin of her family, she earned a degree in political science from Duke University (North Carolina) in 1958. After graduation, however, there was

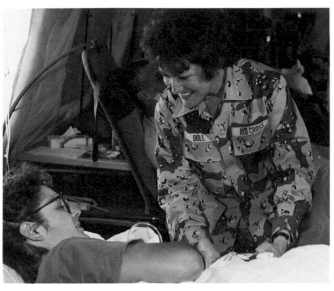

Elizabeth Dole in the uniform of the American Red Cross.

public service. After an unsuccessful bid for a White House Fellowship, she took her first federal job, a position as Deputy Assistant Secretary in a small office of the Department of Health, Education, and Welfare in the Johnson Administration. A series of other bureaucratic positions followed; in every presidential administration from Johnson to George Bush Elizabeth Dole has held a post in government.

uncertainty about the future. As she writes in her book, "It wasn't as if I had a carefully drawn blueprint for the future. Women in that era rarely had one; you might take a job, almost by accident, only to discover ten years out that it had turned into a career."

Yet, politics kept beckoning. After a trip to the Soviet Union and further study, Dole came to Washington, D.C. in 1960, working on Capitol Hill. Her first foray into national electoral politics came that year when she rode on the "LBJ Express," Democratic vice-presidential nominee Lyndon Johnson's campaign train through the South.

On the advice of Margaret Chase Smith, the legendary female Senator from Maine, Elizabeth Dole enrolled in law school at Harvard, becoming one of only fifteen women in a class of 550. There she faced discrimination, both subtle and overt, from fellow students and professors alike. One male student, she recalls, even going so far as to ask, "Don't you realize that there are men who would give their right arm to be in this law school, men who would use their legal education?"

Up the political echelons

As it turned out, Elizabeth Dole did indeed use her legal education, and use it well. Since many of the private law firms were still reluctant to hire female attorneys, her professional career began in the arena where she ultimately found her niche:

She recounts the difficulties of attempting to gain access to the male-dominated strongholds of Washington in the 1960s. She would be invited to meetings which were held at men-only clubs. Politicians questioned her credibility on the basis of her looks. It was, she says now, a battle of constantly "challenging the sexual stereotyping that begins at birth, when a pink blanket is used to identify a girl and simultaneously limit the range of opportunities open to her when she grows up."

Yet, Dole's persistence, her charm, hard work, and obvious skill paid off. She moved to the White House Office of Consumer Affairs, which led to the President's Committee on Consumer Interests, which led to the Federal Trade Commission. In 1974, *Time* magazine called her one of America's 200 "faces of the future."

In the midst of that, she met Senator Bob Dole during a lobbying visit to Capitol Hill. After a two-year courtship, the two married in 1975 at the National Cathedral in Washington. The next six years brought a whirlwind of political activity. After the campaign for Bob's ill-fated run for the presidency in 1980, Elizabeth Dole joined the Ronald Reagan presidential campaign, and after the election, was appointed head of the White House Office on Public Liaison. This was the position that became a springboard for her future Cabinet roles: Secretary of Transportation under Reagan, and, as Secretary of Labor, Bush's first female Cabinet officer.

Spiritual Starvation

Dole speaks with a quiet pride about her long list of accomplishments, but there is a sense of misgiving there too. For, as she came to realize, her political progress did not come without a price. The perfectionism and drive to excel which had brought her so far had at the same time caused a condition she terms as "spiritual starvation."

"As we move along, how often in our busy lives, something seems to get in the way of a more than ritualistic faith," she observes. What are these "somethings"? She continues: "It may be money, or power or prestige. In my case, it was career. More specifically, the Holy Grail of public service became very nearly all-consuming," she writes.

It was that confession that Dole made public during her 1988 National Prayer Breakfast address. She told the story of Queen Esther, and then linked the biblical heroine's story with her own. "I had enjoyed a comfortable life. I had built up my own self-sufficient world. I had God neatly compartmentalized, crammed into a crowded file drawer of my life," she told the group.

She realized, however, that had to change. "For if Christ is who he says he is—our Savior, the central figure in all of history, who gives meaning to a world of confusing, conflicting priorities—then I had to realize that Christ could not be compartmentalized. It was time to submit my resignation as master of my own universe, and God accepted my resignation."

Several actions helped Dole with her newfound resolutions. She joined a weekly "spiritual growth" group at her home church, Foundry United Methodist Church in Washington. The group's main purpose is to help Christians relate their personal faith to everyday experiences. She and her husband also became more intentional about setting Sunday aside as a day of rest. When they are in town, they rarely miss a Sunday at Foundry, congregants say.

Dole also became stricter about her own personal devotional time. Even her husband remarks on it in his portion of *Unlimited Partners*. "She's the early bird, up early most mornings to open her Bible or other devotional reading," he writes.

Such a time as this

After leaving her Transportation post to campaign for her husband's second run at the presidency in 1988, Dole considered getting out of government work. After more than two decades,

she was looking more for private charity opportunities. When George Bush called and offered her the post of Labor Secretary, she decided to accept. "If you want to use a government position to make a positive difference for people, you can consider that your mission field," she told *World Vision* magazine. She stayed there for two years before stepping down late in 1990 to take the helm of the American Red Cross—the first female president of that organization since founder Clara Barton.

As Labor Secretary, she invested much time and energy in getting disadvantaged youths opportunities for the future. And now, at the Red Cross, she has a more direct helping route—something she has desired for a long time. After the Persian Gulf War, she was among the first into liberated Kuwait, bringing relief supplies and setting up planning strategies for further aid to the Middle East areas devastated by war.

"Mine has not been a road to Damascus experience," she explains, "but a continuing search for guidance and the true perspective that comes with the strengthening of faith."

In a town where guidance is often defined as political expediency, and perspective can be myopic and distorted, that is not an easy task. But, as Dole told the National Prayer Breakfast, God requires much of those he calls. "The world is ready, I believe, for men and women who will accept this calling, men and women who recognize that they are not immune to the predicaments of the day, men and women who are willing to accept the privilege of serving, men and women who are ready to see that the providence of God may have brought them to such a time as this."

Further Reading

Dole, Bob and Elizabeth Dole with Richard Norton Smith. *The Doles: Unlimited Partners.* New York: Simon and Schuster, 1988.

Dole, Elizabeth Hanford. "Challenge to Commitment." *Decision*, June 1987, pp. 16–18.

Mission

Hudson Taylor
China's Millions

Until 1842 the mighty empire of China was fast closed to the West except for a small "factory" near Canton where ships might load silks, porcelain, and tea and offload opium from India. No "foreign devils" were allowed to enter China, which thus excluded Protestant missionaries.

Two centuries earlier, Jesuits had been scientists at the Imperial Court, and a few brave Roman Catholic priests traveled in the interior, risking their lives by so doing

Then the Chinese government tried to stop the harmful opium trade. Britain fought a war, and by the "unequal treaties" of 1842 Hong Kong was ceded to Britain and international settlements were formed in five Treaty Ports. A small number of Protestant missionaries began work in these ports, strictly forbidden to go "over the treaty wall" into the interior. Inland China, with its teeming millions, stayed closed to the Christian gospel.

Far away in England, ten years before the Treaty of Nanking (1842), a boy was born to Amelia and James Taylor, an obscure Yorkshire druggist. James Hudson Taylor grew up

to be the catalyst whereby Christianity, against all the odds, spread through every province of China. Under God he laid the foundation of the Chinese church, which astonished the world by its staggering growth in the late nineteenth century.

Druggist

A bored youth of seventeen, apprentice of his druggist father, took out a tray of tracts to find a story to while away an hour off

duty in June 1849. He picked one and went into a warehouse in the stable yard of their shop and home in the Yorkshire town of Barnsley, intending to enjoy the story and skip the moral. James Taylor, his father, was a Wesleyan lay preacher as well as a druggist and apothecary, but Hudson Taylor, his only son, had inwardly distanced himself from religion, having been influenced by a freethinking fellow clerk during a brief spell in a bank.

Taylor began to read about a sick coalman who believed his sins stopped him from reaching Christ, until some pious visitors read him the Bible verse: "Who His own self bore our sins in His own body on the tree." The coalman cried, "Then it's done—my sins are gone!"

Contrary to all Taylor's expectations, the words struck him with force. Underneath

Hudson Taylor's Brethren Assembly Hall in North London.

The young Hudson Taylor.

his uncle, a doctor in the slums. While there, "I felt that one's spiritual muscles need strengthening. When I get out to China I shall have no claim on anyone for anything. How important, therefore, to learn before leaving England to move man, through God, by prayer alone."

His absent-minded uncle generally forgot to pay his nephew, who deliberately never reminded him, but learned to live each day without knowing whether he would have money for the next; once he gave his last coin to a starving woman, and prayed; and by the next post he received a larger coin, tucked in a pair of kid gloves, from a donor he never traced.

In September 1853, at the age of twenty-one, Hudson Taylor sailed for China as the first agent of a new nondenominational society. His medical course at the London Hospital was unfinished, and the girl he had hoped to marry he left behind because she refused to come. He arrived in Shanghai in March 1854, needing to learn the language, and finding a city under fire from rebels.

God's way

He was often depressed and afraid, but his determination to go inland never wavered and he learned Chinese quickly. The inefficiency of the society at home meant that his salary was seldom sent, leaving him debtor or destitute. He therefore broke the connection, and began to live by faith, as he had learned to do in his artificially induced training at Hull. He developed the principles by which he afterward guided his own mission, never appealing for funds except to God, and administering all

his rebellion had lingered a longing for that friendship of Christ that thrilled his parents and his sister, but he had given up the struggle to reach Him. Suddenly, as he read the tract, he realized that Christ had opened the way by dying on the cross. God could not deny His own promise—all that was necessary was to repent and trust Him. This he did instantly, on the warehouse floor.

Celestial Empire

He realized at once that he had been called to serve God, and he knew where. His father, a great reader, had become enthused with the hidden land of China, the "Celestial Empire," which remained fast closed to missionaries except for a very few, clinging to the five Treaty Ports that had been opened for trade seven years before. Hudson Taylor, on that June day in 1849, knew that he was called to China, to the vast inland where no foreigner might go.

He began to train himself. He was small, sandy haired, musical, affectionate, with a strong sense of humor—but within was steel. He moved to the seaport of Hull to learn medicine under gifts with the scrupulous integrity he had learned from his father. "Depend upon it," he would say, "God's work, done in God's way, will never lack for supplies."

Taylor began preaching along inland canals, in defiance of the ban on foreigners, knowing that he was beyond consular protection and could be arrested or murdered. Like all Westerners, he wore European clothes, which included the usual black frock-coat, so different from the robes of a mandarin (teacher), or the pajamas of a peasant.

Honorable garment

At one town in 1855 a rapt listener wished to ask a question. Taylor was delighted.

The man said, "I have been pondering all the while you have been preaching but the subject is no clearer to my mind. The honorable garment you are wearing, Foreign Teacher, has upon one edge of it a number of circular objects that might do duty as buttons, and on the opposite edge, certain slits in the material probably intended for buttonholes?"

The crowd was all attention, text and sermon forgotten.

"The purpose of that strange device I can understand. It must be to attach the honorable garment in cold or windy weather. But, Foreign Teacher, what can be the meaning of those buttons in *the middle of the honorable back*?"

"Why, yes," chorused the crowd, "in the middle of the back!"

The words echoed to Hudson Taylor's footsteps as he walked, as he took off the coat and looked at those three useless buttons. They summed up the absurdity of western dress in an oriental setting.

Going native

Shortly afterward he bought teacher's robes, shaved the front of his head, dyed his hair black, and attached a pigtail. Although Western missionaries were disgusted that Taylor should "go native," but he traveled more freely and was heard with respect, though his blue eyes gave him away as a foreign devil. From that time on, identification with the Chinese became another of his principles: the members of his future mission would always be expected to wear Chinese dress.

He had much to learn. Some years later he confessed, "My greatest temptation is to lose my temper over the slackness and inefficiency in those on whom I depended. It is no use to lose my temper... but O it is such a trial." On one tour, after his medical equipment had been lost in a fire, a servant stole his luggage and he was robbed by Chinese pretending to help. Taylor lost his temper and struck one of them, then walked off alone, thoroughly cross. As he hobbled along uncomfortably in his Chinese shoes, he suddenly realized that he had betrayed his Lord, and at once he sought and found forgiveness.

"At home," he wrote, "you can never know what it is to be absolutely alone, amidst thousands, everyone looking on you with curiosity, with contempt, with suspicion or with dislike. Thus to learn what it is to be despised and rejected of men ... and then to have the love of Jesus applied to your heart by the Holy Spirit... *this is precious, this is worth coming for*."

THE LIFE OF
Hudson Taylor

1832	Born at Barnsley, Yorkshire
1849	Conversion
1854	Arrives at Shanghai
1855	Adopts Chinese dress
1858	Marries Maria Dyer
1865	Founds China Inland Mission
1866	His *Lammermuir* party arrives in Shanghai
1870	Death of Maria
1871	Marries Jane Faulding
1881	Prayer and appeal for 70 CIM recruits
1886	Appeal for "The Hundred"
1890s	Great increase of CIM
1900	Boxer Rising
1902	Retires as General Direct
1905	Dies in Changsha, Hunan

James Hudson Taylor, 1832–1905.

A nobody

Soon he would no longer be alone. He had made his base at Ningpo, where a number of missionaries resided, including a harsh old lady, Miss Aldersey, who ran a school for Chinese girls. One of her helpers was a young English orphan, Maria Dyer. Hudson Taylor and Maria fell in love, but Miss Aldersey demanded that Maria refuse him because he was a "young, poor, unconnected Nobody," all the more unsuitable because he wore Chinese dress.

Maria wrote secretly to her guardians in England, however. The lovers contrived to meet and became engaged "whether the guardians' answer was favourable or otherwise.... I was not long engaged without trying to make up for the number of kisses I *ought* to have had these last few months."

The missionary community was in uproar at the news of the engagement, even when a letter arrived from the guardians with warm consent. Hudson Taylor and Maria were married in January 1858.

Maria sympathized totally with her husband's desire to bring the gospel to the far-flung distant provinces of the Chinese Empire, and in 1858 the Treaty of Tientsin (ratified in 1860) gave Westerners, including missionaries, the nominal right to go anywhere. But Taylor had been seriously ill, and, sadly, November 1860 found Hudson, Maria, and Gracie, their little girl, back in London.

Millions dying

He could not escape the vision of "a million a month dying in the land without God. This was burned into my very soul." He worked on revising a Chinese New Testament; he finished his medical training; he wrote pamphlets; and he urged upon existing societies the claims of Inland China, in vain.

He must found his own mission, but he dared not take the risk of flinging men and women into the unknown. He struggled inwardly until by the summer of 1865 he was nearing a nervous breakdown.

At last, on Sunday morning, June 25, 1865, whilst walking alone on Brighton Beach after

An Overseas Missionary Fellowship worker today.

church, he knew he must make a decision.

He trudged the sands in gloom and fear. Turning, he saw the sea and thought of heaven. "Well, if God gives us a band of men for Inland China, and they go, and all die of starvation even, they will only be taken straight to heaven. And if one heathen soul is saved would it not be worth while?" He walked on, a trifle more cheerful. He stopped, "Why, if we are obeying the Lord, the responsibility rests with Him, not with us!"

The responsibility was God's. Taylor took his Bible from under his arm. It fell open at a chapter in Job. He wrote across the top: "Prayed for twenty-four willing skillful labourers at Brighton, June 25th/65."

"All was joy and peace.... How I did sleep that night! My dear wife thought Brighton had done wonders for me, and so it had."

The twenty-four

Hudson asked for twenty-four laborers as a symbolic figure— two for each province of China

without a Protestant missionary. He had no idea how they would come. To the world his physique was feeble and he was almost a pauper, but he had thrown himself on God and in the next years became indeed an instrument of the Most High: Hudson Taylor's intelligence and charm, his capacity to inspire affection and loyalty, and his gift of leadership, had been touched by the Divine.

Nearly a year after Brighton Beach, on May 26, 1866, the *Lammermuir* windjammer set sail from London Docks with Hudson and Maria and their children, and seventeen recruits— ten women and seven men. The others had gone ahead or would follow. The China Inland Mission had begun. Most of its members would have been rejected by established societies for lack of a university degree or holy orders (ordination).

They survived a typhoon to arrive in Shanghai, a battered near wreck, on September 30, 1866. They had also survived some disagreements between themselves, resolved by the tact of Hudson and Maria, but one or two rejected Taylor's leadership and later left the mission.

The first twenty years of the new China Inland Mission were hard. An English archdeacon in the coastal provinces opposed Taylor's methods and aims, and stirred up strife on the field and slander at home. Taylor refused to reply, except factually and in love, knowing that God and the future would vindicate him.

In the hot summer of 1867 the Taylors lost their beloved eldest child, Gracie, from water on the brain. The following summer, with several others of the CIM, they were nearly killed in a riot, and then falsely accused in the British Parliament of summoning a gunboat to rescue them, almost precipitating war. The pressures and slander brought Taylor "the awful temptation even to end his own life"; only Maria's love held him back. "I hated myself, I hated my sin," he wrote to her when they were parted, "and yet I gained no strength against it."

Abiding

A little later one of his most experienced missionaries told him by letter that he had discovered a secret, not new but misunderstood: "To let my loving Saviour work in me His will.... Abiding, not striving or struggling."

Hudson Taylor was amazed at his own blindness. As in Barnsley twenty years before, as at Brighton four years before, a long inward struggle resolved in a split second. "As I read I saw it all. 'If we believe *not*, He abideth faithful.' And I looked to Jesus and saw (and when I saw, oh, how joy flowed) that He had said, 'I will *never* leave you.'"

Taylor must not struggle for strength or peace but rest in the strength and peace of Christ. "I have striven in vain to abide in Him. I'll strive no more. For has not He promised to abide with me—never to leave me, never to fail me?"

"Think what it involves," he wrote. "Can Christ be rich and I poor? Can your right hand be rich and your left poor? or your head well fed while your body starves?"

He became a new man, and when, the next year, Maria died in childbirth, the heartbroken Hudson was able to cast his grief onto his Lord. Theirs had been one of the deep unions and great love stories of history, and a powerful factor in China's evangelization.

Hudson Taylor was not yet thirty-eight. He could not retire into selfish grief; Inland China had hardly begun to be penetrated. Eighteen months later he married Maria's best friend, Jennie Faulding, for a partnership of nearly thirty years until her death. Once, when demands of work had parted them for too long, he was almost in despair. "I feel as if my heart would break soon if I don't have *you* yourself. I was almost in a mind just to run off by today's P and O, leaving my foreign clothes at Chefoo, and papers and books.... Though the tears will come into my eyes every few minutes, I do want to give myself, and you too, darling, for the life of the Chinese and of our fellow labourers. An easy-going non-self-denying life will never be one of *power*. Pray for me, my own heart's love, that neither my faith nor my patience fail.... I have been so pressed and wearied. The strain very great."

As he often affirmed, "If he had a thousand lives, China should have them. No! Not *China*, but *Christ*. Can we do too much for Him?"

Bombshell

In 1874 Hudson had a serious accident on a riverboat, slipping down a companion ladder onto his heels, and damaging his spine. He was slow to recover, and found the thought of nine provinces still untouched very depressing. But the tide was turning. The international Convention of Chefoo in 1876 opened every part of China in fact, not nominally as before.

Hudson Taylor seized the advantage. "From 1876 to 1880," said a member of the CIM, "Mr. Taylor's advent, we used to say, was like a bombshell scattering us abroad." Yet his strategies were not haphazard; Taylor trusted his men to be cautious as well as brave, and each and every pioneering journey was carefully prepared. The purpose was to preach the gospel, and if other missions reaped where his people had sown, he rejoiced. He was forward in famine relief and in opposing the opium trade; he was before his time in willingness to work with other mission bodies, in allowing women to pioneer on their own, and in his longing for a Chinese-led church.

His writings and his dramatic appeals for recruits—whether for eighteen, for seventy, or for a hundred—stirred the churches of Britain and North America. His words were backed by his own spiritual life, and by his prayers. On the field, he was greatly loved by those he led.

By 1895 his international CIM was the largest single Protestant body in China, though scattered thinly, and in the Boxer Rising of 1900 they suffered most martyrdoms. Taylor was in the West, ill, and yet raising reinforcements. As the terrible news flowed in, he murmured, "I cannot think, I cannot pray, but I can *trust*." The Rising was suppressed, but he refused all compensation for lost lives and ruined buildings: the Mandarins, amazed, issued proclamations applauding the Christians.

In 1905, in the capital of the last province to be opened, Hudson Taylor died, worn out at seventy-two.

The *Lammermuir* Party: The group of 22 CIM missionaries who set out for China on 26 May 1866, on board the *Lammermuir*.

Further Reading

Broomhall, A. J. *Hudson Taylor and China's Open Century*. 7 vols. Kent: Hodder and Stoughton, 1981–90.

Pollock, John C. *Hudson Taylor and Maria: Pioneers in China*. New York: McGraw-Hill, 1962.

Taylor, Howard and Mary Geraldine Taylor. *Hudson Taylor and the China Inland Mission*. London: Morgan & Scott, 1920.

THE CHRISTMAS OFFERING

Few missionaries have had the long-lasting influence of Lottie Moon. Born in old Virginia, she was heir to all the advantages that social status and wealth could provide. Equipped with the finest education a woman could obtain at that time, she found herself as a foreigner and a missionary in China, and the object of scorn and persecution. Her life became a model of genteel and loving service not only to the Chinese but also to her fellow missionaries. In an age when women were seldom allowed to speak in public, Lottie Moon singlehandedly established an outpost of the gospel where others had attempted but failed.

Famine and war in the midst of prejudice and persecution failed to dim her vision or quench her love for the Chinese. While doing the work of three or more missionaries, she kept up a continual barrage of letters calling for missionary recruits and soliciting the finances to support them. In one of her letters published in the December 1887 issue of the *Foreign Mission Journal*, she called for an annual Christmas offering to be taken the week before Christmas for foreign missions.

The idea caught on and the Woman's Missionary Union began to sponsor such an offering in Southern Baptist churches the next year. The first offering raised $3,215.26, enough to send three single missionary women to China. In 1918, six years after Miss Moon's death, the annual offering was named for her. By 1989 the cumulative total given to foreign missions through the Lottie Moon offering amounted to one billion, eighty-three million, five hundred and fifty-six dollars.

In thousands of churches every year, plays and pageants continue to tell the Lottie Moon story to hundreds of thousands who are inspired and challenged by her sacrificial life. Rarely, if ever, has such a little woman cast such a long shadow as Miss Lottie.

Lottie Moon—Missionary to China

A THOUSAND LIVES FOR CHINA

Few missionaries have been as influential as the little vivacious Miss Moon. "Lottie," as Charlotte Diggs Moon became known, was a petite four-foot-three-inch-tall southern belle of aristocratic stock. It would be difficult to conceive of a more unpromising missionary candidate. When Lottie resigned her teaching post in the Female High School of Caldwell, Georgia, to take up missionary service among the "heathen" in China, many of her friends felt her life would be wasted—wasted alabaster. But Lottie near the end of her life,

Charlotte—"Lottie"—Moon as a young woman, c. 1873.

Southern Baptist missionaries in Senegal, funded by the Christmas offering.

said, "If I had a thousand lives, I would give them all for the women of China."

Lottie was born on December 12, 1840, at Viewmont in Albermarle County, the fourth of seven children of Edward Harris Moon and Anna Maria Barclay Moon. As a child she enjoyed all the advantages of the landed gentry of antebellum Virginia. The Moon family lifestyle was made possible by a large plantation with fifty-two slaves and a thriving mercantile business. Tutors in French, English literature, and music were brought to the home for the instruction of the children. The first blow to the tranquility of the family came when Lottie's father grew seriously ill with a disease from which he recovered, only to die from a riverboat accident on the way to New Orleans three months later. Lottie was thirteen at the time. The next year saw Lottie off to a boarding school, the Virginia Female Seminary at Botetourt Springs.

Although Lottie's Uncle James Barclay was a medical missionary to Israel for the relatively new Disciples denomination and her parents were staunch Baptists, Lottie was a skeptic. Apparently, the Moon children were an independent-minded lot, who rarely attended any church. Lottie's church attendance greatly improved during her two years at Hollins Institute (the new name for the seminary) but not her attitude toward religion. Attendance at chapel was compulsory and the Enon Baptist Church, located just across the road from Hollins, made attendance the normal activity on Sundays for the hundred girls enrolled in the school. But Lottie stubbornly resisted this religious influence. The two years she spent at

> *"If I had a thousand lives, I would give them all for the women of China."*

Hollins saw her excel in classical studies, but Lottie did less well in math and science.

A transparent change

On December 22, 1858, Lottie professed faith in Christ as her personal Savior. She reported that during a revival meeting conducted by Dr. John W. Broadus at the Charlottesville Baptist Church, she went to her room to sleep, but due to the barking of a dog she could not. It was during a sleepless night that she determined to examine Christianity honestly and the result was her conversion. She, as so many before her, went to a revival meeting in order to scoff but left to pray.

The change in the gifted but frivolous student was transparent. Her friends wrote of the change which God had brought about in her life. Lottie was then in the second year of her studies in the newly founded Albemarle Female Institute, which a few visionary Baptist ministers and laymen had founded for the education of qualified women. The institute was designed to be the academic equivalent to the University of Virginia, which only admitted men. Here she became as well known for academic accomplishments as for her devil-may-care attitude. Her influence was great and she soon became the object of earnest prayer by concerned Christian friends, her fellow students, and faculty. Shortly after her baptism, Lottie assumed the leadership of the Christian students in the institute.

Four years after entering Albemarle, Charlotte Diggs Moon was awarded the master of arts degree. In the process,

Lottie had become an excellent linguist. In addition to French, Latin, Italian, and Spanish, she had gained a proficiency in Greek and Hebrew. Perhaps her interest in the languages of the Bible had been stimulated by the brilliant teaching of a young professor named Crawford H. Toy, who taught Lottie these languages. Toy's sister, Julia, was Lottie's close friend. Lottie's interest in mission service may also have been encouraged by Professor Toy, who sought for an appointment to become a missionary to Japan.

A clear call

However, Lottie's own call to foreign mission service was not to come until some ten years later. During her second year of teaching in Cartersville, Georgia, where a cousin of Lottie had led a group of businessmen to sponsor a new school known as the Cartersville Female High School, Lottie heard the call "as clear as bell."

Lottie had discussed the possibility of a missionary career with Edmonia, her younger sister as early as 1870. In fact, she and Edmonia were already making generous gifts to foreign mission work in both China and Italy. Finally, Edmonia's dream of becoming a missionary to China became a reality when she was appointed by the Foreign Mission Board of the Southern Baptist Convention to serve in North China in 1872. In reality, although she was emotionally unstable and unsuited for missionary service, Edmonia's efforts were not fruitless. Devout women in five churches in Richmond, Virginia, undertook her support by organizing "Mite Societies." And it was her correspondence which reported that there was much work to be done in China for the Lord which only women could do because Chinese society was segregated. This information struck a resounding chord in Lottie's heart, for she was seeking to discover just where the Lord could make the greatest use of her life.

Once the decision was made, there was no turning back. On July 7, 1873, Charlotte Diggs Moon was appointed a missionary to China and the Baptist women of Georgia were asked to provide her support. On October 7, after a stormy sea voyage in which even the crew of the ship despaired of life, she arrived at last in Shanghai, to be met by veteran missionaries, Matthew T. Yates and Tarleton and Martha Crawford. Some three weeks later, after another trip at sea and a typhoon, she settled at Tengchow (now Qingdao) which was to be her home for the next thirty-nine years. Here, Edmonia awaited her arrival and soon told her about both the privileges and the problems of missionary service.

Tengchow was the principal seaport of the Shantung (now Shandong) Province, at the time reported to be the most densely populated area in the world. Christianity had managed to gain a precarious foothold in the ancient city, especially among the poor.

Foreign devils

Although the government of China was bound by treaty to protect all Americans, the consulate in Chefoo could not shield them from the ridicule and scorn of those who considered them unwanted "foreign devils" and said so. The six Baptist

missionaries, including newly arrived Lottie, and the few more missionaries of the Northern Presbyterian Mission, constituted a tiny minority in the city of eighty thousand. Lottie learnt with delight that Baptists and Presbyterians worked together in the seemingly impossible task of establishing an effective

Qingdao (Tengchow) in 1989; *inset*: Tengchow from "Water City".

witness for Christ in the midst of such great barriers of hatred and prejudice.

Edmonia showed remarkable skill in mastering the difficult Chinese language. However, the primitive conditions of the Shantung Province, the constant barrage of "devil woman" that always accompanied her in the streets of the city, together with the curiosity of children, the denigration of women, and the wanton disregard of human life, was too much for her Her dream of becoming a missionary to China turned into a never-ending nightmare. Culture shock, coupled with poor health, compelled the mission to ask Lottie to take her sister home. Edmonia never returned to China, but Lottie did. Her name was to become a household term, synonymous with missions, for more than a century.

Feeding the hungry

Upon her return to China in 1877, Lottie began to develop her own mission strategy. That which appealed to her most was the educational approach, the most commonly accepted mission methodology at the time. She opened a school in Tengchow. The Bible and a catechism which fellow missionary Martha Crawford had developed for her school comprised the heart of the curriculum. Soon some of Lottie's students could quote from memory the entire Gospel of Mark or Matthew. This was a small victory. She had less success in convincing parents that they should unbind the feet of their daughters, but she persisted and eventually she was able to report progress in this effort as well. Famine, however, which recurred with

devastating frequency, continually frustrated her best efforts. She wrote of the terrible plight of the starving Chinese to the Board and to the *Religious Herald*, published in Richmond. Money began to trickle in, but there was never enough. She fed the hungry at her own doorstep, frequently at her own expense, until her funds were virtually exhausted. For many years she provided for as many as fifteen destitute women at a time in her own home.

Although Lottie longed to win the upper classes to Christ and never gave up this dream, she loved all the Chinese, ignorant and poor as the masses were. Most families could not afford to have a child go to school—Lottie could never reach these masses through education. This is one of the reasons her educational work began to take a back seat to person-to-person evangelism.

Preaching in the country

Day after day, Lottie went with veteran missionary Sallie Holmes, or one of the other Baptist or Presbyterian missionaries, to countless villages. While one missionary witnessed to the women, using the Bible, hymns, and the catechism, the other would instruct the children, girls and boys. Although Chinese taboo kept the women from addressing men, the men found ways to listen—out of sight but not out of hearing. The days were long and privacy was in short supply, but the eager and curious Chinese made the effort worthwhile in spite of hardships.

Afterward, Lottie wrote, "I have never gotten so near the people in my life as during this visit. I have never had so many

Opposite: A painting of Lottie Moon, surrounded by her beloved Chinese.

opportunities to press home upon their consciences their duty to God and the claims of the Savior to their love and devotion. I feel more and more that this work is of God." In the midst of China's war with Japan in 1895, Lottie, together with a younger missionary, made evangelistic excursions to 118 villages in three months. No wonder that back in Tengchow it was increasingly reported that "Miss Lottie Moon is out preaching in the country."

Even before China's war with Japan, Lottie's "country" had expanded. Although she had never been farther than fifty miles from Tengchow, she became determined to work in P'ingtu (now Pingdu), 120 miles from Tengchow. At P'ingtu her mission strategy changed. Instead of going into the streets with her message of salvation she decided first to become a friend and a neighbor and work quietly on a neighborhood basis. She first won the local children with delicious cookies she baked from an old Virginia recipe. With the help of two converts from P'ingtu, she began to make many friends in whose homes she became a welcomed guest.

Friends—then converts

The unbearably cold winter forced her to adopt, for the first time, the padded robe worn by Chinese women. She was amazed to discover the difference the Chinese apparel made. No more did women ask if she were a man or a woman, and no longer was she met on the streets with the epithet "devil woman." Her new strategy was

working, she explained to one of her colleagues. "Demonstrate a Chinese-style Christian life," which means, "we must go out and live among them, manifesting the gentle, loving spirit of our Lord... We need to make friends before we can hope to make converts."

With the help of a Chinese Christian couple by the name of Chao, Lottie became something of a celebrity. As she was the only foreigner living in P'ingtu City, curiosity gradually gave way to friendship, and friendship led to the resumption of her itinerant ministry, now in the innumerable villages in the P'ingtu countryside. A Mr. Dan Ho-bang from Sha-ling, a small village ten miles from P'ingtu City, heard of the woman who preached Jesus and lived on the west side of the city. He sent three men to bring her to Sha-ling, where she found a devout vegetarian group known as the Venerable Heaven Sect, who were earnestly seeking God. She sent for Mrs. Martha Crawford and the two of them reaped a harvest for Christ.

An elderly man who heard Miss Moon teach at Sha-ling longed to know more about the one who could forgive sins and change lives. Lottie gave him a New Testament which he asked his young cousin Li Show-ting, also a brilliant young Confucian scholar, to read to him. At first Li scoffed, but as he read and discussed with Miss Moon the new religion, his attitude began to change. Under her careful witness and that of two other missionaries whom she had asked to come to P'ingtu for that very purpose, he was converted. In 1890, he was baptized and later ordained. He became the most outstanding evangelist in North China, baptizing more than ten thousand converts.

With the growing response to the gospel in P'ingtu came a fresh outbreak of persecution, however. Miss Moon, encouraging the new converts to remain faithful, refused to call upon the American Consul in Chefoo for protection. At the height of the persecution, she placed herself between the persecutors and the Christians, declaring that they must first kill her before harming the Christians. Her faith and courage further endeared her to her beloved P'ingtu Christians—and they remained faithful. Subsequently, the church at P'ingtu became the strongest church in the North China Baptist Mission.

"How she loved us"

Although Lottie returned to Tengchow and re-established her school, she continued to keep in touch with the P'ingtu Christians. She had a special place in her heart for them and they in theirs for her. When, on one occasion, she did not return as expected, two men from Sha-ling walked 120 miles to seek her out. After her death, the P'ingtu church wrote: "How she loved us."

In fact the hardships Lottie had endured and her great love for the P'ingtu Christians brought about her last illness and death. The Boxer Rebellion had partly subsided when the most severe famine of the series hit the Shantung Province. Starvation stalked the land. Lottie fed hundreds at her doorstep, but when she heard that the famine had reached P'ingtu she refused to eat herself. The financial condition of the Foreign Mission Board made it impossible for the Board to help. The situation seemed hopeless. The mission recognized that Lottie Moon's resources were exhausted, both physically and financially. Her fellow missionaries believed her only hope was to return to the United States.

Lottie Moon began the long journey home, only to die on Christmas Eve, 1912, on board ship in the harbor of Kobe, Japan. The nurse attending her saw her lift her frail body and, clasping her hands together in a Chinese greeting, she bowed her head for one last time. She had given her all. She had often written: "I am immortal until my work is done," and during the first, cold, lonely winter at P'ingtu, "I hope no missionary will ever be as lonely as I have been." Now her work was done and what a remarkable work it had been; and now she was no longer lonely.

Further Reading

Allen, Catherine B. *The New Lottie Moon Story*. Nashville: Broadman, 1980.

Lawrence, Una Roberts. *Lottie Moon*. Nashville: Sunday School Board of the Southern Baptist Convention, 1927.

Mission to Calabar

In 1848 a mission was founded at Calabar on the West African coast at the instigation of freed Jamaican slaves who wanted their former countrymen to share in the blessings of the gospel. Poisonous swamps and a debilitating climate made short work of many Europeans who dared to venture there. Nevertheless, reports in the *Missionary Record* of the United Presbyterian Church captured the imagination of readers, many of whom were so touched by conditions in Old Calabar, they dedicated their lives or their resources to God's work among the tribes of the tropics.

Mary Mitchell Slessor of Dundee, Scotland, was one so moved by the accounts in the *Record*. In May of 1875, her heart set on Calabar, she approached the Foreign Mission Board. Thus begins the story of a young woman destined to do what no European woman had ever done— Mary would go alone to live with unknown tribes and carry God's message to the interior of Africa. In spite of chronic illness and often overwhelming fears, with God's constant help she prevailed, and before her death in 1915 she had become known throughout West Africa as *Eka kpukpro Owo—* "Mother of All the Peoples."

Mary Slessor as a young woman.

Mary Slessor of Calabar

MOTHER OF ALL THE PEOPLES

Born to a devout Christian mother and an alcoholic father, Mary Slessor found her early life an exercise in survival tactics. She spent her youth in the slums of Dundee, where she became a "full-timer" at the mill at age thirteen. Frequently beaten and thrown out of the house by her father, Mary had to learn to cope with the unemployed, drunk men who filled the darkened city streets. While she learned to defend herself under dangerous circumstances, she became very shy and developed a great fear of speaking in public, particularly if there were any men present.

Notwithstanding and hardships the family might be suffering, when Sunday arrived Mary and her brothers and sisters were properly attired and taken by their mother to the Wisehart Memorial Church. Mary, a mischievous redhead with sparkling blue eyes and a well-developed sense of humor, did not always take the services seriously, being more interested in engaging in pranks with her friends. As she recalled later, she was finally frightened "into the Kingdom." An old widowed neighbor took interest in her, and holding her hand to the fire in her sitting room said if Mary did not repent, her soul would "burn in the lowin' bleezin' fire for ever and ever!" Shock at the prospect of eternal damnation brought Mary to the Lord, but she vowed never to use such methods on another person.

Aided by constant prayer and frequent trips to the pawn shop, Mary and her mother kept the family together and avoided public disgrace. Her father's passing brought some relief to the family, but Mary nevertheless mourned the death of one who had been so degraded by his inability to cope with what life had dealt him. She developed a great compassion for those enslaved by circumstances, and this force would dominate the rest of her life.

Through these years Mary was never absent from church services. She was fascinated by the tales of returning missionaries and frequently imagined herself teaching the black children of Africa. She carried her Bible to work and read it as much as possible. She felt as if God had written personally to her. To Mary, God was real and close. She wanted to be able to express the same unconditional love toward other people that God expressed to her.

"She's game!"

When James Logie became the minister of Wishart Church he

and his wife took an interest in Mary, and she became a frequent visitor in their home. Logie was so impressed with her commitment to the Lord and her eagerness to learn that, when he organized a mission to reach the people of the slums, he asked if Mary would become his assistant in the youth club. Many slum dwellers opposed the mission because they felt it was avoiding practical matters such as improving salaries and working conditions. Those who attended meetings frequently found themselves pelted with dung or rocks. Once when she was walking to services, Mary was surrounded by a gang whose leader began swinging a

weight on a cord at her head. She stood her ground as the weight came closer and closer, finally brushing her face. Impressed with her courage the perpetrator finally dropped the weight and proclaimed, "She's game!" The gang joined her for services and became her most ardent supporters.

The Dundee mission may not have lasted, but it taught Mary a valuable lesson: by meeting people on their own ground, by living among them, and trying to understand them, she could gain their confidence. Mary herself had been forced to live in dreadful conditions from which there seemed no escape, and she knew the difficulty of trying to

communicate God's love to those who were hungry and plagued by tuberculosis, dysentery, and the many other afflictions which resulted from slum life.

Mary, already driven by a compassion for humanity, was shaken when she read of the death of the great missionary to Africa, Dr. David Livingstone. Moved by Livingstone's plea for someone to "carry out the work I have begun," Mary approached the Foreign Mission Board and requested that she be sent to Calabar. Mary was well aware that the people of Calabar were animists, with minimal Western contacts, but she welcomed the most difficult tasks, knowing her Lord would have done the

Mary Slessor gives first aid to an African child outside her hut.

same and that he was ever with her. In March of 1876, at the age of twenty-eight, Mary left Dundee to receive training in Edinburgh, and in August of the same year she boarded the *SS Ethiopia* bound for Africa. The ship was loaded with alcohol for trade with the Africans, and Mary, realizing what she was up against lamented, "Scores of casks! and only one missionary!"

Stranger in a strange land

As the ship cast anchor off Duke Town on the slave coast of West Africa, romance rapidly faded into reality. A mysterious land awaited Mary—a land governed by witchcraft and superstition, where human life was cheap,

and torture by poisoning and boiling oil was the order of the day. Twins, believed to be children of the devil, were abandoned to die at birth, their mothers banished from their communities. Wives of chiefs were ceremonially strangled to provide company for their dead husbands in the world to come. When Mary arrived the Calabar mission had been in existence for thirty years. During that time only 174 persons had joined the church.

Mary realized that before she could be of any service at all to the African people she had to understand their ways and become one of them. This was not a task she accomplished with

THE LIFE OF	
Mary Slessor	
1848	Born in Gilcomston, Scotland, a suburb of Aberdeen
1859	Family moves to Dundee, Scotland
1862	Works at Dundee mill
1875	Offers services to Foreign Mission Board
1876	Receives instruction at Edinburgh and sails for Calabar
1880	Takes charge of the mission at Old Town
1885	Begins work at Creek Town
1886	Hears of the death of her mother and sister Janie
1888	Begins work among the Okoyong
1891	Is appointed Vice-Consul for Okoyong
1902	Moves to Enyong Creek
1905	Receives office as Member of Itu Native Court
	Mary Slessor Mission Hospital is constructed
1910	Begins work at Ikpe
1913	Receives Maltese Cross for "meritorious service"
1915	Dies at Use

ease. At times her terrors were almost out of control. While Mary had a toughness and determination about her, she was a timid person who would refuse to cross the street alone and was terrified of crowds and speaking in public. Once when speaking at a mission meeting where she had not expected a mixed audience, she had to stop and ask the men to get out of sight before she could continue.

She was also fearful of riding in a canoe, the only available means of long-distance transport in Calabar. She would lie in the bottom of the canoe in terror or sing loudly to keep her mind off her circumstances. The woman who once refused to cross a field because there was a cow in it found herself traveling alone through terrain alive with leopards, poisonous snakes, and crocodiles. She wrote, "I did not use to believe the story of Daniel in the lions' den until I had to take some of these awful marches, and then I knew it was true, and that it was written for my comfort. Many a time I walked along praying, 'O God of Daniel shut their mouths,' and He did."

Stranded alone

Mary contracted malaria soon after her arrival in Calabar. Chronic illness and the loneliness of her work often forced her to the point of despair. In 1886 she received word that her mother and sister Janie had both died, leaving Mary as the sole survivor of her immediate family. She never felt more "stranded and alone," but God gave her the strength to go on. "Heaven is now nearer to me than Britain, and no one will be anxious about me if I go up

Mary Slessor with African twins.

African twins

If all the twins whom Ma Slessor rescued from the hand of death—in Okoyong and other places—had remained alive with their mothers to the present day, they would make up a big town. As soon as this European woman heard that a woman was to die for bearing twins, she would run and find her and take her home with the children. And when she got home, she would take care of the mother and look after her children . And it was her own money which she used in all this business.

Sometimes Ma would walk four or five miles into the bush in order to save people accused of witchcraft who were to be put to death with a cutlass or a rope or "esere" bean (a poison ordeal). More than once Ma looked death in the face, but because she was doing the work of love which is stronger than death, God did not allow death to touch her. No matter how high dispute or strife might rise, as soon as Ma intervened all the disputes and strife and arguments would die away—as if by magic. And so Ma Slessor had this nickname

"Stronger than iron—
Her feet brought peace."

Ma Slessor became an African because of the great love she had for our children. She ate exactly the same food that Africans eat. Little African children would hang round her neck like a string of beads—just as they would do with their own mothers. Sometimes when she went to visit a village, or to walk through the bush, she would go barefoot...

country," Mary wrote, continuing to conquer her loneliness by writing long letters to friends and by her constant communication with God.

Meanwhile, Mary had made her own family among her Calabar orphans, many of them twins whom she had saved from slaughter. One particularly beautiful child whom Mary had named Susie, was the center of attention. But when Susie was fourteen months old she was scalded when she accidentally tipped a jug of boiling water on herself. Mary nursed her for many days, never leaving the child alone. When Susie died in her arms one Sunday morning, Mary's anguish was so great that she could not conduct the service. She later wrote, "My heart aches for my darling. Oh the empty place, and the vain longing for the sweet voice and the soft caress and the funny ways. Oh, Susie, Susie!" Yet there was a victory in the midst of the anguish, for the people dared to attend a twin's burial and a heathen woman prayed that they might all eventually receive the "white Ma's" hope in the beyond.

Probably as a result of her early experience in the slums, Mary was able to confront the most threatening situations. As she was beginning her work with the Okoyong, she heard screams one evening, and forced her way into the center of a crowd that had gathered in the village. She saw a young woman tied to stakes on the ground, with an Egbo man preparing to scald her with boiling oil. The woman's offense was that she had given food to a starving slave man while her husband

Mary Mitchell Slessor.

"Christ sent me to preach the Gospel, and He will look after [the] results."

was away; in local custom this implied unfaithfulness. Mary was furious. Rushing between the woman and the man holding the oil, she refused to budge while the man danced around her in a most menacing fashion. The crowd, animated by drink, became loud with excitement. Mary's courage prevailed, and the assailant backed away. Taking the woman under her protection until she could return to her husband, Mary praised God for standing beside her. The Okoyong held her in respect from that point forward.

Awaiting God's time

Africa did not change rapidly. People would attend services, sing, pray, and profess the gospel—then leave and continue

their feuding and drinking. If ever she became impatient discouraged, Mary reminded herself: "He that believeth shall not make haste." Trying to work one day at a time, she was aware that she might never witness the outcome of her efforts. "Christ sent me to preach the Gospel," she wrote, "and He will look after [the] results."

While victories at times seemed small, in a report to the Mission Board in the late 1890s Mary was able to point to some positive changes she had witnessed. Raiding between tribes and capturing slaves had almost stopped. Women, the greatest victims of the rigid social system, were gaining respect. Tribes were conducting a peaceful trade with the whites. Human sacrifices at the death of a chief had ceased. While drinking continued it had decreased among women, and there was greater value placed on human life.

It was to Mary's credit that many of these positive changes had occurred. She had good relations with British government officials and was appointed to serve several areas as magistrate. She held court, listened to cases, participated in the native "palavers" or discussions, and stood firm against unjust customs. One official noted, "Her judgment was prompt, sometimes severe, but always just." The government allowed her use of every facility and conveyance belonging to it, and highest officials remembered her with letters and sent gifts for the children.

Mary was able to accomplish what she did because she

A Church of Scotland missionary advises on diet and nutrition, Agogo, Ghana.

spot where Mary Slessor had been laid to rest some forty years before. Standing on the bank of the Calabar River it was possible to imagine the day when police and military troops lined the streets at Duke Town waiting for the launch carrying Mary's coffin to arrive from Itu. Mourners gathered, but instead of wailing as they had done at funerals before Mary came to Calabar, they joined in singing "Praise God from Whom All Blessings Flow." There could have been no greater tribute to the life that God had ushered into His kingdom.

gained the trust and respect of the African people. She was one of them. She was not there for personal gain, which was apparent in her every action. She ate African food, gave up material comforts, and lived in huts she helped build, always trusting in God to sustain her and guide her if she lacked knowledge or experience. For example, she preferred cement floors because they kept out the driver ants which had a ferocious bite, but she knew nothing about cement. When asked what lessons she had in making cement she replied, "I just stir it like porridge; turn it out, smooth it with a stick, and all the time keep praying, 'Lord, here's the cement; if to Thy glory, set it,' and it has never once gone wrong."

Meritorious service

In 1913, when Mary was honored with the Maltese Cross from the Order of the Hospital of St. John of Jerusalem in England for "meritorious service," she kept it a secret. She knew she was what she was by the grace of God, and she wanted no credit. The following year World War I broke out. By this time Mary was very ill, and she told a friend, "Oh, if only the war were over and my children safe in the Kingdom, how gladly would I go!" She managed through Christmas in 1914 but steadily weakened as the New Year began. With her children around her, Mary died on the morning of January 13, 1915. Never defeated, whatever the circumstances, Mary had allowed God to mold her to fulfill the requirements of His service. She had now achieved the final victory in a selfless life.

On a 1956 visit to Nigeria Queen Elizabeth II laid a wreath at the base of a large granite cross which marked the

Further Reading

Buchan, James. *The Expendable Mary Slessor.* Edinburgh: Saint Andrew Press, 1980.

Livingstone, W. P. *Mary Slessor of Calabar.* New York: George H. Doran, n.d.

Robinson, Virgil E. *Mighty Mary.* Washington, D.C.: Review and Harold Publishing, 1972.

Syme, Ronald. *Nigerian Pioneer.* New York: William Morrow and Co., 1964.

Amy Carmichael of Dohnavur

Things As They Are

Nineteenth-century missionary biographies were meant to edify. Written to a largely female audience, they recited stories of "beautiful lives," zealous suffering, and miraculous conversions. In the Victorian era, the "romance of missions" was popular adventure fiction with an uplifting moral message.

These books were, in fact, an early form of the computerized fund-raising mailshots of today. Implicit in their message was the need for Christians to give abundantly. They were hugely successful, particularly with women, whose missionary organizations, by the turn of the century, challenged the male-dominated, older societies for the pockets of generous Christians. For years, readers of missionary literature faithfully donated their weekly mites, which, multiplied by thousands, supported an army of evangelists in missions around the world.

No wonder many of these books skimmed lightly over the personal trials and failures of missionary life. Their purpose was to raise support for a worthwhile cause. Loneliness, doubt, and personality conflicts were secrets which had to be kept behind the walls of the missionary compound.

If many female readers guessed the truth, they ignored it. In the nineteenth century, the mission field offered unique opportunities for restless young women, who, in the culture of the Victorian era, were sentimentalized, their varied talents relegated to domestic pursuits. Rewarding occupations were few, and professional opportunities virtually nonexistent; ambitious young women became teachers or nurses, and then usually for only a temporary period. Marriage was the final social promotion most could expect. For many pious, motivated young women, therefore, a career in the "foreign fields"

Amy Carmichael of Dohnavur.

promised challenges for the mind and heart which seemed nearly unlimited.

No haloes

Amy Carmichael is a rare type against this background. "There isn't much of a halo in real life," she once confided to friends at home, "we save it all up for the missionary meetings." A prolific author, she filled her "Scraps," with unflinching descriptions of her experiences, from encounters with "slimy, crawly things" that infested the tropics to the utter foreignness of Western Christianity in Asian cultures. "You go to a hut," she wrote, "and find nobody in, you go to the next and find nobody wants you, you go to the next and find an old woman who says yes, you may talk if you like, and she listens in an aimless sort of way and perhaps two or more drift in, and you go on, a prayer behind each sentence." Her first major book, entitled *Things As They Are*, languished for years without a willing publisher; no one would believe the harsh truths it described.

Amy Carmichael's singular passion, visible even in her

Dr Ponnalari with a young patient in the Dohnavur Hospital.

clothing was for the Great Commission. In Japan, after she realized that the peculiarity of her outfits fascinated her hosts more than the gospel message, she began wearing a kimono. In India she wore the traditional sari, though without the jewels and adornments that were indispensable feminine status symbols in Hindu society. Against the background of a colonial power structure that often regarded non-Westerners with disdain, Amy Carmichael's sari was a potent symbol of both respect and Christian love.

Though certainly inspiring, Amy Carmichael's career belied the triumphant certainty of many a missionary legend. For years she believed she was to work with Hudson Taylor's China Inland Mission, and professed a burden for the Chinese. Turned down by the C.I.M. on health grounds, she went to Japan, where she lasted fifteen months, until debilitating bouts

of neuralgia forced her to Shanghai on furlough. A week later she believed she had received a divine call to Ceylon (Sri Lanka). Against the counsel of many friends in China, she set off to begin the daunting task of mastering yet another non-Western language. A few months later she was on her way home to Britain; her friend and patron, Robert Wilson (fondly known as the Dear Old Man, or D.O.M.) had suffered a life-threatening stroke. When she returned to the mission field a year later—reluctantly turning aside Wilson's pleadings that she remain with him longer—it was to India.

Breaching walls

Raised in the Presbyterian church and a follower of the "higher life" Keswick teachings, she took a post with the Church of England Zenana Missionary Society. She soon found what other Western missionaries had

THE LIFE OF

Amy Carmichael

1867	Born in Millisle, County Down, Northern Ireland
1893–94	Missionary to Japan
1895	Arrives Tinnevelly, South India, as missionary
1901	Begins rescue work for young temple prostitutes
1926	Founds Dohnavur Fellowship
1931	An invalid following an accident, continues writing and Fellowship responsibilities
1951	Dies

already learned: Indian society, rigidly divided by rules of caste and sex, were resistant to open-air preaching or even casual contact between Christians and Hindus. "Zenana" societies tried to breach the wall which separated high-caste women from Christian contact. Amy's friendship with Ponnammal, a gifted Indian Christian, became her own special entry into the perplexing ways of a foreign culture.

In 1901, the arrival of Preena, a young runaway, opened a new dimension of cross-cultural encounter. As an infant, Preena had been devoted to the gods, which meant that she would grow up in the strict seclusion of the temple, and eventually assume the role of ritual prostitute. After one escape attempt, her hands were branded with hot irons. When she heard that Amy, the "child-stealing woman" was in the area, the desperate girl ran from the temple again. Over the objections of the other temple women and the people of the town, Amy and her companions kept Preena. Soon other abandoned children and temple runaways found their way to Amy's bungalow. The work of caring for infants and sickly children became almost overwhelming, and itinerant evangelism became impossible.

Victorians rarely spoke in a direct way about sexual abuse; well-brought-up young women never even referred to those parts of the body above the wrists or ankles. Though Amy was similarly reticent about sexuality, she did not sentimentalize the plight of the young

Amy Carmichael with young Indian children.

girls she rescued. Nor did she gloss over temple life as a quaint foreign custom. It was, in her eyes, a stronghold of principalities and powers which were to be challenged and overcome.

Starry cluster

Amy was not a feminist even by Victorian standards; however, few challenged her authority within the Christian community of men and women known as the Dohnavur Fellowship Victorian women were often strong and determined, usually only in matters relating to their

own feminine sphere. Rarely, if ever, did they directly challenge male leadership. The experience was unique for many of the men, who were always under Amy's spiritual and administrative command. Men who were unable to adapt found their callings elsewhere.

Could this be why she never married? Her correspondence, even with her mother, is extremely reticent on this subject, although there are hints of at least one romantic attraction. Amy's private reasons will probably never surface. It seems most likely that the pool of men able to match her independent drive was already limited; going to India might have narrowed the field even further. Or perhaps, there was simply no one to rival the passion of her first love, the Lord himself, who she believed had called her to the mission field.

It is always tempting to extract a neat historical lesson from an unusually gifted Christian life like that of Amy Carmichael. Certainly her example is personally challenging, but to her time and place it was unique. Her life was more than a few spiritual applications; it has a much broader message for contemporary Christians.

Nobody

Any "lessons" to be learnt from Amy Carmichael's life should be extracted with care. A woman bursting with both literary and artistic talents, she was unusually self-effacing. When the Carmichael children all chose pseudonyms, young Amy called herself "Nobody." She referred to herself as "a cross between a potato and a vegetable marrow" and purposefully defaced her own photographs, when she allowed them to be taken. The Keswick teachings she adhered to further encouraged an extremely deep level of "death to self." At times she seemed unable to enjoy a casual friendship for its own sake.

Although in recent years the language of "self-image" and "self-fulfillment" has certainly been overused, it does resonate with important biblical truths. God does not simply tolerate but loves His creation. Enjoyment of one's self is not always pride; for the Christian it can be a humble act of worship. Life is not just a task—it is also a gift which must be savored.

Much has changed in foreign missions since the Victorian era. Western Christians now hold a far different place in the world. Certainly they need to recapture Amy Carmichael's soldiering spirit and her horror of compromise. Yet at the same time, they must tread carefully. The India of the Raj accepted Christianity in a one-way exchange; Amy Carmichael, who loved the indigenous customs of India, and wore Indian dress, acknowledged spirituality and truth wherever she found it, while holding Christ to be the unique Savior.

In the tilting world of the late twentieth century, American and European believers have new opportunities for exchange. The vitality of the Christianity in Africa, Latin America and Korea at once judges the unexamined lives of western Christians, and is their great hope for the future. Churches in the so-called Third World have much to teach the West about materialism, failed stewardship of natural resources, and compromises with secular power structures. The Victorian missionaries, who helped establish the future of Christianity in Asia and Africa, only laid the groundwork for the spiritual revolution God would ignite through their efforts.

Two world wars and a chain reaction of social and political upheavals have irrevocably changed the world that Amy Carmichael knew. Nuclear proliferation and global warming have introduced fears and a level of hopelessness simply unthinkable to more optimistic Victorians. It would be difficult, if not impossible, to adopt their spirit in the present age.

"Oh, to care..."

What then is the value of Amy Carmichael's life to her spiritual descendants? Neither a rigid guide nor a blueprint, it cannot even be seen as an automatic source of inspiration. It is simply an unparalleled example of spiritual passion. "Oh, to care, and oh for power to make others care," she wrote, "not less, but far, far, more!" The power of Christ's supernatural presence was continually evident in her abiding horror of compromise. Nothing was more precious than her calling, and all of her life she followed a soul-uprooting quest for pure knowledge of God. In a world of increasing complexity, her fiery singleness of purpose re-ignites the power of the simple gospel. In the midst of a thousand conflicting responsibilities, her focused life is a fresh reminder of the untapped power of Christian devotion in our day. No ordinary person; Amy Carmichael's life reflected away from a unique personality to the Creator of life itself. Perhaps she would have wanted it that way.

Further Reading

Elliot, Elisabeth. *A Chance to Die.* Old Tappan, N.J.: Revell, 1987.

Houghton, Frank. *Amy Carmichael of Dohnavur: The Story of a Lover and Her Beloved.* London: S.P.C.K., 1954.

Carmichael, Amy. *Candles in the Dark.* Fort Washington, Pa.: Christian Literature Crusade.

___. *If.* Grand Rapids: Zondervan.

___. *Whispers of His Power.* Old Tappan, N.J.: Revell.

THE LIFE OF
Jim Elliot

Jim Elliot and Elisabeth Howard in May 1952; they were married in 1953.

Jim Elliot—Ecuador Martyr
Heaven Soon

Jim Elliot was a modern nonconformist. His commitment to Jesus Christ being total, he felt responsible to God exclusively and not to man. When he was twenty-two years of age, he wrote the following in his journal, "Do not put yourself in a position relative to any man or groups which permits them to direct policies which you know must be decided upon through your own individual exercise before God. Never let any organization dictate the will of God. A move which so ensnares cannot be of God for me."

After arriving in Ecuador Jim Elliot wrote to a friend, "We have felt great joy in coming to the field as God's free folk. Answering to nobody but Himself, and nobody's support or promise but His very own.... It is most gratifying to look aloft to the God who keeps promises and is sufficient."

Jim Elliot was also a modern mystic, whose writings in his personal journal reflect deep musings about God, profound longings to know God better and to obey Him, and an amazing insight into Scripture for a man so young. His desire to "live to the hilt every situation you believe to be the will of God" was demonstrated in every phase of his life: academics, sports, social life, and spiritual exercises. This worked itself out in reckless abandonment to the will of God that made him not only ready but eager to sacrifice all to God: his career, his love life, even his own blood if necessary.

His greatest contributions to twentieth-century Christianity were, first, that he exemplified a life totally committed to God regardless of cost; and second, the struggles and growth of a great soul which his journals reflect. His early martyrdom at age twenty-eight has inspired and challenged countless others to a similar commitment to Jesus Christ.

All there
"He is no fool who gives what he cannot keep to gain what he cannot lose." These words, written by Jim Elliot at the age of twenty-two, have become the hallmark of his life, quoted more than anything else he wrote. Equally descriptive of his life are these words written less than a year later: "Wherever you are, be *all* there. Live to the hilt every situation you believe to be the will of God." Whatever he was doing—academic studies, Bible study, prayer, preaching, discipling, wrestling, having fun—he was "*all* there," living to the hilt. He was a classic example of Ecclesiastes 9:10, "Whatever your hand finds to

do, do it with all your might."

In the home in Portland, Oregon, where Jim Elliot grew up as the son of Fred and Clara Elliot, the Bible was the foundation, and Christ was honored as head of the home. His father was a Bible teacher and evangelist of the assemblies commonly known as "Plymouth Brethren." The home was saturated with love and with unquestioning obedience. Daily reading of the Bible and constant emphasis on scriptural truth instilled in Jim a lifelong love *for* and amazing insights *into* the Scriptures.

The great outdoors of Oregon, with Mt. Hood spectacularly visible from his home, called Jim to

> *"Wherever you are, be all there. Live to the hilt every situation you believe to be the will of God."*

a rugged appreciation of nature. Frequent camping trips and mountain hikes were part of the fabric of his life.

At an early age he showed an inherent love of beauty and an artistic bent that came out in descriptive writing as well as drawings. His primary school teachers were impressed with

his ability, which was later to be preserved for posterity in the profound journals he started keeping while in college. His ability as a high school orator was transformed into powerful preaching while he was still in his teens.

Approved unto God

In 1945 Jim enrolled in Wheaton College in Wheaton, Illinois. Summing up his freshman year he wrote, "It has been a profitable year drawing closer to my Savior and discovering gems in his Word. How wonderful to know that Christianity is more than a padded pew or a dim cathedral.... And its goal...

Jim Elliot with the other missionary families on the airstrip at Shandia.

bright and unfading, lit up and glowing with the beauties of the Sun of Righteousness."

At that time, however, Jim seriously questioned the value of formal education. During his sophomore year he wrote, "Knowledge puffs up. Culture, philosophy, disputes, drama in its weaker forms, concerts, opera, politics—anything that can occupy the intellect seems to turn aside the hearts of many here on campus from a humble life in the steps of the Master.... No, education is dangerous, and... I am beginning to question its value in a Christian's life. I do not disparage wisdom... that comes from God, not Ph.Ds." He once said that the only degree he coveted was "'A.U.G.'—approved unto God."

Glory boy

This period his contemporaries later dubbed as his "Glory Boy" stage. He was not hesitant on seeing a friend across campus at some distance, to shout a greeting such as, "Glory, Brother! What's your verse for the day?" Whereupon the friend was expected to respond with what God had presumably given him in his morning devotions. Some students began to shy away from eating at the same breakfast table with Jim, fearful that he would ask one's verse for the day. A "holier than thou" attitude came through to others from Jim's words and actions during that period.

This was also evident in his questioning of social activities such as class parties or football games. His dorm companions were sometimes made to feel guilty for dating, attending a party, or going to a ball game rather than spending that time in prayer and Bible study. On the few occasions when he allowed himself to indulge in such activities he would usually return to the dorm with a guilty conscience and spend time in prayer, confessing what he felt had been his carnal excesses.

During his senior year, however, Jim experienced what he termed "the Renaissance." Coming into a fuller understanding of the breadth of God's love, he began to recognize that "God has given us richly all things to enjoy," including the enjoyment of the social side of our nature. Because he always lived "to the hilt," the pendulum swung to the opposite extreme in this period. He began to participate in campus activities with an unbridled zest, wherever he was, becoming the life of the party. His natural sense of humor, often bottled up and inhibited in the past, now was given free rein. And, as they saw him as a "real man" and not as a pious recluse, his spiritual impact on his fellow students became infinitely greater, .

Wrestling for God
God had blessed Jim with a strong body, and he felt that he must use this for the glory of God by doing pioneer missionary work. He chose wrestling as the sport best suited to build up the body with which God had endowed him. Although he was totally inexperienced, he made the varsity team his freshman year. For four years Jim Elliot threw himself into the sport with typical abandon, enjoying it immensely and becoming a champion, winning various medals in his upper-class years.

Jim chose Greek as his major field, believing that a solid grasp of the original language of the New Testament would lead him into adeeper understanding of the truths of God and would also prepare him for translation of the Scriptures on the mission field. His attitude of "live to the hilt" showed itself in academics

as he graduated from Wheaton *summa cum laude* in 1949.

Unreached tribe
After graduating, Jim spent the following year at his home in Portland. This became a time of quiet reflection and personal growth, as he sought God's will for his future. During college days (including attending the first two "Urbana" conventions of InterVarsity Christian Fellowship) God began to speak to Jim about pioneer missionary work in South America. The summer of 1947 had been spent in Mexico with a college friend, where he began to feel the pull of missionary outreach. Information concerning a totally unreached tribe in Ecuador known as the Aucas intrigued him. Impatience to get moving balanced with a recognition that he must not run ahead of God, who was honing him for future usefulness.

During these years Jim Elliot seemed to have an almost divine premonition that he might live a short life and possibly even die a violent death. His journals and letters frequently refer to this possibility. In 1948 he wrote, "God, I pray light up these idle sticks of my life and may I burn up for Thee. Consume my life, My God, for it is Thine. I seek not a long life but a full one like yours, Lord Jesus." Later that year he wrote, "Father, take my life, yea, my blood, if Thou wilt, and consume it with Thine enveloping fire, I would not save it, for it is not mine to save.... Pour out my life as an oblation for the world. Blood is only of value as it flows before thine altars." And again that year, "Now I have nothing to look forward to but a

life of sacrificial sonship... or heaven soon."

One of his favorite hymns, which he sung frequently in his loud and powerful voice, said in part, "Let me burn out for Thee, dear Lord, burn and wear out for Thee." He also sang with great gusto, "Must I be carried to the skies on flowery beds of ease, while others fought to win the prize and sailed through bloody seas?"

In college, Jim Elliot targeted several key campus leaders as potential missionaries and had begun to pray earnestly that God would call them into His service. One of these was Ed McCully, the senior class president. Ed was an outstanding athlete, handsome, suave, and national oratorical champion. After a year in law school following Wheaton, Ed came under the influence of Jim's prayers and felt called of God to head for the mission field. During 1951, Jim and Ed ministered together in home missionary work, scratching out a local ministry in a small town in southern Illinois, which proved to be excellent preparation for later outreach in Ecuador. Jim also took linguistic training at the Summer Institute of Linguistics in Oklahoma.

"Woman hater"
Throughout his high school and college years, Jim was known as a "woman hater." Handsome and personable, he was a prize coveted by numerous young ladies. However, he proved to be unwavering to all approaches. He warned his friends of the dangers of "entanglements" with the debilitating effects of friendships with women, or marriage. He extolled celibacy

as the highest calling of God, at least for him, and by implication for his friends. He was adept at making his friends feel guilty for dating girls.

During his junior year in college, however, he found himself strangely drawn to a fellow Greek major, Elisabeth Howard. Unaware of this, his close friend, and Elisabeth's brother, Dave, invited him to spend Christmas of 1946 with the Howards. For the next few months this attraction (which, unknown to him, was mutual) became stronger. Toward the end of the year he began spending time with Elisabeth regularly, even though he would not admit that he was dating her. A certain hypocrisy came into play here, because to others he still maintained his aura of celibacy. Even Dave, who was his dorm companion and close friend, had no inkling of this friendship.

When the relationship between Jim and Elisabeth finally became known, Dave berated him: "Why didn't you tell me?" Jim lamely replied, "I didn't know what to say." Was it not rather that he didn't want to admit that he had a desire for the opposite sex, a desire he had consistently scorned with lofty declarations of celibacy?

For the next five years a courtship developed that was, to put it mildly, unorthodox in almost every aspect. He and Elisabeth declared their love for each other but placed it "under the cross," as an offering to be sacrificed if necessary. They had no assurance from God that marriage would ever be in His will for them. Jim felt strongly led to Ecuador for pioneer work, which could not be encumbered with home or family responsibil-

Jim Elliot with Quichua schoolboys, Shandia, Ecuador, 1952.

ities. Elisabeth accepted this with an equal commitment to pioneer work and following God's will in her life.

Elements of hypocrisy seem to be present during this period too. At the same time that he made friends feel guilty for dating, let alone holding hands or kissing a girl, he was recording in his journal the steamiest thoughts of a carnal nature about his physical desires for Elisabeth. Much to his credit, however, he never gave in to an overt expression of his desires.

Among the Quichua

Besides cultivating Ed McCully for service together in Ecuador, Jim also developed a friendship with another young man, Peter Fleming. Ed married during this preparatory period but was still headed for Ecuador. In February 1952, Jim and Pete Fleming sailed for Ecuador and were joined shortly by Ed and Marilou McCully. Most of that year was spent in the study of the Spanish language and in cultural orientation in Quito.

Later that year, Jim moved to

the jungle station of Shandia, which had been opened by a veteran Plymouth Brethren missionary but which needed full development. The years 1952–53 saw Jim build a mission station in the jungle, learn the language of the Quichua Indians, and begin to disciple young converts. However, in August 1953, a devastating flood wiped the Shandia mission station off the face of the earth. All that Jim had built was swept away as the river cut into its banks and demolished the station. With no alternative but to start over from scratch, Jim felt led of God that it was now time to marry. Elisabeth had arrived in Ecuador in April 1952 and was working in another Indian tribe, the Colorados, but her friendship with Jim had continued blossoming.

Thus on Jim's twenty-sixth birthday, October 8, 1953, they were married in Quito in a civil ceremony. After a short period in another jungle station they returned to Shandia, where Jim began the rebuilding of home, school, church, and those other facilities needed for an ongoing ministry among the Quichuas.

Operation Auca

Ever since college days, Jim had been learning and praying about a remote Stone Age tribe known as the Aucas. They were known as ruthless killers who would execute anyone, Indian or white, who encroached on their jungle territory. The gospel had never reached them. Jim's total abandonment to the Lord and his desire to sacrifice all for the sake of reaching those who had never heard of Christ made the Aucas a prime target for his prayers and desires.

During 1953–55, while Jim and Elisabeth worked among the Quichuas, he was quietly planning how to find and reach the remote Aucas. In September 1955, the Mission Aviation Fellowship pilot Nate Saint, who served the Shandia station by air, discovered a small Auca settlement. Sighting them from the air in a flight with Ed McCully aboard, he reported to Jim excitedly. For the next three months every week Jim, Ed, and Nate began flying over the Auca settlement, dropping gifts and trying to establish some kind of rapport.

Finally in January 1956, the men believed they were ready for an attempted entrance into the tribe. By this time they had in their team Pete Fleming, and Roger Youderian, of the Gospel Missionary Union. Preparations were made in strict secrecy, as they dreaded the possibility of public exposure and curiosity seekers who might want to be involved. Nate found a stretch of beach on the Curray River where he could land his Piper Cub plane. On January 3, 1956,

Jim Elliot.

Nate began the shuttle flights to land the team of Jim, Ed, Pete, and Roger on the beach. They immediately built a tree house and prepared to contact the Aucas who lived in the jungle.

On Friday, January 6, three Aucas, two women and a man, came to the beach and spent several hours with the men. By gestures and other means the missionaries communicated their desire for friendship with the Indians. All seemed to go well as they gave the Aucas food and gifts and even gave the man a ride in the plane.

Gates of splendor

On Sunday, January 8, 1956, in the early afternoon a group of ten Aucas came to the beach, attacked the men with primitive wooden spears, and killed all five. The missionaries were armed with guns but apparently did not defend themselves with the firearms. When the five wives received no radio communication at the appointed regular hours, they sent another plane to investigate. The pilot saw the ruined Piper Cub on the

beach, destroyed by the Aucas, and realized that tragedy had overtaken the men.

A rescue team comprised of seasoned missionaries, Quicha Indians, and a U.S. Army rescue squadron from Panama entered the jungles to find and bury the five bodies later that week.

Jim Elliot and his four companions died in their attempt to obey the Great Commission. But their testimony, which has gone throughout the world, continues to touch the lives of countless people. Jim's widow, Elisabeth, has written extensively of his life and death. These writings, along with Jim's journals, have been the basis of numberless people giving themselves to God in total commitment as Jim himself had done.

In 1948 Jim had written in his journal, "Saturate me with the oil of the Spirit that I may be aflame. But flame is often short-lived. Canst thou bear this, my soul? Short life? In me there dwells the spirit of the Great Short-lived, whose zeal for God's house consumed Him. 'Make me Thy fuel, Flame of God.'"

For Further Reading

Elliot, Elisabeth. *Through Gates of Splendor*. New York: Harper & Brothers, 1957.

___. *Shadow of the Almighty*. New York: Harper & Brothers, 1958.

___, ed. *The Journals of Jim Elliot*. Old Tappan, N. J.: Revell, 1978.

A. Wetherell Johnson and the Bible Study Fellowship

Miss J.

A. Wetherell Johnson as a young CIM missionary.

Audrey Wetherell Johnson, the founder of Bible Study Fellowship, was born in Leicester, in the English midlands, in 1907. Although she was raised in a home which was devoutly Christian, as a young woman Miss Johnson had not come to faith before going to France to continue her education. Indeed, under the influence of French intellectuals and secular philosophical studies her belief in basic biblical truths eroded. On her return to England she considered herself an agnostic. Stories such as Adam and Eve, Jonah and the whale, were they not simply myths, at least in part? Although careful to keep these misgivings to herself so as not to

When God has a work to do, someone is chosen by Him. His servant is often prepared in the most unexpected ways. It seems that God prepared an Englishwoman, Miss Audrey Wetherell Johnson, for the work of Bible Study Fellowship, an interdenominational, worldwide ministry with about eight hundred classes studying the Bible in depth. Although she had been raised in a committed Christian family in Leicester, England, Audrey Johnson slipped onto the path of agnosticism as a young woman. But later a personal crisis of faith led her to salvation and a life of commitment, with years of sacrificial missionary service in inland China. This missionary service culminated in two and one-half years in prison, internment by the Japanese during World War II, and eighteen months of house arrest by the Communists before she was forced to leave her beloved China. Coming to the United States after the Communist takeover, Audrey Johnson yearned for the mission field. Awaiting the Lord's new direction she spent two years in conference ministry, but her greatest love was teaching the Scriptures to those who had previously experienced little biblical instruction.

Somewhat reluctantly, she agreed to teach five church women the Bible. After a period of prayer, she agreed to teach the class, but determined not to "spoon-feed" the class members. Writing out questions for their preparation, she gradually developed a study method designed to show women from all walks of life that they could come to know God personally and that He could use them to minister dynamically in the lives of others. Her confidence was in a great God and what He could do through any woman committed to Him and to the Bible. She delighted in discerning and developing theother women's gifts. Her teaching and writing were rich with lessons learned from the difficulties she experienced during her years in China.

grieve her godly mother, she could not tolerate any teaching about the cross or the blood of Christ.

Outwardly Miss Johnson seemed to be enjoying new work and old friends; inwardly she was living a life of quiet despair. Without a Christian philosophy, she felt she must find one in which she could believe. Her conundrum was this: if life is indeed "snuffed out" at the end, what difference does it really make how one lives? In an evening of despair and intense introspection, Jesus' words, "And whosoever liveth and believeth in me shall never die. Believest thou this?" (John 11:26) apparently compelled her to grapple with this question of eternal import. And in answer to honest prayer she writes, "Suddenly God's mysterious revelation was given to me. I can only say with Paul, 'It pleased God to reveal His Son in me.' I could not reason out the mystery of the Incarnation, but God caused me to know that this was a fact. I knelt down in tears of joy and worshiped him as Savior and Lord, with a divine conviction of this truth which could never be broken."

After her conversion, she initially took Jesus' words in the Bible as truth. From further careful study she regained her confidence in the "whole counsel of God."

God's path
Because the Bible had been so key in her own conversion, Miss Johnson became deeply committed to the authority of the Scripture. She taught it with power, and lived by it in her life and ministry. The authority of Scripture was to become one of the five guiding principles of her life, which she called "God's Path of Life."

The second and third principles are linked and related to a crisis in her own life. After reflecting on John 12:24, "Except a corn of wheat fall into the ground and die, it abideth alone. But if it die, it bringeth forth much fruit," Audrey prayed this prayer: "Lord, I am willing at whatever cost, for Thy death to be worked out in me, in order that Thy resurrection life may also be manifested."

The principle, that our self-life lost its power at the cross but that we must personally appropriate this truth, and the principle that we must live daily in dependence upon the fullness of the Holy Spirit, became dominant themes in her ministry. We are free to reject our self-protective desire to quit, turn back, or compromise. We are free to choose to continue on the path of obedience under God's direction, trusting the life of Christ within us for strength and power to persevere. We must be willing to go through any difficulty bearing its pain and being comforted by fellowship with Christ.

When in very trying circumstances in her own missionary experience, Miss Johnson was tempted to complain, she chose not to do so. Reminded of her prayer of commitment by God, she chose to resist pushing her own personal agenda for the extension of her ministry into the interior of China. That choice resulted in an unexpected fruitfulness. This is not to imply that her life was one of passivity. When she was certain that God, not self, was leading her, she was ruggedly determined to see the work done in His way. Her willingness to die to self and to personal convenience and comfort became stamped upon the creation and work of Bible Study Fellowship. She set high standards, and selfless service was the expected thing.

The final two principles of her "Path of Life" are: God's love is sufficient for all of life, and, God's grace is abundant in every situation. Miss Johnson came to know intimately the God who loves deeply and supplies grace in abundance for the need of the moment.

Prepared in service
With the Japanese invasion of China during World War II, Miss Johnson learned by personal experience about the love and grace of God in difficult circumstances. She was interned in a camp called Longhua, in huts that had formerly been horse stables. Her hut held eighty-nine cots, with six open toilets and two small washbasins—so that privacy was not an option. Conditions ranged from stifling heat in the summer to freezing cold in the winter, and food was limited to rice and a one-inch cube of meat for each person daily. She dropped from 145 pounds to less than 106 pounds. But even with the pressure of such primitive living conditions, with all the smells and sounds of war around them, her primary memory was of God's daily provisions and lovingkindness. She experienced

His faithfulness in so many little ways during what she had most dreaded—imprisonment. She learned that God was interested in all the details of living. Yet she was the first to admit that she did not always remember this; she had to confess to the Lord a sulking spirit at the end of the war when her few belongings were lost after her release. She was ever flesh, but with a rich experience of communion with God.

After a furlough in England, Audrey returned to Shanghai to teach in the China Bible Seminary, fully intending to remain in China and "die there." But the growing Communist opposition finally required her departure in 1950. With plans to teach in Canada changed by the death of a friend, Miss Johnson arrived in the United States with a six-month visa but uncertain of what lay ahead. A reminder by God of his love for her as His own child and His willingness to assume the responsibility for her future filled her heart with peace as she sailed under the Golden Gate Bridge into San Francisco. She was content to trust the One who had proved Himself so faithful.

Day of small things

While resting under doctor's orders in San Bernardino, California, with her heart longing for China, Miss Johnson was asked to teach the Bible to five women who were already extremely well instructed. Her heart sank. She asked herself, "What have I come to? Am I to give more to those who already have so much?" However, as she prayed about their invitation and poured out to the Lord her longing to teach hungry pagans she remembered the passage in Jeremiah 45:5, "Seekest thou great things for thyself?" (such as training teachers for China's millions), "Seek them not!" and Zechariah 4:10: "For who has despised the day of small things?"

It was as if the Lord had said to her, "Will you not do this one little thing for me?" And so she replied to the five ladies that she would indeed be willing to teach them. However, Miss Johnson, troubled by the prevalence in American Christianity of what she called "spoon-feeding," believers getting all their Bible study secondhand, she requested that each of these women be willing to study the passage personally and share what God had given

---

THE LIFE OF

A. Wetherell Johnson

1907	Born in Leicester, England
1936	Sails for China under China Inland Mission
1937	Assigned to Yu-Kiang in Kiangsi Province
1939	Assigned to Lin Ming Kwan, Hopeh Province
1942	Interned by Japanese during World War II
1945	Returns to England following the war
1947	Serves on faculty of China Bible Seminary, Shanghai
1948	House arrest by Communists in Shanghai
1950	Forced to leave China
1952	Five women in San Bernardino, California, ask for Bible Study
1958	Bible Study Fellowship is incorporated in Oakland, California; grows to almost 300 classes with 100,000 members
1979	Retires due to cancer
1980	BSF Headquarters moves to San Antonio, Texas
1982	Publishes autobiography *Created for Commitment*
1984	Dies on December 22

---

them; she would give them a little wrap-up at then end. She dictated a few simple questions following the method of study she had adopted after her return from agnosticism: (1) What does the passage say? (2) What did it mean to the people in the day it was written? (3) What does it mean to me? The women agreed and the study began.

These sessions were the beginning of what was to prove to be her life work for the next twenty years, the founding of Bible Study Fellowship. But Miss Johnson never forgot that it was God who was the founder and initiator of the classes and that all the glory for the work should go to Him. In fact, after her retirement, when the new headquarters administration building in San Antonio, Texas, was dedicated to her and named the Johnson Center, she commented on her embarrassment in receiving the honor since, she said, she "hadn't wanted to do this work in the first place." She protested that

God deserved all the honor. An aversion to ever touching the glory that belongs to the Lord was another of Miss Johnson's life principles. The principle continues to be emphasized in Bible Study Fellowship to this day.

For such a time as this

God continued to shape through Miss Johnson a unique ministry founded on her deep belief and personal experience that God desired personally to impact the life of anyone willing to go alone with Him, to study prayerfully the Bible for himself, and to do whatever the Holy Spirit taught him. The various aspects of Bible Study Fellowship were developed to encourage this personal, daily interaction with God through a disciplined study of the Bible as well as its application. Miss Johnson's missionary training and disciplined life forged in China permeated the organization and lessons of Bible Study Fellowship.

In the early years, Miss Johnson authored a summary of the lecture which was to be given to class members so that they would not be distracted with note taking. From that early commitment grew five series of studies treating nearly all of the Bible, each thirty-two weeks in duration. Recognizing that the message of Jesus Christ and His work is what brings unity, her notes focused on Him and the application of Biblical truth to everyday living. These notes (revised by BSF International) continue to be read today by class members of Bible Study Fellowship and they bring women and men face to face with the God of the Bible.

In the class sessions discussion is encouraged and those who have little experience in the Bible are free to share what they are learning without fear of being corrected or embarrassed. Miss Johnson's favorite class members were those who had never really studied the Bible before, and it was her delight to see them come alive to Christ through their study.

In the late 1950s a pastor in the San Francisco Bay area asked Miss Johnson to move to northern California and to follow up those expected to come to Christ during the 1958 Billy Graham Crusade there. After moving to the Bay Area with her hostess and helper from San Bernardino, Miss Alverda Hertzler,

Bible Study Fellowship was incorporated and a Board of Directors formed. Miss Hertzler became the Administrator of Bible Study Fellowship for twenty years. Her outstanding administrative gifts provided the perfect balance for the development of the growing work. And this principle of utilizing different gifts for different responsibilities in the classes proved extremely wise and effective. As classes began to multiply, two people were always trained to share the responsibilities, one to teach and the other to handle administration of the classes.

Miss Johnson's experience in China had proved that God could empower simple "Bible women" to share His message of salvation to those who had never heard. Now, again, she saw God choose one woman after another through whom His work could be expanded in the Western world. Her confidence was placed in a great God and His power working through committed and dependent servants.

Transforming lives

The recurrence of cancer after a remission of eight years following a mastectomy brought "Miss J," as she was affectionately called, into closer contact with her chosen successor in the work, Mrs. Rosemary Jensen. Rosemary's husband Bob, a physician in San Antonio, supervised her treatment for bone cancer, which had developed in 1978. It is illustrative of her strength and force of character that following her tenth radiation treatment, with severe internal swelling and unable to eat or take liquids, Miss Johnson embarked upon a series of five leaders' retreats that took her across the country and back. Indeed, such was her love of giving out God's Word, that even when her associates knew she was on the brink of exhaustion before an engagement, they saw her begin a bit weakly but soon grow stronger and stronger and seem to be able to continue indefinitely. She could hold an audience spellbound and wherever she spoke, God seemed to touch hearts. Miss Johnson was extraordinarily gifted, and her teaching was always something that invigorated her. The Bible was always her content and the Lord her subject. Her constant aim was the transformation of individual lives through of Bible Study Fellowship.

Miss Johnson at the dedication of the Bible Study Fellowship headquarters at San Antonio, 1981.

leadership, even as her own health deteriorated. In 1984 she and Miss Hertzler (also retired from Bible Study Fellowship) moved to Carmel, California.

Miss Johnson went into the Lord's presence on December 22, 1984. The attending nurse that evening heard her say, "The Lord is coming for me today. He's at the foot of my bed now." With these words she seemed to experience the lesson often taught from John 8:52: If a person obeys Christ, he shall never see death. She saw not the specter of death, but the face of her Lord Jesus Christ. Those with her saw a light on her face. She departed this life at 7:25 p.m. that evening.

The major legacy of Audrey Wetherell Johnson's life was her leadership in Bible Study Fellowship and her emphasis on disciplined and personal Bible Study. She believed that through the continued, careful study of the Bible many people would come to know, love, and obey her Lord. And in so knowing and so living, they would live out their lives "not just somehow, but triumphantly."

Although constantly busy with the growing ministry of Bible Study Fellowship, Miss Johnson was interested in the work and ministry of many other individuals. Her friendship with Francis Schaeffer of L'Abri Fellowship was a source of mutual encouragement to both. She was a charter member of the Council for Biblical Inerrancy, and for a time was the only woman on its Board of Directors.

All her life Miss Johnson loved history, art, literature, music, nature, and people. She wrote poetry, painted, hiked, read widely, played the piano, and was an expert conversationalist on most current topics.

Retirement
Even though she retired to the position of Director Emeritus of Bible Study Fellowship in 1979, she moved to San Antonio in 1980 when headquarters were transferred there following a generous gift of land for the construction of expanded facilities. She followed with joy the expansion of BSF under Rosemary Jensen's

Further Reading

Johnson, A. Wetherell. *Created for Commitment.* Wheaton, Ill.: Tyndale House, 1982.

For locations and other information about Bible Study Fellowship classes, contact BSF International, 19001 Blanco Road, San Antonio, Texas, 78258.

Tried and tested

The story of Corrie ten Boom is familiar to Christians around the world through her best-selling autobiography and film by the same title, *The Hiding Place*.

Corrie was a very ordinary, obscure Dutch woman until the Nazi occupation of the Netherlands during World War II, when her Christian faith was suddenly put to the test. She and her family could either play for safety and ignore the atrocities being carried out against their Jewish neighbors, or they could risk their lives and stand by their convictions. They chose the latter course, and opened their home as a "hiding place" for Jews seeking refuge. It was a choice that, whilst setting them on a path of high adventure, eventually resulted in Corrie and her sister suffering the indescribable terror of a Nazi death camp.

Unwavering

After she was released, Corrie ten Boom was determined to carry on her family's struggle against the injustice and anti-semitism that had culminated in the Holocaust. She vowed to find some way in which she could make a difference, to insure that she and her family had not suffered in vain. But what could she do—an "old maid" in her midfifties? She was but one of countless thousands who had survived the horrors of Nazism, and she had no special talents or connections. But she had a unwavering faith in God—a faith that had been tried by fire.

Opposite: Corrie ten Boom.

Corrie ten Boom

Shalom

Corrie ten Boom was one of four children born into a devout Dutch Reformed family that for generations had owned and operated a watch shop in the lower level of the family home in the town of Haarlem, in the Netherlands. Business contacts with Jewish suppliers in Germany had alerted the ten Booms to dangers of Nazism long before World War II broke out. They were deeply troubled by the reports, but what could they possibly do to make a difference?

Willem, Corrie's brother who had studied for the ministry, was the first to act. He joined the Dutch underground, who were involved in the provision of escape routes for Jews and the sabotaging of German war installations. Word quickly spread among Jewish refugees that the ten Boom family—the old man and his two unmarried daughters—could be trusted, and the hidden passages and attic nooks of the three-story house became a sanctuary for hunted Jews.

Corrie's family was not the first generation of ten Booms to demonstrate concern for Jews. In 1844, her grandfather began a prayer meeting for the specific purpose of praying for Jewish people, and this concern deepened as the decades passed. Amazingly, it was exactly one hundred years later, in 1944, that the ten Boom home was raided by the Gestapo. Corrie and her father and sister were not betrayed by a German spy but by a fellow Dutchman, who had suspected they were Jewish sympathizers. They were arrested, but miraculously, the Jewish fugitives were so well hidden in their home that they eluded the authorities.

Death camp

The months that followed that cold February morning were filled with terror. Corrie and her sister Betsy were incarcerated at Ravensbruck—a notorious women's death camp—while their father languished in a prison cell. In May, word was received that he had died.

Conditions at Ravensbruck were appalling—long hours of forced labor, rat-infested unheated barracks, malnutrition, disease, and physical abuse. Yet, during their imprisonment, Corrie and Betsy were able to reach out in love to the ravaged women around them and give

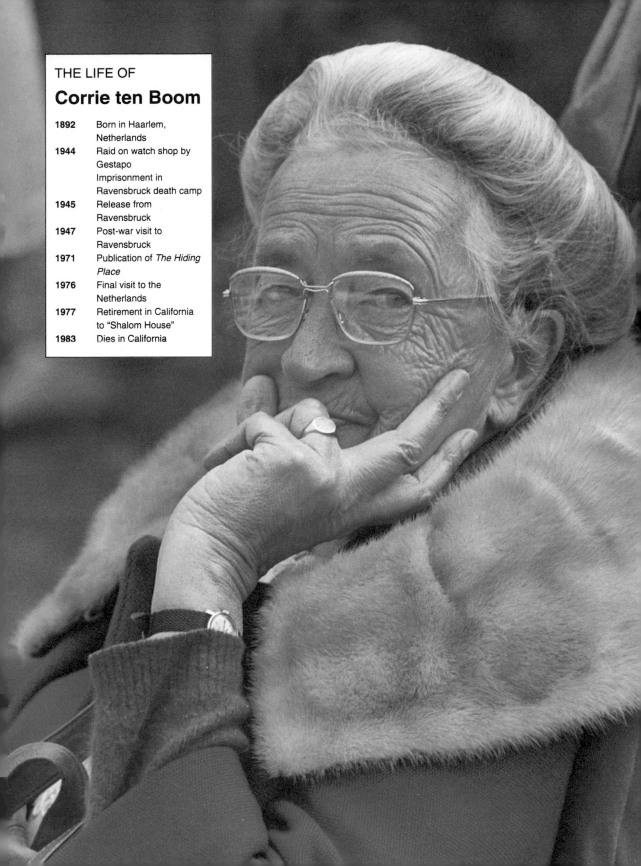

THE LIFE OF

Corrie ten Boom

The ten Boom family: (left to right) Nollie, Corrie, Willem, Betsy.

them encouragement to put their trust in God. At night they would huddle together and read the Bible and pray that they

Corrie on her travels.

would be released. And Betsy was released, but only through death. She died on Christmas Day, 1944. Corrie was released soon afterwards—through a "clerical error" that was no less than a miracle; the rest of the women in her age group were exterminated a week later.

The suffering the ten Boom family endured was not in vain. As she traveled to sixty-four countries during her thirty-three years of public ministry, Corrie's story inspired millions of people. Her focus, however, was not on herself or on her family, but on God's mercy and love. Through all the pain and misery, God was ever faithful. She often told how Betsy had been desperately ill in prison, and how she had only a tiny bottle of medicine. Others needed it as much as Betsy, but Corrie did not want to share, fearing it would run out before her dear sister recovered. But Betsy insisted it be shared, and every day there were enough drops for those in need—with no way of seeing how much was left in the dark glass bottle. Finally,

Cutaway illustration of the Ten Boom House in Haarlem, The Netherlands. The house is today open to the public as a museum.

In Corrie's bedroom, t*op left,* the hiding place can be seen; downstairs the parlour with the family Bible on the table and the clock showroom and workshop.

through the help of a sympathetic guard, Corrie acquired more medicine. She was determined to first finish what was left in the bottle, but to her amazement it was empty. There was not one drop left. God had been faithful, not in giving a month's supply, but in meeting the daily need.

The most difficult moment

One of Corrie ten Boom's most difficult experiences was her visit back to Ravensbruck in 1947. She had come back to Germany to share the gospel with the German people—to let them know that God loved them and that his forgiveness extended to everyone, even to those who had actively participated in the terrible extermination of the Jews. She was sincere as she spoke. Indeed, her heart went out to the German people as she looked out over the audience. She could forgive them even as Christ had forgiven her.

But when the meeting was over, she suddenly discovered that her visit would involve more than forgiving nameless faces. Before her stood one of the most despicable and cruel guards from Ravensbruck; his face had become a terror to her during her months in the death camp. Betsy's painful death flashed before her, and now he was extending his hand, taking her up on her offer of forgiveness. Corrie later reflected on the incident: "It could not have been many seconds that he stood there—hand held out— but to me it seemed hours as I wrestled with the most difficult thing I ever had to do."

Jesus had died on the cross for her sins, and she had been graciously forgiven. Corrie had no other choice, therefore, but to offer that forgiveness to another undeserving sinner.

Corrie died in 1983, on her ninety-first birthday, but she left a living legacy—one that challenges all who follow Christ to be *more than conquerors.*

Further Reading

Rosewell, Pamela. *The Five Silent Years of Corrie ten Boom.* Grand Rapids: Zondervan, 1986.

ten Boom, Corrie, John Sherrill, and Elizabeth Sherrill. *The Hiding Place.* Old Tappan, N.J.: Revell, 1971.

ten Boom, Corrie, with Jamie Buckingham. *Tramp for the Lord.* Old Tappan, N.J.: Revell, 1974.

George Verwer and Operation Mobilization

God is Greater

THE LIFE OF
George Verwer

1938	Born
1955	Conversion
1957	First trip to Mexico
1960	Graduates from Moody Bible Institute
	Marries Drena Jean Knecht
	Moves to Spain
1961	Visits Soviet Union
	Has concept of Operation Mobilization (OM)
1962	OM's first annual summer outreach in Europe and the Middle East
1964	Expands work to India
1970	Purchases ship, *Logos*
1988	Wreck of ship, *Logos*: replaced two years later

"I've got it! I've got it!" exclaimed young George Verwer, leaping from his knees and pulling at the cord of the overhead light in the small dorm room at Maryville College, Tennessee.

"What have you got, George?" asked his startled prayer partner.

"Everyone in the States has a chance to hear the gospel. But not in Mexico. We should go down there this summer and distribute tracts. How about it?"

"Well, George, I don't know." stammered his friend. "I'd have to pray about it."

"OK, let's pray," responded George.

A few minutes later George lifted his head and asked "Are you ready to go now?" On seeing that his friend was still reluctant, he muttered impatiently, "It takes some people so long to decide to do anything!"

Just a year or two earlier, in 1955, two strands of God's weaving had come together in George's life: the faithful prayers of an older woman for students at a nearby high school and a Billy Graham campaign in New York City. The popular senior class president had met

Christ, and his life had been dramatically altered.

God is greater than laws

The summer following his prayer about Mexico he went there with his praying friend and another student. They went again at Christmas and the following summer. By the time George graduated from Moody

---

I can't find it!

"The text is 2 Timothy 2. Let's turn there in our Bibles."
The wiry American preacher had just concluded his lengthy but very lively introductory remarks. Hooking a pair of reading glasses over his ears, George Verwer lifted his Bible and began flipping determinedly through its pages... and kept on flipping.

"I can't find it," he admitted after a long moment, "but here's Acts. It's bigger and easier to find. So let's look at Acts instead."

Reading a few verses that caught his eye, George launched into his message.

Embarrassed

Meanwhile, his British associate cringed with embarrassment in the front row. *Oh George*, he thought, *this is a conference for potential young Christian leaders from all over Great Britain! How can you stand in front of them and preach a message you obviously haven't prepared? I must have a talk with you about this sort of thing.*

But that talk never took place. As the meeting progressed, it was clear that George Verwer's direct, off-the-cuff preaching was striking at the hearts of his hearers. At the end of the week, participants were asked, "Which part of the conference made the greatest impression on you?" The most frequent answer: "George Verwer's message."

This is the enigma of George Verwer. On the one hand, he is utterly human, unconventional, unpredictable, full of weaknesses, with an impressive record of error that he openly acknowledges. On the other hand, he has been used of God in a remarkable way to stir people to a deeper relationship with God and challenge them to become involved in world missions. Countless lives have been affected through Operation Mobilization (OM), the mission work he founded.

Bible Institute in Chicago, where he had transferred, scores of students from various schools were involved in the evangelistic outreach and a small bookstore had been opened in Mexico City.

"Do you know it is against the law to preach the gospel on the radio in Mexico? Let's pray that we can do it anyway!" challenged George during one of the Christmas outreaches.

"But George, we can't pray about doing something illegal!"

"God is greater than laws," stated George, "He can change the laws."

So they prayed. And continued to pray.

The following summer George sent someone to the radio station. "I represent a bookstore," he announced, "and I would like to advertise it on the radio." He went on to explain that the bookstore sold Bibles. "The reason people don't buy the Bible is that they don't know what's in it. We'd like to read from it in our advertisement."

After that, every week for several years the bookstore presented a fifteen-minute program, reading from the Bible and explaining it.

Don't waste the Word

When George graduated from Moody in 1960, he left the work in Mexico in the hands of others and moved to Spain with his wife and a couple of coworkers. Not content with the challenge of a country then closed to the gospel, he looked farther afield to an even more tightly closed land, the Soviet Union. With a friend

he made a trip to Russia by car, concealing gospels, paper, and simple printing equipment in the door panels. Once inside

George Verwer.

the country, the two men began printing tracts, stuffing them in envelopes, and mailing them to addresses which they took from the telephone directory.

A bit of margarine caused their downfall. It made one of the gospels grease-marked.

"Better flush that gospel down the toilet," George's companion advised.

"No, no!" objected George. "We don't want to waste the Word of God! Let's put it where someone will find it and read it. We can drop it from the car sometime when we're out in the middle of nowhere and no one can see us."

That's what they did—they thought. Less than ten miles later they ran into a roadblock. Two days of interrogation resulted in the discovery of all their literature and printing materials. However, instead of the extended "holiday" in Siberia they feared, they were relieved to be given an impressive military escort through Eastern Europe to the Austrian border. Great vision, a lot of planning, much prayer, but then failure.

Operation Mobilization
In Vienna, the two men used the opportunity to pass out thousands of tracts. But haunted by his failure in the Soviet Union, George felt the need to go off alone in the mountains for a time of fasting, prayer and worship. Perched in a tree—one of his favorite places for contemplation—he remembered a Methodist youth group in England he had met at a hostel. *Apparently the church in England, or at least part of it, is alive and doing well,* he concluded. Recalling his experience in mobilizing students to work in Mexico, he began to think in a new direction. *We foreigners can make only a tiny dent in the great need. But what if the churches in Europe could be mobilized to reach their own lands? We could call it Operation Mobilization.*

Going back to Spain, he shared his vision with a few Spanish believers and a short time later with a couple dozen American veterans of Mexico

The *Logos* - the first OM ship - founders off Chile in 1988.

outreaches who had finished their schooling and had come over to Europe.

The concept of short-term missions was virtually unknown at that time. Yet before long, hundreds of Europeans, as well as Americans, were traveling on teams throughout Europe and the Middle East. Their outreaches lasted from two weeks all the way to two years. In 1964 the OM field was extended to India and in 1970 throughout the world by means of a ship. In both expansions, George himself was with the pioneering group.

"Forget the idea!"
"A ship? Forget the idea!" George had been counseled by respected Christian leaders. "OM is good at what it does. Stick to the ministry God has given you. What do you know about running a ship? Nothing! It would be a disaster!"

George saw truth in their words, but he couldn't forget the idea: he was convinced it was from God. Five years of intensive prayer passed before the idea became reality. In 1971,

the 2,319-ton *Logos* set sail from England to India. God blessed the ship ministry so much that a larger ship, the *Doulos*, was added seven years later. Staffed by 400 volunteers from forty to fifty countries, the ships would spend two to three weeks in a port. Working closely with local churches, OMers offered to the public a large selection of both educational and Christian books and carried out an extensive program of evangelism and teaching..

A very black cloud
Providing leadership for a worldwide mission organization brings immense pressures. One of the most difficult experiences of George's life occurred at an OM coordinators' conference in the mid-seventies when OM leaders were wrestling with how to esteem their women workers more. George felt they had made progress in the area, but an older veteran missionary woman, who had just joined as an adviser and Bible teacher, stood up and strongly criticized OM in this area.

"It was as if a very black cloud suddenly came down on me," commented George, describing the emotional impact of her words. "Here we had been working so hard to improve and had apparently gotten nowhere. It all seemed so hopeless."

He couldn't bear to remain in the meeting, his depression was so deep. Slipping away, he went outside into the crisp night air. A huge barrel in a deserted playground caught his eye. He climbed inside, he began to weep and pray. Later, when he returned to his room but was unable to sleep.

When morning finally came, he sought out one of the OM leaders to whom he felt closest. While the leader sat listening, George poured out all that had been bothering him.

And when he was finished, the depression had lifted.

"I've learned how important it is not to bottle up emotions," says George, "but to find someone I can openly share with. Otherwise I couldn't take the pressures of the work."

Disaster

That support was vital in 1988 when he faced an even more traumatic moment—news that the *Logos* had hit a rock in the Beagle Channel, at the southernmost tip of Argentina.

In a state of shocked belief as well as deep concern for those involved, George immediately called his staff together for prayer as they waited anxiously for further news. Word finally came that the ship could not be saved. It had to be abandoned under difficult circumstances, but everyone aboard—including a two-month old-baby—had been safely evacuated.

Overcome with emotion, George struggled to speak but broke down in tears. Thanksgiving for the safety of those aboard mingled with mourning for the loss of a dream become reality, a ship that had become a symbol of warm, challenging, and vibrant faith to millions of people around the world.

The ship was gone but not the ministry. In 1990, the *Logos* was replaced by a larger ship, the *Logos II*. And the work of Operation Mobilization continued on in Europe, Asia, Africa, Latin America, and the islands of the world.

God's laser beam

As a Christian work expands and its leaders grow in maturity and experience, there are those who assume these men and women of God outgrow personal weaknesses. But do they? George relates a pair of temper outbursts that occurred two decades apart:

People were coming to me with their problems all day long. More and more I saw how easily people become self-centered. When I went to my [ship] cabin, my wife began to unload her burdens. I was already keyed up and thought, "She's just like all the others!" I couldn't handle it.

In a burst of temper, I kicked the end of a bed the carpenters had spent days making for us. To my horror, it broke in half! I'll never forget that. I, of course, repented and got it sorted out.

I haven't had too many temper losses in the twenty years since then, but not long ago my wife was using the video recorder. I did something wrong and she gently jumped on me for it. I was under pressure and exploded! Feeling I just had to kick some-

thing, I struck out at a box and kicked it with all my might. Unfortunately, the box was full of heavy notebooks. My foot shrieked with pain! I turned abruptly and marched out the front door.

Immediately under conviction that this was not right I repented, went around to the back of the house, marched in the back door, hugged my wife and gave her a big kiss. Meanwhile she was cracking up with laughter at the behavior of her 'spiritual' husband.

Having a commitment to openness and honesty, I decided to tell my coworkers what had happened. That was a great experience for the soul! Even more embarrassing, I had to go down to the hospital to get my foot X-rayed. In God's mercy nothing was broken, but it was weeks before my foot got back to normal.

And so God continues to work not only *through* George Verwer but *in* him as well. That's the way George wants it. As he told a group of missionaries in Pakistan, "I want to be God's laser beam!"

Further Reading

Rhoton, Elaine. *The Logos Story*. London: STL Publications, n.d.

___. *The Ship Called Logos*. Chicago: Moody, 1989.

Verwer, George. *No Turning Back*. Wheaton, Ill.: Tyndale, n.d.

Verwer, George. *Revolution of Love*. London: STL Publications, n.d.

BROTHER ANDREW
GOD'S SMUGGLER

Brother Andrew's first assignment for God was not behind the Iron Curtain but in his own little village of Witte in Holland. Only a few weeks after he committed his life to Christ, twenty-two-year-old Andrew and a friend were challenged by an evangelist: "Go back home and hold an open-air meeting in the middle of town."

The young men were horror-struck at the thought, but they took up the challenge. The whole town turned out to hear them. When it came Andrew's turn to speak, he walked to the front of the makeshift platform,

looked down into the crowd of familiar faces and promptly forgot his carefully prepared speech. Desperately searching his mind for something to say, he hesitantly began to talk of what he could never forget—his own experience with God.

After that the two young men went out every day to do evangelism of some kind.

Door-to-door evangelist
"I'd get very discouraged," recalls Brother Andrew, "when I'd go door-to-door and people would ask questions I couldn't answer. It would drive me home to study and find answers. Then

Brother Andrew with Joseph Bondarenko in Red Square, Moscow, 1990.

Red Square encounter

The year, 1961—Moscow, two minutes from Red Square. Following the car ahead of them, Brother Andrew and his coworker pulled to the side of the street. They watched as a young Russian man climbed out of the car and headed toward them. They had first met him a few minutes earlier through the arrangements of a dedicated but frightened pastor. Now they were preparing to hand over to him more than a hundred bulky Russian Bibles. If caught, they could be sentenced to many years in prison.

Brother Andrew looked nervously up and down the street, lined on one side by a high wall and on the other by once elegant townhouses. He wondered whose curious eyes might be looking out of the windows. This certainly wouldn't have been his choice of location for such a dangerous transaction, but there on the busy sidewalk the men made trip after trip, hastily transferring boxes from one car to the other.

Bibles for pastors
When the job was finished, the Russian gave Brother Andrew and his coworker each a quick, firm handshake and was gone. Brother Andrew turned to his coworker with a smile of satisfaction. Both knew that within days the Bibles would be in the hands of pastors all over Russia.

This is the Brother Andrew that many people know—God's Smuggler: dedicated, courageous, taking great risks, and accomplishing amazing things for God. Few people know what stands behind his achievements: the hardships, discouragements, loneliness, fears, and hard work.

Opposite: Brother Andrew.

THE LIFE OF
Brother Andrew

1928	Born
1950	Commits life to Christ
1955	Finishes Bible college, Worldwide Evangelization Crusade, in England
	Makes first trip to Czechoslovakia
1958	Marries Corry van Dam on June 27
1960	Adopts name, Brother Andrew, for anonymity
	Joined by first coworker, Hans Gruber
	Expands work to Russia
1972	Begins work in Africa
1980	Begins work in Central America
1981	Delivers one million Bibles to China in Project Pearl
1985	Begins work in Middle East

I'd go out again until I was hit with the next hard question."

The young men persevered and revival came to their town. Almost every one of their church youth group ended up on the mission field.

One day in 1955, Andrew was sitting on a bench beside a busy avenue in Warsaw, Poland. Resting his New Testament on his knee, he thought back over the events of the past three weeks. Having been intrigued by an advertisement in a glossy Communist magazine, he had come to attend an international youth festival. After days of enduring carefully orchestrated speeches and sightseeing tours, Andrew had managed to sneak away to see the real Warsaw. The shock was still with him. The sight of the poverty and filth of rubble-strewn bombed-out areas. The stories of fortunes being made by those smuggling Bibles into Russia. The readiness with which the people received the "Way of Salvation" booklets which he'd stuffed his suitcases with. The heartrending words spoken by a Baptist pastor, "We want to thank you for just *being* here. We often feel we are all alone in our struggle."

Strengthen what remains

Looking down at his New Testament, he read the words, "Awake and strengthen what remains and is on the point of death." Tears welled up in his eyes as he began to sense that this was God's mission for him. He was to help the struggling church behind the Iron Curtain.

In 1957 that commission was reinforced in a small church in Belgrade, Yugoslavia. Word had spread quickly about the visit of

a foreigner, and the building was packed. Responding to an invitation at the close of his message, everyone in the congregation raised a hand to indicate a desire to follow Christ. Astonished, Andrew launched into an enthusiastic challenge to daily prayer and Bible reading in order to grow in the faith.

His enthusiasm turned to bewilderment as people began to shift uneasily in their seats, carefully avoiding eye contact with him.

"Andrew," whispered the pastor, obviously embarrassed, "praying we can do. But reading the Bible? Andrew, these people don't *have* Bibles."

Stunned, Andrew turned back to the congregation. "How many of you have a Bible?" he asked.

Only seven hands, including the pastor's, went up.

Providing God's Word

After that experience Andrew knew that whatever it might cost him, he was going to see to it that God's people behind the Iron Curtain had His Word.

That was the beginning of the work which would be called Open Doors and would take Andrew throughout Eastern Europe and the Soviet Union, risking his own freedom to bring Bibles, Christian literature, and messages of encouragement to the church behind the Iron Curtain. Frequently he would be moved to tears by the deep love and gratitude of believers. Again and again he would see God's protection in amazing ways.

How does Andrew feel about this dramatic ministry?

"After two years," he admits, "I pleaded, 'Lord, let me go back to the job I had at a factory in

Holland. I can win more souls there. And I can have a home, security, and a modest income as well.' From the outside my work may have looked glamorous, but inside, it was a daily struggle. I was in a new mission field so there was no one to ask for advice, no one to keep me from making mistakes. I was always on the road alone that first year because no one wanted to join me on those crazy trips. I had a serious problem with a slipped disc and was always tired, sick, and in pain. I was lonely and very poor."

After experiencing the family life and warm hospitality of Eastern European believers, Andrew found it hard to think of returning to his lonely little room in Holland.

"Many times, I'd stay just outside my village to try to find myself," he says, "or I'd go to someone experienced where I could cry a bit and be pampered till I got over culture shock. Inner restoration takes time."

Marriage in 1958 to Corry van Dam relieved some of the loneliness, but along with the joy it brought its own pressures. Once he returned after a

trip of 14 weeks and his baby didn't even recognize him. Having a family made Andrew want to avoid the risks inherent in his work.

Dangerous encounters

Crossing the border with a car full of forbidden Bibles was one of the greatest points of danger. On one occasion, while waiting at the Romanian border, he watched as the half dozen cars ahead of him underwent long,

Brother Andrew in Beirut, Lebanon, 1989.

"Project Pearl": 1 million Bibles for China, 1981.

intensive searches—with car contents being spread out on the ground, the hub caps and seats removed, one engine even taken apart. Four hours of fervent prayer passed before Andrew finally made it to the guard, handed over his papers and watched apprehensively as the guard flipped through the passport, scrutinized the photo and compared it with Andrew's face. Handing back the papers, the guard waved Andrew on. The process had taken thirty seconds! As Andrew drove off, he looked in his rearview mirror and saw the driver of the next car climb out, walk around to open the hood of his car for the guard's inspection....

God had come to the rescue again. However, seeing God work again and again didn't keep Andrew from experiencing fear, he admits:

"I've driven toward the Iron Curtain with my carload of Scripture, arrived at the border, seen the controls, and gotten so scared I've turned around and *driven back to a hotel in the nearest village where I could pray and fast. I'd stay there until I had faith that with God I was a majority; and that I could cross over with Scripture and preach on the other side and not be caught."*

Into China

Prayer has always been the cornerstone of Brother Andrew's work. In 1975, at a Love China seminar, he heard Christian leaders saying, "The Bamboo Curtain must be God's will; otherwise it wouldn't be there."

Greatly disturbed, Andrew protested. "Now wait a minute. Let's not be fatalists. This is not the time to accept the circumstance, but to intercede and say, 'God, it must change. Use me.'"

God did use Andrew in China; in a massive operation his workers were able to smuggle in one million Bibles in a single night. His work expanded into other parts of Asia, into Africa, Central America, and finally, the Middle East.

"Communism is dead," he says. "The real revolution is taking place in the Middle East. Nowhere in the world is the church weaker."

Brother Andrew and his coworkers are still willing to pay the price to be in the forefront of God's work.

Further Reading

Brother Andrew. *Building in a Broken World.* Wheaton, Ill.: Tyndale House, 1981.

Brother Andrew with Sherrill, John and Elizabeth. *God's Smuggler.* Lincoln, Va.: Chosen, 1970 [1965].

Brother Andrew with Williams, Susan Devore. *And God Changed His Mind.* Old Tappan, N.J.: Revell, 1990.

Brother Andrew with Wooding, Dan. *God's Agent.* Basingstoke, England: Marshall, Morgan and Scott, 1983.

Writers

Best-seller!:
Harriet Beecher Stowe   *Margaret Bendroth*

Notes from the Underground:
Fyodor Dostoievski   *Beatrice Batson*

To God be the Glory:
Fanny Crosby   *Richard Stanislaw*

Mentor to C. S. Lewis:
George MacDonald   *Lyle Dorsett*

Scholar Pilgrim:
C. S. Lewis   *Henry William Griffin*

Jungle Doctor:
Paul White   *William Gilliver*

Unshackled!:
Eugenia Price   *Kay Marshall Strom*

Living Word:
Ken Taylor   *Peter Gunther*

Harriet Beecher Stowe and *Uncle Tom's Cabin*

Best-seller!

When Abraham Lincoln first met Harriet Beecher Stowe in 1862, he leaned over benevolently and remarked, "So you're the little woman who wrote the book that made this big war." He was speaking of an all-time national best-seller, *Uncle Tom's Cabin.* The controversial novel turned over 300,000 copies its first year in print.

The book first appeared in 1851 as a serial in a small abolitionist newspaper, *The New Era,* and quickly attracted an eager following. In March 1852 a Boston publisher gathered the chapters into a two-volume set. The first printing of 5,000 copies was gone in two days; by May it had sold 50,000. Americans bought two million copies of the book in the next ten years; in proportion to population it was the best-seller of all time.

Harriet Beecher Stowe was an unlikely author for this literary bombshell. The wife of a college professor in Brunswick, Maine, she had never been an ardent abolitionist. Much of her life was spent in the shadow of her famous father, Lyman Beecher, her talented sister, Catharine, and her erudite husband, Calvin Stowe. In 1850, she was the busy mother of five active children, living on the shoestring budget of a scholar's wife.

Fugitive Slaves

Uncle Tom's Cabin was Mrs. Stowe's answer to the Fugitive Slave Law of 1850. This act of Congress, part of a cynical compromise between North and South, was meant to pacify Southerners who were angry at the addition of free territory in California and the Southwest. It meant that slaveowners could retrieve their property in any Northern state, aided by federal marshals; no slave could ever be free within the borders of the United States.

The Fugitive Slave Law brought many Northerners face to face with the agonizing injustices of slavery. The abolitionist community in Boston organized to protect a young escaped slave named Shadrach, who was seized in the coffeehouse where he worked as a waiter. Before

---

A troubled family

Harriet Beecher Stowe's family filled the center stage of nineteenth-century American Protestant society. Her father Lyman Beecher was a nationally known evangelist, temperance campaigner, and social critic. All of his sons entered the ministry, and one, Henry Ward, went on to become the most gifted preacher of the post-Civil War era. The daughters were equally brilliant: Isabella Beecher became a leading suffragist, Catharine an innovative educator, and Harriet the most celebrated American author of the century with the publication of *Uncle Tom's Cabin* in 1852.

Yet Lyman Beecher's fame was a complicated legacy. Two of Harriet's brothers, George and James, died by their own hand. Catharine, the oldest, suffered severe religious doubts, and rejected her father's Calvinism after her fiancé, Andrew Fisher, died before undergoing Christian conversion. Charles, another brother, was tried for heresy for his belief in evolution and the pre-existence of souls. Accusations of adultery against Henry Ward led to the infamous Beecher-Tilton scandal, in which his personal life became a salacious subject for Victorian-era gossip. Harriet's half sister Isabella, who was mentally unstable, led the public charge against Henry Ward's reputation.

Success amidst tragedy

Harriet's personal success also occurred in the midst of family tragedy. Married to Calvin Stowe, a widowed Bible scholar nine years her senior, she gave birth to six children, and only three survived her. In 1849 she lost an infant during a cholera epidemic; Calvin was off on business and she buried the child alone. In 1857 her oldest son, Henry, drowned in the Connecticut River during his freshman year at Dartmouth College. Her youngest son, Frederick, never recovered from the physical and psychological wounds he received during service in the Union Army. He vanished from sight after sailing to the San Francisco gold fields in 1870. Georgiana died in 1887 after years of mental instability and abuse of morphine.

The emotional power of Harriet's most popular book galvanized a generation grown apathetic about slavery. Clearly, her own acquaintance with personal loss, even by 1851, gave the story of Uncle Tom's martyrdom its special urgency and conviction. Though no literary masterpiece, *Uncle Tom's Cabin* is a deeply human book, and one that would forever change the terms of slavery in American life.

he could be returned to slavery, vigilantes forced their way into the courtroom, snatched the prisoner, and spirited him away to Canada on the Underground Railroad. In return the government seized another fugitive, one Thomas Sims, sealing the courtroom with a chain. While the abolitionists tried every legal recourse to free the man, three hundred armed marshals escorted him to a vessel in Boston Harbor where two hundred and fifty U.S. soldiers were waiting to him back to slavery.

Mrs. Stowe witnessed these events through the eyes of her brother Edward, a leader of the Boston abolitionists. She was moved to write by a chance remark from Edward's wife: "Hattie, if I could use a pen as you can, I would write something that would make the whole nation feel what an accursed thing slavery is."

Unforgettable scenes

The book, with its unforgettable scenes and characters, more than succeeded in doing so. Thousands of readers from Maine to Minnesota cheered on Eliza escaping the slave-catcher

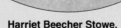

Harriet Beecher Stowe.

Haley and his bloodhounds across the icy Ohio River. When Uncle Tom was sold to Augustine St. Clare in New Orleans, they learned to love

the irascible slave girl Topsy and the starchy Miss Opheila, St. Clare's visiting Yankee cousin. They wept when St. Clare's daughter, the pure Little Eva, languished and died, and clenched their fists as the righteous Uncle Tom succumbed to the wrath of Simon Legree. It was ironic that most Americans formed their strongest impressions of slavery from this book, which was based on secondhand accounts and a vivid imagination. Mrs. Stowe freely admitted that she had never been to the South, apart from a brief trip to a Kentucky plantation.

This best-seller of the last century is seldom read today, however. The book's melodramatic plot and sentimental characters have certainly diminished its appeal to a modern audience. And, over the course of time, the very name "Uncle Tom" gained the racial stereotype of a fawning, spineless collaborator. This is ironic, since it was the reverse of Mrs. Stowe's intent in creating the character. The

THE LIFE OF

Harriet Beecher Stowe

1811	Born on June 14 in Litchfield, Connecticut,
1816	Her mother, Roxana Beecher dies
1824	Harriet moves to Hartford, Connecticut, to attend Hartford Female Seminary
1836	Marries Calvin Stowe in Cincinnati, Ohio, on January 6
	Twin daughters born on September 29
1850	Moves to Brunswick, Maine
1851–52	Writing and publication of *Uncle Tom's Cabin*
	Family moves to Andover, Massachusetts
1853–78	Literary career, including publication of four novels, travel books, and numerous articles
1886	Death of Calvin Stowe
1896	Dies in Hartford, Connecticut

stereotype owes more to the endlessly popular, vulgarized minstrel-show versions of the book, played by white actors in blackface.

All the same, any modern reader is struck by Mrs. Stowe's constant racial assumptions about the relative "strengths" of white and black characters: those with the most African blood, like Uncle Tom, are shown as the most submissive, those with the most "Anglo-Saxon" ancestry being portrayed as possessing the most fire and determination.

Mrs Stowe's vision

But still, the book has a curious eloquence. Mrs. Stowe readily admitted that its climactic scene, the death of Uncle Tom, came to her in a vision. As she was coming forward to take communion at a church service in February 1851, she saw the scene in vivid detail— an elderly black man being flogged to death by a vicious tormentor. As the slave died, he implored God's forgiveness for his tormentors. Harriet Stowe returned to her seat deeply shaken. The power of this image left her physically prostrated for days, until she began to weave it into a larger story.

That sense of urgency carried her through the next year of monthly installments. As she confided to her son, "I write with my heart's blood. I suffer exquisitely in writing these things." The death of Little Eva left her unable to lift a pen for weeks. She was in no doubt about where the power derived. When asked about what sources she used for her writing, she always gave the simple answer: "God did it!"

The book's eloquence— then as much as now—comes from its ability to convey spiritual truth in deeply human terms. The emotional core of *Uncle Tom's Cabin* was Mrs. Stowe's intense love for her own children in the midst of loss; it is this that gives life to Eliza's love for her son Harry, St. Clare's for Eva, and Uncle Tom's for his own family. She described this love strikingly: "I seemed to understand what Christ meant when he spoke of

Above: Harriet Beecher Stowe; below: Topsy from *Uncle Tom's Cabin*.

Uncle Tom was Mrs. Stowe's representation of a very human, suffering Christ. The simple old man endured more bereavement, injustice, and physical pain than any other character in the book. And perhaps nineteenth-century readers recognized in him what today's readers, too often intent on a pain-free existence, cannot—a Christ who did not so much triumph over sin and pain, as dwelt in the midst of it.

The death of Uncle Tom, from an early edition of Stowe's classic novel.

himself as being made bread and giving his flesh and blood as the vital food for his own."

The sin of slavery

Americans who had never walked south of the Mason-Dixon line learned that slavery was a sin because of what it did to families. The pathos of *Uncle Tom's Cabin* brought home the awful truth: that the agony of losing a child is in every way as real and as horrifying to an African parent as it is to an "Anglo-Saxon" one.

Further Reading

Stowe, Charles Edward. *Harriet Beecher Stowe: The Story of Her Life*. Boston: Houghton Mifflin, 1911.

Gerson, Noel. *Harriet Beecher Stowe; a Biography*. New York: Praeger Publishers, 1976.

Wilson, R.H.F. *Crusader in Crinoline: The Life of Harriet Beecher Stowe*. 1941. Reprint. Westport, Conn.: Greenwood, 1972.

Opposite: Fyodor Dostoievski;
portrait by V. Perov.

Notes from the Underground

Calling Dostoievski more than a conqueror in his spiritual pilgrimage may strike some readers as the oxymoron of the nineteenth century. That he came to hold faith in the Incarnate God as crucial to Christian belief is incontrovertible; that his own journey was far from being conflict-free is equally undeniable.

Dostoievski was not the type of believer who refers to a particular date or occasion on which he becomes a Christian, nor was he the kind who brings conceptually stated convictions and dogmas to the riddles of human existence. However, it is possible to trace his development from his boyhood in a pious orthodox family, to a strong association with utopian socialism, to a radical socialistic outlook, bordering on atheism.

It is also possible to observe his return to orthodoxy, following a clear understanding of the plight of unredeemed existence and an acquired disgust with any form of social reform. There then followed something resembling a Christian perspective on humanity's basic need to believe in the Divine Christ, the ultimate revelation of God. His Christianity, however, can hardly be seen as radically fideistic. He constantly weighed the proofs of faith with arguments of negation.

In his *Diary of a Writer*, Dostoievski tells of his early training in his Russian Orthodox faith: the family went on pilgrimages, participated in church services, received the bread and wine of Holy Communion, and enjoyed friendships among fellow worshipers. The family also read the Old and New Testaments.

Sentenced to death

While attending the University at Petersburg, where his father sent the impetuous young man to be trained as an engineering cadet, his interest in religion began to wane. Becoming preoccupied with social reform, Dostoievski soon wondered, after periods of action and reaction, whether reform has any relation to religion or to God. In his judgment, social reform begins with denial of God, and reform is absolutely necessary. Although he still appeared to hold a high regard

The human condition

Albert Einstein once stated that he had learnt more from Dostoievski than from a certain distinguished physicist whom he named. Such a comment is not hard to believe, if one recognizes that great writers are to be appraised not by the facts they convey but by the vision they reveal and the way in which the transform the readers' experiences. It is impossible to measure the profound influence of Dostoievski for more than a century on individuals from every walk of life.

Whatever their background, profession or creed, all find his sensitivity, range, and depth irresistible.

To read Dostoievski, especially The Brothers Karamazov, is to face large human questions and profound moral and spiritual concerns, not in the language of discursive statement but in the contradictions of human experience. While the pressure of nihilism, atheistic humanism, and radical socialism in Russia were all too familiar to him, his writings focus primarily on the seething revolutions, agonizing doubts, and confusing paradoxes within the soul and spirit of the individual.

A seer and a prophet, Dostoievski gives voice to the inner contradictions known by most mortals. What he reveals so clearly about the human condition, he saw first within himself and made no attempt to hide. Few writers draw so near to each of us and perhaps fewer so definitely intertwine their own lives and vocations as did Fyodor Dostoievski, who spent his entire creative energy on a single theme, the individual's need for and relation to God.

THE LIFE OF

Fyodor Dostoievski

1821	Born in Moscow
1849	Faces firing squad; receives a reprieve; sentence commuted to four years at hard labor and five years imprisonment
1861	*House of the Dead*
1864	*Notes from the Underground*
1866	*Crime and Punishment*
1868	*The Idiot*
1872	*The Possessed*
1875	*The Raw Youth*
1880	*The Brothers Karamazov*
1881	Dies

---

for Christ, not as Savior but as an ideal, he discontinued attendance at communion in 1845.

His interest in reform grew more intensely when he joined the Petrashevsky circle, advocates of utopian socialism, and met with a group of young men to discuss the disparity among social classes in Russia. One of the radical members of the circle persuaded Dostoievski to follow an extreme position, verging close to atheism. Dostoievski and several revolutionary-minded young men united to prepare the people for an uprising, but no such turmoil occurred. He, with others, was arrested and sentenced to death, but at the moment of execution, each was reprieved.

Following the reprieve, Dostoievski spent four years in hard labor and five years in prison in Siberia, as a "common soldier in a disciplinary platoon." While in prison, he came face to face with evil and suffering and saw the debilitating effects of these upon human lives, whether those of the peasant or the aristocrat. He also spent much time in prayer, meditation, and thought, as well as in reading the New Testament, the only book permitted him during imprisonment. In his reading he found spiritual sustenance for each day and a renewed resolve to know peace in God.

What seems unmistakable is that this was the time that he began a search, with a mixture of faith and disbelief, that led to his renewed belief in Christ. These years in Dostoievski's life, from age twenty-nine to thirty-four are crucial in his spiritual pilgrimage. It was at some point during these five years that he met and married his first wife, a marriage that was without happiness. The

unhappiness was due in part to the violence of his epileptic attacks and a compulsion for gambling.

The House of the Dead

Dostoievski's creative powers, deepened by his prison experience, began to focus on the suffering of individuals, robbed of freedom. Something of the harrowing experiences of prison life are unfolded in *The House of the Dead*. The book also recognizes that social reform has no power over sin, and that Jesus, if perceived only as a moral reformer, has little transforming effect in lives. There is little to suggest that Dostoievski actually became a dedicated Christian during those years, but from the markings in the New Testament, particularly John's Gospel, he understood that the essential message for anyone in bondage is the freeing power of love for God and others. As indicated, beginnings of a search are evident.

The House of Death exemplifies his vocational life: it is a novel which examines the problems of freedom and bondage, issues of doubt and belief, facts of evil and good, and questions of a good God's relationship both to creation and to human society. In each major novel, which becomes a testing ground for various points of view, Dostoievski shows the human spirit's restless questionings and the tangling consequences of moral actions. For him, his struggling faith was intertwined with his developing vocation.

The problem of freedom

Crime and Punishment, completed in 1866 with the help of his second wife (his first wife died two years earlier), emerged from his questioning experiences during his prison term. What if one consecrates himself to what he believes to be the service of mankind, the main character wonders, even if such service means murdering an old woman? Is a man through his own might and power not free to set right what he calls the ways of God? Is crime ever a virtue and is evil ever a good? Even if the powerful have the right to restrain individual freedom, does not an individual have the freedom and right to commit crime? Yet, why cannot one kill and be indifferent? Why does one feel guilt? After tracing the course of "freedom from God," it becomes self-evident that man becomes his own god if he rejects freedom in God. So-called freedom from God leads only to disaster and ruin. The problem of freedom constantly tears at Dostoievski, but the author leaves no doubt regarding its true source. No freedom exists apart from freedom in Christ.

In *The Brothers Karamazov* the problem of freedom receives its most intense treatment. By the time he wrote this novel (1881), his struggling movement toward faith had become a reality. He had freely chosen the Christ. Although his commitment to Christ is unmistakable, he demonstrated its outworkings in the world, where doubters are still capable of compellingly arguing their unbelief. A reader sees this not through abstractions and discursive statements, but through characters who embody convictions.

The fictional character Ivan Karamazov, embodies the strongest possible argument against a belief in God who creates a world and supposedly loves it; yet fails, Ivan says, to stop the horrible atrocities rampant in this world. His repudiation of the belief that people are capable of freely choosing Christ is equally compelling. Why does He "mistakenly" think individuals capable of willingly choosing Him through love even though He offers Himself as guide? Do not most people in the "herd" of humanity prefer that someone make choices for them? Do they not prefer servitude to freedom? Aren't they primarily concerned over food for the body, caring little for food for the spirit? Do not hundreds of years of history show that human beings are incapable of handling freedom? These and similar questions haunt Ivan (and haunted Dostoievski as well).

Ivan admits the existence of God; but equally undeniably, he refuses to accept the world that God created. He does, however, have a "longing for life;" he loves the "sticky little leaves as they open in spring;" and "the blue sky," and he loves some people "whom one loves without knowing why;" but what life really means defies explanation. Almost unbearable, he finds, is the cruelty and brutality of one human being toward another, and no amount of pious talk concerning a final harmony alleviates the suffering and pain some must endure because of cruelty freely inflicted by others. Even if one could somehow defend adult suffering, who can possibly explain the suffering of little children? As long as there is one innocent child in the world, then so long is Ivan unwilling to accept God's world. Yet, Ivan acknowledges that he has a "Euclidian earthly mind," and as a mortal being, how can one ever solve problems not of this world? Why Dostoievski chose to write as he did at this stage is difficult to ascertain, but throughout his life he weighed the hard questions, ultimately purporting the only sure response to the "Euclidian mind" of any Ivan of any era.

Light of our darkness

The response lives not with Ivan but with another character, Alyosha (and to some extent, Father Zossima). His answer does not attempt to explain away intellectual difficulties. Evil atrocities exist; longings for certitude are human characteristics. Problems have to be faced, but no exclusively intellectual or ethical solution is sufficient. Faith in the crucified and risen Christ, in whom no person is compelled to believe, is the path each individual must take. This faith is without conditions and to be freely accepted. In the acknowledged dilemma between exclusively rational responses and free choice which may entail suffering, Dostoievski (as Alyosha) chose Christ.

A free faith in Christ manifested through vigorous and active love for God and the world was the stance of Dostoievski. But he showed a fearless inquiry into difficult questions and problems. Never did he suggest that believers avoid large questions and focus only on simple ones. He was aware that perplexities of the human situation may bring doubts and that human beings can inflict suffering. It is no wonder, then, that Berdyaev says: "He showed that the light of our darkness is Christ.... Dostoievski takes us into the very dark places but he does not let darkness have the last word." That he showed the triumph of Christ and His Word gives evidence that Dostoievski had a vision of what it means to be more than a conqueror.

Further Reading

Berdyaev, Nicholas. *Dostoevsky.* Translated by Donald Attwater. New York: Meridian, 1957.

Gibson, A. Boyce. *The Religion of Dostoevsky.* Philadelphia: Westminster Press, 1973.

Panichas, George A. *The Burden of Vision, Dostoevsky's Spiritual Art.* Grand Rapids, Mich.: William B. Eerdmans, 1977.

Wasiolek, Edward. *Dostoevsky, the Major Fiction.* Cambridge: MIT Press, 1964.

"Fanny" Crosby—Hymnwriter

To God be the Glory

"If perfect earthly sight were offered to me tomorrow, I would not accept it. Did you ever know of a blind person's talking like that before?" So writes Fanny Crosby in the pages of her first autobiography. A doctor's mistake, "if mistake it was," she writes, caused blindness from the age of six weeks. Yet this nineteenth-century active preacher-writer-influencer more than conquered her handicap in a day when little help was provided. Listen to her own conquering faith:

Although it may have been a blunder on the physician's part, it was no mistake of God's. I verily believe it was His intention that I should live my days in physical darkness, so as to be better prepared to sing His praises and incite others so to do. I could not have written thousands of hymns—many of which, if you will pardon me for repeating it, are sung all over the world—if I had been hindered by the distractions of seeing all the interesting and beautiful objects that would have been presented to my notice.

Fanny Jane Crosby was born to a proud revolutionary period family. Early she heard stories of courage and heroism, and of writing (one ancestor, she claims, was a character in a James Fenimore Cooper novel). Active physically, she participated in sports and travel, her blindness never seeming to slow her involvements.

At the age of nine she experienced "the greatest piece of good fortune," the twin influences of the study of the Bible and the study of poetry with a Mrs. Hawley of Ridgefield, Connecticut. "She was an old Puritan Presbyterian, and took everything in the sacred writ as literally as the most orthodox Scotchman could do; but she loved at the same time the green meadows and singing brooks of imagination." From Mrs. Hawley's "line upon

9000 hymns

Fanny Crosby established the style of poetry that still characterizes gospel songs. Her diction and rhyme resurface in today's contemporary Christian music, and her simple memorable texts are the basis of expression for evangelical Christianity a century later: "All the Way My Savior Leads Me," "Blessed Assurance," "I Am Thine, O Lord," "Jesus, Keep Me Near the Cross," "Praise Him, Praise Him," "Rescue the Perishing," "Redeemed, How I Love to Proclaim It," "Tell Me the Story of Jesus," "To God Be the Glory."

Crosby's nearly nine thousand hymns made her familiar to her entire generation as she traveled, witnessed, and preached. Her texts were set to music by every popular American tunesmith of the nineteenth century: Doane, Lowery, the Sankeys, Kirkpatrick, Sweeney, Gabriel, Main, Bradbury, Stebbins, Root. The author index of any evangelical hymnal is testimony to her influence, yet she is largely unrepresented in denominational hymnals.

Blind from a baby

Blind from six weeks of age because of mistreatment by a man claiming to be a physician, she memorized Scripture and poetry—she never became adept at braille. She studied, then taught at the New York School for the Blind. There she met her husband, Alexander "Van" Van Alstyne (she was always called "Mrs. Crosby").

She was a social guest of six presidents—and Grover Cleveland was a personal friend. She traveled independently, often preaching at rescue missions when she visited new communities. She humbly accepted only about two dollars for each of her compositions and deliberately lived simply.

Her papers are collected at the New York Public Library's Lincoln Center Music Division. She wrote two autobiographies—delightful personal testimonies of a life of joy and thanksgiving along with stories of many of her hymns.

THE LIFE OF
Fanny Crosby

1820	Born March 24, Putnam County, New York, to an old family of the revolutionary period
1820	Father dies
	Moves to Ridgefield, Connecticut
1830	Fanny able to recite the first four books of both Testaments
1835	Begins at New York School for the Blind
1844	First publication—*The Blind Girl and Other Poems*, including her first hymn
1850	Conversion, November 20, at Broadway Tabernacle—New York City
1853	Writes cantata, *Daniel*, with Bradbury and Root (Civil War composers)
1858	Marries Alexander Van Alstyne, a blind musician (piano and cornet) [date of marriage is incorrect on her tombstone]
1864–89	Most hymns written; secular poems also produced
1897	Publishes *Bells at Evening and Other Verses*
1915	Writes last hymn, "In the Morn of Zion's Glory," February 11, to comfort a neighbor family who had lost a young child
	Dies, February 12, Bridgeport, Connecticut

Right: Mrs Fanny Jane Crosby, 1820-1915.

line, and precept upon precept" approach to Bible study combined with her "secular poems almost without number" came the foundation of a life of literary service for Fanny Crosby—and the confidence to see past her blindness. Like the biblical Timothy, Fanny too had a Christian mentor in Grandmother Eunice—and her entire family of devout believers.

Sick ... of Arithmetic
Studies at the New York School for the Blind were another inspiration, including "Grammar, Philosophy, Astronomy, and Political Economy"; she writes "With these I was in love." Crosby's academic trials came, not from the more predictable difficulty of moving among a sighted world, but from the study of mathematics: "I have never been a very good hater, even when the best material was provided for the purpose; but I found myself adept at the art of loathing, when it came to the Science of Numbers." That down-to-earth schoolgirl concern resulted in a couplet somewhat

less insightful than her hymns: "I loathe, abhor, it makes me sick / To hear the word Arithmetic."

Her autobiographies are never self-pitying. Her rich expressions of faith in hymns were lived out in a remarkably normal life. Crosby's entire life was a demonstration of matter-of-fact confidence in Christ. The "Blind Girl" self-description of her first book became a highly competent poet with stunning memory and worldwide influence. The student became teacher. The strong Christian witness invaded rescue missions and White House events. She became the best-known woman in nineteenth-century America.

Following her own education, she returned to teach at the New York School for the Blind and, in the process, became self-supporting. Her immense output of verse flowed because "the sweetness and grandeur of the religion of our Savior sank into my heart."

She was not strong in braille, so she relied on her phenomenal memory. Poems were composed and edited in her mind, then dictated. If today

The birthplace of Fanny Crosby, Putnam County, New York State.

some lyrics seem clichéd, it is because a hundred years ago, Crosby created the expressions that have become the overused words of her gospel song progeny.

Writing and toothache

Fanny wrote out of deep faith, not for financial security. She refused to exploit her popularity and took only moderate fees for her compositions—another lesson to today's popular Christian entertainers. How did she do it? A charming chapter in her *Life-story* traces the process. Here are her own colorful words:

There are some days, or at least hours, when I could not compose a hymn if the world were laid at my feet as a promised recompense. Fancy writing verses when one has that "hell of a' diseases," as Robbie Burns called it, the toothache! The silent cry of the suffering molar would run through it all.... Sick people have written good poetry, but I fancy it was in their intervals of partial convalescence.

I am not subject to very many unpleasant sensations on account of ill health.... But there are times when I am not in the mood to write, [so] I would build a mood—or try to draw one around me.

I should sit alone, as I have done on many a day and night, praying God to give me the thoughts and the feelings wherewith to compose my hymn.... It may seem a little old-fashioned, always to begin one's work with prayer: but I never undertake a hymn without first asking the good Lord to be my inspiration in the work that I am about to do....

Often I take in my mind some tune already known ... this, however, does not imply that the tune will ultimately be chosen as the companion of the works: for it has probably already its own true and lawful mate, with which it is to be happy and useful. Sometimes a tune is furnished me for which to write the words. "Blessed Assurance" was made in this manner....

After a particular hymn is done, I let it lie for a few days in the writing-desk of my mind, so to speak, until I have leisure to prune it, to read it through with the eyes of my memory, and in other ways mould it into as presentable shape as possible. I often cut, trim, and change it....

I have no trouble in sorting and arranging my literary and lyric wares within the apartments of

Fanny Crosby with Ira D. Sankey, Moody's colleague.

my mind. If I were given a little while in which to do it, I could take down from its shelves, hundreds if not thousands of hymns, that I have written during the sixty years in which I have been praising my Redeemer through this medium of song.

Fanny Crosby is remembered for those thousands of hymns. In her lifetime they gave her a platform for preaching and for witness. In her independence, she modeled leadership both as a handicapped person and as a woman—long before the status of either was recognized by national policy. She kept her maiden name, although she was called "Mrs." Crosby in acknowledgment of her marriage to Alexander Van Alstyne. But she traveled alone, finding her own way to new cities. On one occasion she considered serving as a missionary in Africa with the maverick Methodist bishop William Taylor.

Her poetry was admired by Presidents John Tyler, John Quincy Adams, Andrew Johnson, and Grover Cleveland (who also was a close personal friend and secretary at the New York School for the Blind); she was a White House guest of each of them. She knew James Buchanan, Lincoln's

Secretary of State William Henry Seward, William Cullen Bryant, Stephen A. Douglas, and even Jefferson Davis. She was a friend of President James Polk, Horace Greeley, Hannibal Hamlin (Lincoln's first vice president), Henry Clay, and soprano Jenny Lind. Through all that fame, she faithfully presented the gospel message of "To God be the glory, great things He hath done, so loved He the world that He gave us His Son." Friends mentioned her personal evangelistic work—kneeling beside a derelict or a sophisticate and leading that man or woman to faith in Christ.

Broken cord

Crosby's final familiar hymn was "Someday the silver cord will break.... And I shall see Him face to face and tell the story—saved by grace." British hymnodist Frances Havergal, who corresponded frequently with Crosby, wrote (and Crosby particularly remembered) this tribute: "Sweet blind singer over the sea, / Tuneful and jubilant, how can it be ... / How can she sing in the dark like this? / What is her fountain of light and bliss? / Oh her heart can see, her heart can see!"

When she died, her funeral was the largest ever seen (in the same town where P. T. Barnum had been buried a few weeks earlier), with people standing for blocks, according to eyewitness George Stebbins (one of her many composers). Charles Gabriel, another gospel songwriter, in 1916 correctly prophecied that Fanny Crosby's "name, suspended like a halo above modern hymnology ... will live on as long as people sing the Gospel."

Further Reading

Crosby, Fanny J. *Fanny Crosby's Life-story, By Herself.* New York: Everywhere Publishing Co., 1903.

_____. *Memories of Eighty Years.* Boston: James H. Earb, 1906.

Jackson, Samuel Trevena. *Fanny Crosby's Story of Ninety-Four Years.* New York: Revell, 1915.

Ruffin, Bernard. *Fanny Crosby.* Philadelphia: United Church Press, 1976.

Lewis' debt

"I know hardly any other writer who seems to be closer, or more continually close, to the Spirit of Christ Himself." This is high praise coming from C. S. Lewis, who was undisputedly one of the most influential Christian writers of the twentieth century. Lewis, the author of nearly forty books, went on to say that he regarded MacDonald "as my master; indeed I fancy I have never written a book in which I did not quote from him."

C. S. Lewis was not alone in acknowledging a great debt to George MacDonald. In 1924, over two decades before Lewis published his tribute, the celebrated G. K. Chesterton, author of over one hundred volumes, extolled the nineteenth-century writer's story-telling power when he revealed that *The Princess and the Goblin* was "the most real, the most realistic, in the exact sense of the phrase the most like life." That book, Chesterton testified, "made a difference to my whole existence."

George MacDonald, whose writing touched such literary giants as Lewis and Chesterton, was born in Huntly, Aberdeenshire, Scotland a few days before Christmas in 1824. He died in the south of England in the autumn in 1905. During his lifetime he wrote over fifty volumes of fiction, poetry, sermons, and Christian commentaries, as well as numerous essays on sundry topics. Although he suffered from poor health, a meager income, and a family racked by pain and death, he exuded a deep love for Jesus Christ and a passion for life. Through his writing, preaching, and teaching, he passed this love for Christ to countless others on both sides of the Atlantic.

George MacDonald—a Victorian Writer

Mentor to C. S. Lewis

In October 1872 a handsome man with warm eyes, dark hair, Roman nose, and a beard that reached about eight inches below his chin, walked up to the podium of the crowded Lyceum lecture hall in Boston, Massachusetts. Dressed in an English-cut black suit complemented by black shoes and black tie, George MacDonald spoke for over an hour using neither notes nor manuscript. Holding only a volume of Robert Burns' poetry in his hand, this visitor to America read passages of verse every few minutes as he illustrated points during a passionate presentation on the life and art of the renowned poet of Scotland.

The following day an article on the lecture appeared in a Boston newspaper. The reporter noted that those who regularly attended Lyceum lectures frequently encountered great minds: last night, however, "we were in the presence of a great soul." The reporter captured the essence of George MacDonald. None of the British author's devoted readers would argue that he was one of the greatest English authors of the nineteenth century. In truth much of his writing style, especially his fiction, is awkwardly contrived, wordy, and preachy. Nevertheless his books are magnetic.

They draw in those who are spiritually hungry and alert. In brief, the writings of George MacDonald exude the Spirit of God and they have nourished hungry souls for over a century.

Making disciples

If George MacDonald was not a writer comparable to Charlotte Brontë or Jane Austen, he was a teacher who had few equals. Indeed, no nineteenth-century British author did more to fulfill Christ's Commission to "make disciples ... teaching them to obey everything I have commanded you" (Matt. 28:19-20). His books, both fiction and non-fiction, brim to overflowing with the teachings of Christ. For those who want to learn about God's love and mercy, as well as how to know God and love Him with the heart and soul rather than just the mind, MacDonald is a master teacher.

This man whose soul was ablaze for Christ like a hot, burning ember was born in 1824 in a troubled, pain-racked part of the world. MacDonald was born at Huntly, in northeastern Scotland, on December 10. The Scots battled with economic hardship as they sought to make a living on windswept, hilly, and rocky land in a northern climate that was often shrouded in mist, rain, and

George MacDonald.

THE LIFE OF
George MacDonald

1824	Born in Huntly, Aberdeenshire, Scotland
1845	Graduates from King's College, Aberdeen
1848	Enters Highbury Theological College, London
1851	Ordained at Trinity Congregational Chapel, Arundel, England Marries Louisa Powell Publishes his first collection of poems
1853	Pressured to resign from Trinity Chapel Embarks on full-time writing
1855	Publishes *Within and Without*
1858	Publishes *Phantastes* and establishes his literary reputation
1880	Publishes *Diary of an Old Soul*
1881	Begins to spend part of each year in Italy due to poor health
1905	Dies in England

clouds for much of each year's short growing season.

The Calvinism that had evolved in Scotland by the nineteenth century was nearly as dreary and burdensome as the weather. Although John Calvin and his followers helped liberate Christianity from the bondage of Roman Catholic law, generations which followed—especially in Scotland—gradually slipped into a new legalism, which was wholly out of character with the spirit of the Reformation. The attributes of God, in particular His holiness and justice, were so accentuated in some congregations that divine love and mercy were all but ignored.

The burned violin
Likewise joy, pleasure, and even beauty were criticized as the work of Satan. MacDonald's grandmother, for example, burned his uncle's violin, as to

her mind and religion it was an instrument conceived by Satan. MacDonald's own father, in a similar spirit, urged the lad to stop writing poetry because it was a "fruitless" enterprise that would not glorify God.

Many Scottish Calvinists of this era emphasized the need to memorize creeds and catechisms with the good intention of teaching truth and combating heresy. Nevertheless, at its worst this enterprise led to mere head knowledge of God and biblical truth; it became an angle of vision from which to look for error rather than a vantage point to encourage a living relationship with Christ.

Young George MacDonald grew up on a farm on the outskirts of Huntly village. His mother died shortly after his birth and his father did not remarry until a decade and a half later. Although the boy grew up without a mother, his father, in spite of his austerity and exaggerated manliness (he had to have his leg amputated and refused to drink the customary shot of whiskey to dull the pain) brought him up quite well.

His father was so kind, loving, and gentle that he would not, like the vast majority of churchgoing Scotsmen, grouse hunt because he thought the sport cruel. As C. S. Lewis noted, the boy learned, if not from the local Congregational pastor then certainly from his own father, "that Fatherhood must be at the core of the universe. He was thus prepared in an unusual way to teach that religion in which the relation of Father and Son is of all relations the most central."

The senior MacDonald gave George every encouragement to get an education, sending him

to school in Huntly. When the young man was sixteen years old he won a small scholarship to King's College at Aberdeen. While he was there he eked out a living by tutoring children of middle-class families, and in 1845 he was awarded an M.A. after reading the classics in history, philosophy, literature, and theology.

For the next three years MacDonald, by this time in his twenties, lived in London, where he supported himself by giving tutorials. It was during this period that he felt God leading him to spend his life communicating what he had not learned in his local church or at King's College—that God loves His creation and wants to walk in mystical union with the men and women He created.

In answer to this call George MacDonald enrolled at Highbury College, a Congregational theological college. He remained there one year and then in 1850 accepted a call to Trinity Chapel, a Congregational fellowship at Arundel, West Sussex, where he was ordained in 1851.

Within and without
The early 1850s brought some important changes that would set the pattern for the remainder of MacDonald's life. First was illness. In 1850 he was stricken with pulmonary tuberculosis. Although he regained his strength after several weeks of bed rest, he battled the debilitating effects of this disease for the next half century. A second change was that he started writing for publication. While convalescing he wrote a long dramatic poem entitled *Within and Without*. Although he was

unable find a publisher for the poem until 1855, he did publish his translations of *Twelve of the Spiritual Songs of Novalis* in 1851.

Beginning a life of writing for publication and fighting tuberculosis were only two of the changes in MacDonald's way of life. In 1851 he married Louisa Powell, thereby beginning his beloved role as a husband and father. He loved Louisa with his heart, mind, and soul. She loved him unconditionally in return, and gave him eleven delightful children.

In the midst of his newfound joy as a family man, published author, and parish pastor, MacDonald fell on some trying times with his new congregation. In his rebellion against the coldness of doctrinaire religion, he began to stress the necessity of a personal relationship with Christ through the teachings of the Scriptures and nudgings of the Holy Spirit. Becoming something of a mystic, MacDonald increasingly devoted himself to prayer. He believed that God spoke to him during prayer time as well as through dreams and the beauty and activity of His creation.

It was in this vein that he wrote to his father in 1851, telling him that he had little confidence in the "shorter Catechism system." As his letter said "I firmly believe people have hitherto been a great deal too much taken up about *doctrine* and far too little about practice. The word doctrine, as used in the Bible, means teaching of duty, not theory." He went on to explain that he had "preached a sermon about this. We are far too anxious to be definite and to have finished, well-

A photograph of George MacDonald by Charles Dodgson, "Lewis Carroll".

polished, sharp-edged *systems*—forgetting that the more perfect the theory about the infinite, the surer it is to be wrong, the more impossible is it to be right." The letter, quoted in Grenville MacDonald's *George MacDonald and Wife*, ended with these words: "I am neither Arminian nor Calvinist. To no system would I subscribe."

Hardship
Because of MacDonald's stand against Calvinism a faction of his congregation began to criticize his teaching and preaching. Although his opponents did not have the temerity to fire him, they did cut his salary several times. In consequence, by 1853, with responsibility for a wife and two children, the nearly

destitute pastor was forced to resign.

After 1853 George MacDonald was without a church and a steady income. Indeed, blessed with an ever-growing family, plagued by a weak body, and driven by a definite sense of calling from God, he was forced to preach wherever he could wrangle an invitation, lecture on theology or literature whenever opportunities arose, and write books during the times in between. The income from these enterprises was meager and sporadic. Nevertheless, God provided the family's needs and neither he nor Louisa ever complained about the spartan-like life style they were forced to maintain.

Over the next thirty-five years MacDonald preached and lectured all over Great Britain and Ireland, and he even made one speaking tour of the United States. During these three and a half decades he published over fifty books, which included some thirty-seven novels of fantasy and fiction, two collections of short stories, a half dozen books of poetry, and five volumes of sermons. His most productive decades for writing were the 1870s and 1880s when he wrote thirty-one books.

Christian fantasist

Most of his writing is Christ-centered. Among his best-loved adult novels are *Annals of a Quiet Neighborhood*, *The Seaboard Parish*, *Thomas Wingfold, Curate*, and *Paul Faber, Surgeon*. These works are still read with profit, as are his children's stories, which include *At the Back of the North Wind*, *The Princess and the Goblin*, and *The Princess and Curdie*. C. S. Lewis argued in his *Introduction to George MacDonald: An Anthology* that the fiction as a whole is "undistinguished, at times fumbling." Nevertheless, Lewis admired the teaching in many of these novels. He also agreed with most critics that MacDonald was at his best with "fantasy that hovers between the allegorical and the mythopoeic. And this," Lewis insisted, "he does better than any man." These books include *Phantastes*, *The Portent*, and *Lilith*—which are all widely read and acclaimed today.

Amongst his most influential writings are the sermons, in particular the three volumes which are entitled *Unspoken Sermons*. These books have been printed and reprinted in numerous editions, as well as anthologized by C. S. Lewis.

George MacDonald is remembered today, nearly a century after his death, because he wrote so many influential books. He is less known for his admirable personal qualities. Perhaps more important than writing more than fifty books was the strength of his faith and perseverance in the face of much adversity. MacDonald and his wife Louisa were "more than conquerors" in the face of his many illnesses and periods of convalescence which resulted from his tuberculosis.

They weathered these difficult times valiantly, but even more impressive was the way they kept their focus on Christ and continued to praise and obey Him when death claimed four of their children. In 1878 their daughter, Mary, died at age twenty-four. Less than a year later their fifteen-year-old son, Maurice, succumbed to tuberculosis and died of pneumonia. Five years later they buried Caroline, age twenty; she also had tuberculosis. Then their beloved firstborn, Lilia, died of the same disease within a few years.

Following Christ

In the midst of all this sorrow George MacDonald not only wrote his books, lectured, and preached, he ministered to his family and to the poor in their midst. For example, every Christmas—even when his own poverty was such that he barely had enough to feed his family—he would bring home the poor children of the neighborhood and tell the Christmas story of how God so loved the world that He sent His only Son to save those who would trust Him. One Christmas the MacDonalds were so poor that there was only a modest-sized pudding and a few oranges for celebration and gifts. Yet several impoverished children were brought in and the pudding was shared with them. Finally, the oranges—the family's only presents—were peeled and divided with the guests.

In 1946, C. S. Lewis wrote of MacDonald: "the Divine Sonship is the key conception which unites all the different elements of [his] thought. I dare not say that he is never in error; but to speak plainly I know hardly any other writer who seems to be closer, or more continually close, to the Spirit of Christ Himself." These sentences get at the heart of MacDonald's thought and contribution, yet the Scotsman certainly was not without error.

Indeed, in his reaction against the ultra-Calvinistic emphasis on God's holiness, justice, and the biblical doctrines of final judgment and hell, MacDonald went to the opposite extreme. In his desire to help people see the love and mercy of God he went beyond Scripture and argued that God will send no one to hell. While never maintaining the universalist position that all people are saved from eternal damnation, he did argue that God loves His children and will never stop pursuing them. And, according to MacDonald, God will offer salvation even after death to those He has created. People must *choose* hell, he wrote in numerous ways and places, because God will not send them there.

George MacDonald taught and preached what he hoped to be true on this doctrinal issue, rather than what the Bible clearly teaches. This obvious flaw notwithstanding, he was an unusually anointed man whose writings then and now have guided countless seekers to become disciples of Jesus Christ. His sermons, too, led many drifting souls to a place of peace and rest in Christ. Furthermore, his writings have had a profound impact on many Christian writers whose works are extremely influential. C. S. Lewis, for example, acknowledged that, although he was never to meet him, he regarded MacDonald, "as my master." Frederick Buechner, a well thought of American author, has spoken of his enormous debt to the Victorian writer, and G. K. Chesterton has extolled the importance of his fellow Briton, confessing that MacDonald's writing "has made a difference to my whole existence."

Further Reading

MacDonald, George. *George MacDonald: An Anthology.* Edited by C. S. Lewis. New York: Doubleday, 1946.)

MacDonald, George. *George MacDonald: Selections from His Greatest Works.* Edited by David Newhouser. Wheaton, Ill.: Victor, 1990.

MacDonald, Greville. *George MacDonald and His Wife.* London: George, Allen & Unwin, 1924.

Phillips, Michael R. *George MacDonald: Scotland's Beloved Storyteller.* Minneapolis: Bethany House, 1987.

C. S. LEWIS

Opposite: Lucy, Susan, Edmund and Peter have dinner with Mr Beaver; from *The Lion, the Witch and the Wardrobe*.

Scholar Pilgrim

On November 22, 1963, newspapers of the world reported the deaths of John F. Kennedy, Aldous Huxley, and C. S. Lewis. At the time, the horror of Kennedy's death overshadowed the news coverage of those of Huxley and C. S. Lewis. Now, it is Lewis who is remembered with increasing respect and admiration.

C. S. Lewis in his rooms at Magdalen College, Oxford.

The reputation of C. S. Lewis has grown for almost three decades. He is remembered for his spiritual and theological writings such as *The Screwtape Letters* and *Mere Christianity*; for his children's books—*The Lion, the Witch and the Wardrobe*, plus the six others that form *The Chronicles of Narnia*; for his fiction, such as *The Great Divorce* and *Till We Have Faces;* and for his science fiction titles *Perelandra, That Hideous Strength*, and *Out of the Silent Planet*. In addition, he is remembered for his scholarship, especially for *English Literature in the Sixteenth Century*. But few remember him as a man of prayer.

Clive Staples Lewis spent his working life, from 1925 to 1962, at the universities of Oxford and Cambridge, tutoring two generations of students in medieval and Renaissance literature. A bachelor, he nonetheless acquired a family. While training for World War I at Oxford, he befriended Paddy Moore. As so often happens when young men face the possibility of imminent death, a bonding took place.

Lewis volunteered to take care of Paddy's mother if he did not return, and Paddy promised to do the same for Lewis's father.

Bachelor life
Paddy was killed in action. Lewis, slowly, awkwardly, took up the painful task of looking after Mrs. Moore as she took up the painful task of grieving for her own son whilst attempting to resign herself to her new "son." With Mrs. Moore and her daughter Maureen, he lived in a succession of digs around the Oxford area, eventually landing in The Kilns, a rickety house on Headington Hill, just outside the city limits. It seemed to be an arrangement that suited

Lewis, giving him some sort of regularity and stability; but as Mrs. Moore grew older, Lewis's filial attitude toward her was severely tested. She died in 1949.

In 1957 C. S. Lewis acquired another family, this time marrying a dying divorcee from New York, named Joy Davidson Gresham. At first he had acted out of pity, but then, after she underwent a remission from her cancer, out of love. She came with two sons, Douglas and David; the three of them enlivened The Kilns for both Lewis and his brother, Warren. When Joy died in 1960, Lewis felt the loss as though he had been married a lifetime.

Lewis the writer
Lewis was first and foremost a teacher. He set out to master his material; his lectures grew more refined; and his academic writing had a fine oral quality about it. He wrote books such as *The Allegory of Love: A Study in Medieval Tradition* (1938), *The Personal Heresy* (1939), *A Preface to "Paradise Lost"* (1941), and *English Literature in the Sixteenth Century* (1954). The last has been called by his English biographer, A. N. Wilson, the most entertaining work of literary criticism ever written.

With his friend and colleague on Oxford's English faculty, J. R. R. Tolkien, whose specialties

The gleaming spires of Oxford.

were Icelandic and Anglo-Saxon, Lewis devised a more limited curriculum. This being completed, they both proceeded, in their spare time, to add their own compositions to what they considered the already swollen corpus of English literature.

Lewis wanted to be a poet, but failed to achieve popularity. He continued to toil in prose—in science fiction—producing a number of false starts and eventually penning three creditable works: *Out of the Silent Planet* (1938), *Perelandra* (1944), and *That Hideous Strength* (1945). In 1950, he began writing a children's story, *The Lion, the Witch, and the Wardrobe*, and followed it with six more titles,

Lewis's house, The Kilns, Headington Quarry, Oxford.

ending in *The Last Battle* (1956). These detailed the adventures of some English school-children, loosely based on the children who had been evacuated from London during the Blitz and stayed at The Kilns.

Screwtape and pain

As for spiritual works, Lewis was invited one day in 1939 to write a popular book on suffering; no one else wanted to do it, but Lewis took it on. After *The Problem of Pain*, which was a modest success, he wrote something as an entertainment for the Inklings, a group of Oxford Fellows who had literary aspirations and who also happened to be Christians. This was a series of letters from a senior devil named Screwtape to a junior devil named Wormwood. They appeared as a serial in the Anglican newspaper, the *Guardian*, and eventually in book form as *The Screwtape Letters*.

All these volumes he wrote in his university vacations. And, beginning in 1941, Lewis also made five series of popular radio talks on theological subjects for the BBC, which were broadcast at the odd hours relegated to religious programming. The talks made him something of a celebrity, and the texts were printed and published in a number of booklets, eventually being bound within one cover and entitled *Mere Christianity* (1952).

Soul–searching

At a young age Lewis was something of an atheist; he was a member of the Church of Ireland who quite simply lapsed his way into noncommunion with his Church. His return to

Clive Staples Lewis, known to his friends as Jack.

the Church was accompanied with all the agony and soul-searching that one has come to associate with conversion. He had to think and read himself back in, and the process seems to have had several notable moments.

First, on the night of April 27, 1926, Lewis was reading in his

rooms at New Buildings, as his residence at Magdalen College was called, when he was joined by another Fellow of the college, Thomas Dewar Weldon. The same age as Lewis, he taught philosophy at Magdalen. The talk turned to *The Golden Bough*, James Frazer's study of comparative folklore, magic,

Magdalen College, Oxford.

and religion. According to Frazer, there were many parallels between the rites and beliefs of early cultures and those of the early Christians. Frazer's thesis was that magic seemed to have preceded religion everywhere; Weldon, or so Lewis thought, would surely agree that man turned toward religion only after magic failed.

After admitting the Gospels were more or less true, Weldon went on to reveal that he believed in the Trinity, at least as presented by the nineteenth-century German philosopher Hegel. The kingdom of the Father was expressed in logic, the kingdom of the Son was expressed in philosophy of nature, and the kingdom of the Spirit was expressed in the philosophy of spirit, which appeared in the union of God and the faithful in the Church. The triune God, said Weldon, attempting to quote Hegel from memory, consisted in the Father

and the Son, and this differentiation in the unity as the Spirit. The whole thing seemed to fit in. Lewis was stunned to realize that the tough-minded, cynical Weldon was a Christian, even of this vague and philosophical sort.

A revolutionary bus trip

Lewis had read George Bernard Shaw and H. G. Wells, Edward Gibbon and John Stuart Mill, writers who were definitely not in the theistic tradition. He had found them mildly entertaining, but on the whole they put him to sleep. Christian writers, on the other hand—such as Donne and Browne, Spenser, Milton, Johnson and Chesterton—with whom he was bound to disagree, he read again and again. The Christians might be wrong, but they were not boring. That is what he thought one spring day in 1929—and this is the second notable moment—as he boarded a bus outside Magdalen College

for the trip up Headington Hill.

If books had the power to move men's souls, then he was feeling the pressure. Earlier, in the winter term, he had reread Euripides' *Hippolytus*, which made chastity into a martyr, and Alexander's *Space, Time, and Deity*, which distinguished "enjoyment" from "contemplation." He reconsidered Hegel's philosophy of the absolute and festooned it with Berkeley's conrception of the spirit. The result was a philosophical construct which was called God. He could not know this God any more than Hamlet could have known Shakespeare. But with this sort of concept he felt comfortable. In fact, he felt free to accept it or reject it. When the bus reached Lewis's stop, he got off believing something that he had not believed when he got on, that is, that an absolute spirit, or God, did indeed exist.

The most reluctant convert

Third, in that same year Lewis spent time in self-examination, and was appalled by what he saw: "a zoo of lusts, a bedlam of ambitions, a nursery of fears, a harem of fondled hatreds." Simultaneously, he seemed to have had a vision of Hegel's Absolute Spirit, Someone who said: I am, I am that am, I am the Lord. It was a traumatic experience—a theological shock taking place in his life. It was as though climbing up the staircase of New Buildings, passing through the oak door of his room, was the person that Lewis the agnostic, Lewis the atheist, or perhaps just Lewis the lapsed, feared most of all. "I gave in, and admitted that God was God, and knelt and prayed: perhaps, that night, the most dejected and reluctant convert in all England."

Shafts of light

The fourth moment was on September 19 of the same year, a Saturday evening. It was after dinner at Magdalen College; Lewis and his guests, J. R. R. Tolkien and H. V. Dyson, set out for a stroll along the River Cherwell. It was a warm, still night. The conversation turned toward myth and metaphor.

Myths are enjoyable in themselves, argued Lewis; he had certainly enjoyed them more than most, but they were only believed by children. Adults knew better; myths were lies; although the better ones had been breathed through silver, they were not the more believable for that. Tolkien and Dyson were quick to disagree. However untrue they might seem to be, myths contained elements of the truth. Created by God as man was, the mythmaker too was a creator, albeit a subcreator, when he undertook to spin a tale or develop a plot, and when he did so, shafts of truth were bound to illuminate the floor of the fores.

A rush of wind interrupted the argument. It began to rain, or so they thought at first. Leaves pattered down on their shoulders, not raindrops, but they decided to head back to New Buildings, where the conversation turned toward Christianity and its doctrines.

Sacrifice

Lewis was having difficulty, he said, not so much in believing a doctrine as in knowing what a doctrine meant. When he was asked to give an example, he gave the doctrine of redemption.

Drunkenness could lead a person down the primrose path where only a redemptive act could save him. He could see that, but what he could not see was how the life and death of someone else (whoever he was) two thousand years ago could help them there and then— except insofar as his *example* helped them. He had read the New Testament, but nowhere did he find this *example* business; instead he found "propitiation" and "sacrifice" and "blood of the lamb"— expressions that he could interpret only in a sense that seemed to him either grisly or shocking.

And what was wrong with sacrifice? asked Tolkien, who was Church of Rome, and Dyson, who was Church of England. There was nothing wrong with the idea of sacrifice, Lewis had to concede. In fact, hee had always liked the idea of sacrifice in a pagan story, the idea of a god sacrificing himself to himself, the idea of a dying and reviving God. But notions of sacrifice such as these seemed entirely out of place when it came to interpreting the New Testament.

If pagan stories were God expressing himself through the minds of poets, using such images as He found there, then Christianity might very well be construed as God expressing Himself through real things.

Myths and truths

Why could not the story of Christ be construed as a myth, argued Tolkien and Dyson with vigor, but a myth that was true? A myth working on them in the same way as on the others, but with this tremendous difference,

that it really happened.

And what about the doctrines derived from the one true myth? Were they in any sense truths? Whatever else they were, they were translations into *concepts* and *ideas* of that which God has already expressed in a language that was more adequatethan that found in any myth, that is to say the actual incarnation, crucifixion, and resurrection.

As the evening wore on, Lewis grew more and more certain that the Christian story had to be approached in the same way as he approached other myths. By three in the morning he was almost certain that it had really happened. He and Dyson let Tolkien out by the little postern on Magdalen Bridge. Then they returned to New Buildings where they paced the colonnade until four o'clock.

A day at the zoo

The fifth moment was on Monday, September 28, 1931 on an excursion to Whipsnade Zoo with his brother, Warren, and Mrs. Moore and her daughter Maureen. At 11:15 Warren and "Jack," as Lewis was familiarly known, set off from Headington on motorcycle, and the others followed by car.

They arrived at the village of Whipsnade before 1:00. There, after spreading the motorcycle's waterproof on a slope of short turf, they opened bottles of beer, and recovered from the vibrations of the forty-mile run. At 2:20 the car arrived. Maureen emerged from behind the wheel, followed by her mother, a friend of her mother's, and the dog, Mr. Papworth. Sandwiches were passed around.

At 3:00 they all entered the zoo, except Jack, who had to

Magdalen Tower from the banks of the River Cherwell, Oxford.

mind Mr. Papworth. He felt pleasantly relaxed, emotionally refreshed—as a man after a long sleep, still lying motionless in bed, becomes aware that sometime during the last few hours, he has come to a conclusion without the intervention of the intellectual process. When he set out, he had not believed, and when he arrived in Whipsnade he did believe, that Jesus Christ was indeed the Son of God.

"I have just passed on," he wrote on October 1 to his life-long friend Arthur Greeves in Ireland, "from believing in God to definitely believing in Christ—in Christianity."

Changes
By the end of 1931 Lewis was going to Church; by the end of February the following year he was going to Holy Trinity Church, Headington, for com-

munion; he was praying on a regular basis; and he began to consult the Cowley Fathers, a order of Anglican priests, about the proper way to conduct one's spiritual life.

At the end of October 1940, by dint of prayer, his lusts, ambitions, fears, and hatreds had become more manageable in size, and so he could gaze on them regularly and plan what to do about them. He decided to start going to confession, although he was afraid that he was indulging in an egoistic practice, or so he wrote Anglican Sister Penelope Lawson; the reason he wrote her was that he would not back out gracefully. Back out he did not, and when he wrote to her after the event, he admitted that he had come though the wall of fire. "The suggestion about an orgy of egoism turns out, like all the Enemy propaganda, to have just a grain of

truth in it, but I have no doubt that the proper method of dealing with that is to continue the practice, as I intend to do."

Thus all the spiritual pieces were in place. From then on, Lewis's religious practice— churchgoing, communion, and spiritual direction—continued apace until the end of his life. This did not mean that his life was a morally perfect one. It was filled with the peccadilloes of a fallen world. It was not that he fell down so much, as that when he did, he had more than one means to rise quickly and proceed on.

The life of prayer
By the end of this life, C. S. Lewis had even been able to write a book about prayer— *Letters to Malcolm, Chiefly on Prayer*. It was cast, as *The Screwtape Letters* had been, in the form of an epistolary novel.

"I am in favor of your idea that we should go back to our old plan of having a more or less set subject—an *agendum*—for our letters," the unnamed main character writes to one of his friends. "Prayer, which you suggest, is a subject that is a good deal in my mind. I mean, private prayer. If you were thinking of corporate prayer, I won't play. There is not a subject in the world (always excepting sport) on which I have less to say than liturgiology."

Lewis had read Loyola and De Sales and indeed drawn some fruit from *Spiritual Exercises* and *Introduction to the Devout Life*, but no one in the history of ascetic literature had written a book for middle-aged, middle-class academics.

Mechanics of prayer

Like De Sales and Loyola before him, Lewis had to deal with the mechanics of prayer. When? Almost anytime; at the end of the afternoon; just before dinner; never before bedtime. Where? Never in a church; churches are too cold nine months of the year; in the other three, there was either a woman in rubber boots swabbing the sanctuary floor or a mad organist practicing in the loft. In what position? It mattered not a whit whether one knelt, sat, or stood, for it mattered not to the Person prayed to.

De Sales suggested that the meditator, at the beginning of each meditation, should put himself into the presence of God; which might be an easy task for a peasant, wrote Lewis, but which, for intellectuals like himself and Malcolm, was an intricate, if not an impossible, task.

In the course of the twenty-two letters, Lewis elucidated two kinds of prayer, the prayer of adoration and the prayer of petition. There would also be consolation and desolation, the one following the other as surely as waves hitting shore. He would even reveal his practice of festooning, garlanding some formula like the Lord's Prayer with all sorts of personalized reflections and particularized petitions.

The book summed up Lewis's own life of prayer, long and actively cultivated, plus the fruit of the spiritual direction he had been receiving from the Cowley Fathers for two decades. It was published in 1964, after his death, and remains the divining rod, ever quivering, signifying the spiritual aquifer that ran deep in his life.

His funeral, on November 26, 1963, was attended by a variety of friends and acquaintances, but not by his brother Warren, who was drowning his sorrows. After the service at Holy Trinity, the group moved out to the graveyard which surrounded the church, their feet crunching the hard frost on the ground. It was a cold, sunny, brilliant day. Cloud puffballs were everywhere. A single candle burned on top of the coffin as it was carried from the catafalque and put over the open grave, which lay, Tolkien noticed, under a larch. After the final prayers, as the earth was being returned into the grave, people talked.

"We've certainly lost a friend," said Dundas-Grant to Havard as they passed out the churchyard gate.

"Only for a time," replied Humphrey Havard.

Further Reading

Lewis, C. S. *The Great Divorce: A Dream*. Collins Fontana, 1972.

_____. *Letters to Malcolm, Chiefly on Prayer*. Collins Fontana, 1966.

_____. *Mere Christianity* (A revised edition of *Broadcast Talks, Christian Behaviour* and *Beyond Personality*). Collins Fontana, 1955.

_____. *Poems*.

_____. *The Screwtape Letters*. Collins Fontana, 1955.

Out of testing

During the last half century, Paul White's Jungle Doctor books and other works (totaling more than eighty titles) have been published in nearly ninety languages. And this says nothing of the filmstrips, the cassette tapes, the thirty-five years of radio broadcasting, the involvement in television, the training and support of others committed to the ministry of spreading the gospel.

Nor does the list of publications tell of Paul White's involvement with the Church Missionary Society, Scripture Union, Fact and Faith Films, InterVarsity, African Enterprises, and a host of other Christian ministry organizations.

Paul White has given his life to sharing the gospel message with as many people in as many places as he, under God, possibly could...and God has seen that work bear fruit.

Yet his story is only partially told if his accomplishments alone are cited. For Paul White faced daunting personal challenges at the beginning of his ministry—difficulties that from a human perspective seemed beyond repair. In them he found his God to be faithful.

Paul White

Jungle Doctor

P aul White was born in Bowral, Australia, on February 2, 1910. His childhood was far from easy, with his chronic and, at times life-threatening, asthma, and the death of his father when Paul was only five years old. His father had been a farmer, who had served in the Boer War, and who died of meningitis at the Liverpool army camp.

But childhood proved a sound foundation to Paul White's Christian life and ministry. First, it was during times of

Dr. Paul White, "Jungle Doctor".

convalescence that he devoured the many boys' adventure books and magazines popular early in the twentieth century. These readings helped stimulate his love of writing and storytelling. Second, his godly mother made him aware of Christ's love and taught him Christian stewardship. Even during times of terrible deprivation, she would continue to give financially to the wider work of God. Third, his successful involvement in middle-distance running had toughened him, and had taught him the importance of training and endurance.

It was on December 3, 1926, that Paul White came to faith in Jesus Christ under the preaching of a well-known Irish evangelist, W. P. Nicholson. Within days of his decision, White displayed a passion for sharing the gospel with others.

He studied long and well at Sydney University (1930–35). Despite his asthmatic condition, he continued a notable running career and served as captain of the Sydney University Athletics team in 1932.

In his last few years of medical school, White's life took a dramatic turn. In 1935, he was preparing for his final medical examinations. A successful outcome would—at last—transform Mr. Paul White into Dr. Paul White. Now, he presumed, was the right time to ask the woman he had loved since "Med II" to marry him. Mary Bellingham agreed.

Bewildered

A few days later a bewildered White received a phone call from his fiancée at two in the morning. "Is that you, Paul?" she trailed off, followed by the

---

THE LIFE OF

Paul White

1910	Born in Bowral, Australia
1923–29	Attends Sydney Grammar School
1926	Conversion to Christ
1930–35	Attends Sydney University, studies medicine
1937	Marries Beatrice Mary Bellingham (dies 1970)
1938–41	Ministers in Tanganyika
1942	Begins Jungle Doctor Broadcasts, which continue until 1945
1945–51	Honorary Secretary Inter-Varsity Christian Fellowship
1945–73	Works as Rheumatologist
1978–	Serves as Chairman of African Enterprises—Australia

---

click of the receiver. The phone rang again. This time it was Mary's mother, informing the alarmed medical student that "Mary is acting very strange; she is screaming and threatening to take her life." This was Paul White's introduction to Mary's endogenous depressive psychosis.

In the mid-1930s, there was no real treatment for this kind of mental illness. Many doctors thought it best to let it "work itself out." For Mary, this meant weeks of raving until fatigue lulled her into confusion and temporarily abated her physical violence. She lost weight, her skin became infected, and death seemed inescapable. Paul White recounted his feelings in *Alias Jungle Doctor*:

Over those bitter days the peace of God that is beyond all human reason kept my heart, my emotions, and my mind in the knowledge and love of God. This was real, positive, almost tangible support. Maurice and Neville (two of Paul's closest friends) stayed very close to

---

me.... They and many others gave me the greatest help that anyone can give: regular understanding prayer.

Slowly, over many weeks, Mary began to recover. By Christmas, she seemed to be back to her normal self again.

In 1937, Paul and Mary got married, knowing full well that Mary's problem could reoccur at any time and without warning. Mary's depressive psychosis was the cause of the severest testing in Paul White's life.

Tanganyika

In 1938, Paul and Mary White, along with their infant son, David, traveled to Tanganyika (now Tanzania) where Paul assumed the post of Superintendent of the Church Missionary Society hospitals. In Africa, the White family experienced both struggles and blessings; they saw God at work in the flurry of activity at the hospital, and they rejoiced when people began to abandon their superstitions to follow Jesus. On the mission field, they realized their own shortcomings, and recognized their need to rely on the faithful provision of God.

During their first three years of service in Tanganyika, Mary experienced—and bounced back from—brief bouts of illness. But then came the turbulence. Mary suffered a relapse that lasted for more than eight agonizing months. As each week passed, she deteriorated. The doctor begged for his wife's recovery, but the answer from heaven seemed to be "No." He clutched onto the assuring promise that God will not test his children beyond that which they could endure. He then forced himself to shoulder the work.

Some familiar characters from the Jungle Doctor books.

The old enemy returns

Mary's disorder, his demanding medical and managerial work in the hospital, and the domestic demands of caring for two young children battered Paul White's body. His old enemy, asthma, returned with a vengeance. At times, he was so weak that coworkers rolled him from his residence to the hospital in a wheelbarrow. In the course of delivering babies, he frequently would wheeze, "Quick! Inject one-half cc of adrenalin in my leg!" Assisting midwives would set him on a stool, and actually hold him up as he worked.

The last blow was a telegram he received from the Senior Medical Officer. He never forgot the words: "There is practically no prospect of recovery for your wife. We must regard her case as hopeless." Devastated and numb, White showed the telegram to two of his African friends—a lame evangelist named James, and Daudi. Daudi urged, "We must pray."

"I can't, I can't," came White's strangled reply.

But they persisted. James and Daudi knelt down beside the shattered missionary and stormed the heavens. Recalling the intensity of the experience, White confesses: "I felt like Moses when Aaron and Hur held up his arms, one on each side of him."

Three days after the first telegram had arrived, a second message followed, announcing that Paul White's replacement, Dr. Wellesley Hannah, was to arrive shortly. In desperation, Dr. White appealed to Wellesley Hannah to come quickly to Africa: "If God opens the way, come, and come soon. You are urgently needed."

Miracle

Dr. Hannah appeared, bringing with him a miracle in the form of a new treatment. Dr. White narrated Mary's treatment in *Jungle Doctor's Progress*:

Wellesley Hannah was with her day after day. For a time, she gained ground only to lose it again. A week went by; and dramatically, full recovery was reached. To me Mary's recovery is as clear a miracle as anything in the Bible. It was a clear-cut, direct answer to effective and fervent worldwide prayer.

Yet, in spite of all the trauma, sickness, and despair, Paul White believes it was all worth it. He looks at it this way, "Testing puts muscles on your soul." Paul White depended and leaned on God's Word; Proverbs 3:5–6 especially comforted him during these murky days. When Mary first became ill, he found an obscure verse that only made sense to him in retrospect: "You do not realise now what I am doing, but later you will understand" (John 13:7).

Monkeys mean trouble in the Jungle Doctor books.

Through Mary's disease, the husband-and-wife team were led into deeper realms of obedience and blessing. The testing of Paul White's faith—like iron in a crucible—resulted in greater dependence upon and trust in God. Through the affliction shared by the Whites, ministry opportunities expanded that enabled Paul White to share the gospel more effectively.

On the way back to Australia from Africa, he "developed a boil in such a spot that I bought a chair, cut a hole in it, and sat with care. It hurt to walk, so I sat and wrote, and wrote, pages and pages of things that happened. That was the beginning of the Jungle Doctor books." From copious notes and photos which he amassed from his 100th trip around Tanganyika, he shaped a fascinating series.

After all the missionary hardships, a little comic relief is overdue—a nettling boil on a tireless Jungle doctor. If Dr. Paul White had not been forced to sit down, a ministry spanning fifty years may have never been launched.

Further Reading

White, Paul. *Alias Jungle Doctor: An Autobiography*. Exeter: Paternoster Press, 1977.

White, Paul. *Doctor of Tanganyika*. Grand Rapids: Eerdmans, 1955.

Eugenia Price
Unshackled!

Radio. Television. Books. Two things are true of all of them: They are an undeniable part of our everyday lives, and they are largely the domain of secular writers.

In the 1950s, Christians had even less of a presence in the entertainment field than they do today. Back then there was relatively little Christian radio. And although there were Christian publishers who produced fine books, very few of those works fit into the fiction category. Fewer still could be considered popular novels with the historical accuracy, exciting storytelling, attractive settings, and compelling characters that so appeal to the secular mass market. Could such a novel be built on a foundation of Jesus Christ and His divine involvement in human life? Impossible, many insisted.

In a stylish apartment in a fashionable section of Chicago lived a successful young radio writer–producer. She had ability and she had experience. But the chances of her being interested in Christian writing? About zero. Less than zero, she would have said. But that was before the October 1949 night in a New York City hotel room when Eugenia Price fell into the hands of the living God.

What a life Eugenia Price led! A beautiful apartment in a fashionable section of Chicago, lovely clothes, the best restaurants in town, travel by limousine, influential friends—ah, the life of a radio writer who owned her own production company. What more could a young woman want?

Yet Eugenia Price was desperately miserable.

From childhood, Genie had been accustomed to the good life. Her father, a successful dentist, provided his family with a succession of lovely homes. Genie grew up feeling loved, special, and important. She was the center of the world, she believed, a position she was convinced was rightfully hers.

As a child and teenager, Genie attended church. All nice girls did. But once she started college, she quickly declared her freedom. Proclaiming herself an agnostic, she insisted, "There is no God!"

In her junior year, Eugenia declared a major in pre-dentistry. "I figured I could be really free in a lucrative career like dentistry," she said. The only woman accepted at Northwestern Dental School that year, Genie was an honor student. Yet after three years, she grew bored and quit.

"Life is heavy"

For the next ten years, Eugenia wrote for radio shows. Yet with each passing year, she grew more and more miserable. "Life is terribly heavy," she wrote, "when you have spent your life convincing yourself and everyone else that you are a success and then you have to be—or find a way out of it all."

Then in 1949, Eugenia re-met her childhood friend, Ellen Riley, "the girl with the slanty green eyes and naturally curly brown hair." But much to Eugenia's dismay, her friend was no fun anymore; she had become a Christian. Ellen did not drink. (Eugenia did—a lot.) She did not smoke. (Eugenia was up to three packs a day.) She was insufferably patient and kind and honest. (Not a bit like Eugenia.) Yet Ellen understood Eugenia as no one else did. Despite herself, Genie was irresistibly drawn to her friend with the slanty eyes. It was through Ellen she fell into the hands of the living God.

"The strain of knowing that one is separated from God is the worst strain of all," Eugenia was later to write. "Especially after one has lived so many years believing there is no God."

Kicking into the Kingdom

Some people come to God gently. Not Eugenia Price. She kicked and fought every inch of the way. But finally, on October 2, 1949, in a New York City hotel room, Eugenia Price was born for the second time.

From the beginning, Eugenia knew that wherever she went, she carried the reputation of Jesus Christ with her. It was a responsibility she took seriously. She turned down a high-salaried TV dramatic show and closed Eugenia Price Productions. No longer could she write murder stories for children to watch, nor could she talk adults into doing things she could not do as a Christian. Her old life was gone—all but her crushing debts, that is.

Together Ellen and Eugenia set up housekeeping in a dumpy basement apartment. It was a hard adjustment for Genie, who had been used to earning an excellent salary. She was out of touch with the free-lancers' market, but she was sure she would soon be on top again. After all, she had been the top writer in the country's biggest talent agency.

"All I could do was write and direct radio scripts," Eugenia wrote. "But no one seemed to need anything played or written for money."

Through God's grace, and Ellen's and Genie's willingness to do anything—even carry out garbage and scrub halls—the girls managed to survive, and even to pay off Genie's debts. And Genie had plenty of time to pray and study

God's word and to read the works of Christian authors. Day by day, she drew closer and closer to her Lord.

"A Visit with Genie"

Just when things seemed hopeless, the program director of a Catholic FM station called Eugenia and asked her to host an hour-and-a-half show, five days a week. She would only get a nominal salary, but it was a job she could do. And it was work for the Lord. "A Visit with Genie" made its debut.

Although she loved doing the show, by September Eugenia was getting restless. She longed to write again. In answer to her prayers, she was introduced to Harry Saulnier. He and his board had been praying about a possible half-hour dramatic program in which the true stories of lives transformed at the Pacific Garden Mission would be told. They had both the stories and the radio time. What they needed was a writer-producer with professional and Christian experience. When she was offered the job, Eugenia said, "My writer-heart leaped with delight."

On the first Saturday night of October 1950, Eugenia directed the first broadcast of "Unshackled!" a program that was to become world famous.

Before long "Unshackled!" was attracting a great deal of attention. Eugenia was deluged with invitations to speak to groups of all kinds, up to fifteen engagements a week.

"Isn't it wonderful that they want me?" Eugenia exclaimed in amazement.

Then suddenly, on the very heels of the greatest success of her life, Eugenia was overtaken by what she calls "the great darkness," an agony of soul and mind and spirit.

"I pushed myself doggedly through one 'Unshackled' script after another," she says. "I stood before hundreds of people telling them what Christ had done in my life. Night after night I forced myself to stand in pulpit after pulpit when I wanted to break and run for the nearest bar!"

Discoveries

Slowly Eugenia began to realize that what she had was not a true walk with the Living Christ at all. It was nothing but a fascination with her own concept of who He was. "It began to settle," she said of the darkness, "when I observed with pride the effect of my words of persuasion." She used all the right words. She quoted the right Scriptures. And to her it was all a source of great pride. That is when darkness rushed in.

For weeks Eugenia wrestled with the darkness. She fought and suffered and made Ellen's life miserable. Finally Genie demanded of her friend, "Why do I feel like this?"

"Don't ask me!" Ellen responded. "Ask God!"

But Eugenia was not about to give in. She fell across her bed and tried to pretend she had never known Christ. It did not work. "I missed Jesus so much," she says. "He had to be alive. I knew He was there in the room with me, waiting just outside my self-pity." And to Eugenia, on her knees beside her bed, healing finally came. The darkness was gone.

In 1952, Eugenia was approached about the possibility of doing a book. *Discoveries Made from Living My New Life* was the first of many.

Beloved Invader

Eugenia's already successful writing career took a new turn in 1961 when she became fascinated by St. Simons Island off the coast of Georgia. Almost one hundred years before, a man by the name of Anson Greene Dodge, Jr., had rebuilt Christ Church Frederica in memory of his bride who died on their honeymoon.

"Wow!" Eugenia exclaimed when she heard the account. "What a story!" Then and there she resolved to write a novel about Dodge.

Beloved Invader, the first of her historical novels, was published in 1965. It is from them that her renown as a writer largely stems. Several have achieved best-seller status.

To date Eugenia Price has authored thirty-five books of which more than fifteen million copies have sold. Her work has been translated into seventeen foreign languages.

"I am a believer in Jesus Christ," Genie says. "Since I would be bored to write a book which did not include Him, I attempt sincerely to show His divine intervention and involvement with all human life."

Some look at Eugenia Price and say, "Sure,

Eugenia Price, author of *Beloved Invader*.

but she has such exceptional talent!"

Eugenia says, "I know I have no burning literary talent. And that is not undue modesty. I think I have a very realistic point of view about my writing."

Of her decision to leave everything she knew to follow Christ, Eugenia Price only says, "His yoke is easy, His burden is light."

Further Reading

Price, Eugenia. *The Burden is Light!* Old Tappan, N.J.: Revell, 1955.

_____. *Beloved Invader*. 1965.

_____. *St. Simon's Memoir*. New York: Lippincott, 1978.

Ken Taylor reads to his young family at bedtime.

Ken Taylor and the Living Bible

Living Word

The forty-sixth edition of *Who's Who in America* gives a detailed list of Ken Taylor's recognitions and accomplishments. At the end of the entry, Taylor has himself written, "Who but God could make an unending universe, sized by billions of light years? And who could dream of knowing such

a God personally? I am one who believes this, and have based my life on the Bible as God's message to mankind, and to you and me. But how to manage Bible reading when it is in such an ancient language? How to crack the shell of the coconut and find the milk and meat? That is why I spent 16 years translating the Bible into living English.

Since early childhood, Ken Taylor has demonstrated a deep respect for the Word of God. An event in his boyhood days helped shape this attitude. The

Dr. Kenneth Taylor in his office in Wheaton.

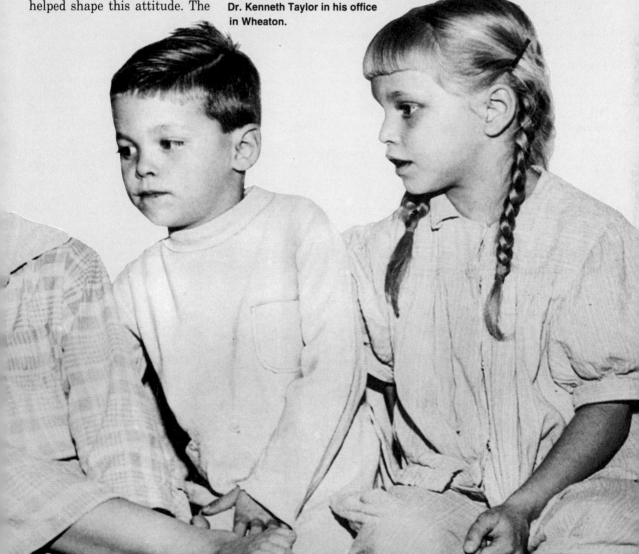

family Bible on the living room table was brushed off onto the floor. His father, a Presbyterian minister, rushed over to pick it up and carefully laid it back on the table. Ken Taylor has never forgotten this.

Bible reading and prayer had a high priority in the Taylor household. His father would tell his boys, "Unless you fellows get into the Word of God and get the Word of God into your lives, you'll never amount to much as Christians." Despite his parents' example, Taylor encountered "constant difficulty in reading the Bible from the King James Version, which was the only accepted translation" in his youth. As years went by his frustrations only increased at his inability to enjoy the Word of God. He longed to grow spiritually and knew this would not happen without regular feeding on God's Word.

Ken Taylor faced personal tensions as well. He was very close to his brother Doug, for whom he felt both jealousy and pride. Doug became a successful medical doctor, something Ken had always wanted to be. In fact, Ken always felt a concern for the poor and elderly. He has also remained a man of high moral principles. Daily he prayed that God would keep him from temptations, and it is for this reason that no television was allowed in the Taylor home.

Timidity also constituted a lifelong problem. Fear of public speaking has not left him; he is a "dreader" of audiences. And yet he became Student Body President in high school and the most enjoyable part of his high school and college days was participating on the debate teams. Taylor has always felt much

more comfortable reaching out to others through journalism. His father provided him with a role model as he had a regular newspaper column in which he clearly presented Christ as the Savior of mankind. One of Ken Taylor's first salvation booklets was entitled *Is Christianity Credible?* This has been the means of salvation for many.

Making decisions has been another lifelong problem. All through high school he had a girlfriend of sorts, but he had been looking for that perfect girl, physically, socially, and spiritually. Margaret West did not quite measure up to that perfection. It was not until after his college days when Margaret began dating someone else that he decided to ask her to marry him. They eventually had ten children.

Thwarted ambition

Ken Taylor's early ambition was to be a medical doctor. This came to a sudden end when he flunked a medical aptitude test and his college zoology professor wisely suggested that perhaps his talents might better be used elsewhere.

Early on, Ken Taylor had a strong urge to be rich. While at college he came across a book entitled *Borden of Yale*, which he read during the summer. This book changed his life. William Borden was not only an athlete and a millionaire, but also a spiritual giant—three goals Ken had for himself. Yet William Borden had a love for God and his fellow man. Money meant nothing to him. He gave away millions and offered his life for service to the Muslim world. He died in Cairo, Egypt, enroute to his first missionary

assignment. Taylor had made a public confirmation of his faith around twelve years of age, but it was after reading the life of Borden that he prayed, "Lord, here is my life. Take it and use it in any way you want to."

"Why doesn't it say so?"

After Taylor got married and began having children he made sure that time was set aside each evening for family Bible reading and prayer. Not only did he read the Scriptures, he also had a time for discussion of the text, and asked the children questions. He often became discouraged when the children did not seem to understand what had been read. His burden to make the Bible understandable became more evident night after night. Often he would put the Scriptures in his own words during family devotions. He found that his children listened more attentively to his rephrasing than when he read from the King James Version. One evening when he rephrased a certain verse, his daughter responded, "Well, if that's what it means, why doesn't it say so?"

Over and over again Taylor prayed, "Lord, how can our family devotional time become more interesting and valuable to my children and how can I myself learn to read the Bible with more interest?" One day he decided to experiment by summarizing a Bible verse to make it more understandable. Taking a sheet of paper, he reached for his Bible, and turned to 2 Timothy 2. He read the first few verses and then returned to verse one. He analyzed it word by word and phrase by phrase. The King James reads, "Thou, therefore,

Ken Taylor with his wife, Margaret.

my son, be strong in the grace that is in Jesus Christ." Taylor wrote instead, "Oh, Timothy, my son, be strong with the strength Christ Jesus gives you." He did the same with the verses that followed.

That night he read these rephrased verses to his children, and he was elated; the discussion and question time showed they had understood.

This rephrasing led to other rephrasings, at first simply for family devotions. Gradually the conviction deepened that he ought to rephrase all the epistles—the letters of Paul, James, Peter, John, and Jude and the Epistle to the Hebrews. It was only later that he thought perhaps other children and parents would be helped by such paraphrasing, and he began to work in earnest that the material might be published.

The commuting writer
Since Taylor had a full-time job as Director of Moody Press, the only logical time to work on the paraphrase seemed to be on the commuter train. Day after day, with the Bible on one knee and a pad of paper on the other, he rephrased the Scriptures. He started with Romans, chapter one, taking about a year to paraphrase all the epistles, and ending with Jude. He used the American Standard Version of 1901 as the basic text.

In the evenings, after the children had settled into bed, he would go over the work done on the train, using commentaries and Greek word studies to tighten up the paraphrase. It took seven revisions and seven years before he felt satisfied that the *Living Letters* could now be published. A handwritten note framed on a wall in his home reads: "Finished final revision of paraphrase *Living Letters* at 3:00 p.m. today with praise to the Lord." The date was December 27, 1960.

Up to this point Taylor had given little thought as to who would publish the paraphrase. To his shock and surprise various publishers turned him down, including his own Moody Press. He therefore decided to publish it privately. A printer friend offered to print them on a "pay me when you can" basis. His first print order was for 2,000 copies.

Multiplying the loaves
While the type was being set, Taylor was asked to go on a nine-week trip overseas. Galley proofs were sent to him in Jerusalem. One day while sitting on the Mount of Olives overlooking Jerusalem, the miracle of the five loaves and two fish which fed five thousand people came to mind. He asked himself, "Since five thousand people were fed by five loaves (of bread), how many people would be fed by 2,000 loaves (of Living Letters)?" After a quick calculation he found the answer: two million. So Taylor asked God to multiply the copies to two million.

Living Letters was introduced at the Christian Booksellers Convention in 1962, where 867 copies were sold. Within a year, 75,000 copies were sold. Billy Graham had received a copy of *Living Letters* when he was in a Honolulu hospital. Eventually he ordered 600,000 copies for his television broadcasts.

Taylor named his new publishing venture Tyndale House Publishers as William Tyndale, 440 years earlier, had felt called of God to give the Bible to the English-speaking world to be read and helped by it.

Published on credit
It soon became apparent that Taylor should resign from

Dr. Kenneth Taylor with Dr. Billy Graham.

Moody Press and devote full time to paraphrasing the entire Bible. This was an act of faith. He published the first edition on credit, despite having a family of ten children to feed. The complete *Living Bible* was published in 1971. Twenty-seven years after his first 2,000 copies of *The Living Letters*, more than thirty-six million copies of *The Living Bible* have been sold.

Taylor decided that since God was the author of the Bible, all royalties should be set aside for the furtherance of God's work. The first royalty check was for $30,000. There was no thought to use it for himself though the Taylor family was living in an old, crowded farm house that was in great need of repair. Instead the Tyndale Foundation was established, and to date, millions of dollars have been re-invested in various ministries around the world through the Foundation.

Ken Taylor is an innovator. Sometimes he did not do enough research on a project, which led to serious cashflow problems in Tyndale House Publishers. One project investment spree, all for legitimate causes, almost led to financial ruin. Projects such as a weekly newspaper, *Christian Life and Times* were good ideas, but they did not pay for them-selves, and eventually these programs drained his resources by $250,000 and he had to aban-don them. In their place came *Church Around the World*, a monthly summary sheet now issuing a million copies per month. So out of disaster came great usefulness. *The Christian Reader*, begun in 1964, reached 100,000 copies per issue within the first year. Its circulation peaked at 310,000.

Spreading furrows
One morning as Taylor wak-ened, he was given a vision. He found himself walking in the woods, and saw where the earth had been plowed—first one fur-row, then a second furrow, then another until the furrows spread wider and wider and cov-ered the whole earth. It came to him that God would use *Living Letters* all around the world. He later found that 90 percent of the world population speaks one of 100 major languages. Why not translate *The Living Bible* into those one hundred lan-guages? This was the genesis of Living Letters Overseas in 1968, later called Living Bibles International. His goal was to complete this program in ten years, a dream not yet fulfilled. Living Bibles International now has a worldwide staff of one thousand. To date, translators have completed fifty-six *Living New Testament* translations and fifteen translations of the entire Bible. Altogether, 114 lan-guages are being worked on in 107 countries.

Taylor has written numerous books such as *Stories for the Children's Hour* and *Devotions for the Children's Hour*. Over a million copies of his *Bible in Pictures for Little Eyes* have been sold, in more than sixty languages.

Prayer has always been a cen-tral part of Ken Taylor's life, and he has discovered the secret of setting time before breakfast or late at night to meet with God. He confesses, "After so many years of ups and downs, of success and failure, I realize there is no solution except to make a regular appointment with God and to do my best to stick with it."

Further Reading
Taylor, Kenneth N. *My Life: A Guided Tour: The Autobiography of Kenneth N. Taylor.* Wheaton, Ill.: Tyndale, 1991.

Evangelists

D. L. Moody—Evangelist

A Zeal for Souls

Dwight L. Moody at age thirty; portrait by G. P. A. Healy

D. L. Moody preferred speaking to the general masses, not the college elite. But here he was at Cambridge University because Christian students had pleaded with him to speak to their classmates. Moody knew some students would disdain his fifth-grade education and his American ways. He did not know, however, that November 5 was Guy Fawkes Day, when throughout the country, English people held bonfire parties and firework displays.

Ira Sankey, his song leader at all campaigns, began playing the pump organ. The students responded with an unmelodious tap, tap, tap of umbrellas and canes on the floor, and shouts of "Hear, hear!" When Sankey led singing of the famous "Ninety and Nine," several students yelled "Encore!" at the end of each verse.

Finally Moody spoke. The young audience responded to his New England accent with unmuffled laughs and mimicry, his American pronunciations met with bursts of laughter, and sharp cries of "Well done!" The evangelist continued bravely to the end.

Ungentlemanly reception

The Oxford University students showed more courtesy after Moody began his second night, by launching a direct rebuke. The previous night he had needed to delay his reading of Ezekiel until students had stopped stamping their feet. Now he appealed to these men, saying that they had acted "ungentlemanly," that apologies were in order, and that students could show their contriteness by listening quietly to his remarks. His cleverness and directness

The First Mass Evangelist

During the nineteenth century when mass media consisted of only printing presses and public oratory, more than 100 million people heard or read the gospel message of D. L. Moody. The evangelist spoke to "at least 1.5 million in London [during four months] in 1875, long before radio and television made mass audiences usual."

Moody challenged middle- and lower-class Britons with the gospel message of hope during four more visits. He evangelized Americans with equal fervor, visiting twenty-three states before deteriorating health forced him to give up six-a-day meetings in Kansas City only months before his death. Moody also led a strongly evangelical Young Men's Christian Association. He served as President of the Chicago chapter, addressed national conventions, and became the chief fundraiser for Farwell Hall, where the YMCA held evangelistic meetings.

Children's work

Before focusing on the evangelization of adults, Moody was a trailblazer in children's missions. He brought Chicago's street urchins to his Sunday school, and when his church refused them, he began his own Sunday school and eventually hosted fifteen hundred children.

Moody stimulated interest in Bible conferences in America with his popular Northfield conferences. He also brought Bible training to secondary students with two Northfield schools, and tuition-free education to collegians with his Chicago Bible Institute, renamed Moody Bible Institute upon his death. Moody inspired young adults to consider missions through the Student Volunteer Movement. The physical vigor of the five-foot-seven, two-hundred-plus-pound evangelist matched his remarkable zeal to evangelize and educate his world. He was motivated by a love for Christ.

THE LIFE OF
D. L. Moody

> *"Only the mouthpiece and expression of a deep and mysterious wave of religious feeling now passing over the nation."*

won their respect. His authority in later sessions at Oxford was obvious. One news account called the evangelist "an earnest man, face to face with [the students], searching them with his glance, pointing at them personally, unveiling their hearts to them."

Earlier, one of the front-row mockers at the Cambridge meetings, Gerald Lander, had told the student sponsor, "If uneducated men will come to teach the varsity, they deserve to be snubbed." But next morning Lander came to Moody's hotel room to apologize and read a letter of apology from the other rowdies. Moody listened and then had a long talk with the student. Moody asked Lander and his friends to come to the next meeting to prove their apology sincere. Lander came. Three days later, during Moody's final meeting, fifty-two men left their seats for Moody's inquiry area, a fencing room in the university gym. One was Gerald Lander. Later Lander would serve in South China as a missionary bishop.

A little-educated American caught between the intellectual elite of England's twin towers of higher education though Moody may have been, he nonetheless held his own there as well as with the lower- and middle-class masses during three decades. He appealed to many, this humble evangelist who felt he preached at God's request.

Crazy Moody
"I am the most overestimated man in America," Moody told reporters in the 1870s after his successful revival meetings in Philadelphia and New York. He called himself "only the mouthpiece and expression of a deep and mysterious wave of religious feeling now passing over the nation."

It is a real wonder that God used Moody in helping propel this "mysterious wave." Moody acted abruptly at times toward people and plans, once resigning from the board of his budding Chicago Bible Institute, another time offending leaders of an evangelistic campaign. His early brashness in evangelism earned him the title "Crazy Moody" from one uncle.

He was never ordained to ministry. In fact, he had no college degree and never attended college. Misspelled words dot his sermon outlines, and his letters to friends and family contain enough grammatical and spelling errors to make Victorian English teachers shake their heads.

In spite of little formal education and occasional abrupt manners, Moody presented the gospel to more than 100 million people in more than forty years of ministry. How did he overcome these weaknesses? In whatever he was doing, Moody humbly sought God's direction. Moreover, he readily admitted his mistakes. He apologized as quickly to his sons for being harsh as to colleagues for being shortsighted. Findlay, one of his biographers, was surprised at his tender heart: "At the inner core of his being he lacked the toughness of fiber and ruthlessness of attitude that seemingly ought to have accompanied his unquestioned ambition, drive and determination." When his wife, Emma, rescued an oil portrait of him from their burning home during the Great Chicago Fire, he protested. Though the picture by American portrait painter G.P.A. Healy showed a thoughtful evangelist at age 30, Moody was more interested in a

Moody gives free rides on his "gospel pony" as he gathers neighborhood children for his Sunday School classes.

practical item that his wife had located—his Bible.

Moody the tenderhearted

God used Moody the tender-hearted. After returning in 1875 from a successful two-year campaign in Scotland, Ireland, and England, the evangelist began a three-year tour of the United States, preaching in large cities and small towns alike. He spoke in abandoned railroad depots, grandiose churches, and even outdoors. He began in Brooklyn, New York, at a skating rink decorated for the occasion. In Philadelphia, the arena reportedly held twelve thousand and often was full one hour before the meeting.

A year later Moody returned to New York City and spoke at the Hippodrome, the future site of the original Madison Square Garden. The *New York Times* had opposed the campaign, but when it ended, declared, *"The work accomplished this winter by Mr. Moody in this city for private and public morals will live. The drunken have become sober, the vicious virtuous ... the ignoble noble, the impure pure.... A new hope has lifted hundreds of human being, a new consolation has come to the sorrowful, and a better principle has entered the sordid life of the day, through the labors of these plain men."*

Moody kept no tallies of converts, feeling he could not know for sure whether a claimed conversion was genuine. "That record is on high," he once told reporters. Yet the staying power of his converts was noteworthy. Twenty years after Moody's 1876 Hippodrome meetings, Pastor James Hoadley, of the New York Faith Presbyterian

Church wrote Moody that 139 people became church members in 1876, 121 as new Christians. "The large part of these [came] to Christ under the influence of your great revival meetings. Only a very small percent have fallen away."

The sun shines brighter

The young Moody had a zeal for souls soon after his conversion. The sixth child of Edwin and Betsey Moody, he lost his father at age four and left for Boston at age seventeen to become a shoe salesman. Moody worked for his uncle, Sam Holton, who insisted the boy attend Mt. Vernon Congregational Church. There he heard the church's pastor, Edward Kirk, who preached with "fiery eloquence" that "had melted hardened sinners to penitence and love." One day Moody's Sunday school teacher, Edward Kimball, called on his student at the shoe store, and found him in the back, wrapping and stacking shoes. Kimball put his large hands on Moody's stooped shoulder and, looking in the youth's eyes, asked his student to come to Christ, "who loves you and who wants your love and should have it."

The next morning Moody saw a new city. "The old sun shone a good deal brighter than it ever had before. I thought that it was just smiling upon me; and as I walked out upon Boston Common and heard the birds singing in the trees, I thought they were all singing a song to me.... I had not a bitter feeling against any man, and I was ready to take all men to my heart."

This love of people caused him to present his faith to nearly all

that he met, beginning with children. Though he continued in the shoe business after he moved to Chicago, his heart was in evangelism. He recruited children in the near northside slum called The Sands, where youngsters played surrounded by neighborhood saloons, gambling, and prostitution houses. He greeted children and their families, distributed coal, food, and clothing, and he invited them to his church's Sunday school. When church leaders complained that his group of ragamuffins was too loud and too many for them to handle, he organized his own class in a freight car. Within a few weeks children had packed the car, so he moved the class to a former saloon. Numbers grew, and the class soon met in North Market Hall near the Chicago River.

Moody attracted the children to class by his zeal and compassion, qualities that would mark his evangelistic campaigns. Moody roamed the streets, pulling candy and trinkets from his pocket like a young, happy uncle. He also gave the children smiles, head pats, and invitations. The children loved free rides on his gospel pony, a gift from friend and supporter John Farwell, a prosperous dry goods merchant. By the summer of 1859, six hundred children came each Sunday. By 1863 he opened a building with classrooms and an auditorium and soon filled it with fifteen hundred. Moody's compassion and honesty attracted both children and adults to the gospel.

Moody escapes a thrashing

Once during his weekly visit in the slums, he found a mother of six children with little food or

Moody preaches at the Agricultural Hall, London, during his British campaign of 1875.

money; her husband had wasted it on liquor. Another time he found the children alone, a full whiskey jug nearby. He emptied the whiskey into the street and took the children to his school. The incensed father stopped Moody during the preacher's next visit.

"Did you pour away my whiskey?" The man rolled up his sleeves. "I'll thrash you!"

"I broke the jug for the good of yourself and family. If I am to be thrashed, let me pray for you all before you do it."

Moody's heartfelt prayer surprised the man, who had expected either a lecture or a whining plea. Quietly he mumbled, "You had better just take the kids, not a whipping."

His zeal for souls caused him to abandon the shoe business in 1860 for full-time evangelism, even though one year earlier he

had earned the princely sum of five thousand dollars in commissions. He focused on evangelism in the streets and through the YMCA, which he served as Chicago chapter president in the 1860s and for which he raised funds to build Farwell Hall.

"Are you a Christian?"
Though Moody and others held evangelistic outreaches at the then evangelical YMCA, he was equally comfortable in the streets. "Are you a Christian?" he asked people passing by. "He shouted it from the platform," recalled Farwell's daughter Abbey. "He whispered it in the narrow passageway, seated at your side at the dinner table, as he joined you on the sidewalk; in fact, everywhere."

Sometimes people would ridicule Moody for his fervent

faith. When he preached on the streets, heckling and catcalls sometimes came his way. Moody remained unwavering, however. Once he asked a man leaning against a lamppost, "Are you a Christian?" The stranger cursed and told the young evangelist to mind his business, and later told a friend the evangelist had insulted him. Three months later Moody stumbled to his door after midnight to answer a persistent knocking. "There stood this stranger I had made so mad at the lamppost, who declared he had known no peace, and pleaded with me: 'Oh, tell me what to do to be saved.'" During this time Moody had vowed not to let a day pass without telling someone about Christ.

Moody's regret
The evangelist only regretted one thing in his life, and that

was that he had not asked an audience to receive Christ as Savior on April 8, 1871, the night of the Chicago Fire. That night Moody spoke to his largest audience ever in Chicago. His topic was "What Then Shall I Do with Jesus Who Is Called the Christ?" At the conclusion, he asked listeners to consider the question and respond the next Sunday, when they returned. But they did not return. Fire bells rang even as they rose, and the building burned, and the congregation scattered.

On the fire's anniversary twenty-two years later, Moody told another audience, "I have never seen that congregation since. I have looked over this audience and not a single one is here that I preached to that night. One lesson I learned that night ... is that I [must] preach to press Christ upon the people then and there, and try to bring them to a decision on the spot. Ever since that night I have determined to make more of Christ than in the past."

Moody chided himself for his divided loyalties. "The Chicago Fire was the turning point of my life. I had become so mixed up with building Farwell Hall and was on committees for every kind of work, and in my ambition to make my enterprises succeed ... I had taken my eyes off the Lord."

In major mode

Only months earlier Moody had declared he would no longer let the attractive non-evangelistic speaking offers in the U.S. distract from a larger work. He began to prepare for a tour of evangelism in Great Britain, even as he realized he was too busy with the details of his church and the YMCA. Soon he concentrated solely on preaching and winning people to Christ, and Moody realized he had slipped back into the minor mode. It was time to major on evangelism alone. The Chicago Fire was at one and the same time his greatest loss and God's greatest preparation.

Moody began his first overseas campaign slowly in 1873, with uneven crowds in York and Sunderland, England. But in Newcastle, the response changed. Attendance climbed steadily, and the crowds were enthusiastic. At Newcastle, Moody began several successful practice; an inquiry room where those who had responded to the message might be counseled; specialized gatherings including services for women, children, and laborers; and notification of local churches of his upcoming visit, so members would be able to invite guests.

Greater success awaited in Scotland. In Edinburgh, crowds overflowed the six-thousand-seat Corn Exchange; and the Glasgow Crystal Palace, also seating six thousand, filled to capacity. The messages during his five months in Scotland were brief compared to the church sermons of one hour or more which congregations there were used to; and he presented the gospel simply, with stories to illustrate and humor to keep attention. A divinity professor from Edinburgh noted that Moody avoided "articulate wailings, prostrations [or] sudden outbursts of rapture which we have heard in former revivals."

Moody also downplayed God's wrath, moving listeners with reminders of God's goodness and forgiveness. Still, he called sin "corrupt," "black," and "vile." Fortunately, Adam's fall "brought out God's love," Moody explained. "If your sins rise up before you like a dark mountain, bear in mind that the blood of Jesus Christ cleanses from all sin." He preached for decisions, and a cross section of Edinburgh's residents were drawn to his inquiry room.

Contagious joy

Moody's four months in London capped his England tour. His emphasis on the love of God contrasted with the hellfire of earlier revivalists. "He exulted in the free grace of God," wrote one observer. "His joy was contagious. Men leaped out of darkness into light, and lived a Christian life afterwards."

Moody's oratory was powerful, although his enunciation was slurred and his pace rapid. Still, his strong, straight-ahead delivery, mingled with anecdotes, quickly captured his audience. With his fast speaking rate, he would contract words so that "Sam'l" anointed David, and "Dan'l" stayed unharmed when thrown to the lions. In Moody's sermons, one reporter said, there is a "scuffle among the words for suitable places in his hasty sentences, [and words] become chipped and mutilated. Final letters disappear, middle syllables [slip], and the outer ones run together." Perhaps this fast, truncated style made the crowds listen more carefully to the stoop-shouldered evangelist who earnestly confronted them with the gospel.

Free tuition

In the 1880s, education was added as a tool of evangelism. Moody opened the Chicago Bible

Institute andthe Northfield secondary schools to train students for ministry in the cities. In 1881 he founded the Mount Hermon School for boys with thirteen students at Northfield, while Northfield Seminary, his two-year-old school for girls, had 100 students. Both boys and girls worked after classes to keep operating costs and tuition low. His greatest educational legacy is the Moody Bible Institute (originally the Chicago Bible Institute), which has sent more than six thousand missionaries to foreign fields. But the school almost never began.

The evangelist had challenged supporters in 1885 and 1886 to raise $250,000 to provide an operating budget and to endow the Institute for tuition-free education. He was sure God would provide the funds. "God never had a work but what he had men to do it," he told supporters in 1886. But his desire for the Chicago Evangelism Society (CES) to quickly raise funds and the stress from his campaigns caused him to resign abruptly from the CES in 1887.

Nettie McCormick, CES supporter and widow of inventor Cyrus McCormick, had written Moody about disagreements over the duties of trustee board members and concern over the role of the "ladies' work" in the constitution. She suggested changes in the constitution. Moody, however, thought her suggestions were demands, and, upset, the evangelist wrote a letter tendering his resignation from the Society. "For six months I have had to oppose some of the dearest friends I have ever had, and I am tired and sick of it."

CES members were shocked,

> ## *"God never had a work but what he had men to do it."*

and Mrs. McCormick quickly wrote a second letter, offering her own resignation in place of his. His wife Emma helped her husband to reconsider, and it was not long before he wired Mrs. McCormick his decision to withdraw his resignation.

Thus Moody possessed several personality traits that genuinely hampered his ministry. He was headstrong, impatient, and perhaps overly sensitive to criticism. But he also had an open mind and a readiness to admit his mistakes.

Getting things going

Whatever his shortcomings, Moody fired followers with zeal for Christ. Through him, seven English cricketers, all of them men of great athletic ability, status, and wealth, dedicated themselves to missions in China. The Cambridge Seven brought many other university students to Christ with their message before sailing to China. One of the Seven, C. T. Studd, founded Worldwide Evangelization Crusade, a mission board with a thousand missionaries. Later Moody led a Northfield Bible Conference exclusively for students, resulting in about one hundred students pledging themselves to international missions. Within one year, more than two thousand students had joined what was to become the Student Volunteer Movement for Christian service overseas.

Although Moody organized the movement, he let others lead it. "It's my job to get things

going," he said simply. Moody, the direct yet plain-spoken evangelist, did indeed get thigs going—in the lives of the poor, the young, and the masses—by turning them to the gospel. Years after Moody's death his son Paul wrote how amazing he found "the use that God made of him despite [his obvious] handicaps." In Moody, God had used someone who, in spite of his handicaps, was available to start Bible schools, to inspire missionaries, and to win many thousands to Christ.

Further Reading

Findlay, James F. *Dwight L. Moody, American Evangelist: 1837–99.* Chicago: U. of Chicago, 1969.

Getz, Gene. *MBI: The Story of Moody Bible Institute.* Rev. ed. Chicago: Moody, 1986.

Maas, David. "The Life and Times of D. L. Moody." *Christian History* 25 (Vol. 9, 1990).

Moody, Paul. *My Father: An Intimate Portrait of Dwight L. Moody.* Boston: Little, Brown, 1938.

Pollock, John C. *Moody: A Biographical Portrait of the Pacesetter in Modern Mass Evangelism.* New York: Macmillan, 1963.

Sadhu Sundar Singh

Apostle with the Bleeding Feet

Jesus belongs to India
Sadhu Sundar Singh disappeared in the foothills of the Himalayas in 1929. As a Christian witness he had been rejected as well as welcomed, persecuted, and even left for dead. By many missionaries and even Indian Christian leaders he had been regarded as a highly eccentric convert, totally out of step with contemporary Christianity as he wandered the roads in his yellow robe and turban. And yet, even though he never heard the later vogue-word "indigenization," he had done more than any man in the first half of the twentieth century to establish that "Jesus belongs to India." He made it clear that Christianity is not an imported, alien, foreign religion but is indigenous to Indian needs, aspirations, and faith. He remains one of the permanently significant figures of Indian Christianity.

Sundar Singh was born in 1889 into an important landowning Sikh family in Patiala state, North India. Sikhs, rejecting Hindu polytheism and Muslim intolerance in the sixteenth century, had become a vigorous nation with a religion of their own. Sundar Singh's mother took him week by week to sit at the feet of a sadhu, an ascetic holy man, who lived in the jungle some miles away, but she also sent him to a Christian mission school where he could learn English.

Her death when he was fourteen plunged him into violence and despair. He turned on the missionaries, persecuted their Christian converts, and ridiculed their faith. In final defiance of their religion, he bought a Bible and burned it page by page in his home compound while his friends watched. The same night he went to his room determined to commit suicide on a railway line.

Poisoned

However, before dawn, he wakened his father to announce that he had seen Jesus Christ in a vision and heard His voice. Henceforth he would follow Christ forever, he declared. Still no more than fifteen, he was utterly committed to Christ and in the twenty-five years left to him would witness heroically for his Lord. The discipleship of the teenager was immediately tested as his father pleaded and demanded that he give up this absurd "conversion." When he refused, Sher Singh gave a farewell feast for his son, then denounced him and expelled him from the family. Several hours later, Sundar realized that his food had been poisoned, and his life was saved only by the help of a nearby Christian community.

On his sixteenth birthday he was publicly baptized as a Christian in the parish church in Simla, a town high in the Himalayan foothills.

For some time previously he had been staying at the Christian Leprosy Home at Sabathu, not far from Simla, serving the leprosy patients there. It was to remain one of his most beloved bases and he returned there after his baptism. Then, in October 1906, he set out from it in quite a new way. He walked onto the road, a tall, good-looking, vigorous teenager, wearing a yellow robe and turban. Everyone stared at him as he passed. The yellow robe was the "uniform" of a Hindu sadhu, traditionally an ascetic devoted to the gods, who either begged his way along the roads or sat, silent, remote, and often filthy, meditating in the jungle or some lonely place. The young Sundar Singh had also chosen the sadhu's way, but he would be a sadhu with a difference.

"I am not worthy to follow in the steps of my Lord," he said, "but, like Him, I want no home, no possessions. Like Him I will belong to the road, sharing the suffering of my people, eating with those who will give me shelter, and telling all men of the love of God."

Bleeding feet

He at once put his vocation to the test by going back to his home village, Rampur, where he was shown an unexpectedly warm welcome. This was poor preparation for the months that were to follow. Scarcely tough enough to meet physical hardship, the sixteen-year-old sadhu went northward through the Punjab, over the Bannihal Pass into Kashmir, and then back through fanatically Muslim Afghanistan and into the brigand-infested North-West Frontier and Baluchistan. His thin, yellow robe gave him little protection against the snows, and his feet became torn from the rough tracks. Not many months had passed before the little Christian communities of the north were referring to him as "the apostle with the bleeding feet." This initiation showed him what he might expect in the future. He was stoned, arrested, visited by a shepherd who talked with strange intimacy about Jesus and then was gone, and left to sleep in a wayside hut with an unexpected cobra for company. Meetings with the mystical and the sharply material, persecution and welcome, would all characterize his experience in years ahead.

From the villages in the Simla hills, the long line of the snow-clad Himalayas and the rosy

Sadhu Sundar Singh, in his characteristic dress of a sadhu.

peak of Nanga Parbat, rose in the distance. Beyond them lay Tibet, a closed Buddhist land that missionaries had long failed to penetrate with the gospel. Ever since his baptism Tibet had beckoned Sundar, and in 1908, at the age of nineteen, he crossed its frontiers for the first time. Any stranger entering into this closed fanatical territory, domin-ated by Buddhism and devil-worship, risked both terror as well as death. Singh took the risk with his eyes—and his heart—wide open. The state of the people appalled him. Their airless homes, like themselves, were filthy. He himself was stoned as he bathed in some cold water because they believed that "holy men never washed." Food was mostly unobtainable and he existed on hard, parched barley. Everywhere there was hostility. And this was only "lower Tibet" just across the border.

Sundar went back to Sabathu determined to return the next year.

A cup of water

He had one even greater desire—to visit Palestine and re-live some of the happenings in Jesus' life. In 1908 he went to Bombay, hoping

THE LIFE OF
Sadhu Sundar Singh

1889	Born at Rampur, Punjab
1903	Conversion
1904	Cast out from home
1905	Baptized in Simla; begins life as a sadhu
1907	Works in leprosy hospital at Sabathu
1908	First visit to Tibet
1909	Enters divinity college, Lahore, to train for the ministry
1911	Hands back his preacher's license; returns to the sadhu's life
1912	Tours through north India and the Buddhist states of the Himalayas
1918–22	Travels worldwide
1923	Turned back from Tibet
1925–27	Quietly spends time writing
1927	Sets out for Tibet but returns due to illness
1929	Attempts to reach Tibet and disappears

to board a convenient ship. But to his intense disappointment the government refused him a permit, and he had to return to the north. It was on this trip that he suddenly recognized a basic dilemma of the Christian mission to India. A brahmin had collapsed in the hot, crowded carriage and, at the next station, the Anglo-Indian stationmaster came rushing with a cup of water from the refreshment room. The brahmin—a high-caste Hindu—thrust it away in horror. He needed water, but he could only accept it in his own drinking vessel. When that was brought he drank, and revived. In the same way, Sundar Singh realized, India would not widely accept the gospel of Jesus offered in Western guise. That, he recognized, was why many listeners responded to him in his Indian sadhu's robe.

There was still sharper disillusionment to come. In 1909 he was persuaded to begin training for the Christian ministry at the Anglican college in Lahore. From the beginning he found himself being tormented by fellow students for being "different" and no doubt too self-assured. This phase ended when their ringleader heard Singh quietly praying for him, with love in his tones and words. But other tensions remained. Much in the college course seemed irrelevant to the gospel as India needed to hear it, and then,

as the course drew to an end, the principal stated that he must now discard his sadhu's robe and wear "respectable" European clerical dress; use formal Anglican worship; sing English hymns; and never preach outside his parish without special permission. Never again visit Tibet, he asked? That would be, to him, an unthinkable rejection of God's call.

With deep sadness he left the college, still dressed in his yellow robe, and in 1912 began his annual trek into Tibet as the winter snows began to melt on the Himalayan tracks and passes.

Extraordinary accounts

Stories from those years are astonishing and sometimes incredible. Indeed there were those who insisted that they were mystical rather than real happenings. That first year, 1912, he returned with an extraordinary account of finding a three-hundred-year old Christian hermit in a mountain cave—the Maharishi of Kailas—with whom he spent some weeks in deep fellowship. Other stories were more credible, even if more terrible. He had been sewn into a wet yak-skin and left to be crushed to death as it shrank in the hot sun ... tied into cloths laced with leeches and scorpions to sting him and suck his blood ... roped to a tree as bait for wild animals. At these and at other times he had been rescued by members of the "Sunnyasi Mission"—secret disciples of Jesus wearing their Hindu markings, whom he claimed to have found all over India.

Whether he won many continuing disciples of Christ on these hazardous Tibetan treks will never be known. For the Tibetan it was Buddhism or nothing. To acknowledge Jesus Christ was to ask for death. But the Sadhu's own courageous preaching cannot have been without effect.

Fighting Satan

As Sundar Singh moved through his twenties his ministry widened greatly, and long before he was thirty years old his name and picture were familiar all over the Christian world. He described in terms of a vision a struggle with Satan to retain his humility but he was, in fact, always human, approachable and humble, with a sense of fun and a love of nature. This, with his "illustrations" from ordinary life, gave his addresses great impact. Many people said: "He not only *looks* like Jesus, he talks like Jesus must have talked." Yet all his talks and his personal speech sprang out of profound early morning meditation, especially on the Gospels.

In 1918 he made a long tour of South India and Ceylon, and the following year he was invited to Burma, Malaya, China, and Japan. Some of the stories from these tours were as strange as any of his Tibetan adventures. He had power over wild things, like the leopard which crept up to him while he stood praying and crouched as he fondled its head. He had power over evil, typified by the sorcerer who tried to hypnotize him in a railway-carriage and blamed the Bible in the sadhu's pocket for his failure. He had power over disease and illness, though he never allowed his healing gifts to be publicized.

For a long time Sundar Singh had wanted to visit Britain, and the opportunity came when his old father, Dher Singh, came to tell him that he too had become a Christian and wished to give him the money for his fare to Britain. He visited the West twice, traveling to Britain, the United States, and Australia in 1920, and to Europe again in 1922. He was welcomed by Christians of many traditions, and his words searched the hearts of people who now faced the aftermath of World War I and who seemed to evidence a shallow attitude to life. Sundar was appalled by the materialism, emptiness, and irreligion he found everywhere, contrasting it with Asia's awareness of God, no matter how limited that might be. Once back in India he continued his ministry, though it was clear that he was getting more physically frail.

Christ of the Indian road

His gifts, his personal attractiveness, the relevance of Christ as he presented Him to his Indian people could have given Sundar Singh a unique position of leadership in the Indian church. But to the end of his life he remained a man who sought nothing for himself, but only the opportunity to offer Christ to everyone. He was not a member of any denomination, and did not try to begin one of his own, though he shared fellowship with Christians of all kinds. He lived (to use a later phrase) to introduce his own people to "the Christ of the Indian road."

In 1923 Sundar Singh made the last of his regular summer visits to Tibet and came back exhausted. His preaching days were obviously over and, in the next years, in his own home or those of his friends in the Simla hills he gave himself to meditation, fellowship, and writing some of the things he had lived to preach.

In 1929, against all his friends' advice, Sundar determined to make one last journey to Tibet. In April he reached Kalka, a small town below Simla, a prematurely aged figure in his yellow robe among pilgrims and holy men who were beginning their own trek to one of Hinduism's holy places some miles away. Where he went after that is unknown. Whether he fell from a precipitous path, died of exhaustion, or reached the mountains, will remain a mystery. Sundar Singh had been seen for the last time.

But more than his memory remains, and e has continued to be one of the most treasured and formative figures in the development and story of Christ's church in India.

Further Reading

Appasamy, A. J. *Sundar Singh*. Cambridge: Lutterworth, 1958.

Francis, Dayanandan, ed. *The Christian Witness of Sadhu Sundar Singh*. Alresford: Christian Literature Crusade, 1989.

Streeter, Burnett and A. J. Appasamy. *The Sadhu: a Study in Mysticism and Practical Religion*. London: Macmillan, 1923.

Watson, Janet Lynn. *The Saffron Robe*. London: Hodder and Stoughton, 1975.

THE LIFE OF
Billy Sunday

Billy Sunday

Acrobatic Evangelist

Billy Sunday was born on November 19, 1862, to Mary Jane and William Sunday in Story County near Ames, Iowa. His father, "a ne'er-do-well bricklayer," had joined the Union Army, but had died of pneumonia at Camp Pendleton, Missouri, without seeing his third son. Mary Jane, a Christian, subsequently remarried. Her second husband, Heizer, proved to be derelict in his family duties, however. He abandoned his wife, two natural children, and three stepsons in 1874. Mary Jane was unable to provide for her children. Billy and his brother Edward were sent to the Soldier's Orphanage

Billy Sunday as a young ball player.

The sawdust trail

In the often-colorful and rarely dull history of gospel preaching in America, Billy Sunday occupies a very prominent position between Dwight L. Moody and Billy Graham. In the glitzy idealism of the Progressive Era, from Theodore Roosevelt to Warren G. Harding, Sunday had no equal for audience appeal, enthusiasm, and name identification.

Acrobatics
His robust manly image, vaudevillian acrobatics, and florid rhetoric (some have estimated that he on occasion spoke 300 words a minute!) combined with a direct, simplistic appeal for moral and spiritual change catapulted him to a career that encompassed four decades.

Sunday held audiences spellbound by his remarkable theatrical delivery. He offered assurance of the steady triumph of Christianity to the Christian public and hope through Christ to the perplexed unreached.

Crusades
During his lengthy career he was heard by 100 million Americans in over three hundred crusades. They crowded into specially built wooden tabernacles, which held up to twenty thousand people. His thunderous voice was audible without amplification. With one million of his hearers "hitting the sawdust trail" (i.e., going forward to shake the evangelist's hand), Sunday became one of the most productive professional soul winners in history.

Home in Glenwood, Iowa, and later to Davenport.

Billy received "a good schooling and proper religious instruction." When Edward turned sixteen in 1876, the boys left the orphanage returning to their grandfather's farm near Ames. Billy then determined to strike out on his own by moving to nearby Nevada, Iowa, where he was employed by Colonel John Scott. After high school, Billy Sunday worked as a laborer in Marshalltown, and joined the volunteer fire brigade.

"Where is Jesus?"
He also played on the local state-champion baseball team.

His amazing speed attracted the attention of A. C. "Pop" Anson, manager of the Chicago White Stockings (now the Chicago White Sox). Billy Sunday could round the bases in only fourteen seconds. From 1883 to 1891, he played professional ball for Pittsburgh, Philadelphia, and Chicago. He achieved celebrity status when he stole ninety-five bases in a single season. This was an amazing feat.

His life took a dramatic turn in 1886 when he experienced a genuine religious conversion at the Pacific Garden Mission in Chicago. Later, in his sermon "Heaven," he declared:

When I reach Heaven, I won't stop to look for Abraham, Isaac, Jacob, Moses, Joseph, David, Daniel, Peter, or Paul. I will rush past them all saying, "Where is Jesus? I want to see Jesus who saved my soul one dark stormy night in Chicago in 1887 [real date 1886].

Subsequently, he joined the Jefferson Park Presbyterian Church and received religious instruction at the local YMCA. In 1888 he married Helen A. Thompson, who was the sister of the bat boy of the White Stockings, a woman of strong Presbyterian convictions. The couple had four children— Helen, George, William, and Paul.

Advance man
Retiring from baseball, Billy Sunday began to work with the YMCA (1891–93), before being invited by J. Wilbur Chapman to serve in his evangelistic team as "advance man." The group dissolved after two years, and Chapman invited Sunday to come to Garner, Iowa, to hold evangelistic meetings. This summons brought Sunday to his career as a full-time evangelist. At Garner, he used his former boss's sermon material, and preached in the local opera house.

Sunday's evangelistic career can be divided into three parts: first of all, the building years (1896–1905), from Garner to Burlington, Iowa; then came the booming years (1905–17), from Burlington to New York City; and then, the bleak years (1917–35), from New York City to rural America. Sunday's meetings in the initial period were in the rural Midwest, mostly in Iowa. In those years he tried to wear the mantle of

Two photographs showing Billy Sunday's dramatic preaching style.

Chapman: to adopt a conservative style and a reserved demeanor, prohibiting Lord's day meetings in deference to local pastors, and excluding inquiry rooms.

After 1900, Sunday's approach to evangelism changed. His rhetoric became increasingly colloquial. He attacked apostate churches and ministers directly. He demanded that church functions cease during his campaigns, which more and more took on an atmosphere of entertainment. In 1901, he began to use a wooden tabernacle for his services. Starting in 1904, he required that the expenses for an entire campaign (including the wooden tabernacle) be pledged before he would commit to come. In this early period of

ministry, ninety of Sunday's one hundred campaigns were in towns with populations of less than 10,000.

The Sunday Party

From the Burlington (Iowa) Crusade in 1905, Sunday began to reach into larger centers of population in the Midwest and East. His influence crested especially in New York City, where in ten weeks, 98,264 "hit the sawdust trail." Sunday had become a national figure.

Business efficiency characterized the "Sunday Party" staff, in which Mrs. Sunday played a critical role. At the peak of Sunday's evangelistic activity, twenty-three full-time staffers performed a dizzying array of activities. His most famous song-leader was Homer "Rody" Rodeheaver, whose lively, joyful, and even jazzy songs set an optimistic, self-confident mood for Sunday's invitation (the choir being used after Sunday's messages, not before as in Moody's crusades).

J. Gresham Machen, the great evangelical scholar at Princeton Seminary, gave a first-hand account of what it was like to hear Billy Sunday preach:

The sermon was old-fashioned evangelism of the most powerful and elemental kind. Much of it, I confess, left me cold—I "took" some of the touches of humor and did not "think that they were mine." But the total impact of the sermon was great. At the climax, the preacher got up on his chair—and if he had used a step-ladder, nobody could have thought the thing excessive, so dead in earnest were both speaker and audience!... In the last five or ten minutes of that sermon, I got a new realization of the power of the gospel....

Disappointments

It was in the years after 1918 that Billy Sunday's evangelistic activity began to recede from the spotlight of national attention. His poignant optimism, so culturally relevant in the pre-war years, began to sour into pessimism as some Americans turned away from traditional Christianity. Although he still continued with his campaigns through the 1920s, he shifted his activities from the urban Northeast to the rural South and Midwest. In addition, the crusades were shorter in length and the numbers of staff were greatly reduced.

Evangelist Billy Sunday.

On July 3, 1927, song-leader Homer Rodeheaver wrote the evangelist a letter in which he tried to persuade Sunday to be less angry in the pulpit, to be less interested in offerings, to preach shorter sermons, and not to drive himself and his staff so hard. Sunday did not take the letter well.

Billy Sunday spent his last days in semi-retirement at his home in Winona Lake, Indiana, near a conference auditorium named in his honor. He was weakened by the effects of age, disappointed by a generation of Americans who increasingly disdained evangelical religion, saddened by two wayward sons, George and William, and pained by the death of a daughter,

Helen, in 1933, he nevertheless continued to preach, and the Lord blessed his ministry. On October 27, 1935, he preached his last sermon, which his wife Nell described in this way: "It was a good Gospel message, and Billy presented it well. He gave the invitation and forty-four people came forward. Billy was thrilled and so was I." On November 6, 1935, after three heart attacks, Sunday passed into the presence of his Lord.

Much controversy has ensued over how Sunday's ministry should be assessed. Recently, Lyle Dorsett has provided what appears to be a balanced assessment. Not glossing Billy Sunday's shortcomings, Dorsett nevertheless concludes:

Through his preaching and teaching, through his zealous promotion of Bible conferences such as those at Winona Lake, he did more than anyone else in the first half of the twentieth century to keep Christianity vital.

Further Reading

Dorsett, Lyle. *Billy Sunday and the Redemption of Urban America*. Grand Rapids: Eerdmans, 1991.

Frank, Douglas W. *Less Than Conquerors: How Evangelicals Entered the Twentieth Century*. Grand Rapids: Eerdmans, 1986.

McLoughlin, William G., Jr. *Billy Sunday Was His Real Name*. Chicago: U. of Chicago, 1955.

Rodeheaver, Homer. *Twenty Years With Billy Sunday*. Winona Lake, In.: Rodeheaver Hall-Mack, 1936.

China's greatest evangelist

John Sung ranks alongside Billy Graham as one of the great evangelists of the twentieth century and is considered by many to be the greatest evangelist ever to come out of China. Hundreds of thousands of people were touched through his ministry as he traveled throughout China and elsewhere in Southeast Asia. Though a powerful speaker himself, the key to his far-reaching evangelistic outreach was his remarkable ability to recruit others to become effective evangelists themselves. Under his able leadership thousands of Christians were mobilized in evangelistic bands to go out into cities and villages to share their faith with others. His ministry was further augmented by the many Bible conferences and training centers that he established.

Crossing divides

Sung's roots were in the Methodist church, but his ministry crossed all denominational lines as he received invitations to speak from faith mission societies, as well as from Anglicans and Presbyterians. Yet, he himself was strictly independent and shunned close ties with mission organizations. Indeed, he was often very critical of Western missionaries—so much so that his ministry provoked controversy wherever he went. He had little time for social graces or diplomacy, but his single-minded commitment to Christ earned him respect from Christians worldwide.

John Sung

Revival in the East

John (*Ju-un* in Chinese) Sung was born in the Hinghwa district in Southeast China in 1901, the sixth child of an impoverished Chinese Methodist preacher and his wife. Mrs. Sung, a fervent Buddhist, was surely not a typical Methodist pastor's wife. Their marriage had been arranged before she and Mr. Sung were even born, and his conversion to Christianity had not altered his obligation to marry her. But following a near-fatal fifth childbirth, she became a Christian, and so it

was that *Ju-un* (meaning God's grace) was born into a truly Christian home.

During the great Hinghwa revival—often called the "Hinghwa Pentecost"—young John Sung was converted. Though only nine years old, he was so convicted by sin that his tears of remorse soaked right through his outer coat as his head was bowed in a spirit of contrition. The spiritual awakening began with the powerful Passion Week messages of a little-known Chinese preacher; he ignited a

John Sung meeting in Java in 1939.

spark that set revival fires burning for several months.

"Little pastor"

John Sung was one of some thousands in this Buddhist stronghold of Hinghwa to be converted, and as such, his transformation might have gone unnoticed. But God's grip on this young Chinese boy was un- shakable. Within a few short years he became known as the "little pastor" of Hinghwa. He accompanied his father on preaching missions, and when his father was ill or engaged in other activities, he preached the very sermons he had memorized by listening to his father. Soon he began formulating his own sermons, and through his open- air ministry men and women were brought to faith in Christ.

In 1919, after he completed secondary school Sung received a letter that would change the course of his life. It was from a woman in America, offering to finance his education at Ohio Wesleyan University. Accepting the offer, John Sung was soon heading for a scholarly career in scientific research.

A brilliant student, after only three years of undergraduate study, Sung graduated in 1923, with highest honors. He was elected to Phi Beta Kappa, and was awarded a gold medal and a cash prize for physics and chemistry. So remarkable were his achievements that his story appeared in newspapers nation- wide. He received scholarship offers for graduate studies from Harvard and other prestigious schools, but chose to remain in Ohio and continue his studies at Ohio State University. In 1924, Sung was awarded a master's

degree, and two years later a Ph.D. in chemistry.

By any standard he was an extraordinary success. Univer- sities in America and abroad sent invitations for him to join their faculties. But amidst all the accolades, John Sung was distraught. He could not forget the deep fulfillment he had found in preaching the gospel years earlier, and he sensed God calling him back into the ministry. He could not accept a teaching position. Instead he would go on for fur- ther training. On the advice of a friend, he deci- ded to enrol at Union Theolog- ical Seminary, and became acquainted with notables such as Henry Sloan Coffin, the seminary's president, and Harry Emerson Fosdick, one of his

professors. It was here he also became acquainted with liberal theology. In one class after another he was taught that the Bible could not be trusted—that the Creation account was a myth and that the miracles of Jesus were fanciful tales told by disillusioned disciples.

John Sung.

THE LIFE OF

John Sung

In the wilderness

Although a brilliant scientist, John Sung found himself unable to respond to their seemingly well-reasoned arguments, and soon he found himself doubting the very Word of God that had once so empowered him. In some desperation, he turned to the religion of his ancestors and began to chant Buddhist scriptures. He also studied Taoism, hoping to find peace, but the more he searched the more confused and distressed he became. "My soul wandered in a wilderness," he later confessed. "I could neither sleep nor eat. My faith was like a leaking, storm-driven ship without captain or compass. My heart was filled with the deepest unhappiness."

In the midst of his doubt and depression, Sung was invited to attend an evangelistic campaign at New York City's Calvary Baptist Church, where the great Fundamentalist preacher John Roach Straton served as pastor. John Sung had been told that the speaker would be Dr. Haldeman, a renowned Bible teacher. Instead, the speaker was Uldine Utley, a fifteen-year-old evangelist. Her message was simple, yet powerful, and Sung found himself under conviction no less than he had been years earlier at the beginning of the Hinghwa revival. He returned the following four nights, awed by the presence of God and vowing that he would entreat the Almighty until he was empowered to preach even as this young woman was.

Dramatic dream

The following weeks and months were difficult for John Sung. He devoured Christian biographies, read the Bible, and defended the faith before unbelievers, but the weight of his sin crushed him down. Then one night he had a dream in which he saw himself lying in a coffin with his academic degrees and gowns; He was dead. In his dream, the brilliant scientist had died; but the new John Sung was alive to preach the gospel.

From that point, dramatic changes began to take place in his life. The gift of a globe from a stranger a week later was the sign that he was to carry the gospel around the world, but his starting point would be Union Theological Seminary. He set aside the liberal textbooks and began reading only the Bible. He prayed late into the night and sang hymns and shared his faith as he walked through the corridors of the seminary.

Confined!

When he was chanting Buddhist scriptures, Sung's behavior was accepted by the seminary, but now he was deemed abnormal. Indeed, some of the officials in the seminary were convinced he was mentally deranged. They scheduled him for psychiatric testing and then admitted him to the psychopathic ward at Bloomingdale Hospital. For more than six months he was confined against his will—six months that became for him his own personal theological seminary. He read through the Bible forty times—each time with a different focus—and he reached out to other patients with the gospel. He was finally released in August 1927—through the intervention of the Chinese consul, and soon afterwards he went back to China to preach, ignoring the invitations to teach that came from universities in his homeland.

In the months and years that followed he preached wherever he could gain a hearing—in the open air, in village churches, at universities, and at evangelistic campaigns and Bible conferences. An animated speaker, not unlike Billy Sunday—John Sung paced back and forth as he preached, pleading with sinners to repent.

"China needs Christ!"

As he traveled from place to place, he discovered that his months in seminary had prepared him well for his work in China. On hearing a Western missionary praise the teachings of Harry Emerson Fosdick and Mahatma Gandhi, Sung offered an angry rejoinder: "China does not need the teaching of Fosdick or Gandhi. The teaching of Confucius is far better than theirs. What the Chinese need is Jesus Christ and His Cross. People talk about Fosdick, but what do they know about him? I have studied under him and I rejected his teachings utterly and finally."

For the next few years John

devotion to preaching the gospel of Christ serves as a powerful model for Christians today.

John Sung in China; he is in the back row next to the woman.

Sung worked closely with the Bethel Mission, an evangelistic organization directed by Dr. Mary Stone, a Chinese medical doctor who like Sung had been educated in America. Through their effective partnership, the Bethel Mission arranged a full schedule of meetings—nearly nine hundred in one six-month, thirty-three-city tour. During that time, some fourteen thousand Chinese professed faith in Christ, and nearly three thousand volunteered to serve as full-time evangelists in small teams known as Bethel Bands. Indeed, during those months more than seven hundred new bands were formed. Other tours saw similar results.

Revival!

But Sung could not be confined to one organization. He was independent and did not work well with others. By 1934, he was on his own, and for the next eight years he traveled through China, often speaking to crowds of several thousand. People came from miles around to hear him preach and to ask him for prayer for healing. His travels also took him to Formosa (Taiwan), the Philippines, Singapore, Malaysia, and Thailand, where thousands more were converted to Christ and Bible training centers were established. Revival broke out wherever he spoke. Indeed, in Thailand, one missionary referred to his ministry as the answer to thirty years of one prayer: "Lord, send revival."

Many missionaries, however, regarded Sung a sensationalist performer and they resented his criticism of Westerners. Yet, they recognized that he had a rapport with the Chinese people that they could never have, and that through his ministry and the ministry of his evangelistic teams in China and abroad, hundreds of thousands had committed their lives to Christ.

In 1942, after fifteen years of exhausting ministry, Sung retired—his health spent. He died in 1944, at the age of forty-two. John Sung was a singular instrument of God, whose total

Further Reading

Lyall, Leslie T. *Flame For God: John Sung and Revival in the Far East.* London: Overseas Missionary Fellowship, 1976.

Seamands, John T. *Pioneers of the Younger Churches.* Nashville: Abingdon, 1967.

Sung, John. *Allegories.* Peking, China, 1951.

Charles E. Fuller

Old Fashioned Revivalist

The United States changed so swiftly after World War II that many conservative Christians, often called "fundamentalists," felt like uncertain aliens in a new land. They crossed no oceans to enter this foreign environment; and they clung to their traditional beliefs (the beliefs of most nineteenth-century Americans) while the larger American culture experienced its twentieth-century revolution.

New attitudes toward traditional Christianity were clearly evident in America's educational and media institutions. Scriptwriters, entertainers, and professors came to look upon fundamentalists as one does items in a museum, as quaint and bizarre reminders of a distant past.

During the 1930s and 1940s Charles E. Fuller, who became the most popular revivalist between Billy Sunday and Billy Graham, sensed instinctively the cultural revolution that was taking place in America and led hosts of evangelical Christians in a renewal of their traditional faith. He demonstrated for them how radio, the greatest

advance in communication, and Christian higher education could address the needs of people in the days of post-Protestant American culture. His spiritual roots were in fundamentalism's resistance to modern America, but he contributed significantly to a new progressive movement among evangelical Christians that emerged in the United States after World War II.

Charles E. Fuller at the radio microphone.

Orange groves

Fuller's parents were dedicated Christians who lived in Southern California near Redlands, and he grew up surrounded by orange trees and family devotions. Every day the family gathered around the Scriptures and the ranch house pump organ. Unfortunately, the Scriptures appeared to have had little influence upon Charles through his years at Pomona College and early married life.

As the manager of an orange growers' cooperative packing plant in Placentia, he remained a nominal member of the Presbyterian church in town until July 1916 when he read in the newspaper that Paul Rader, former wrestler and boxer, would be preaching at the Church of the Open Door in Los Angeles. With nothing better to do, Fuller, who had played football at Pomona, decided to drive to Los Angeles to hear the former athlete speak.

As he listened to Rader, he grew uncomfortable. Leaning forward on the seat in front of him, he trembled under deep conviction. At the invitation he could not muster the courage to move forward to express his faith in Christ. But then, after the meeting, he drove to Franklin Park in nearby Hollywood, and in the shade of a eucalyptus tree he yielded his life to God.

The unearthly hour

A family friend soon introduced him to William E. Blackstone's *Jesus is Coming*, one of the most widely circulated books of the early fundamentalist movement. Fuller became so excited about Bible prophecy that he began teaching a class which began at 8 o'clock on Sunday mornings called "The Unearthly Hour Bible Class." The study focused on the Book of Daniel.

On Sundays after teaching the class, Fuller and his wife Grace often drove into Los Angeles to hear evangelist Reuben A. Torrey at the Church of the Open Door. Thus from the beginning of his spiritual pilgrimage his associations were with the center of fundamentalism in the Los Angeles area. Naturally when, in 1919, he decided to prepare to preach the gospel, he entered the Bible Institute of Los Angeles (BIOLA). It was there Torrey's influence upon him deepened, especially in the basic Bible doctrine course taught by the evangelist.

The emphases of fundamentalism were all there at the school: Bible doctrine centering on prophecy, evangelism, foreign missions, and the Spirit-controlled life. All became a part of Charles E. Fuller's concept of ministry.

Given these deep roots in fundamentalism, Fuller's tensions with the Placentia Presbyterian Church appear predictable. In 1920, when he began teaching an adult class in the church, his dissatisfaction with the social emphasis of the church surfaced. By early 1924 he resigned as an elder of the church and the Bible class he taught separated from the church. A little over a year later the Bible class became Calvary Church with

THE LIFE OF	
Charles E. Fuller	
1887	Born
1910	Graduates from Pomona College
1916	Confesses Christ as Savior due to ministry of Paul Rader
1919	Enters the Bible Institute of Los Angeles
1931	Broadcasts first program of what becomes the "Old Fashioned Revival Hour"
1944	The "Old Fashioned Revival Hour" is one of the most popular radio programs in the United States
1947	Founds Fuller Theological Seminary
1968	Dies

Fuller as pastor. During the next eight years under his leadership the church grew sevenfold, from fifty members to three hundred and seventy.

Fuller's greatest gifts, however, were soon to surface. In February 1929, while he was on an evangelistic tour sponsored by BIOLA, he was asked to take the place of the regular speaker on a local radio broadcast from Indianapolis, Indiana. He left Indianapolis for Philadelphia, impressed with the results of his experience at the microphone. While on the train returning to Southern California, he spent a sleepless night considering the possibilities of spreading the gospel by radio.

Thus, in December 1929 Charles Fuller seized the opportunity to broadcast the Sunday evening service at Calvary Church over a new station in Santa Ana. That was his beginning in radio.

The power of the air

The 1920s were not particularly conducive to broadcasting the gospel. Numbers of fundamentalists felt that the Bible taught the air waves were the domain of Satan, "the prince of the power of the air" (Eph. 2:2, KJV). But a few hearty pioneers had already ventured into enemy territory including Donald Grey Barnhouse, who in 1927, began preaching by radio from his Presbyterian church in Philadelphia.

Early in 1931 Fuller moved beyond the local broadcast by launching "The Pilgrim's Hour," aired on seven stations of the Columbia Broadcasting System (CBS) from San Diego to Seattle.

Major success in broadcasting did not come, however, until he had undergone the trials of the

Depression years and had resigned from Calvary Church. Some of the members of the church felt Fuller's broadcasting was hindering his pastoral work, and he interpreted their attitude as a lack of vision. Late in 1932 he decided to leave the church.

Fuller had no way of knowing that the morning after his last sermon in March 1933, President Franklin D. Roosevelt would close the banks across the country or that five days later Long Beach, the location of his broadcasts, would suffer a severe earthquake, killing 115 people and inflicting damage totaling $40 million. Hardly the best circumstances for launching a full-time radio ministry!

On his way to the studio for his first Sunday broadcast the radio preacher was stopped by a U.S. Marine sergeant sent with others to guard Long Beach from looters. Fuller argued his way through the barricade and made that broadcast. Only two months after this the Gospel Broadcasting Association was created to sponsor his radio ministry.

Old Fashioned Revival Hour

The following months were marked by financial struggles but on the first Sunday in October 1934, Fuller, with only fifty people present at the Women's Club House in Hollywood, broadcast the first hour-long program of what was later called the "Old Fashioned Revival Hour." For the next twenty-three years the hour-long service reached a Sunday audience.

A wider ministry opened to Charles Fuller in October 1937, when the newly formed Mutual Broadcasting System provided him with a coast-to-coast network. Starting with fourteen stations of MBS in 1937 carrying the "Old Fashioned Revival Hour," Fuller dared to grow with the network, until 456 stations aired his program in 1942. By December 1941, when World War II suddenly swept over the country, the "Old Fashioned Revival Hour", in the heart of Sunday evening listening time, was the most widely heard broadcast in America, reaching at least ten million people.

During the four years of international conflict— years before the introduction of television— America was held together by air waves. Radio news reports made H.V. Kaltenborn and Edward

Fuller Theological Seminary, Pasadena, California.

R. Murrow household names, and funnymen Jack Benny and Edgar Bergen helped make bearable sacrifices for the war. Still, the most widely heard voice was neither newscaster nor comic. In May 1943, *Coronet* magazine observed, "If you're inclined to wager that America's largest radio audiences tune in on Charlie McCarthy or Bob Hope, ignore your hunch and save your money. For while these comedians are indeed aces of the air,

Inset: Cutting the ground for the new seminary.

a couple of preachers operating on shoestring budgets are giving them a run for their money.... They are Walter A. Maier of St. Louis...and Charles E. Fuller of Los Angeles.... Fuller is the founding father of the 'Old Fashioned Revival Hour,' which has so many outlets there probably isn't a radio set anywhere in the United States which can't pick up his hymn singing and sermons on Sunday Nights."

Coronet magazine was proved right. After 1944 Charles Fuller had to move the broadcast from a small studio to the five-thousand-seat Municipal Auditorium in Long Beach, California, where meetings were accented by many servicemen's uniforms. Sunday after Sunday an estimated twenty million Americans heard the California evangelist follow his message with this familiar appeal:

If you want the joy of being a child of God simply by exercising your faith in Jesus Christ, raise your hand... God bless you down there. I see you, and God bless you... How about those in the first balcony? I see you... Raise your hands way up high. Show the Lord you mean business... Yes, I see... God bless you.

And all across America, mothers thought of their boys in uniform and wondered if they were listening too.

Through these years the radio evangelist built a base of financial support by holding massive public gospel services in the major cities of America: Portland, Seattle, Salt Lake City, Des Moines, Chicago, Boston, Minneapolis, and in many others.

Playing Carnegie Hall

No one could ever be quite sure what Charles Fuller would do in these meetings. Once during a service in New York's Carnegie Hall he said, "When a singer gets to sing in Carnegie Hall, he feels that he has arrived. Now here I am in Carnegie Hall, and I don't want to lose my opportunity to sing." So he asked the pianist to accompany him while he sang, "What Can Wash Away My Sins? Nothing but the Blood of Jesus." In all probability that was the first and last time anyone ever sang "Nothing but the Blood" in Carnegie Hall.

During his years of broadcasting Fuller had nurtured a dream of founding a college of missions and evangelism, and he took the first step toward implementing this vision in the summer of 1944 when the Fuller Evangelistic Association secured a piece of property near the California Institute of Technology in Pasadena. Unfortunately, early attempts to gather a faculty for such a school went awry.

After these initial frustrations Fuller, in April, 1946, wrote to Harold J. Ockenga at Park Street Church in Boston. The two men were drawn together by their shared vision for a school. Ockenga, however, urged the evangelist to consider a seminary rather than a college and under his stimulus four men, Carl F. H. Henry, Wilbur Smith, Everett F. Harrison, and Harold Lindsell agreed to help launch the school. Classes began in September 1947. According to surveys during the early years of the seminary more than half the students who enrolled said their chief reason for entering Fuller Theological Seminary came through the influence of the "Old Fashioned Revival Hour."

Risks for God

From its modest beginnings Fuller Seminary eventually grew to a school of over three thousand students, the largest nondenominational seminary in the country. More importantly the seminary represented a scholarly and socially sensitive evangelical vision of ministry, markedly different from the earlier fundamentalism of the school's aging founder. Fuller, in fact, was often at odds with positions of the seminary but continued to give the school his support by relying on the advice of his son, Daniel. He lived to see his missionary vision find concrete expression in the seminary's highly respected School of World Mission, founded in 1965 under the leadership of church growth scholar Donald McGavran.

Three years later, on March 18, 1968, the popular voice of the "Old Fashioned Revival Hour" fell silent. Speaking at his funeral, Harold John Ockenga, who knew him well, said of Charles E. Fuller: "Here was a man of faith who took risks for God."

Further Reading

Fuller, Daniel P. *Give the Winds a Mighty Voice: The Story of Charles E. Fuller*. Waco, Texas: Word, 1972.

Marsden, George M. *Reforming Fundamentalism: Fuller Seminary and the New Evangelicalism*. Grand Rapids: Eerdmans, 1987.

Discipling

Known to his friends and colleagues as "Daws," Dawson Earle Trotman singlehandedly shaped evangelical thinking and methodology regarding the follow-up procedures for evangelistic meetings during the second half of the twentieth century. Instead of viewing the public profession of faith as the end product of revival meetings or youth rallies, Trotman strove to make such a commitment the beginning of a discipling relationship that would culminate in the new believer bringing others to faith in Christ and ultimately to Christian maturity.

Stressing one-on-one accountability over a period of time, Trotman's plan included memorization of Scripture for the discipline of godliness and the preparation for personal witness. Beginning with naval personnel in southern California in 1933, The Navigators was among the first of a series of dynamic evangelical parachurch agencies that reshaped the pieces of fundamentalism shattered by the Scopes "Monkey Trial" in 1925.

After World War II, the G.I. Bill allowed veterans to attend college. Dawson Trotman's movement followed them, expanding to college and university campuses nationwide. Interestingly, the founder himself had a limited higher education. The ministry flourished and expanded to include a training center at Glen Eyrie in Colorado Springs, and discipleship ministries in cooperation with local churches, and in 1975 NavPress. Today's Navigator staff of forty-four nationalities work in more than 80 countries to multiply laborers for Christ.

Dawson Earle Trotman, "Daws".

Dawson Trotman and the Navigators

Daws

The police officer could not help noticing the young man with reddish-brown hair staggering aimlessly along the street near the Long Beach Pike amusement beach. Twenty-year-old Dawson Trotman was so drunk he could not find his red Buick or even remember where he had parked it. At last they stood face to face. The officer looked at him and bluntly asked the drunken man, "Do you like this kind of life?"

"I hate it, sir," was Trotman's response. In fact, he despised his habitual pattern of lying, his propensity to gamble, and the long black pipe that he often smoked. Even his joy of gliding across the floor of the Silver Spray dance hall until the wee hours of the morning had begun to lose its glamour.

Dawson Trotman had been a natural leader and an outstanding student in high school. President and valedictorian of his class, he had also effectively

THE LIFE OF
Dawson Trotman

1906   Born in Bisbee, Arizona
1926   Becomes a Christian in
          Lomita, California
1932   Marries Lila Clayton
1933   Founds The Navigators
1956   Drowns at Schroon Lake,
          New York

headed the Christian Endeavor Society which met at Lomita Presbyterian Church. He would pack his Model-T with his friends and attend the Los Angeles Christian Endeavor conventions. All the while the boy with the infectious personality from Bisbee, Arizona, led a double life. After graduation, however, he turned his back on his spiritual charade and opted for the partying life of the Roaring Twenties.

Rescue!
Perhaps the turning point in Trotman's life came when he was swimming with a girlfriend in a mountain lake a month before his confrontation with the law. When the girl was unable to reach shore, Trotman struggled to rescue her. Both began to sink. Had it not been for a couple in a boat who fished the two out of the water, the history of evangelical discipleship might have been very different

This sobering "baptism" began a process which in a matter of months brought Trotman into a firm commitment to Jesus Christ. A change in lifestyle followed. Having been disciplined by memorizing the Scriptures, Trotman established a pattern of evangelism and follow-up that has been used or imitated by nearly every evangelistic

parachurch agency and many churches in America during the remainder of the twentieth century. It is ironic that the pioneer of discipleship, in another mountain-lake rescue attempt, on the other side of the continent would lose his life thirty years later.

Dawson Earle Trotman, weighing only two-and-a-half-pounds, was born on March 25, 1906, in Bisbee, Arizona. Early life was a struggle. Physically frail, young Dawson found that the combination of his father's gregarious personality with his mother's protective instincts were to produce conflict in the family. Dawson's father, Charles, professed little in the way of religious beliefs, while his mother became enamored with the evangelist, Aimee Semple McPherson. The contrast in his parents' religious values was ultimately to lead to their divorce and forced Dawson to find his own direction in life.

When he was twenty years old, Trotman made a lasting commitment to Jesus Christ and started attending Christian Endeavor meetings once again. Although at first his motivation was to earn points for his team, the young man memorized as many as ten Bible verses a week and in so doing, discovered a discipline that would shape his future life.

The Fishermen's Club
His newfound passion compelled him to join the Fishermen's Club, a group dedicated to public witness for Jesus Christ. His Scripture memorization provided knowledge and confidence. Soon his opportunities as a leader in Christian Endeavor and his boldness in sharing the

gospel on the streets produced a number of converts.

Twice Trotman enrolled in Christian colleges, only to withdraw because of the urgency he felt for continuing the ministry in which he was already engaged. His own determination to memorize the Bible, as well as the willingness to undertake what amounted to a systematic study of theology as part of his daily devotional life, became the educational force behind his development. Throughout his life, the trainer of disciple-makers was a layman with a minimal amount of formal training.

Dawson Trotman with Navigator workers in 1950. Left: Lorne Sanny; Trotman standing.

On July 3, 1932, one month after his fiancée's high school graduation, Trotman married Lila Clayton, to whom he had been engaged since her sophomore year. Lila shared her husband's vision and energy. Together they labored, using their own home as a center for witnessing and discipleship.

Minute Men

Dawson Trotman saw his life's ministry as working "with young men [in] a ministry of training spiritual guerrillas, Christian soldiers who would give no quarter in battle for their Commander in Chief." The discipline that he had lacked as an adolescent became the main ingredient of the ministry he shaped. He began with the International Fisherman's Clubs, but soon felt the need to build his own ministry. With a few friends he organized the Minute Men, using the image of the Revolutionary War, when people were ready to respond at a moment's notice.

Within a year, his vision crystallized. Through contact with a sailor on the *U.S.S. West Virginia*, he recognized the potential of training sailors to initiate ministries on board ship, in effect creating floating seminaries. In 1933 the Minute Men ministry dissolved; in its place, The Navigators emerged, their motto "To Know Christ and To Make Him Known."

Born to reproduce

Over the years, Daws Trotman "the Navigator" became known as the apostle of follow-up. He persisted in his conviction that evangelism was only the beginning of a long process that would enable Christians to reach and train others to reproduce their spiritual lives. *Born to Reproduce*, one of the few booklets written by Trotman, was an articulate expression of his philosophy.

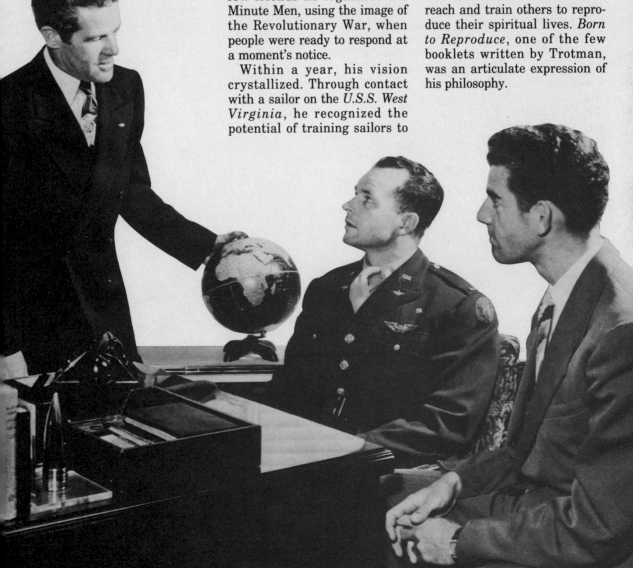

Dawson Trotman influenced others in ministry, including Bill Bright of Campus Crusade for Christ before Bright became a believer. Jim Rayburn's Young Life Campaign adopted some of The Navigators' tools for Bible Study and Memory after they joined forces for several youth rallies in 1942. Charles E. Fuller, the radio evangelist, was so impressed with Trotman's ministry that his evangelistic foundation purchased a home in Pasadena, California, which he rented to The Navigators for a nominal fee.

In 1950, Billy Graham asked Trotman to develop a follow-up program for his crusades. After declining three times because of the extensive commitment of time required, Trotman finally agreed. Acceptance of this project proved to be a turning point in The Navigator ministry, for many evangelical churches and ministries adopted the methods, emphases and strategy which Trotman developed.

Navigating

Research by Robert Walter Felts suggests significant Navigator influence on a variety of other missionary organizations including Overseas Crusades, Mission Aviation Fellowship, Wycliffe Bible Translators, the Foreign Mission Board of the Southern Baptist Convention, Campus Crusade for Christ, and Operation Mobilization. Two of these, the Southern Baptist Foreign Mission Board and Wycliffe, are reported to be the largest mission organizations in the world.

Dawson Trotman's life was well suited to the military motif suggested by The Navigators'

name. He was forceful and brusque, ready to confront. Time, however, honed within him a willingness to be confronted. It has been suggested that he had a greater difficulty relating to women than men. Thus it is ironic that when he drowned in Schroon Lake, New York, he was holding above the water a young girl who had fallen from a speed boat. She was rescued, but he sank into the depths.

The caption given under his obituary picture in the July 2, 1956, edition of *Time* magazine simply reads, "Always holding someone up." Perhaps that is the role of the apostle of follow-up.

Further Reading

Foster, Robert D. *The Navigator*. Colorado Springs: NavPress, 1983.

Skinner, Betty Lee. *Daws*. NavPress, 1974.

Trotman, Dawson. *Born to Reproduce*. Colorado Springs: NavPress, 1955.

Jack Wyrtzen and Radio Ministry

Words of Life

Though his grandfather, Count Caspar von Wyrtzen of Denmark, was a renowned Danish sea captain, and his grandmother worked for Queen Victoria, Casper John von Wyrtzen was born on April 22, 1913, into the home of a humble dispatcher for the Long Island Railroad. His mother, with a cocktail in one hand and a cigarette in the other, ruled as the matriarch of the family. Margaret was strong enough to keep her husband Harry in line along with her three young sons—Harry, Jimmy, and Casper.

Hard work and study ordered the Wyrtzen weekdays, but Sundays were reserved for fun. They jumped on the subway, swam, rode ponies, and went to the amusement park. One hot Sunday afternoon at Coney Island, Margaret Wyrtzen invited her Casper to take a sip of beer. "Yuck!" He spat it on the ground. "That stuff tastes like cough medicine!" Young Casper Wyrtzen, tired of high school teasers, changed his name to "Jack." Together with his change of name, he developed

"Hi, everybody! Jack Wyrtzen speaking from high, high up here in the heart of the beautiful Adirondack mountains at Scroon Lake, New York. This program is dedicated to youth and is known around the world as Word of Life."

For over fifty years, Wyrtzen's clear voice has proclaimed over the air waves that he is just as sure of heaven as if he had already been there for a thousand years. Jack Wyrtzen, founder and director of Word of Life International, never graduated from high school, yet he became a pioneer in Christian radio, innovating youth evangelism, camping, and training. Under his leadership, Word of Life's distinctive blend of enthusiastic evangelism and committed edification has flourished to influence the world, from South America to the Ukraine.

Thousands locked out
The fuse that ignited this world outreach was a mass evangelistic rally held in New York City near the end of World War II. On April 1, 1944, Jack Wyrtzen preached to a packed house of twenty thousand inside Madison Square

Jack Wyrtzen (right) with evangelists, including Billy Graham (center) in 1956.

Garden. During the 1950s and 1960s, Word of Life's facilities at Schroon Lake mushroomed into a complex capable of ministering to over twenty thousand per summer. In the ensuing decades, Wyrtzen created a free forum for evangelism on the talk show circuit. A heated, four-hour joust with the atheist Madalyn Murray O'Hare jammed CBS Chicago phone lines with over nineteen thousand calls.

Jack Wyrtzen is recognized as one of the foremost youth evangelists. How did this poor Brooklyn kid raised in a Unitarian home become a voice of fundamentalism in the United States and around the world? How did God blend the creative salesmanship of a Walt Disney with the passionate laymen's concern of a D. L. Moody in the personality of one man?

THE LIFE OF

Jack Wyrtzen

1913	Born in Brooklyn, New York
1932	Born again
1933	Dedicates his life to the Lord
1936	Marries Marge Smith
1940	Begins Word of Life Ministry
1941	First Word of Life radio program on WHN, Brooklyn, N.Y.
1947	Camping ministry at Schroon Lake, N.Y., begins
1948	Yankee Stadium rally in New York City
1958	Word of Life Brazil initiates overseas ministry
1959	Word of Life Bible Club ministry founded
1970	Word of Life Bible Institute founded at Schroon Lake
1984	Marge Wyrtzen goes home to be with the Lord
1986	Marries Joan Steiner
1990	Word of Life Florida conference center dedicated

his candid, straight-from-the-hip style of oratory.

Occasionally Mr. and Mrs. Wyrtzen did take their sons to church. As a three-year-old, Casper stood before a Unitarian Church and sang "Jesus Loves Me." At eleven, he begged his dad to allow him to attend a woodworking class at the local YMCA. Remembering the organization's fervor, and picturing his youngest son being perverted by a "Billy Sunday" type of religious fanaticism, the elder Wyrtzen hesitated. The son persisted; finally his dad relented. The eleven-year-old arrived at the YMCA expecting instruction in the use of saws, hammers, and nails. Instead, an old man began to expound from the Bible about a woman who was changed into a pillar of salt. Jack giggled and joined in mocking the teacher. He then walked out and found the woodworking class down the hall. At nineteen, Jack continued to ridicule religion. That all changed when his closest friend in the 101st Cavalry Mounted Band handed him a copy of the Gospel of John.

Born again

In the summer of 1931, George Schilling guzzled more alcohol than any of his New York National Guard buddies. However, at the following summer camp, Schilling no longer drank, but would kneel beside his cot each night, pray, and read his Bible. Wyrtzen joined in the cussing and the shoe throwing against the kneeling believer, but secretly admired his friend's courage. Schilling persisted in handing him copies of St John's Gospel. The word "saint" galled Jack. The last thing he aspired to be was a saint. After the two-week camp, however, Jack stopped tearing up the Gospels and finally sat down to read one.

"How about playing a trombone solo at a gospel meeting over in Brooklyn?" Curious and wanting to do a favor for George Schilling, Wyrtzen accepted the invitation, quickly memorized a hymn, and showed up. He performed and then listened. The religious jargon—"new birth," "personal salvation," "trusting in Christ"—irritated him. And then the preacher stepped forward. Unlike the gentle tones of the liberal ministers of his youth, this man pounded out a message of judgment and hell. "Obviously the 'lake of fire' was a real place to this revivalist, but could this mean heaven was also real?" The thought disturbed Wyrtzen. The pious talk and the scare tactics angered him, however. He left.

Alone in the darkness of his bedroom, and unable to evade the conviction of the Holy Spirit, he confessed "I'm angry—angry because I'm proud and afraid. Does Jesus love me like it says in the Gospel of John? Maybe He did die for me." Jack Wyrtzen slipped from his bed to his knees, and was born into the family of God in the fall of 1932.

The next morning George Schilling called to apologize. "Jack, I'm sorry about last night. The guy came on strong!" "Yeah," Wyrtzen responded, "when I got home I got saved!" For several months, only George Schilling knew of the conversion. Wyrtzen followed his friend's example of daily Bible study and prayer, practicing what was to become a habit throughout his life.

"Honey—I'm saved!"

Jack Wyrtzen had good reasons to remain silent. His dance band, known as the Silver Moon Serenaders, played at prestigious places. His girlfriend, Marge, known among his friends as the "Fifth Avenue Belle," could hardly be enthused about his conversion. Through the winter and spring he kept his secret. In July, however, he received a letter, "Honey, I'm saved and I want you to be saved. But don't get saved until I get home because I want to save you. Love, Marge."

Jack responded instantly, with a telegram, "Dear Marge, Praise the Lord! I've been saved for the last few months but I've been afraid to tell you. I'm so thankful the Lord has saved you. Jack."

On April 18, 1936, Jack and

Evangelist Jack Wyrtzen.

Marge married in her parents' living room. The couple insisted on having one of their young gospel team members sing for the wedding over the objection of Marge's distinguished physician father. The bride won the argument, however, and George Beverly Shea, then an unknown baritone, sang for the Wyrtzens' wedding.

During the autumn of 1933, Jack Wyrtzen maintained his old lifestyle—insurance salesman by day, dance-band leader by night. With Marge, he studied the Bible, prayed, and struggled over the difference their faith should make in daily life. On the evening of December 3, he was wrestling with the verse, "Whatsoever ye do in word or deed, do all in the name of the Lord Jesus" (Col. 3:17, KJV).

"You never told me!"
After playing his trombone for the holiday dance at the Hotel Ambassador, a friend offered to save him the train ride home.

"Hear about my brother?" His friend's voice interrupted the silence as they drove across Manhattan.

"No! What about him?"

"He was killed! Head-on collision two weeks ago. Died instantly."

When the initial shock subsided, Wyrtzen found his voice and began to share with his friend how in the promises of Jesus he had found peace concerning life after death. Smoldering, his friend took his eyes off the road, and glared at Wyrtzen.

"Jack, I can't understand it. If you knew all about this heaven thing, and that hell is for real, how come you never told me or my brother about it? If my brother had known, he might have believed. He could have been in heaven right now. But you never said a thing!"

They drove home in icy silence. Down on his knees in his room, Jack prayed, "Lord, never again will someone that I know die without hearing the gospel."

Though he had never heard of George Whitefield, a legendary eighteenth-century evangelist, Wyrtzen's prayer echoed the vow made by Whitefield, "God forbid that I should travel with anybody a quarter of an hour without speaking of Christ to them."

The fervent passion of an evangelist kindled in his heart. Reaching people became his consuming purpose.

Christians Born Again
With George Schilling and two other friends, Jack created Chi Beta Alpha (Christians Born Again). They witnessed to their friends, and the group expanded to twenty-one. Convinced they were the only born again believers among millions of New Yorkers, they prepared one sermon and started preaching on street corners. When crowds multiplied, Chi Beta Alpha moved to a large Brooklyn church to conduct a three-month Sunday night series. Over two hundred people were attracted to the first Sunday-night service, and to this audience Jack delivered his one message. Twenty responded to the invitation to receive Christ. Three months later, with six hundred present, and Rev. Charles J. Woodbridge the guest speaker, fifty-five people came forward. The embryo of Word of Life began to form.

Wyrtzen's speaking schedule intensified, and by 1939 he faced a critical decision—should he leave the insurance business and go into evangelism full time? A mature, godly friend wisely counseled, "If you can do anything else, don't become a full-time preacher. But if you must preach, go ahead." Jack went forward trusting the Lord to provide for the needs of Marge and their two-year-old daughter, Mary Ann. In June 1942, three years later, taking his motto from Philippians 2:16 "holding forth the word of life" (KJV), he founded Word of Life Fellowship.

Network coverage
At the conclusion of a gospel meeting in 1940, a Christian business executive named Mortimer Bowen approached Wyrtzen. "Son, you have the gift of an evangelist. Next Tuesday morning, I want you, the quartet, and the brass trio to be at WBBC. I'll pay the bill for a half hour on the air for one year." Thus Word of Life radio began on a small Brooklyn station. Yet although the program was popular, unfortunately the station went bankrupt!

Jack Wyrtzen's inherited strong will prompted him to approach the sales offices of the powerful 5,000-watt sports station WHN. The manager greeted him with, "No religion on my station!" Two weeks later Marty Glickman, a young salesman in the office, picked up Wyrtzen's letter of inquiry. Unaware of the rejection and anxious to sell time, he contacted Wyrtzen, admired the evangelist's aggressive style, and signed him to a thirteen-week contract for a Saturday-night youth broadcast. All Wyrtzen needed was a downpayment of $1,750 and a place to meet.

The ministry team prayed, and by the first rally, a total of $1,760 came in. Old Alliance Gospel Tabernacle in Times Square was procured. Two hundred and fifty young people hardly filled the auditorium, but the program went on the air. At 7:30 p.m., October 25, 1941, the WHN announcement rang out: "From Times Square, New York, Word of Life presents Jack Wyrtzen with words of life for the youth of America."

During the first month of broadcasting, WHN increased its transmission wattage to 50,000 and the potential listening audience swelled to millions. By the third Saturday of January 1942, Gospel Tabernacle could no longer contain the crowds.

Madison Square Garden
The days before his first Madison Square Garden rally should have been filled with anticipation, but instead Jack Wyrtzen was filled with dread. A high fever attacked Don, his five-year-old son; Marge's third pregnancy was not going well;

and only two days before the meeting, the War Department informed Word of Life that no military personnel would be permitted to give testimony. These testimonies were the heart of the program. "The Victory Rally" looked like it would become "Wyrtzen's Garden Fiasco." Fear mocked faith: "Where would the $6,000 needed to cover expenses come from? How would they ever fill the twenty thousand seats. Maybe the prominent clergy in New York were right. The age of mass evangelism was dead." Helpless and desperate, Jack Wyrtzen and his team beseeched heaven.

Victory!
The day before the rally, Don's fever broke, Marge safely gave birth to Betsy Lee, and a major official in Washington lifted the restricting order—the testifying military men could appear. At 4:30 p.m., April 1, 1944, the proud new father arrived at the Garden. Masses of people were already congregated outside the Garden. By 6:30 the police urged Wyrtzen to begin. With twenty thousand jamming the stadium, another ten thousand pressed together outside in order to listen to the amplifiers blaring the message. By Word of Life's eighth anniversary, on a rainy day in June 1948, forty thousand came to Yankee Stadium to hear the gospel and celebrate. More than eleven hundred decisions for salvation were made. Jack Wyrtzen had arrived in the world of big-time evangelism.

Word of Life's mass rallies in the forties influenced the establishment of other organizations such as Youth for Christ. In

1945, Torrey Johnson of Chicago called a twenty-seven-year-old suburban preacher to become YFC's first full-time evangelist; by his 1957 New York crusade, Billy Graham had become a household name and the preeminent mass evangelist of the world.

Although Graham welcomed the help of ministers who did not necessarily agree with his theology, Jack Wyrtzen would only cooperate with those who accepted the fundamentals of the faith. When Graham asked Wyrtzen to cooperate with the liberal Protestant Council of Churches in the New York campaign, a crisis arose. Wyrtzen and Graham could not resolve the dilemma, and like Paul and Barnabas, they went separate ways but they remained close friends.

Castles in Germany
The last thing the Wyrtzens wanted was to direct a Bible conference center, yet God chose to make Christian camping the centerpiece of their ministry. With the miraculous purchase price of $25,000 for a ninety-acre island in the middle of Schroon Lake, the first camp opened for teenagers in the summer of 1947. With the purchase of the Inn in 1953 and the Ranch in 1955, Word of Life's camping ministry could meet needs from the cradle to the grave. Following the legacy of their mentor, Percy Crawford of Pinebrook, and from their own experience, Jack and Marge Wyrtzen committed the camps to proclaim the gospel, to challenge believers to dedicate themselves to personal growth in godliness, and to obey Christ's command to reach the

Word of Life rally at Madison Square Garden, New York City.

married in 1986. Since then Jack and Joan have traveled in the United States and Canada, behind the Iron Curtain, in Africa, and in every country of South America. Today, Jack Wyrtzen continues his energetic pace, ministering around the world. What enables him to endure, to conquer for Christ? Four elements stand out: (1) His focused purpose to proclaim Christ; (2) his consistent daily Bible reading and prayer; (3) his willingness to obey God; and (4) his willingness to adapt and change, even in his later years.

world. Ultimately, camps were established in Kenya, Brazil, Argentina, Germany, Hungary, Poland, and elsewhere.

Focus on the family
With the birth of Ron in 1952, Wyrtzens' family was complete. The demands of sixty thousand miles a year by car on the evangelistic circuit were too much, and Marge decided to stay home to raise her family. Like most young entrepreneurs consumed by their work, Wyrtzen had little time for the mundane but necessary tasks of caring for a family. He believed sinners went to hell unless he was out preaching. Exasperated by Marge's weak physical condition, his conviction created intense conflicts. How could she make him stay with her in the hospital when thousands waited to hear him proclaim the gospel? In the fifties and sixties, he went, but by the end of the sixties, Marge emotionally broke down. Hospitalization and loving care eventually restored her. Their last fifteen years of life together produced some of the richest and tenderest times of their marriage.

On the first day of January, 1984, Wyrtzens arrived at a friend's home for a New Year's celebration. As they walked to the door, Marge struggled for breath. Jack had to help her back into the car, but before he could turn on the ignition, she slumped over on his shoulder. He knew she was gone.

A year later on James Dobson's "Focus on the Family" radio broadcast, Jack Wyrtzen was asked about losing Marge. The independent, powerful, fundamentalist leader broke down. The silence and tears allowed a national audience to experience firsthand his tenderness, his grief, his humanity.

While struggling with his loneliness, God brought Joan Steiner into his life. They were-

Further Reading

Bollback, Harry. *The House That Jack God Built.* New York: Word of Life, 1988.

Hunter, Jack D. *Jack Wyrtzen.* New York: Simon and Schuster, 1976.

Celebrate! Fifty Faithful Years. New York: Word of Life, 1989.

Billy Graham

Pathfinder in Evangelism

O n January 16, 1991, when President George Bush ordered the United States to spearhead the Allied air strike against Iraq, Billy Graham was summoned to the White House in Washington, D.C., to pray with the president of the United States and to spend the night. Once again he was being called to minister to the spiritual needs of a world leader just as he had been asked to do throughout four decades for other American presidents, for British royalty and prime ministers, and for politicical authorities of many nations.

Throughout the past forty years this same person has been chosen repeatedly by the American public as one of its most highly esteemed men. During that time the Gallup Poll Organization has polled American adults for its annual list of the ten men in the entire world they admire most. Out of those forty surveys this man has been named an astounding thirty-two times, which is well ahead of Dwight Eisenhower and Winston Churchill, the next closest runners-up.

In November 1990, this man preached for five nights in Hong Kong. Each time he reached more people with the gospel of Christ than had ever before been contacted at one time. Beamed by satellite across Asia, this preacher's messages each reached an estimated one hundred million people in more than thirty countries.

Even in his seventies, when this evangelist speaks for Jesus, the world listens. His name is Billy Graham.

A life of achievements

For many people Billy Graham is a familiar voice on the radio or a face on the television. *The Hour of Decision* began in 1950 on 150 ABC radio stations and has continued ever since on an expanding network to an audience estimated in the tens of millions. Series of one-hour segments of various crusades have been televised several times each year from 1957 onward.

In 1951 a Graham subsidiary, World Wide Pictures, produced its first of a hundred films, *Mr. Texas*, a feature centering on the Fort Worth Crusade.

Dr. Billy Graham, evangelist.

Graham's pen has reached millions of readers through his newspaper column *My Answer*. He was also a major force in the founding of America's leading magazine of evangelical thought and news, *Christianity Today* (1955), and has written for it often. In 1958 he established the magazine *Decision*, which regularly carries his feature articles as well as news of past and future crusades. Books like *Peace with God* (1953), *Angels* (1975), and *How to Be Born Again* (1976) quickly became best-sellers.

In addition, in order to foster the spread of the gospel, Billy Graham has organized or strongly influenced a number of training and support structures. Some thousands have attended seminars at his Schools of Evangelism. The Billy Graham Center in Wheaton, Illinois (1975, evangelism resources and research, Graham archives), and the Cove near Asheville, North Carolina (1987, lay training in Bible, evangelism) have served many more.

The most important of all Graham's organizations is the Billy Graham Evangelistic Association (BGEA), formed in 1950 to coordinate and oversee his many diverse ministries.

A goal achieved

But without doubt the most impressive feature of Billy Graham's impact on the world has been his evangelistic crusades. BGEA records show that Billy Graham has personally preached more than three hundred crusades since he first began his ministry in 1937. The New York Crusade of 1957 was his longest. It lasted sixteen weeks. The attendance was

> *"My goal is to proclaim the gospel to as many people as possible and to build bridges of friendship and peace regardless of political or economic systems."*

2,357,400, and 61,148 decisions for Christ were recorded. Many other crusades have been conducted by Graham's associate evangelists.

Over the years Billy Graham has received many honors from academic, governmental, and religious groups. Through the gospel, he has brought together, and gained their respect, those from America and foreign lands, northerners and southerners, blacks and whites, men and women, Protestants and Catholics, Christians and Jews, fundamentalists and liberals, and royalty and commoners.

Billy Graham's own words give both an explanation and a commentary on his remarkable achievements. He says "My goal is to proclaim the gospel to as many people as possible and to build bridges of friendship and peace regardless of political or economic systems."

A farm lad

But who is the man behind the voice on the radio and the face on the television? William Franklin Graham, Jr., was born on a dairy farm near Charlotte, North Carolina, on November 7,

THE LIFE OF

Billy Graham

1918	Born in Charlotte, N.C.
1934	Commitment to Christ as Savior
1937–40	Studies at Florida Bible Institute
1937	Commitment to Christ as Lord; commitment to preach
1938	Baptism by immersion
1939	Ordained a Southern Baptist minister
1943	Graduates from Wheaton College Marries Ruth Bell
1945	Full-time evangelist with Youth for Christ
1949	Commitment to biblical authority Los Angeles Crusade
1950	Beginning of *Hour of Decision* Billy Graham Evangelistic Association incorporated
1951	Beginnings of TV ministry
1953	Publishes first book, *Peace with God*
1954	London Crusade brings international fame
1960	Founds *Decision* magazine
1974	Lausanne Congress for World Evangelization Speaks to largest crowd ever in Seoul, Korea; 2,700,000 people present
1982	Preaches in USSR (again in 1984)
1983,1986	Convenes Amsterdam congress for itinerant evangelists
1990	Hong Kong Crusade reaches 500,000,000

1918. His ancestors had been residents of the Carolinas since pre-Revolutionary days. His family life was a happy one, with loving, godly parents and three younger siblings. His grandfathers gave the family three legacies: Scots-Irish blood, Presbyterian faith, and strong loyalty to the South—they both had fought for the Confederacy in the Civil War.

Billy Graham's parents were both faithful members of the

Associate Reformed Presbyterian Church. Though the house commonly rang with laughter, the solemnity of daily Bible reading and prayer nurtured a serious, purposeful view of life. Billy Graham's parents prayed that he would live for God and perhaps one day become a preacher of the Word. When he was ten years old he was required to memorize the Westminster *Shorter Catechism*. Thus, years before he became a Christian, he learned the essential doctrines of the faith and was rooted in the sovereignty and security of God.

His father was one of a number of Charlotte Christians who were burdened for the salvation of their families and friends. They arranged for meetings with evangelist Mordecai Ham. His soul-stirring preaching brought Billy Graham under conviction of sin. In his seventeenth year Graham, destined to be soul-winner extraordinare, was himself born again.

A number of friends influenced Billy Graham in his youth. He enjoyed farm life and was often up at 3:00 a.m. to help milk the twenty-five cows. A black foreman named Reese Brown provided both verbal counsel and a daily model for Christian living. No doubt this relationship contributed to Graham's later hatred of racial prejudice and segregation.

Grady Wilson was Graham's boyhood companion. They were saved side by side the same night. Of the two, Grady Wilson started preaching first, and he urged Graham to become an evangelist. Later he became Graham's first associate evangelist, a bond that continued for forty years until Wilson's death in 1987.

Christ shall have all

Three other friends were to play important roles in Graham's life at Bible school and college. During his brief experience as a student at Bob Jones College in

Possibly the world's biggest evangelistic meeting, at Seoul, South Korea in 1974, addressed by Billy Graham.

Tennessee and during his three years at Florida Bible Institute, Graham's friend, roommate and confidant was Wendell Phillips. It was he who had encouraged Graham to become a student at the Institute, and he who had comforted him through a disappointing romance. When the girl whom he was courting chose someone else, Graham wrote to Phillips: "I have settled it once and for all with the Lord. No girl or friend or anything shall ever come first in my life. I have resolved that the Lord Jesus Christ shall have all of me. I care not what the future holds. I have determined to follow Him at any cost."

The dean of the Institute, John R. Minder, also became Graham's friend. He served him as a spiritual adviser and preaching coach, available to him at all hours of the day or night. "If Dean Minder hadn't taken a hand in my life, I'm not sure where I'd be or what I'd be doing," says Graham.

During Graham's time in Florida relatives of V. Raymond Edman, professor at Wheaton College, Wheaton, Illinois, got to know him. Their recommendation regarding the student's preaching ability and Christian character prompted Dr. Edman to arrange for him to attend Wheaton. By the time Graham

graduated three years later, Edman had become the college president and Graham's fast friend. His wise counsel greatly benefited Graham until Edman's death in 1967.

Graham met his future wife, Ruth Bell, at Wheaton College. She grew up in China, where her parents were Southern Presbyterian missionaries. She was an unusually beautiful woman, popular, and a devoted Christian. That she accepted Graham's proposal of marriage said much because her ideals for a marriage partner were high. In her eyes he measured up to these standards. Graham often says, "The Lord certainly knew

what He was doing when He chose her for my wife and number one adviser."

During and shortly after his student years, Billy Graham was active in numerous ministries. None of these were to be his life work, but each would contribute to his growth and effectiveness. While at the school in Florida he began preaching on street corners, at rescue missions and at small churches. Much of this early preaching was in fellowship with the Southern Baptist Convention, which in time came to be his lifelong denomination. Convinced, through his Baptist associations, of believer's baptism he was himself immersed, and was later ordained in the Baptist ministry.

Songs in the Night

Billy Graham became pastor of United Gospel Tabernacle for a short time while studying at Wheaton. Upon graduation he pastored for a year in Western Springs Baptist Church in a Chicago suburb. He spoke on a local weekly radio broadcast *Songs in the Night.* Thus he gained the pastoral perspective and the media experience that facilitated his later involvement with thousands of pastors and broadcasters.

After his brief pastorates Billy Graham joined Torrey Johnson in establishing and extending a new ministry called Youth For Christ (YFC). For four years he traveled in America, Canada, and Europe preaching at rallies and organizing YFC chapters. At the same time he was unwittingly creating personal and group alliances for his future ministry through his personal winsomeness, physical attrac-

tiveness, dynamic delivery, and vital spirituality.

In 1947 Graham reluctantly agreed to become president of Northwestern Schools in Minneapolis, a role which he was to fill until he resigned in 1952. Though short-lived, Graham's college presidency gave him a lasting legacy: valuable training in administration, finance, promotion, and teamwork. It also resulted in several personnel additions to his later evangelistic organization and in the selection of Minneapolis as the home base for the BGEA. His call and his commitment to evangelism were strong and continued to intensify. Then in 1949 Graham suddenly gained national prominence through the Los Angeles Crusade.

Is he genuine?

Billy Graham has not led a charmed, trouble-free life. But his adversities make his ministry all the more remarkable and inspiring.

Among the more obvious challenges that Graham has had to overcome are criticisms from various directions. Early on, some critics wondered if he practiced what he preached. As a reporter once put it: "One of Billy Graham's drawbacks is his appearance. Tall, handsome, athletic, he has all the physical attributes and charm of a potential film star—a glamour boy in fact. The question is at once asked: 'Is he genuine?'"

First in 1950, then in 1977, Graham had to field allegations of financial irregularities. Suspicious critics attempted to cast Billy Graham in an Elmer Gantry mold. When investigative reporters learned about a trust that had been established

quietly in the seventies in order to further evangelism worldwide—the World Evangelism and Christian Education Fund—some insinuated sinister implications. But Graham's immediate offensive (radio broadcast, press conference, regular published accounting reports) made the facts self-evident, and the charges collapsed. Graham's words to his BGEA team sum up his attitude: "There are many people who read the Bible from cover to cover and do not have integrity or holiness. We must have both."

Graham's principle of cooperative evangelism has been the source of severe and recurrent criticism. From the beginning of his large campaigns, he welcomed the help of church officials who themselves were not evangelical.

Fundamentalist?

Billy Graham has repeatedly tried to clarify his own theological position and his view of gospel outreach to all people and churches. On the one hand although Graham vigorously professes his faith in fundamentalist doctrines—he was, after all, educated in fundamentalist circles. But on the other hand, he says, "If by fundamentalist you mean 'narrow,' 'bigoted,' 'prejudiced,' 'extremist,' 'emotional,' 'snake handler,' 'without social conscience'—then I am definitely not a fundamentalist." His comments, made at the opening of the All-Scotland Crusade, reveal Billy Graham's goodwill and commitment to all fellowships: "I am here to serve the church, whether it be a humble Brethren assembly or the congregation of this ancient cathedral."

About liberal people serving on crusade committees Graham observes, "If they want to come and endorse what I am saying, thank God!" But he does not use doctrinal compromise to enlist liberals: "I will never go anywhere where there are strings on my message. I ask all to attend and cooperate who wish to, regardless of what identification they may have. Who serves on what committee seems to me to be rather incidental. It is what is proclaimed from the platform that counts."

American and foreign politics have occasionally created their own challenges for Graham's ministry. Riots in Bombay in 1956 and the denial of his visa for Poland in 1966 forced the postponement or cancellation of meetings. Then the Watergate scandal threatened to tarnish Graham's reputation because he enjoyed close friendship with President Richard Nixon. Billy Graham reaffirmed his interest in political matters, his intention to remain publicly neutral in party conflicts, and his opposition to wrongdoing in every area of life. But he did not break off his friendship with the beleaguered president.

Graham and race

Some of the most explosive challenges Billy Graham faced in his early national ministry were racial segregation and ethnic hatred. He was inwardly repulsed—"burned inwardly" is the way Graham puts it—by racial discrimination, which so clearly contradicts the gospel. Preoccupied by the logistics and stresses of his early ministry, Graham initially allowed existing social customs to go unchallenged. However, in early 1953,

Billy Graham in a domestic setting.

more than a year before the U.S. Supreme Court decision that struck down the separate-but-equal doctrine and more than a decade before the Civil Rights Act, he preached at Chattanooga, Tennessee, in the first deliberately integrated crusade held in any southern city. Graham described his thinking in these words: "I had become convinced in my own heart that segregation in religious meetings was wrong. Not only was it against the dignity of the Negro, but it was a sin against God."

Just as real as the more obvious external adversities in his

ministry were internal problems with which Graham wrestled. There were occasions when he suffered grave doubts about his abilities to live for God or preach His Word. He faced temptations to accept alluring career opportunities such as Fuller Brush leadership, professional baseball, the military chaplaincy, social action, film acting, politics, and, of course, the pastorate, youth evangelism,and college administration. To all his doubts and diversions Graham's answer has always been, "I am an evangelist for the same reason the Apostle Paul

Billy Graham's 1949 Los Angeles Crusade.

was: 'Woe is unto me, if I preach not the gospel'" (2 Cor. 9:16, KJV).

Judging by the craggy good looks of this seventy-two year old man, one would never guess that Billy Graham's most recurring adversity has been poor health. Through the years he has suffered from common ailments like fevers, the flu, heat prostration, and exhaustion. In addition he has had bouts with mumps, insomnia, high blood pressure, kidney stones, eye trouble, an infected salivary gland, heart valve malfunction, prostatitis, pneumonia, spinal pain, and thrombophlebitis. Although he takes routine care of himself through exercise and diet, he also schedules a thorough physical examination once each year at Mayo Clinic in Minnesota. At times he could have chosen the easier way, which would surely have been

to escape from the pressures of evangelism and retire to his mountaintop in North Carolina. Billy Graham did not do this.

The Lord's doing

Graham has all the qualities generally associated with a nice person: friendliness, kindness, reliability, stability, and so forth. But beyond these traits that some seem to manifest from birth, this man possesses other qualities that only adorn those who are teachable and self-disciplined—qualities that distinguish a godly person.

Billy Graham is a man of faith, prayer, and thanksgiving. The man who as a student once walked and prayed in the Florida bush an hour each day now prays as naturally as he breathes, whether for a pressured moment or an entire day. And when great blessings come, he loves to quote Psalm 118:23,

"This is the Lord's doing; it is marvelous in our eyes" (KJV).

Humility—unaffected, spontaneous, genuine—is another trait of the evangelist. About his own life he has said, "I am not the holy, righteous prophet of God that many people think I am. I share with Wesley the feeling of my own inadequacy and sinfulness constantly. I am often amazed that God can use me at all." When talking of his mental and theological abilities, the man who long ago canceled his application to chaplaincy training at Harvard acknowledges, "I'm no great intellectual. The Bible has been my Harvard and Yale. If God should take His hands off my life my lips would turn to clay."

In 1949 when he first realized he was famous he said something that still characterizes his attitude about his preaching: "I feel so undeserving of all the Spirit has done, because the work has been God's, not man's. I want no credit or glory. I want the Lord Jesus to have it all."

Commitments

As impressive as Billy Graham's virtues are, one factor above the rest explains the direction and impact of his life: commitment. When confronted with the truth and claims of Christ, Graham made certain decisions—four in particular—that account for both the purity and power of his ministry.

First, in his teen years at home, he decided to receive Christ as his savior.

Second, as a Florida student, he surrendered to the lordship of Christ in every area of his life: "I have resolved that the Lord Jesus Christ shall have all of me." As a direct consequence

"The Bible has been my Harvard and Yale. If God should take His hands off my life my lips would turn to clay."

of this commitment Graham has made it a point to ask the Holy Spirit's help in guarding his thought life, as he believes that spiritual power requires personal purity.

Third, again in Florida, Graham agreed to a deep-felt call to preach. In some ways like Moses before him, he had argued with the Lord that he could not preach, could not learn to preach, that he did not want to preach, and would not be invited to preach. At last, past midnight, while walking beside the eighteenth hole of a nearby golf course, he said, "All right, Lord, if you want me you've got me." According to one account, on that very night he wrote a one sentence letter to his parents: "Dear Mother and Dad: I feel that God has called me to be a preacher." By God's grace, the world, yet unaware, had just received an evangelist.

Fourth, in 1949, Graham took his stand for the total authority and reliability of the Bible. His own inner questions, as well as the criticisms of others, had raised in him some doubts about the Scriptures. These misgivings were profoundly upsetting for him. This spiritual crisis was the reason for an ineffective crusade in Altoona, Pennsylvania. Grady Wilson called Altoona "the greatest flop we've ever had

anywhere." A short time later, while Graham was at Forest Home conference grounds in California, he did some intense soul-searching and late one night, alone in the woods, broke through the problem. He recalls his words: "Oh, God, I cannot prove certain things. I cannot answer some of the questions, but I accept this Book by faith as the Word of God." One month later the Los Angeles Crusade began.

Graham looks to his future with these words of commitment and hope: "I intend to keep on going, preaching the gospel, writing the gospel, as long as I have any breath. I hope my last word as I am dying—whether by a bullet wound, by cancer, a heart attack, or a stroke—I hope my dying word will be *Jesus*."

Further Reading

Frady, Marshall. *Billy Graham: A Parable of American Righteousness*. Boston: Little, Brown, 1979.

Lockard, David. *The Unheard Billy Graham*. Waco, Tex.: Word, 1971.

Pollock, John. *Billy Graham: The Authorized Biography*. New York: McGraw-Hill, 1966.

_____. *Billy Graham: Evangelist to the World*. New York: Harper & Row, 1979.

Luis Palau—Evangelist
Calling Nations to Christ

A university professor challenged Luis Palau, "How can you go to country after country, where people have so many economic and social problems, and preach about the resurrected Christ? Can't you do something practical for them?"

The international evangelist replied, "There isn't a better way to help them." For Luis Palau, the professor's question immediately brought back memories of his own upbringing in Argentina, South America, which was under a dictatorship. His family had been in poverty for several years after people unjustly took advantage of his widowed mother.

The question also brought back memories of his dream, as a young man, of becoming a lawyer, of changing the world, and of making South America a decent place for troubled, poor people to live without getting walked on. Then, slowly, came the realization that even the best he could do as a lawyer would not be enough.

Discipled by both British and American missionaries, Luis Palau became convinced that "the people of this world create the problems of this world. If we can lead them to Christ, we will create a climate for other positive, practical changes to take place." In Palau's heart grew an intense desire to become an evangelist—an ambassador for Jesus Christ to the nations.

Argentina
Palau is a third-generation transplanted European who trusted Jesus Christ and who, as an Argentine lad, came to the United States to take an intensive one-year graduate course in Bible, and now is an evangelist to the world.

Equally at ease in English and Spanish, Luis Palau commands audiences' attention wherever he goes. His solidly biblical, yet practical messages hit home in the minds and hearts of listeners.

"Sometimes it seems I have been preaching all my life," Palau states. "Actually, although I started preaching in Argentina as a teenager, it really wasn't until I was in my thirties that God opened the door for me to pursue full-time mass evangelism."

That door did not open until several years after Palau had discovered what he calls "the most important lesson I've ever learned." Although Palau had trusted Jesus Christ at the age of twelve and dedicated his life to Christ at age seventeen, he went through an intense period of spiritual struggle when he was a young man.

For Palau, the struggle came to a head several months after he had arrived in the U.S.A. at the insistence of Ray Stedman. "The first two months, I lived in his home. I was argumentative and wanted to discuss theology and doctrine for hours. I had come to learn, but maybe I wasn't ready to admit I didn't have all the answers. Ray and Elaine and their four daughters were so patient and understanding. Their harmony pervaded the place, despite the fiery Latin who had invaded their home."

After serving a brief pastoral internship that summer under Stedman at Peninsula Bible Church, Palo Alto, California, Palau enrolled in the graduate course at Multnomah School of the Bible. By the end of his first semester at Multnomah, dedicated as he was, Palau was on the verge of giving up on the Christian life.

The problem was not that Palau saw any lack in God,

But because I was weary of fighting and struggling and seeking on my own to persevere through sheer dedication. I was exhausted, and exhaustion can breed cynicism.... I knew the other side of life was hopeless. But there is a monumental emptiness when you know you're looking in the right place and still not finding the answer.

Any Old Bush
The answer came right before Christmas break. During a twenty-two-minute address at the chapel service held daily at Multnomah, Major Ian Thomas (founder of the Torchbearers in England) delivered his famous message, "Any Old Bush Will Do." This short message about the Christ-centered life proved

to be a tremendous answer to prayer for one very frustrated grad student from Argentina.

After hearing Thomas preach, Palau "ran back to my room and in tears fell to my knees next to my bunk. I prayed in my native Spanish, 'Lord, now I understand! The whole thing is "not I, but Christ in me." It's not what I'm going to do for You but rather what You're going to do through me.'"

For Palau, discovery of the Christ-centered life "marked the intellectual turning point in my spiritual life. The practical working out of that discovery would be lengthy and painful, but...what peace there was in

Luis Palau preaches in Trafalgar Square, London, during his Mission to London (1983–84).

"The whole thing is 'not I, but Christ in me.' It's not what I'm going to do for You but rather what You're going to do through me."

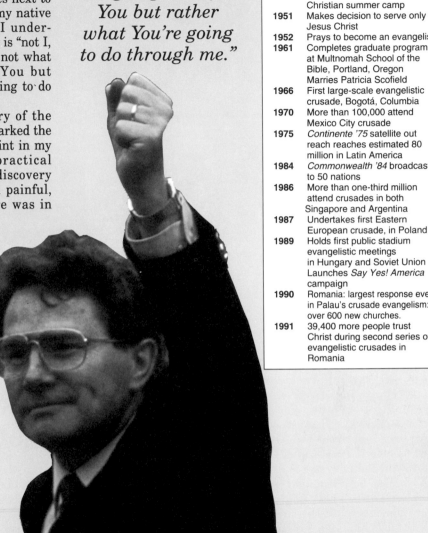

THE LIFE OF
Luis Palau

1934	Born in the province of Buenos Aires, Argentina
1947	Trusts Jesus Christ at a Christian summer camp
1951	Makes decision to serve only Jesus Christ
1952	Prays to become an evangelist
1961	Completes graduate program at Multnomah School of the Bible, Portland, Oregon Marries Patricia Scofield
1966	First large-scale evangelistic crusade, Bogotá, Columbia
1970	More than 100,000 attend Mexico City crusade
1975	*Continente '75* satellite out reach reaches estimated 80 million in Latin America
1984	*Commonwealth '84* broadcast to 50 nations
1986	More than one-third million attend crusades in both Singapore and Argentina
1987	Undertakes first Eastern European crusade, in Poland
1989	Holds first public stadium evangelistic meetings in Hungary and Soviet Union Launches *Say Yes! America* campaign
1990	Romania: largest response ever in Palau's crusade evangelism: over 600 new churches.
1991	39,400 more people trust Christ during second series of evangelistic crusades in Romania

knowing I could quit struggling" with both frustration and with fruitlessness.

I preached many of the same messages I had preached before, only now I saw fruit. People were being converted. Now I experienced power. There was authority; there was victory; there was freedom; there was joy.... The Lord changed the way I thought, the way I felt about people, the whole way I went about life.

It soon was apparent that God's hand was upon the gifted young evangelist. He and his American bride Patricia went to Cali, Colombia, as missionary-evangelists with OC International. But by the end of their first term, Palau was feeling much like a racehorse still at the starting gate. He wanted to break away, to go out on his own and hold mass evangelistic campaigns throughout the Spanish-speaking world.

"Be patient," Ray Stedman advised him. "If God is in it, it will happen."

One cold, dark afternoon in West Berlin, where Palau was participating in the World Congress on Evangelization, he received a call from two OC board members. They wanted to take a walk and have a chat.

"We walked for a long time before they got to their point," Palau remembers. Finally Dick Hillis said, "Luis, we feel you should go home on furlough in December as planned. Once your furlough is over, begin to develop your own evangelistic team with your sights set on Mexico."

For once the young evangelist was speechless.

Palau's opportunity to preach Christ to the masses came sooner than he expected. Before he

Palau preached in the USSR in 1989, before the fall of communism.

left Cali for furlough, a group of young evangelicals asked him to help them reach the capital city of Bogota with the gospel. The presidential plaza was jammed with twenty thousand people for the opening rally; three hundred of these raised their hands to indicate that they wanted to trust Jesus Christ, and during meetings over the next four nights, several hundred more trusted Christ.

A new Billy Graham

What a way to end one mission term and start looking forward to the next. On furlough, Palau and two others assigned to the new evangelistic team announced that they were ready to take Mexico for Christ. Palau's Mexico City crusade in 1970 attracted 106,000 people with 6,670 making decisions for Christ. Word soon spread of the new "Billy Graham of Latin America."

During the 1970s Palau and

his team conducted evangelistic campaigns and rallies throughout the Americas. Invitations started coming from other parts of the world also. By the early 1980s, the evangelist's ministry had taken Britain by storm and new doors were opening all around the globe.

Since then, huge crowds have packed out concert halls, arenas and stadiums to hear Palau speak, in countries as diverse as Argentina and Hong Kong, Guatemala and Hungary, Brazil and India, Indonesia and Costa Rica, Colombia and Japan, Peru and Romania, Mexico and New Zealand, Singapore and the Soviet Union, the Philippines and the United States.

The impact? Hundreds of thousands of people have come to trust Jesus Christ and have become established as disciples in local churches. Towns, cities and nations have heard a clear-cut proclamation of the Gospel.

Luis Palau takes time to talk to a little girl during one of his campaigns.

Palau's dream

"I wholeheartedly believe in one-on-one evangelism. I practice it, I teach it," says Palau. "But it can only be a complement to the greater movement of God within a nation.... You can prepare the groundwork, but eventually it's necessary to move the masses, sway public opinion, influence the thought patterns of the media. A nation will not be changed by timid methods.

My dream is that people from other nations will look at a country that is being revived and ask, "What is happening over there?" And also that they will get the answer, "A nation has been turned around, and God did it."

As I see it, we're in a last surge of evangelism in which many hundreds of thousands of new Christians are added to the fold every day. Look how many millions have been converted in just *the last 50 years! There are more Christians now, in total number and in percentage of the total world population, than ever before in history.*

I don't think the Bible teaches a defeatist philosophy. If it did, we should have given up decades ago. I am looking for the return of Jesus Christ, but until then, I will work and hope and pray for the salvation of tens of thousands and for the betterment of as many countries as possible.

To date, Luis Palau has proclaimed the good news of Jesus Christ in person to ten million people, and to many tens of millions through radio and television broadcasts in ninety-five countries.

"Luis is probably more in demand among evangelicals to preach and speak than almost any other person in the world," Billy Graham says of him. "Wherever there is an evangelical conference they try to get Luis Palau, because he is a powerful preacher. But more than that, he is an evangelist that God has given a multiplicity of gifts to, and thousands of people come to hear him every year, and other thousands are won to Christ."

Further Reading

Palau, Luis. As told to Jerry B. Jenkins. *Calling the Nations to Christ.* Chicago: Moody, 1983.

Tucker, Ruth A. "Luis Palau." In *From Jerusalem to Irian Jaya,* pp. 449–53. Grand Rapids: Zondervan, 1983.

Dr. Joon Gon Kim

Heart and Seoul

D r. Joon Gon Kim's decision to proclaim the Word began during the Korean War. During that time when Communists occupied Korea, fear and horror, torture and slaughter dominated the lives of the inhabitants. Before his very eyes, first Kim's father and then

his wife were brutally killed. He was beaten by a club several times, almost had his throat cut with a sword, and was put into a sack to be thrown into the sea from the top of a cliff—only to be miraculously spared.

It was in the midst of these trials that he discovered a new

and deeper fellowship with his Savior. He emerged from this crucible no longer the kind of man who feared men—only God. Wanting others to know Jesus as he did, Kim responded to God's call upon his life to reach Communists for Christ. Here is the fascinating story of how God has used one man in remarkable ways to reach his countrymen for Christ.

Hermit Kingdom

Viewed at dusk from a hilltop in Seoul, symbols of Korea's growing spiritual revival glow brightly with the city's lights. Tiny orange crosses, perched on church steeples or high atop iron towers, dot suburban landscapes of colorfully tiled roofs and high-rise apartments.

Sunday morning finds traffic jammed around the Christian churches in Seoul, which claim some of the largest membership rolls in the world. Church bells chime. Music from choirs in smaller neighborhood churches drifts through empty market places. A visitor does not need to look far to discover evidence that 25 percent of this Asian country claim Christianity as their faith.

But revival hasn't come to the country of 43 million people without sacrifice. In 1866 Koreans burned the ship that brought the first Protestant missionary to the Hermit Kingdom as it was docking. Although American Robert Thomas escaped the burning ship, a Korean killed him as he reached lande. Later, this killer committed his life to Christ.

During the occupation of Korea by the Japanese between 1910 and the Korean War in the 1950s, a crucible of suffering

Dr. Joon Gon Kim.

and persecution further refined the church. The Japanese made their Shinto beliefs the religion of the state. They forcibly closed the churches. In one case, the Japanese burned a church with the Korean worshipers inside.

Out of this crucible rose a church leader who helped to stimulate a spiritual revival that expanded the Christian population in Korea from 2.9 million in 1974 to more than 11 million today. Joon Gon Kim, the director and founder of Korea Campus Crusade for Christ, suffered his own personal trauma and loss before being used of God in a mighty way to stir up his country.

Communists invade

After World War II, Korea was divided into two parts when the Communists gained control of the northern state. Joon Gon Kim was studying to become a Presbyterian minister when North Korean soldiers invaded South Korea in 1950 and began murdering any civilians who disagreed with the Communist ideology.

Kim and his family, hoping to find safety, fled to his father's house on Chi-do Island off the southwestern coast of Korea. When Communist partisans cut off escape routes, the island's twenty thousand inhabitants tensely awaited a blood bath.

"The rebels began confiscating property on the island and killing people and families without trial," Kim recalls. "The zeal to kill was highly honored among them as a token of their revolutionary spirit. It was under this atmosphere that my family and I had to live."

One night at family devotions, Kim's wife Junjin prayed for each family member, asking God to prepare them for death. She asked all of them to put on the white mourning clothes that she had prepared for them.

That same morning at two o'clock the Kims awoke to harsh voices calling for "comrade Kim." The partisans seized Kim, his wife, and his father, but left Unhi, Kim's three-year-old daughter, asleep in her bed. The Kims, along with sixty others, were taken to a mountain top, lined up and, one after another, savagely beaten. Kim recalls:

"Just a stone's throw away from me, my father was struck on the head several times and fell dead. Then my wife, trying to keep back her tears, said good-bye to me and said she would see me in Heaven. Before my eyes, she was brutally killed."

Left for dead

The Communist leader beat Kim with a club and left him for dead. He regained consciousness, but later in the day was beaten two more times. Kim, while close to death, remembers his consciousness returning and then fading again. Finally, Kim regained consciousness once more and miraculously escaped.

He rushed home, grabbed his daughter and fled to the mountains. They hid for three weeks in caves along the coast, subsisting on sweet potatoes for which they scrounged during the daytime in the empty fields. When the killing spree over the island ended, two thousand lay murdered.

On one occasion, a military man was about to cut Kim's throat with a sword when a Communist woman shouted at him not to shed blood in her

THE LIFE OF
Joon Gon Kim

1924	Born March 28 on Chi-do Island, Korea
1942	Conversion
1945	First marriage (his wife was martyred during the Korean War)
1948	Graduates from Korea Presbyterian Theological Seminary
1951	Second marriage; ordained as a pastor
1957–58	Studies at Fuller Theological Seminary, California
1958–	Director and founder of Korea Campus Crusade for Christ
1966	Honorary Doctor of Literature (Chunbook National University)
1967	Initiates Korean Presidential and Congressional Prayer Breakfast
1973	Honorary Doctor of Divinity (L.A. Bible College and Seminary)
1974	Preparatory chairman for EXPLO '74
1980	Preparatory chairman for the World Evangelization Crusade
1981–89	Campus Crusade director of East Asia
1983	Honorary Doctor of Education (Sejong University, Seoul)
1984	Preparatory chairman for International Prayer Assembly (IPA)
1988–90	President of Korea Evangelical Fellowship

house. Another time, he was put into a sack to be thrown into the sea from the top of a cliff. But at that moment a message came for all militia to go to a certain spot. The two men who had been in charge of him fled and left him on the verge of death.

"All during this persecution, I was not at peace with God,"

says Joon Gon Kim. "Although I was a Christian then, I was at the bottom of human tragedy."

"Then I recalled my Savior— God heard my crying. As I looked upon my Savior on the cross, I renewed my fellowship with Him."

Forgiveness

A supernatural peace and joy replaced his anguish. His fear and hatred for the Communists vanished, and he prayed for the Communist who murdered his family.

"I learned that day, in the midst of human tragedy, to confess fear as sin," he says. "Then I could experience God's cleansing and forgiveness."

Kim's strength returned and, with his fear of the Communists gone, he took his daughter to visit the home of his enemy. Shaken by Kim's boldness, the man invited him into his house.

"As I spoke to him of salvation through Christ, he wept over his sins," Kim recalls. "We prayed together, and this man later became a faithful witness among the Communists."

The experience convinced Kim that he had been called by God to proclaim the gospel to the Communists. When United Nations soldiers later retook the island, Kim asked them to spare the lives of the Communist partisans who had killed his family. This act of mercy enabled Kim to later pastor a church in Communist-controlled territory where he won a great number of Communists to Christ.

After hostilities ended in South Korea in 1953, Kim began preaching at youth rallies to reach college students for Christ. But the response was not encouraging..

Campus Crusade

Soon realizing that he needed to be better equipped for his work, Kim traveled to the United States in order to study at Fuller Theological Seminary in Southern California. There he met Campus Crusade staff members who arranged for him to meet with Bill Bright, the founder and president of the interdenominational Campus Crusade organization.

"I saw that Campus Crusade's simple, basic message was the key that God could use to open the hearts of men," Kim says. "They talked of Jesus Christ, the new birth, the Holy Spirit, prayer, and Scripture."

Bill Bright convinced Kim to join the organization's staff, and to return to Korea to begin Campus Crusade's first overseas ministry. Kim returned to Korea in 1958 burning with a vision for his country. Shortly after his arrival, he met with forty college professors, who he trained to reach students for Christ.

In 1960, accompanied by two hundred Christian students, Kim climbed a mountain for a day of prayer, dedication, and fasting, asking God to evangelize Korea. The rest is history.

Since the late 1950s, more than 230,000 college students have become Christians through the ministry of Korea Campus Crusade for Christ. Today there are nearly a thousand full-time and associate staff at Korea Campus Crusade, who work with 19,800 students on 223 Korean college campuses. The Nazareth Brothers, a special branch of Korea Campus Crusade, begun by a group of college graduates who wanted to have ministries in their vocations, continues to influence those in the professional realm.

"Our goal is to win our whole nation for Christ, not just the campuses," Kim says. "The campus ministry is simply a means which contributes to that end."

Here's Life

Although he started with evangelizing college students, Kim organized two immense evangelistic training conferences that shaped the course of Korean church history: 323,419 delegates were attracted to EXPLO '74, and the evening meetings were attended by between 1 to 1.5 million people each night for five nights. In 1980 Here's Life South Korea drew about ten million. As the delegates went out to witness during the week, 1.3 million people responded to the invitation to receive Christ into their lives and 1.8 million indicated that they had been filled with the Holy Spirit.

Under Kim's leadership, Korea Campus Crusade has trained businessmen, military personnel, and school teachers, as well as college students, to tell others about the claims of Christ and has taught new Christians the basics of their new-found faith. The pastors of the eight largest churches in Korea have attributed the increase in their congregations to the evangelism and discipleship training received from Korea Campus Crusade.

"God has used Dr. Kim as the key person to help evangelize Korea," says Nils Becker, one of Kim's assistant's since 1968. He states that without Joon Gon Kim's ministry, the number of Christians in Korea would not have reached 25 percent of the population. And, in addition, 1.8

Dr Kim at a student summer conference in Korea in 1991.

million Korean Christians would not have been trained in how to share their faith and how to be filled with the Holy Spirit.

Transferable concepts

Kim's influence can be seen in the lives and ministries of Korean Christians everywhere. Once Bill Bright was traveling to Seoul on Korean Airlines. When the meal was served, he bowed his head to pray. When he looked up, a steward who was standing in the aisle asked, "Are you a minister?"

"No," Bright replied, "but I am a Christian." He handed the steward a *Four Spiritual Laws* booklet to identify himself.

At that point, the steward became excited and said that he was greatly influenced by Korea Campus Crusade for Christ. He was then teaching a class at his church, and was using Campus Crusade's *Ten Basic Steps* and *Transferable Concepts*. He ran to fetch his materials, which he had been studying on the plane, to show Bright.

Today, there are Korean Christians all over the world who trace their spiritual origin to Kim. Among them are students, engineers, and even maids who have gone to other countries to get jobs so that they can be missionaries. Some practically sell themselves into slavery to be servants of Christ.

Samuel Moffett, a former Presbyterian missionary to Korea and son of one of Korea's great missionary pioneers, acknowledges Kim's major role in the dramatic growth of the Korean church. "The campuses are pretty well reached now, thanks to Dr. Kim," Moffett says. "Young people are a very large part of [Korea's] Christian constituency."

"He is remarkably low-key for someone who has accomplished so much and organized such huge meetings," Moffett says. "He obviously spends a great deal of time in meditation and prayer. That's where he gets his spiritual energy. But he's not the organizing, bustling type."

While that may be true, Kim's preaching style is anything but low-key. Many Koreans know him as a man of great personal charisma. He has an eloquence with words that melts the hearts of students.

Bill Bright says, "He is truly one of the most visionary, incredibly godly, dedicated men I have ever known in my life." It was Kim's vision that inspired

Dr. Kim preaching.

coming the unified Christian nation he envisions. The proliferation of rapidly growing churches in Korean cities and the spiritual ardor of Koreans attending all-night prayer and fasting conferences suggests that Kim's dream is well on its way to becoming reality.

three thousand Koreans to go to Manila in the summer of 1990 for an international outreach designed to saturate the city with the claims of Christ. Although delegates came from 102 countries, the Korean group was the largest. At some time in the near future, Kim plans to send ten thousand students to Japan. Later he intends to send up to one hundred thousand Koreans on outreaches to other Asian countries.

No short cut
A distinctive of Kim's leadership is his devotion to prayer and fasting. "There is no shortcut for evangelism apart from prayer," Kim says. "That is the secret to the victorious life."

Although Kim is an elderly man, he still fasts, sometimes for up to forty days and particularly during times of financial hardship for the ministry or during periods of grief. (After the Korean War, he remarried and had three other daughters. He lost one of these daughters to stomach cancer in 1982.)

Many Korean Christians still faithfully follow Kim's discipline of prayer and fasting.

Kim points out that fasting is not a major biblical doctrine, but he compares it with conducting a demonstration before God. The Korean students, who have seen many political demonstrations, understand. Many follow his example.

Kim has expressed concern that, as the Koreans become more affluent, the students will become apathetic. But monthly air-raid drills, sonic booms from reconnaissance planes, and the ever-present war readiness of the North Korean Army serve as constant reminders to Koreans in the midst of their prosperity that their country could again become a crucible for suffering. The threat of a North Korean invasion is one reason many Korean Christians attend weekly all-night prayer vigils, and prayer and fasting conferences.

Kim knows from experience that only through prayer will Korea ever have a chance of be-

Further Reading
Howell, Steve, "Heart and Seoul," *Worldwide Challenge* 18, no. 1 (January/February 1991), pp. 56–59.

Kim, Joon Gon, "Give Christ the Glory," *Worldwide Impact* 1, no. 9 (September 1974), pp. 8–20.

Kyte, Vickie, "Korea's Incredible Crusade," *Worldwide Challenge* 7, no. 11 (November 1980), pp. 37–38.

Preachers

Slave/Free-Man Preacher:
John Jasper   *Samuel Hogan*

Prince of Preachers:
C. H. Spurgeon   *Arnold Dallimore*

Chicago Prophet:
A. W. Tozer   *Rosalie de Rosset*

The Doctor:
Dr. D. Martyn Lloyd-Jones   *R. B. Lanning*

Operation Everything!:
Pastor E. V. Hill   *Rupert Simms*

John Jasper

Slave/Free-Man Preacher

On July 4, 1812, John Jasper was born in Williamsburg, Virginia, under the yoke of slavery and had to endure the hatred and bitterness fostered by this institution. His mother, Nina, lived in the big house with white people and was forced into Southern white culture and manners, and his father was a well-known slave preacher in his own right. The parents passed on certain traits to their son. He liked to dress well and carry himself as a gentleman, with honor and dignity. The air of an "aristocrat" marked his bearing, some said.

In his youth John worked on a tobacco farm and later in a tobacco factory. According to his own witness, he had not yet turned his back on sin in these days.

In 1831 during a celebration on a public square, John heard a message which troubled his soul. Deeply convicted by the Holy Spirit, twenty-five days later he openly confessed his sins and united with a church. By God's grace he began to lose his hatred for those who had enslaved him and to love the unlovable.

Eight years after his conversion he became convinced that the power of the Holy Spirit had been given to him to preach the gospel. After reading what God had said to others in His Word when calling them to the ministry, Jasper accepted the call of God, believing that whom God calls, He will also qualify. He had not had the opportunity to receive a formal education; he had only been taught seven months of spelling from the *New York Speller* by a slave named William Jackson. But even with this

Slavery and the Gospel

Slavery was a horrendous institution. But many men, women, and children had no choice but to submit to it. Only by the grace of God did some survive its ravages. Slavery often caused black men and women to hate their oppressors. It also caused many to hate themselves. Some became afflicted by what we would call today a chronic inferiority complex. The Christian faith provided large numbers of blacks with hope. Ironically, a white preacher or missionary was frequently the bearer of the gospel.

The real Master

In a Richmond, Virginia, cemetery a large monument stands in memory of John Jasper, a preacher famous for delivering spellbinding funeral services. Jasper had been a slave for fifty years. He preached for twenty-four years as a slave and thirty-nine years as a free man. Even after he became a free man, he never outgrew his dialect or manners from his slavery days. Educated black preachers, the role models for the religious community, never seemed to have much respect for such a preacher, who seemed to them deficient in culture, manners, and the language of a trained pulpiteer. The testimony of other contemporaries, however, tells a different story: John Jasper was deeply beloved and esteemed as one of the greatest preachers of his day. Wherever he preached, both blacks and a good number of whites thronged to hear this man of God. They sensed the Holy Spirit's presence with him.

The inscription on the monument erected over Jasper's grave gives evidence that the former slave had no second thoughts about having served his real Master, the Lord Jesus Christ: *I have finished my work. I am waiting at the river, looking across for further orders.*

THE LIFE OF
John Jasper

1812	Born, a slave, in Williamsburg, Virginia, on July 4
1831	Converted
1839–1901	Preaches 24 years as a slave, 39 years as a free man
1901	Dies a free man (lived 50 years as a slave, 39 years as a free man)

limited education, he boldly went forth to preach the gospel.

Funeral preacher

Jasper was indeed a remarkable preacher. When he spoke about his own conversion, his audiences were transfixed. He told them in vivid verbal strokes about that conversion morning when the Lord sent him out with the good news of the kingdom. Although his step slowed, and his voice was breaking down, and he sometimes felt "awful tired," he kept telling the good news and would do so until his last breath. Jasper was especially well known as a funeral preacher. Funerals for black people were often a large community experience. When he preached at funerals, his audiences seemed to be swept into another world, some even lying prostrate on the ground in order to listen to his descriptions of the triumphant Lord in the heavens.

An observer who attended Jasper's meetings at the time was awed by his oratorical skills: "I have always liked fine speaking. Oratory has a resistless charm for me. I bow to the man who thrills me. If Jasper wasn't the soul of eloquence that day, then I know not what eloquence is. He painted scene after scene. He lifted the people to the sun and sank down to despair. He plucked them out of hard places and filled them with shouting." People from far and wide came to hear the famous preacher who possessed so much conviction of soul, so much reverence for the Bible, so much love of the Lord. Thousands wanted to know better the Christ about whom Jasper spoke with such loving and yet firm conviction and utter sincerity.

John Jasper, 1812–1901.

Jasper did face numerous difficulties during his ministry. The first night of his marriage to Elvry Weaden, a slave from Williamsburg, Virginia, Jasper's owner sent him to Richmond. He would never see his new bride again. Because the slave owner thought he might try to go north to freedom, he was never permitted to revisit Williamsburg. Months later his wife wrote a letter asking him to return. When Jasper was not allowed to do so, she decided to remarry. This was possible because no civil laws existed regarding slave marriages. Jasper's church gave clearance for him to remarry based on the fact that his wife had already remarried and no children had been born to this marriage. In 1844, John Jasper married Candice Jordon, a slave, and to this marriage were born nine children. However this marriage also ended in disappointment.

Domestic problems such as these would have destroyed the faith of many servants of God, but Jasper was an overcomer. He looked upward for his strength and believed that God's grace was sufficient. He weathered the storm.

"The Sun Do Move"

Another area of difficulty for Jasper was prompted by his beliefs regarding celestial activity. Using the Scriptures as authority, he argued that the sun moved. Many astronomers taught otherwise, following Copernicus. But Jasper believed that it did move, and this was true "according to the Scriptures."

Educated preachers were often embarrassed by Jasper's insistence on this point and what they perceived to be his mishandling of biblical text. Nonetheless, large numbers of white preachers came to hear sermons such as "The Sun Do Move" (preached perhaps 250 times), not because of Jasper's astronomical analysis, but because of the way God used him to deliver these messages. Many blacks and whites confessed Jesus Christ as Lord and Savior, even after hearing a sermon that included among other points that the sun moves.

John Jasper went from the slave house to the church house where all who heard him—white and black, rich and poor, slave and free—were touched by the power of his preaching about the Savior whom he faithfully served. Why was this? Certainly, he was a very gifted preacher, capable of enthralling his audiences with rich imagery and histrionics. But more than this, contemporaries recognized the Holy Spirit's anointing on his preaching.

Richmond Institution

When Jasper died, a writer for the *Richmond Dispatch* commented, "It is a sad coincidence that the destruction of the Jefferson Hotel and the death of the Rev. John Jasper should have fallen upon the same day. John Jasper was a Richmond Institution, as surely as was Major Ginter's fine hotel. He was a national character, and he and his philosophy were known from one end of the land to the other.... His implicit trust in the Bible and everything in it, was beautiful and impressive. He had no other lamp by which his feet were guided. He had no other science, no other philosophy. He took the Bible in its literal significance; he accepted it as the inspired word of God; he trusted it with all his heart and soul and mind.... He followed his divine calling with faithfulness, with a determination, as far as he could, to make the ways of his God known unto men, His saving health among all nations. And the Lord poured upon His servant, Jasper, 'the continual dew of His blessing.'"

Further Reading

Day, Rubard Ellsworth. *Rhapsody in Black: The Life Story of John Jasper*. Philadelphia: Judson, 1953.

Hatcher, William E. *John Jasper: The Unmatched Negro Philosopher and Preacher*. Harrisburg, Va.: Sprinkle, 1985.

C. H. Spurgeon

PRINCE OF PREACHERS

S purgeon's life abounded in blessing to such an extent that one may easily forget that it also had its bitter trials.

Charles Haddon Spurgeon, 1804–92.

Unparalleled success crowned his early labors. When he was only seventeen he filled to overflowing the church of which he

was the pastor, at nineteen he was called to a historic church in London, and at twenty-six he built the Metropolitan Tabernacle, the largest Baptist church on earth. And the divine approval continued to rest upon his efforts, as evidenced in the great number of those converted under his ministry, in the worldwide circulation of his printed sermons and his several books, and in the constant prosperity of the various enterprises he founded. Even his courting of the young woman he married seemed clothed with charm and their union was blessed with unusual happiness.

Nonetheless, his life had also its severe difficulties. Although his ministry was praised by some newspapers and admired by various preachers it was also the subject of hostile criticism in numerous editorials and many a sermon. Following the birth of

Above: Spurgeon's birthplace, Kelvedon, Essex.

Right: Spurgeon's Metropolitan Tabernacle, London .

twin sons his wife was too unwell to leave their house for fifteen years. He himself suffered from gout, and experienced not only incredible pain but also its accompanying agony of mental depression. His stand for the truth of the Scriptures finally brought on the harsh opposition of numerous former friends.

Yet amid all such trials his ministry continued in strength, and his sense of triumph in the Lord was unabated.

Puritan

Spurgeon's English boyhood was spent in an atmosphere of rich piety. Though born at Kelvedon, Essex, he was taken when an infant to the home of his grandparents and was there for six years. His grandfather, the Reverend James Spurgeon, was pastor of the Independent church in a village by the name of Stambourne, and was a man of thorough learning, of Puritan doctrine, and of unusual ability as a preacher. He possessed an unquestioning confidence in the infallibility of the Bible. His countenance showed his inward goodness, and under his care the little grandson experienced a discipline characterized by kindness.

When he was a child of only three or four, Charles spent much time digesting the meaning of the pictures in Bunyan's *Pilgrim's Progress*. When he was five or six and had learned to read, he grasped something of the teaching of this and other Puritan books. He learned that he bore a burden, the heavy burden of sin, and that it could be removed only at the foot of the cross of Jesus Christ.

His parents' home, to which he returned at the age of seven, was of similar spiritual quality. His father, though he worked in an office, was also a minister of an Independent church and a firm believer in the truth of the Scripture. His mother was a woman of spiritual fervor and he often heard her pray that God would save Charles, her strong-minded son. Through reading various books in his father's library, by the time he was ten the young boy began to realize something of the holiness of God, to know his own lost condition, and painfully to feel his need of Jesus Christ to be his Savior. This conviction was to remain upon his consciousness as time went by and

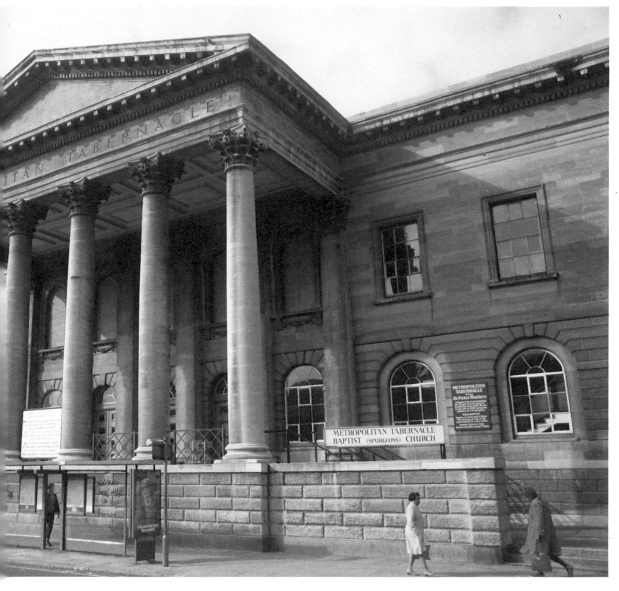

was, indeed, so severe that the depth of his longing to be saved can hardly be exaggerated.

A snowy morning

Spurgeon's account of his conversion is well known. While he was attending a small Primitive Methodist chapel one snowy Sunday morning, at the age of fifteen, he heard an unlettered layman try to preach. This man, despite his lack of ability, told the young visitor to "look to Jesus and be saved." And in that instant Charles Spurgeon looked to Christ. His burden was removed, he knew he had been made a child of God, and his joy was immeasurable.

Within weeks he preached for the first time, addressing a handful of people in a cottage. He soon preached again, and, although he was teaching school throughout the day he preached virtually every evening. When he was seventeen he was called to become pastor of the Baptist church in the village of Waterbeach. The little building soon overflowed with hearers, and he witnessed many lives transformed under his ministry.

News of his extraordinary success carried to London and

at nineteen he was invited to become pastor of the New Park Street Baptist Church, succeeding the theologian John Gill, and John Rippon, a popular preacher. But the work had gone down and a building that could seat twelve hundred housed a congregation of little more than a hundred. Under the ministry of the new young preacher it was crowded out in a few weeks and services had to be transferred to a large auditorium. In order to accommodate the crowds, Spurgeon went on to obtain the Surrey Gardens Music Hall, a building that could seat seven thousand. At the age of twenty-six he led his people in the construction of the Metropolitan Tabernacle and from that time on, Sunday by Sunday, some five thousand people crowded themselves in to hear him.

Charles Spurgeon was equally successful in his literary undertakings. His sermons began to be printed at the close of his first year in London. Every month, five appeared in print, until 1917—twenty-five years after his death—when only the wartime shortage of paper stopped publication. Circulated in all English-speaking countries, Spurgeon's sermons were translated into several foreign languages. He also published a monthly magazine, wrote a commentary in seven-volumes on the Psalms, and produced an amazing number of other books. He likewise founded a Pastors' College, an almshouse, and an orphan house, besides various schools and missions, and led in the forming of several churches.

One would feel that with such constant success Spurgeon had no difficulties. But this was far

The young Mr. and Mrs. Spurgeon.

from the case. Along with his joys he had many sorrows, and together with his blessings he met numerous trials.

Attack!

Spurgeon had been in London merely a few months when one of the city's most prominent Protestant pastors published an anonymous article in a widely circulated magazine, cruelly criticizing him. The article was subtle, for the writer, the Reverend James Wells, began by praising Spurgeon's abilities, but then went on to question whether his professed conversion was real. He warned his readers to "beware of words that are smoother than butter," of a ministry that is "a mixture of truth and error," and of "a halfway Gospel." Since arriving in London, Spurgeon had preached the great doctrines that are the essentials of Calvinism and had declared his intention of restoring Calvinism to the place it had held among the Puritans. But Wells, being a Hyper Calvinist, sought to belittle Spurgeon's bidding sinners to believe on Christ and be saved then and there. He assumed the position of a very righteous man who was condescending to correct a youth, but his spirit was that of a person whose pride was wounded in the loss of his prominence.

Wells' attack was followed by cutting remarks in several newspapers. One of them, under the title "A Clerical Poltroon" stated, "All his discourses are redolent of bad taste, are vulgar and theatrical, an insult to God and man." Also, Spurgeon was keeping company with a young woman in his congregation whom he was soon to marry, but this relationship was unknown among his people. This paper however went on to state that he announced from the pulpit that he did not want any young ladies sending him presents or "making worsted slippers for him as he was already engaged." This utterly false and silly story was soon copied by several other papers across the land, and provoked numerous letters to the editors bitterly criticizing him, although others spoke strongly in his favor.

As was constantly manifest in his preaching, Spurgeon was a highly sensitive man. Although he was deeply wounded by this treatment he made no reply of any kind, but strengthening himself in God he went on about his ministry.

Fire! Fire!

But an utter calamity awaited him. While he was awaiting the completion of his new church,

Spurgeon preaches to huge crowds in London's Crystal Palace.

the Metropolitan Tabernacle, he hired the largest auditorium in London. This was the Surrey Gardens Music Hall, which had three galleries and seated more than seven thousand. But on his first Sunday evening there, some men raised a previously planned cry of "Fire!" and "The building is falling!" Spurgeon tried to quiet the congregation but a large number made a rush for the doors, a stair rail broke, and some people fell to the floor and were trodden on. Seven lives were lost and numerous others were seriously wounded.

Spurgeon asked the people to retire in an orderly manner. He was then led out of the building, and being in a highly distraught condition he was taken to the home of one of his deacons, a quiet place in the country. For days he felt he would never preach again. In the meantime several newspapers asserted that he was to blame for the tragedy; one said he should be tried for murder. Certain Christians declared it was the judgment of God, the divine condemnation of his ministry. The catastrophe, however, left its scar on Charles Spurgeon's soul for life and an overcrowded building never failed to bring fears to his mind.

A false notion has spread abroad that Spurgeon was a chronic jokester, that people came because he gave them a good laugh. Admittedly, when he was giving the Friday afternoon lecture to the students of his Pastors' College, knowing they had been through a tense week of study, he would often allow his inner mirth to bubble to the surface. Although he spoke of the serious work of the minister he also had a free and easy time with these young men. But his labor of the Lord's Day was very different. As the time of the service approached, upon leaving his vestry he was so overwhelmed with the responsibility of preaching that his face was white and showed great strain, but by the time he reached his pulpit the blood had returned and he stood before his congregation strong in the strength of the Lord. With the sense of the holiness of God he gave out the hymns, and as he prayed he was overwhelmed with the realization that he was speaking to God. With a mighty earnestness he preached, declaring the Word of God and beseeching sinners to believe in Christ and be saved.

A frail frame
Spurgeon was unwell throughout much of his ministry. Although he began full of youthful vigor he labored to such an extent that his health soon was

drained. He preached ten times a week on the average, often in places that were far removed from London. He oversaw his Pastors' College, his orphanage and almshouses, and bore the responsibility of raising the funds to keep them all vibrant and healthy. Every Monday he edited a sermon preached the previous day to prepare it for the press, and each month he produced his magazine *The Sword and the Trowel*. He was also constantly producing books. His *Autobiography* lists seventy-eight separate volumes that he wrote besides the volumes of sermons, one appearing at the end of every year.

By the time he was thirty years of age, Spurgeon's frame began to show signs of wear. The disease known as gout had developed in his body, and as time went on he was often confined to bed, suffering great pain. He says, for instance:

It is mercy to be able to change sides when lying in bed.... Did you ever lie a week of one side? Did you ever try to turn and find yourself quite helpless? Did others lift you and by their kindness only reveal to you the miserable fact that they must lift you back again to the old position, for as bad as it was it was preferable to any other.... What a mercy I have felt to have only one knee tortured at a time.

This sad ailment continued throughout the balance of Spurgeon's life. Gout is well known for causing unbelievable depression of spirit, and this was often his experience. Moreover in later years on many a Sunday he entered his pulpit on a crutch, suffering great pain, and with his hand and foot heavily swathed in bandages. Yet he overcame his anguish sufficiently to preach, seemingly with his usual fervor and following the service to meet with the several who came to his vestry seeking spiritual counsel. Sad to say, there were people who asserted that the condition was either evidence of God's judgment or a sign of his lack of faith.

Mrs. Spurgeon also endured a long period of suffering. In 1869 she said that she experienced a crisis in her life that would mean either a restoration to health—or death. Sir James Simpson, the eminent surgeon from Scotland, came to operate and would take nothing for his professional labor. She was confined to the house from that time onward until 1884 when her husband's fiftieth birthday was celebrated at the Tabernacle, and to his great joy and that of the congregation she was able to be present. But her lengthy illness put added strain upon him.

Down-grade

The greatest trial of Spurgeon's life was caused by the entrance of skepticism among certain Baptist pastors of England. A disbelief in the truth of the Bible was increasing noticeably in all denominations throughout the latter half of his career, and by 1887 Spurgeon began to denounce it in his paper, *The Sword and the Trowel*. He conferred with the Secretary and several prominent men of the Baptist Union, and although fully gracious in his manner Spurgeon was very definite in his protest. But it was evident that unbelief had spread widely among the churches. Finally, in October of that year, 1887, he withdrew from the Baptist Union and in a unanimous vote the Tabernacle followed him. But at the next convention of the Union a motion of censure was passed upon Spurgeon, two thousand voting in the affirmative and only seven in the negative.

Spurgeon possessed a soldier's heart and, in his defense of the Scriptures he showed a militant fervor. But this strife, which was later termed the Downgrade Controversy, cost him dearly, further enfeebling his already weakened constitution and hastening his death. On January 31, 1892, while seeking health in the south of France, he was taken home by God.

Charles Spurgeon's career presents as with a magnificent example of triumphing for God whatever the trials, and going on in victory.

Further Reading

C. H. Spurgeon. *Autobiography*. 2 vols. , condensed from 4 vols. by Iain Murray. London: Banner of Truth, 1981.

Arnold Dallimore. *Spurgeon: A New Biography*. London: Banner of Truth, 1985.

Spurgeon's Sermons. *The Metropolitan Tabernacle Pulpit*. 56 vols. Pasadena, Texas: Pilgrim Publications.

A. W. Tozer

Chicago Prophet

Prophet, scholar, mystic, theologian, pastor, poet, missionary, author, editor—these are the titles given to Aiden Wilson Tozer. Yet he had humbe origins. Born April 21, 1897, in La Jose, now Newburg, Pennsylvania, he was the third of six children. As he was forced by circumstances to do the work of a hired hand on the family farm, he could only complete elementary school. However, his grandmother taught him all she knew, and he became an avid reader, a habit which persisted throughout his lifetime.

In 1912, the Tozer family moved to Akron, where Tozer worked at the Goodrich Rubber Company. There, he attended church for the first time. In 1915, just before he turned 18, Tozer was converted and transformed. While standing on a busy street corner one day, he overheard an older open-air preacher say, "If you don't know how to be saved, just call on God, saying 'Lord, be merciful to me a sinner.'" He went home and wrestled with God. After this experience, Tozer began to witness, attaching himself to street preachers and conducting neighborhood prayer meetings.

Southside preacher
Tozer's conversion not only gave him a zeal for the lost, but also awakened his intellect and softened some of his hard edges. As a young man he had a tendency to be cynical and doubtful, but Christianity refined those outlooks into gifts of insight, discernment, and critical thinking.

Aiden Tozer grew spiritually under the ministry of strong Christians, among them his mother-in-law, Ada Pfautz, whose daughter, Celia, Tozer married in 1919. Ada gave him encouragement to study and loaned him her religious library. The discipline of study bore fruit, his gifts being recognized by a Christian Missionary Alliance district superintendent. Without Bible school training, he was appointed pastor of the Alliance church in Nutter Fort, West Virginia, and ordained a year later. This appointment led to other pastorates, culminating in his greatest ministry at the Southside Alliance Church in Chicago, from 1928 to 1959.

The congregation grew under his leadership, as did Tozer's reputation. Missionary giving mushroomed, and dozens of young people, still active today in churches and missions worldwide, responded to the call to Christian service.

When one looks at Tozer's life and vision, several qualities distinguish him from the common run of preachers, editors, and

A Preacher's Goal

"Save me from the curse that lies dark across the face of the modern clergy, the curse of compromise, of imitation, of professionalism. Save me from the error of judging a church by its size, its popularity or the amount of its yearly offering. Help me to remember that I am a prophet; not a promoter, not a religious manager—but a prophet."

Ordination vow
In these words, written as part of his ordination vow in 1920, Aiden Wilson Tozer set forth the goal of his life. That he became a twentieth-century prophet seems clear when one reads the tributes of those who knew him and the memorable essays, devotionals, and editorials which remain as his legacy.

Uncompromising
Here is a man who pursued God uncompromisingly. His standard for quality in Christian preaching, writing, scholarship, church practice, and personal lifestyle was rigorous, biblical, and inspiring. His insights into twentieth-century Christianity are distinctive for their intellectual yet readable quality; they challenge the secularism with which the church at times seems comfortable.

THE LIFE OF	
A. W. Tozer	
1897	Born in Newburg, Pennsylvania
1915	Conversion
1928–59	Pastor at Southside Alliance Church, Chicago
1950	Becomes editor of *The Alliance Weekly*
1963	Dies

> *"The only book that should ever be written is one that flows up from the heart, forced out by inward pressure."*

writers. His message was marked by originality, spiritual depth, and grace in writing. People listened when he spoke; they were inspired and moved to action by what he wrote.

Tozer pledged himself to learn to think, read, and write for the sake of Christ, his own denomination, and the church universal. His lifelong love for reading contributed greatly to this end; he spent much time in second-hand bookstores of the large cities where he preached. He read theology, philosophy, history, poetry, and literature, with a special interest in the church fathers and Christian mystics. He kept a dictionary and lexicon with him to look up words and spent many hours memorizing Scripture and great poetry. He incorporated this material into his sermons, editorials, and books. He delighted in quoting Shakespeare, Emerson, and Burns, together with Wesley, Watts, and Fénelon. He believed that one's faith should not be falsely protected.

The pursuit of God

Artistic awareness led Tozer to have high standards about publishing, his own and that of others. He agreed with Solomon that "of making many books there is no end" (Eccles. 12:12, KJV). One should only write, he said, from a burdened soul. He practiced what he preached; he wrote *The Pursuit of God* in his study, praying on his knees. He said, "The only book that should ever be written is one that flows up from the heart, forced out by inward pressure." That his books came out of such personal struggle may explain their wide popularity today. They have been translated into a number of languages. In 1950, Tozer was also named the first elected editor of *The Alliance Weekly* (his denominational magazine, now *The Alliance Witness*) and became known for his editorials.

The decline of good reading among evangelicals troubled Tozer, who felt that attendance to good books could change one's character and was a privilege and an obligation. Reading poor books was a tragedy which had at its root a spiritual problem. It's not that good books are difficult to read, he wrote: it's that modern Christians resist what makes them think. Or, if they do read what is good, they do not read to obey the truth they find. Christians, especially preachers, he concluded, should read widely.

Tozer also understood the importance of knowing who he was before God. He recognized the dangers of being in Christian leadership and built into his life safeguards to protect himself against the sins which can beset the influential. The last thing he would have wanted is for someone to write his biography; praise could be dangerous. As an executive he would not agree to accept gifts. Invited to serve on many boards, he refused with one exception—membership on the Board of Managers of the Christian and Missionary Alliance, on which he remained till his death.

"What's the hurry?"

Tozer tried to avoid anything that smacked of materialism. He owned neither a car nor real estate; had no bank account, and refused any ventures that might have brought financial profit. He sometimes turned down salary increases. He felt that one reason for the absence of desire for Christ's return among Christians was that they had made themselves so comfortable in this world that there was little reason to leave it. Furthermore, he said, religion was being presented in such an entertaining way that people were asking, "What's the hurry about heaven anyway?"

He boasted that he never took a vacation; if given one, he would go off on a preaching trip. Such a life was hard on his family because he was seldom at home. If guests arrived at the house, Tozer, a loner, went outside or to the kitchen to eat by himself. Although he loved his children, six boys and one girl, their primary care was left to his wife.

Through the discipline of a lifetime of Biblical and classical learning and the relentless pursuit of God, Tozer resisted both slick professionalism and compromise. Prayer had marked his life from the time of his conversion, and was the foundation for everything he did; he preached it and he practiced it. Carrying a notebook with him, he noted requests for himself and others. His prayer was like his preaching and writing: honest, open, colorful, intense, and sometimes humorous. Often he lay on the floor, humbling himself before the Lord.

Tozer knew his strengths and weaknesses and narrowed his outreach to those things he felt most called to do. His loves were study and the pulpit, while he avoided the everyday duties such as visitation, counseling, and committee work, turning them over to his associates. More than anything else, he was a preacher. His sermons treated every aspect of Christian living. He preached the great doctrines and through the books of the Bible. And his messages were marked by the same direct, in-depth quality that was reflected in his writing.

Tozer believed that the achievment of precise wording was crucial to effective ministry and he kept a notebook of the clichés he heard other preachers use. Clichés, he said, were the enemies of religion because they bored the hearer and dulled the understanding. He used images which helped his listeners see and feel vividly, and he was not

A. W. Tozer, 1897–1963.

afraid to engage in down-to-earth humor.

The knowledge of the holy
Tozer's message was not only fresh but it was also uncompromising. He would not keep quiet for the sake of a false peace when he noted how preachers with little spiritual insight were giving their congregations a poor diet. He wrote: "We dare not be silent. Error is not silent; it is vocal and aggressive. We dare not be less so." He felt that Americans, known worldwide as an enthusiastic people who are , "always doing [their] stuff with an exaggerated

flourish," have a "low level of moral enthusiasm"; are "slow and apathetic ... in the field of personal religion." He complained that the church is no longer producing saints; rather it is in danger of making religion a form of entertainment. He wrote *The Knowledge of the Holy* in order to emphasize the attributes of God and to demonstrate what their significance is for Christian living.

By speaking in such a very direct manner, Tozer was sometimes accused of being both cynical and negative. But while he admitted that he sometimes failed to say things graciously, he also insisted, "I guess my philosophy is this: Everything is wrong until God sets it right."

Possessed by the Spirit
Other emphases of Tozer's ministry included worship ("to feel in your heart and express in some appropriate manner a humble but delightful sense of admiring awe and astonished wonder and overpowering love"), his worldwide missions, and the power of the Holy Spirit in individual lives. He also encouraged Christians not to be afraid of the Holy Spirit in spite of the extremes into

which segments of the church had fallen.

Once, when at prayer, aged nineteen, he had what he called "a mighty infusion of the Holy Ghost." After this he wrote that "nothing on the outside held any important meaning" except "to be possessed by the Spirit of the living God." He regretted that "we are turning out from the Bible schools of this country ... young men and women who know the theology of the Spirit-filled life, but do not enjoy the experience."

In 1959 Tozer felt that he had completed his work in Chicago and he accepted a call to the Avenue Road Baptist Church of the Christian and Missionary Alliance in Toronto. His reputation preceded him and the church was crowded, especially with university students. On May 12, 1963, he suffered a heart attack and died in the hospital just after midnight. Funeral services were held in Toronto and in Chicago, where he was buried. Tozer once wrote the following words:

In this day when shimmering personalities carry on the Lord's work after methods of the entertainment world it is refreshing to associate for a moment even in the pages of a book with a sincere and humble man who keeps his personality out of sight and places the emphases upon the in-working of God.

Perhaps more than any other twentieth-century Christian, Tozer asked for no praise and remained uncorrupted by fame. He felt himself happy when the glory went to God. Because his life was a testimony to his word, God has honored A. W. Tozer by allowing him to be remembered. And he remains today, a godly example, disturbing our complacency, provoking us to raise our standards, and calling us back to Christian truth as we live out our lives in a secular world.

Further Reading

Reid, Daniel G., ed. "Tozer, A. W." In *Dictionary of Christianity in America*, p. 1182. Downers Grove: InterVarsity, 1990.

Dr. D. Martyn Lloyd-Jones

The Doctor

The twentieth century has been largely a dark age for the Christian pulpit in Great Britain as it has elsewhere in the world. At the beginning of the century there were many preachers of note in British pulpits, and preaching evidently had wide appeal, for most Britons were churchgoers. But most of these preachers had long since abandoned both the theology of the Reformation and the piety of the eighteenth-century Evangelical Awakening. The "new theology" proclaimed a low view of Scripture, a high view of man, and a great faith in the inevitable progress of the human race. In its day, the new faith had seemed triumphant, but it suffered a terrible setback and lost much of its credibility in the horrific and dark ordeal of World War I. In the 1920s, people began to desert the preachers in ever growing numbers.

By the middle of the twentieth century, Christianity in Britain seemed everywhere on the retreat, with an ever smaller fraction of the population turning out for the Sunday services. Almost alone, by way of exception, stood the preacher of London's Westminster Chapel, Dr. Martyn Lloyd-Jones. Thoroughly biblical and quite old-fashioned and uncompromising both in his message and method, he drew thousands of hearers to his services in the heart of the nation's capital.

Even more impressive were the numbers who were converted under Lloyd-Jones' preaching. The effects of his ministry reached many parts of the nation and the world even before his retirement and death, and since that time books containing his sermons and lectures have gone to the ends of the earth. He was God's faithful witness in an age of apostasy and decadence; as such he was a mighty instrument. To many he was the greatest preacher of the age; no doubt he deserves to be ranked among the greatest preachers of all time.

A man sent from God

"There was a man sent from God, whose name was John" (John 1:6, KJV). The gospel writer gives this terse accounting for the ministry of that extraordinary prophet and preacher, John the Baptist. After a long silence the voice of prophecy had sounded forth once more. Here was a prophet, and more than a prophet: a mighty preacher whose words shook the people of his day and turned many back to God. The only explanation for such a ministry is that given by the evangelist: "There was a man sent from God." David Martyn Lloyd-Jones (1899–1981) was likewise a man sent from God. God raised him up in an extraordinary way and for more than fifty years honored his ministry with extraordinary success.

No other explanation for Lloyd-Jones's power as a preacher does justice to the facts. His conversion to the evangelical faith owed nothing to the moderate and modernistic religious climate in which he grew to manhood. He was called to the ministry while he stood on the threshold of a very promising career in his chosen field of medicine. He devoted himself to preaching when many were saying that the day of the pulpit was over. Finally, in an age when television is the communication medium of choice, Lloyd-Jones's ministry has reached around the world, attracting an ever-growing audience through the publication of books of his sermons and lectures in the years since his retirement and subsequent death.

Called to preach

"Preacher" is the term that best describes Lloyd-Jones. "To me the work of preaching is the highest and the greatest and the most glorious calling to which anyone can ever be called." So he believed and he acted on this conviction. From the time he began his ministry at Aberavon in 1927 until 1980 when illness at last shut him out of the pulpit,

THE LIFE OF

D. Martyn Lloyd-Jones

1899	Born December 20 in Cardiff, Wales
1914	Joins Calvinistic Methodist Chapel, Llangeitho, Wales
1921	Awarded medical degrees
1923–24	Brought to personal faith in Christ
1925	Becomes a Member of the Royal College of Physicians
1926	Finally decides to enter the ministry
1927	Marries Dr. Bethan Phillips, January 9
	Ordained to the ministry in Whitefield's Tabernacle, October 26
1939	Settles at Westminster Chapel as copastor with Dr. Campbell Morgan
	First book of sermons published, *Why Does God Allow War?*
1959	Publication of *Revival* and *The Sermon on the Mount* in 2 volumes
1968	Illness ends his ministry at Westminster Chapel, March 1
1970	Publication of his sermons on Romans
1972	Publication of his sermons on Ephesians
1980	Illness forces him to give up preaching
1981	Dies on St. David's Day, March 1

Lloyd-Jones gave himself unstintingly to preaching. When not actually in the pulpit he was preparing to preach; and when public ministry was not possible, he busied himself preparing sermons for publication. Such devotion to his calling did not prevent his freely giving time to people and organizations that called on him for help; but this involvement grew very largely out of what he was accomplishing in the pulpit of London's Westminster Chapel.

The preacher G. Campbell Morgan had spent many years building up and maintaining a large following at Westminster Chapel when he called upon Lloyd-Jones to join him in the work in 1938. Lloyd-Jones came to London after eleven years of powerful ministry in South Wales. A year of sharing the pulpit with Campbell Morgan culminated in the church extending a call to Lloyd-Jones to settle permanently. Thus a new period of ministry commenced at the beginning of September 1939. This date was also the beginning of World War II, and in fact the induction service for Lloyd-Jones scheduled for September 4 was canceled for fear of enemy air attack. This was to be the first of the many hardships and difficulties experienced during the long years of war. Under such conditions the large congregation of Campbell Morgan's time melted away to a few hundred, many of these being service personnel living in London temporarily in connection with wartime duty.

Supreme test

At the war's end, Lloyd-Jones found himself in charge—Morgan having passed away in 1945—and preaching to a very small congregation in a very large and badly dilapidated chapel. In spite of such discouragements, Lloyd-Jones rallied his convictions for a supreme test. Years were to pass before he reaped fully the fruit of his labors, but it was by his preaching alone that he built up a new congregation at "the Chapel." Throughout the 1950s and beyond his hearers numbered in the thousands. Success of this kind and on this scale was not granted to any other British preacher of that period.

It is tempting to account for it all in terms of Lloyd-Jones's nationality. Wales is renowned for its land of poetry and preaching, and in the words of his daughter, Lloyd-Jones was "a Welshman through and through." However flattering it may be to the Welsh people, to attribute the power of Lloyd-Jones's ministry to his Welshness is both superficial and misleading. Not only in content bit also in style he broke with the Welsh pulpit of his day. Pulpit histrionics were abhorrent to him, and he warmly embraced a theology that most of his Welsh colleagues attacked and rejected.

Welsh faith

Yet one important part of his Welsh background must not be overlooked, and that is the great synthesis of theology and piety that was forged under revival conditions in eighteenth–century Wales and was known as Calvinistic Methodism. Here was a marriage of Reformed theology and the intense spirituality of early Methodism. The result was a powerful religion of light and heat. Calvinism's majestic vision of the sovereign God, emphasising the depravity and utter helplessness of fallen man, mingled with Methodism's fervent preaching of repentance and regeneration. The revival swept through Wales, the result of which was that the Calvinistic Methodist Connexion (today known as the Presbyterian Church of Wales) became more or less the national church of the Welsh people.

Sadly, by the time Lloyd-Jones was born, this kind of Calvinistic Methodism had been given up in favor of a religion of which embodied respectability, chapel-going, and faith in human goodness and social progress. Martyn grew up in that tepid spiritual climate both at home and in the chapel he faithfully attended with his family and most of his neighbors.

Yet two influences began to work on him in those days and continued with him to the end of his life. One was knowledge of the Bible in Welsh and English, something fostered in the Welsh chapels of those times in spite of the unbelief that had come into the pulpits; the other was a profound acquaintance with the treasure store of hymns which are widely known and

Dr D. Martyn Lloyd-Jones.

73:27). What men needed most was the new birth, and, as he pondered upon these things, Martyn Lloyd-Jones was born again. Led by the Spirit, he soon possessed a radiant and joyful assurance of faith in Christ. His heart was now turned to the work of gospel preaching, and Martyn felt compelled to leave medicine and answer God's call to the gospel ministry.

Martyn entered into the work of a lay preacher but shortly after taking up a post at the Bethlehem Forward Movement Hall (a Calvinistic Methodist work in Sandfields, Aberavon, in South Wales), he was ordained to the ministry of his denomination. The year was 1927, and his destination was Whitefield's Tabernacle in London, afterwards destroyed

loved in Wales even today. Lloyd-Jones's sermons are sometimes faulted for their lack of illustrations; but such criticism overlooks the vast array of citations from Scripture and the hymns. These were skillfully used by the preacher both to illumine his meaning and to give force and point to his applications.

Medicine abandoned

But it was not in a chapel that Lloyd-Jones was converted. Rather it was in his study as he engaged for his superior and mentor, Lord Horder, the most renowned medical man in England at that time. The junior physician became convinced that the root of his patients' ailments ran far deeper than the purely physical, or even the psychological, level. To live apart from God is death: "Those who are far from you will perish" (Psalm

by wartime bombing. Even at that early date the name of Whitefield was connected with Lloyd-Jones, for, like Whitefield, Lloyd-Jones first won a wide hearing with his evangelistic preaching. And like the eighteenth-century revival preacher, he was saying things from the pulpit that had not been heard for a very long time. Soon Lloyd-Jones was in demand for preaching services in many parts of Wales. The results were profound; large numbers gathered to hear him, and many were converted. Best of all were blessed days of revival that came in the work at Sandfields.

A preacher's training

It has been noted that Lloyd-Jones entered the ministry without the usual seminary training. Certainly this was not because he despised education and training as such; he himself was both highly educated and thoroughly trained as a medical man. In many ways that background left its mark on him and was far from being detrimental to his ministry. His approach to preaching was very much the diagnostic method he had learned from Horder. Once in the ministry, the habit of study and research that had guided his scientific work led him into a lifelong course of theological reading and enquiry. Whatever he may have lacked by way of seminary training was more than made up in the early years of his ministry; nor did he make a mistake common to many seminary graduates. He never gave up the effort to inform and improve his mind.

He read deeply and widely. He had received the *Works of John Owen* (16 volumes) as a wedding present in 1927, and always valued Owen as the greatest of the Puritans. In 1929 he discovered the *Works of Jonathan Edwards* (2 volumes) in a used bookshop and was later to say, "I devoured these volumes and literally just read and read them. It is certainly true that they helped me more than anything else." In 1932 he came upon the works of B. B. Warfield on the new acquisitions shelf of a theological library in Toronto, the ten volumes newly published by the Oxford University Press. Warfield's blend of Bible scholarship and profound faith conquered the young preacher, and from this source came the strong, compelling doctrinal interest and the emphasis that characterized his preaching in all the years that followed.

Physician of souls

Nonetheless, it is true that he never was nor ever wanted to be an academic theologian. He studied to be a theologian of the pulpit in the manner of Edwards and the Puritans. He practiced as a physician of souls, using the pulpit as consulting room and operating theater; his instruments, the classic methods of sound rhetoric and Puritan homiletic, and his medicines the remedies prescribed in the Word of God. Beside his rigorous Calvinism stood his commitment to that vital spirituality of eighteenth-century Methodism and its stress on the work of the Holy Spirit in regeneration and sanctification. So it was that he came to embody and express the long-forgotten Calvinistic Methodism of his Welsh forbears.

The result has been that people are drawn to Lloyd-Jones's preaching for a variety of sometimes conflicting reasons. Some are drawn for intellectual reasons, and they admire his staunch Calvinism and "logic on fire." Others are attracted by his emphasis on the work of the Spirit and are eager to recruit him posthumously for the charismatic movement. Still others are perplexed and even put off by what they variously conceive as rationalism or even mysticism in Lloyd-Jones. Few, it seems, are prepared to appreciate the integration, balance, and completeness achieved by Lloyd-Jones as he drew upon Scripture and the resources of the Christian past.

A conservative Christian

From all this it is clear that Lloyd-Jones was conservative in the best sense of the term. He believed that the Lord Jesus Christ had provided His church and her ministers with both a message and a method adequate and relevant to the needs of every age or period. He found ample confirmation for this view in the history of the Christian church. The need of the hour was not to discover some new approach to meet a newly-emerged and supposedly unique contemporary situation; rather we must go back and rediscover what was given to the church at the beginning. He illustrated the point by appealing to the example of Isaac digging again the wells of water that had been dug in the days of his father Abraham, and so finding the supplies of water he needed (Genesis 26:17–19).

Such tough-minded and thorough-going conservatism put Lloyd-Jones out of sympathy, though never out of touch, with twentieth-century thought and culture and, in particular, with twentieth-century theology and preaching. He stood apart from great contemporaries such as Donald Soper and Leslie Weatherhead, and even Billy Graham, though for very different reasons in the latter's case.

Martyn Lloyd-Jones's unique positions on many issues brought him into conflict with the English evangelical establishment, which resulted in a public breach with Anglicans such as John Stott and James Packer after 1966. The occasion of this breach was the refusal of these men to heed Lloyd-Jones's appeal for evangelicals to leave their mixed and compromised denominations, and to unite in a new fellowship of evangelical churches. In their eyes he was encouraging separation and division; whereas in fact his own aim was to promote a new and vastly higher degree of evangelical unity and cooperation.

Westminster Chapel, London.

Proclamation

American readers must not imagine that Lloyd-Jones was a militant fundamentalist of the sort they are familiar with. In fact, he rebuked such tendencies whenever he had opportunity to do so. Though firmly opposed to error and fully alert to present dangers, Lloyd-Jones insisted that the preacher's calling is proclamation and instruction, and not mere diatribe or polemic. The gospel must be preached in its fullness, and the Scriptures expounded in their totality. Moreover, he did not relish his position of relative isolation in the wider church scene of his day and even among evangelicals of the period. But he accepted that isolation was the consequence of his remaining true to his principles, something he did with remarkable consistency from beginning to end.

Remarkable also is the fact that Lloyd-Jones has won even greater renown in the years since his death than he knew in his best days of active ministry. When illness brought his thirty years of ministry at Westminster Chapel to a sudden end in 1968, he took up the task of editing transcripts of his sermons for publication. By the time he died in 1981 many had appeared in print, and since that time many more and, with them, the noteworthy biography issued in two volumes by his long-time friend and colleague, Iain H. Murray. Lloyd-Jones titles currently in print will now fill a fair-sized bookshelf, and more awaits publication. Lloyd-Jones himself believed that the Lord took him out of the pulpit for this very thing, and the present demand for these books throughout the world confirms this view.

Preaching and preachers

Unique among the books of Martyn Lloyd-Jones is the volume, *Preaching and Preachers*. Not a textbook for homiletics, the book is presented rather as a sort of autobiography. The book reveals much about his spiritual outlook and experience, and shows how he went about his work and what principles guided him along the way. It is a personal and even intimate book, providing a good starting point for anyone setting out to make a thorough study of the preacher and his preaching. A most important questionwhich Lloyd-Jones asks is:

"What is the chief end of preaching? I like to think it is this. It is to give men and women a sense of God and His presence."

If success be the attainment of a stated aim, then Lloyd-Jones was a most successful man. Both those who heard him preach and those who today read these sermons in print agree that here is preaching that imparts a vivid sense of God and His majestic presence.

Devoted though he was to preaching, Lloyd-Jones was far from being one-sided as a human being. He had an immense capacity for friendship and love. His marriage to Bethan Lloyd-Jones was singularly happy, as were the close relationships he enjoyed with his children and grandchildren. He maintained close friendships across many years, and was well known for his ability to win the respect and regard of those who differed from him on issues or matters of belief or principle. In his reading and study he pursued many interests outside the realms of theology and medicine, including history, literature, politics, and current events. He enjoyed serious music, though oddly not that of J. S. Bach. His skill as a counselor brought to him many people seeking help with personal and spiritual problems. Though he kept it out of his sermons, he also had a keen sense of humor and a capacity for good fun. But the most significant fact about him was that there was no disparity between the private man and the public image. This authenticity as a man was no small part of the authority that came so naturally to him in the pulpit.

Dying well

Never was this more true than at the time when he approached his death. He had always been impressed by what John Wesley said about the early Methodists: "Our people die well." Accordingly, he was determined to die in a manner worthy of all he had preached and lived for. While disease consumed him physically by slow degrees, he seemed to grow in spiritual strength, becoming radiant at times and knowing greatly the peace of God.

In the end he bore profound witness to his faith in the power of prayer and to his conviction of things not seen. "On Thursday evening, February 26, in a shaky hand, he wrote on a scrap of paper for Bethan and the family: 'Do not pray for healing. Do not hold me back from the glory.'" On the following Lord's Day, March 1, 1981, the day known as St. David's Day, Martyn Lloyd-Jones was admitted to that glory which he had spoken of so often and for which he had been waiting so longingly at the end. The man sent from God had returned home at last, his labors ended and his mission fully accomplished.

Further Reading

Catherwood, Christopher, ed. *Martyn Lloyd-Jones: Chosen by God.* Westchester, Ill.: Crossway Books, 1986.

Eaton, Michael. *Baptism with the Spirit: the teaching of Dr. Martyn Lloyd-Jones.* London: InterVarsity, 1989.

Murray, Iain H. *David Martyn Lloyd-Jones.* Edinburgh: Banner of Truth, 1982; 1990.

Pastor E. V. Hill of Los Angeles

Operation Everything!

Radio listeners throughout America heard a man's soul in dialogue with God through the message, "My Wife's Death from a Biblical Perspective." Pastor Edward V. Hill's sermon at the funeral of his spouse, Jane, revealed the intimacy and depth of his relationship with the Lord.

This relationship began at age eleven when Edward accepted Jesus as his personal Savior. By the time of Jane's burial, he had served the Lord for over three decades, walking in harmony with Him daily. His trust in God's goodness and inscrutable wisdom compelled him to confess at the death of his wife, "The Lord has given, and the Lord has taken away. Blessed be the name of the Lord."

Again, during the funeral, with his heart convulsed with grief, Edward Hill revealed God's supernatural provision, crying out, "I am experiencing tears, and I am experiencing strength— a rare combination."

Edward Hill's biography parallels the life story of many biblical characters. It is the fascinating record of how the Lord in His grace nurtured a faithful little boy to become a remarkable man of God.

THE LIFE OF

E. V. Hill

1933	Born in Columbus, Texas
1944	Accepts Christ as Savior
1955	Graduates in Agronomy from Prairie View College, Texas Marries Jane Edna Coruthers
1961	Assumes pastorate of Mount Zion Missionary Baptist Church, Los Angeles
1970	Founds the World Christian Training Center, Los Angeles
1984	Speaks at the Dallas Republican Convention

Report for duty!

Edward V. Hill, the featured speaker at Moody Bible Institute's 1987 Pastors' Conference, approached the pulpit with the ease and confidence of a patriarch of gospel ministers. After teasing his host and fellow preachers with inimitable homespun eloquence, Pastor Hill went on to verify his credentials as one of America's most dynamic pulpiteers with his forceful sermon: "Report for Duty!" In one spontaneous motion, the normally reserved audience of pastors from across the nation responded to the message with a resounding standing ovation.

Pastor Hill's international reputation as one of today's most charismatic orators and as a trend-setting leader in urban evangelism contrasts with his humble beginning in Columbus, Texas, where he was born in 1933. He was raised by a friend of his mother in a two-room log cabin, where the family was rich in spirit although materially poor. In spite of growing up in a racially tense community characterized by hatred and discrimination, Hill accepted the Lord as his Savior in 1944 and began to know God's grace and experience His love for all mankind.

After being reared in rural San Antonio, Texas, he attended Prairie View A&M College, graduating with distinction in 1955. In the same year he married Jane Coruthers of Prairie View, Texas. The Hills have two children, Norva Rose, a practicing attorney in New York, and Edward V. Jr., a student studying for the ministry.

Hill's first pastorate was at the Mount Corinth Missionary Baptist Church, Houston, Texas, where he ministered from 1955 until 1960. Since 1961 he has been pastor of Mount Zion Missionary Baptist Church, Los Angeles. While full time in this ministry, he pursued further education at Union University of Los Angeles, graduating with a masters in psychology.

All power in His hands

E. V. Hill is committed to conservative evangelicalism, believing that all man's problems are fundamentally spiritual and that Christ is the solution to every difficulty in life. In relating his theology to the sufficiency of Jesus, he testifies, "I believe that, when they crucified Him, they stretched Him wide, and raised Him high, and dropped Him low. I believe that He was buried and that on Sunday morning He arose with all power in His hands." Though Hill has sometimes been criticized by both blacks and whites as a political turncoat, his leading role in Black Clergy for Reagan and his speech at the 1984 Dallas Republican convention, being cited as examples, Pastor Hill maintains that his preeminent allegiance is to Christ and to winning lost souls.

At Mount Zion the thrust of both his life and his ministry is firstly, to meet the spiritual needs, and secondly the survival needs of the urban poor. In an interview with Lloyd Billingsley of *Christianity Today*, Hill observes, "Those who will save the city are not the politicians, the educators, the media, the police, the businessmen or the man on the street, but the Christians."

> *"Those who will save the city are not the politicians, the educators, the media, the police, the businessmen or the man on the street, but the Christians."*
>
> **Pastor Edward V. Hill.**

diversified." In order to give context to the Gospel, he ingeniously devised "Operation Everything," a ministry employing all his parishioners, over two thousand in number, in over fifty committees specifically designed for the evangelization of South Central Los Angeles. Hill delights in sharing the soul-winning triumphs of his pimp committee, prostitute committee, alcoholics committee, gang committee, street corner committee and a number of others. Mount Zion members are intent on achieving their goal, that of overcoming every obstacle to reaching urbanites for Christ.

WCTC, established in 1970 and located in South Central Los Angeles, embodies the second aspect of Hill's evangelistic program. The target community here comprises both the impoverished and the unchurched Blacks and Hispanics.

WCTC's objective is to train blacks from neighborhood churches in the techniques of soul-winning, discipleship, and Christian living, preparing them to evangelize their blocks. Over a hundred and fifty assembly members participate in the program, studying such subjects as the person of Christ and the theology of salvation.

Fifty committees

This battle to save the city was to involve a two-fisted strategy, in which the Mount Zion Baptist Church and the World Christian Training Center (WCTC) assumed the vanguard. As Pastor Hill explains, "It is readily apparent that evangelism in the complexity of the urban situation must be

A cell on every block

When a believer, having been trained to share his faith, leads someone from his block to Christ, he submits the new Christian's name and address to headquarters. The office dispatches a mature

Christian to contact the new believer and a prayer group and Bible study is begun with him in his block. The overriding aim is to establish a cell on every block of South Central Los Angeles, enabling believers to win their neighbors to Christ street by street.

The center concerns itself not only with the spiritual lives of its contacts, but also ministers to their physical and emotional needs. Convinced that if the poor are assisted they are willing and capable of overcoming their circumstances, Hill has implemented several self-help programs with the aim of helping the unemployed to find jobs and the uneducated to attend school. He heartily believes that the inner-city poor must be told two foundational truths—"God loves you" and "You have the potential of being somebody."

Hill heads a spiritual attack on the strongholds of poverty, prejudice, and spiritual destitution not only in Watts, the site of the 1965 race riots, but throughout America and the rest of the world. As president of the STEP Foundation, a national association of Christians who fight poverty, he has expanded his agenda beyond Los Angeles to include Dallas and other cities. In concluding his message, "The Evangelist Lifts Up Jesus," delivered at the International Conference of Itinerant Evangelists in Amsterdam in 1983, Hill challenged his audience: "O the world is hungry for the Living Bread. Lift the Savior up for them to see, trust him, and do not doubt the words that he said, 'I'll draw all men unto me.'"

The Lord has graciously raised E. V. Hill from poverty and insignificance to the Board of Directors of both World Impact and the Billy Graham Evangelistic Association, to become the Consul General of Liberia, Vice President of the National Baptist Convention, and to many other honors. His first love, however, is his church in Watts, where he ministers to those who have been rejected by society as he once was.

Further Reading

Hill, E.V. "Inner-City Evangelism." *Religious Broadcasting*, October 1981, 52–53.

_____. "A Call to Prayer for Washington, D.C." *Decision*, April 1986, 15–16.

Sport &
Entertainment

C. T. Studd

Cricketing Missionary

The crowd at the Oval, the Surrey County cricket ground in London, south of the Thames, was so tense with excitement on an August day in 1882 that one spectator gnawed right the way through the handle of his umbrella. The English Test match score, to decide the series, was creeping closer to that of the triumphant Australians. Only once were the Australians beaten—by the Cambridge University team,

C. T. Studd, founder of Worldwide Evangelization Crusade.

thanks to a brilliant century (one hundred runs) by a twenty-one-year-old undergraduate, C. T. Studd, who thus became a national cricketing hero.

The England captain now put him in last, to clinch victory; but it was an error, for the tenth man was bowled before Studd had taken a single ball: England lost by eight runs.

Brilliant cricketer

During the next two years Charles Studd was a household name and the idol of schoolboys. He was reckoned the best all-round cricketer of his day, "the most brilliant member of a well-known cricketing family." The world of fashion and sport was therefore astonished when he threw it all away to become a missionary in China.

Studd had been brought up to luxury. His father was a retired planter who had made a fortune in India. He was spending this freely as a racehorse owner and hunting man, with a country mansion and a house in London, when in 1875 he was converted to Christ through D. L. Moody and became at once what C. T. Studd called "a real live play-the-game Christian." His three boys, Kynaston, George, and Charlie were at Eton and he did not cease to pray and persuade until each of them, unknown to the others, accepted Christ and wrote to his father; who wrote back—a joint letter of joy and encouragement. A few months later he died.

The boys went to Cambridge University and captained the Cambridge cricket eleven one after another. But while George and Kynaston gave a strong witness to the love of Christ, C. T. (as he was known) "was selfish and kept the knowledge all to

---

No Plaster Saint

Steamships were bringing the countries of the world closer together, and electric cables brought news fresh from distant lands to the great industrial nations of the West. In Britain and America, by 1885, a fresh surge of Christian conviction and discipleship had strengthened the churches, but in Asia, despite a few valiant missionaries, the age-old dominance of Buddha, the Hindu gods, and Islam, kept millions from the light of Christ. If these were to hear the gospel, many more dedicated men and women must leave ease and security and penetrate the unknown.

The best reservoir of reinforcements lay in the universities of the West, yet these were almost without missionary concern, except for a brief flurry of excitement nearly twenty years earlier when David Livingstone had returned from "darkest Africa."

Then C. T. Studd blazed across the colleges with a call to follow him to the unknown. Young Studd was a household name for his athletic prowess. His charm and his wealth put him on a ladder to the top of any profession he chose. And now he was about to abandon fame and fortune to bury himself in inland China for God.

After being sent home from China because of poor health, he served in India and Africa for twenty-five years and founded WEC, one of the largest mission societies in the world.

Yet C. T. Studd—one of the Cambridge Seven—was by no means a plaster saint.

---

myself. The result was that my love began to grow cold, the love of the world came in."

Rededicated

In the autumn of 1882 Kynaston Studd organized D. L. Moody's great mission to Cambridge, but C. T. was away in Australia with the English cricket team, recovering "The Ashes". When he returned, he continued his cricketing triumphs. He was tall, good looking, with black, wavy hair and a pleasant manner, but as a Christian witness he was a nonentity. Then, in

November 1883, his brother George fell desperately ill and was believed to be dying. Keeping watch by the bedside in their London home, C. T. began to realize how seduced he had been by the honor, riches and pleasures of the world. "All these things had become as nothing to my brother. He only cared about the Bible and the Lord Jesus Christ; and God taught me the same lesson."

Rededicated, Studd threw himself into Christian service. The disciplined zeal that had made him a great cricketer was switched to soul winning, for his mind worked in single tracks and whatever he did must absorb his energies to the exclusion of all else. Moody was back in London for his second campaign. Studd brought all his cricketing friends to hear him, and worked night after night in the enquiry room and spoke at subsidiary meetings. Aware of his prestige and influence, he tried to discover his life's work—but no guidance came, until frustration and impatience threw him into such an emotional tangle that his health gave way.

Only after a convalescence in the country did he realize, at a quiet drawing room meeting in September 1884, that he was still his own master, denying Christ the right to direct and control. He surrendered. Then the call came. One of his sporting friends from Cambridge, the great oarsman, S. P. Smith, had been accepted for missionary service in the little-known China Inland Mission, founded nineteen years before by Hudson Taylor. Smith took Studd to a service of farewell to a missionary returning to China, and as the missionary spoke, Studd knew that God "was leading me to China."

The sudden decision caused uproar in the Studd home. C. T. did not mind throwing up his fame; he relished the prospect of hardship; but his widowed mother was distraught at losing him. He wavered but the guidance was clear and at last his mother, tearfully but sincerely, withdrew her objection.

Smith and Studd set off on a farewell tour of universities and youth meetings in Scotland and the north of England. The effect

was astonishing. "Smith was eloquent," recalled one student many years later, "but Studd couldn't speak a bit—it was the fact of his devotion to Christ which told, and he, if anything, made the greatest impression."

The Cambridge Seven

They were joined for China by five others of social prestige, wealth, or sporting prowess: the "Cambridge Seven," as they were dubbed, shook the nation by the splendor of their sacrifice. Their farewell meeting on February 5, 1885, had a decisive influence on the growth of overseas missions, and on Christian witness in Britain.

"Dear fellow!" wrote Mrs. Studd to Hudson Taylor. "He is very erratic and needs to be with older and more consistent Christians," Stanley Smith and Charlie were, she felt, "too much of the same impulsive nature and one excites the other."

The Cambridge Seven sailed for China, and wherever they stopped they held public meetings for British and American expatriates, and in Shanghai, with the same spiritual impact as before. Then they put on Chinese clothes, with pigtails and shaven heads, and were sent up-country, though not all together because seven rather large men (and C. T.'s big feet were most un-Chinese) would arouse suspicion.

C. T. was soon irked by the drudgery of learning Chinese. On the slow journey up the Han River he and two others of the Seven put away their books, fasted, and prayed for a miracle of tongues. But Hudson Taylor deplored "such extreme views.... How many and subtle are the devices of Satan to keep the

Chinese ignorant of the gospel." He wrote firmly, and by October 1885 was relieved to learn that "Charles Studd and the others have restarted language study and seen through some of their mistakes."

Revelling in discomfort

C. T. revelled in discomfort—as if to compensate for his earlier life of luxury he amused others by refusing to sit on a chair if a backless bench was around— but the frustrations and delays of missionary life, and the niceties of Chinese etiquette, made him restless. Though he was become a fluent Chinese speaker, and did good work in difficult conditions, he alarmed the wise, experienced Hudson Taylor by "reckless" methods.

On his twenty-fifth birthday C. T. Studd came into absolute control of a considerable fortune that had been held in trust for him since his father's death. Unlike the Rich Young Ruler, he determined to give it away, and to "live by faith," a decision strengthened when he was unexpectedly sent to help missionaries in a riot-torn city where a British consul could witness the deeds of gift. He kept back a reasonable amount to provide for his wife, for he wooed and won a beautiful Irish missionary, Priscilla Stewart, in 1888, but she refused to keep it and they wrote a letter together to General Booth of the Salvation Army, giving him the remainder of the fortune.

The controversial renunciation was not approved by the Studd family. Yet when, later, C. T. and Priscilla had nothing with which to educate their four daughters, the elder Mrs. Studd gallantly sent them to the best English schools and never ceased to ensure that they did not suffer from their parents' self-imposed poverty.

Studd remained restless in the China Inland Mission, of which he was never a full member, until in 1894 his asthma (relic of an attack of typhoid) and Priscilla's heart condition made them return to England, to the sorrow of the Chinese in the inland city where they had built up a work through much suffering and hardship.

US tour

Very soon Studd was invited to tour universities in the United States, where Kynaston, his brother, was already helping Moody to fan the great Student Volunteer Missionary movement, which arose as a result of the Cambridge Seven.

In the years 1896–98 Studd passed through the American campuses like a whirlwind. He was not a natural speaker, but his pithy style, backed by the fame that he had gained as an athlete and because of the great renunciation, gave the Student Volunteers strong impetus. He refused to let Priscilla join him, and despite his broken health he spent long hours in personal counseling, scorning comforts and shaming those Christians who would not sacrifice ease or ambition for Christ.

Then he went to North India, to Tirhoot, the town and district where his father had won his fortune from indigo. Not knowing Indian languages, Studd could do little other than to exhort his relations in the indigo business, but this foray led to six years in a south Indian hill station as pastor to a church, mostly of Anglo-Indians, and to

C. T. Studd as a young cricketer.

The English cricket team which toured Australia in 1882-83. Studd is seated, with arms folded.

a ministry among British army officers and officials, including the Governor of Madras, who welcomed the great cricketer. These years were happy for his growing daughters, but when they all returned to England in 1906 Studd was sure he had not yet met his destiny.

Cannibals need missionaries

In 1908, happening to visit Liverpool as a freelance evangelist, he noticed a poster outside a hall which read: *Cannibals need Missionaries*. He went in and heard a German missionary pleading the needs of unevangelized tribes in the forests of Central Africa—pygmies and cannibals included. C. T. Studd responded at once. He rejected the verdict of doctors, who had said that he would die if he went to an equatorial climate; he resisted the pleadings of his wife and his mother that he should stay at home; and in 1910 he sailed for Africa to find a field. He travelled in the company of an Anglican Bishop among the naked tribesmen of the southern Sudan, but finally concluded that he would not be happy to work with the Church Missionary Society.

Returning to Britain C.T. teamed up with the American-based Africa Inland Mission and swept through the universities, thrilling young men with the call of Africa so that several abandoned their degrees to join him and his new Heart of Africa Mission, which had split away from the AIM almost as soon as C. T. Studd had landed in East Africa. With Alfred Buxton, a young man already engaged to one of his daughters, he set off by bicycle for the Belgian Congo, to choose an area where Christ was not named; and he was convinced that his venture was not for the Heart of Africa only, but for the world. Priscilla, who was now fully reconciled to his plans, helped him to set up a home base.

While nations were engulfed in World War I, and in the years after the Armistice, C. T. Studd exerted a remarkable sway on the African tribesmen, seeing hundreds turn away from the worship of spirits and demons, to Christ. Recruits joined him, including another son-in-law, Norman Grubb, a young war hero. In 1919 the mission had been renamed the Worldwide Evangelization Crusade and Studd was soon sending young men to find pioneer fields in other parts of the world.

Korean WEC missionaries at work in West Africa.

Soldiers of Christ

C. T. said that he did not care "a brass button" for the opinions of men. "Every true Christian is a Soldier of Christ—a hero 'par excellence'! Braver than the bravest—scorning the soft seductions of peace and her oft-repeated warnings against hardship, disease, danger, and death, whom he counts among his bosom friends." But he grew dictatorial, his own man in all matters, scorning not only "the soft seduction of peace" but the advice of his board and his colleagues. He even dismissed the Alfred Buxtons, his daughter and son-in-law, because they disagreed over a point in policy.

He began to age, having already astonished the doctors by his survival in an exhausting climate. They prescribed morphine. Determined to fight to the last he obtained, through innocent friends at home, more of the drug than his doctors realized. When the news broke, many of his home supporters deserted the mission, already rent by disputes. Priscilla came to Africa, hoping to persuade him to retire. She was shocked by his physical deterioration and sadly returned alone to England, dying in 1929. He fought on, preaching to the last, until his death at Imbambi in the Belgian Congo on July 16, 1931. Two thousand tribesmen despite pouring rain, attended his funeral.

The Worldwide Evangelization Crusade (WEC), was on the verge of collapsing. Norman Grubb pulled it together and, under God, developed it into a truly worldwide, great pioneer mission. In 1933 Grubb wrote *C. T. Studd: Cricketer and Pioneer*, which became one of the most widely read missionary lives of the twentieth century.

Whatever his defects, C. T. Studd, with his intensity and his red-hot faith, remains a supreme example of those who renounce wealth and fame for the cause of Christ.

Further Reading

Buxton, Edith. *Reluctant Missionary*. London: Lutterworth, 1968.

Grubb, Norman. *C. T. Studd: Cricketer and Pioneer*. London: Lutterworth, 1933, and many later editions.

Vincent, Eileen. *No Sacrifice too Great*. Gerrards Cross: WEC Publications, 1992.

Eric Liddell, Olympic champion.

Eric Liddell

Olympic glory—and after

Eric Liddell ascended to the very heights of world athletics, beginning to win awards for his all-around skill at rugby and general sportsmanship when he was only sixteen and still in school. He also captained the school cricket team and set a school record in the 100-yard dash. When he entered Edinburgh University in 1920, Liddell soon began running in athletic events, and playing rugby for the university and for Scotland in international matches. Before long, he had won races for both Scotland and the entire British Empire in worldwide competition.

Chariots of Fire

Among the sports figures of the 1920s, the name of Eric Liddell is one that is instantly recognized today, long after the names and exploits of others of his colleagues in athletics have been forgotten. But thanks to a major 1981 film, *Chariots of Fire,* the account of Liddell's Olympic victory at Paris in 1924 has made him a familiar personality in many households. Eric Liddell, athlete, enjoys renewed fame.

Eric Liddell the man, however, remains largely unknown. True, *Chariots of Fire* highlighted Liddell's Christian witness and convictions, from his evangelistic messages at trackside to his refusal in Paris to run the 100 meters on a Sunday, the idea of running on the Lord's day being abhorrent to him. But what did he do during the remaining twenty years of his life after winning the gold medal? And what, in fact, did he do in those twenty years *before* his Olympic success?

Eric Liddell may not have had the theological genius of a John Calvin, the literary gifts of a C. S. Lewis, the political commitments of a Jimmy Carter, or the international ministry of a Billy Graham. Yet his life deserves review, not only because of his athletic prowess, or because of his courage and steadfastness in standing by his convictions, but because it reflects radical obedience to Jesus Christ.

Triumphantly he traveled to Paris in 1924 to contend for and secure two medals: bronze for the Olympic 200 meters, and gold for the 400 meters, in which he broke a world record.

Olive wreath

Scotland loved this young man. He demonstrated on the field just the sort of determination, stamina, and honest excellence that—though perhaps not flashy—the Scots love to see in a native son. On the day of his graduation from the university, Liddell was crowned with the emblem of Olympic mastery— an olive wreath. He was also presented with a poem etched in Greek acclaiming his honor. He was literally paraded around the streets of Edinburgh to the adulation of its inhabitants.

The following year when Liddell departed for missionary service in China, he was again lauded publicly and was escorted to the train station in an elaborately decorated carriage. In China and Japan, remote from the scene of his early achievements, he continued to be asked to appear at sporting events. He was cheered by spectators who had heard about this fleet-footed foreigner from halfway around the world. On the two occasions when he returned to Britain on furlough, he again attracted crowds that proved his celebrity status. When he died, he was honored by memorial services around the globe. In the following years numerous memorial awards, foundations, and clubs have been established in his memory.

The Lord's Day

Liddell's most famous decision was at the Paris Olympics, where he refused to compete in the 100-meter race because the event was held on a Sunday. Though the 100 was thought to be his best chance for the gold, medal, Liddell found the idea of participating in sports on the Lord's Day abhorrent. And he refused to run.

His decision led the press and a majority of public opinion to criticize him roundly. He was accused of being unpatriotic (denying Scotland a chance at glory) and legalistic (taking the letter of the law to an absurd extreme). Yet, for sticking to his principles in the face of great pressure, Liddell deserved—and in the end received—the highest admiration. It was the sort of spiritual obedience that Liddell himself wrote about when he challenged all Christians:

Ask yourself: If I know something to be true, am I prepared to follow it, even though it is contrary to what I want, [or] to what I have previously held to be true? Will I follow it if it means being laughed at, if it means personal financial loss, or some kind of hardship?

Liddell's personal experience in Paris speaks loudly and clearly through these words, which he penned fifteen years later in China.

Whatever one thinks of such a strict Sabbath rule, Edinburgh University's paper, *The Student,* was respectful:

What he has thought it right to do, that he has done, looking neither to the left nor to the right, and yielding not one jot or tittle of principle either to court applause or to placate criticism.... Devoted to his principles, he is [nevertheless] without a touch of Pharisaism.

"He that honours me"

In refusing to run the 100, Eric Liddell steadfastly obeyed what he believed his Master asked of him, even if his more immediate masters might scold. One of the men who assisted Eric's trainer slipped him a note just before the 400-meter race: "In the old book it says, 'He that honours me, I will honour.' Wishing you the best of success always."

The man was right, and, providentially, Liddell won the gold medal for the 400 rather than for the 100. Even if he had not—particularly since he was not expected to—his obedience was exemplary. This larger-than-life incident offers an exception in Liddell's life—not because he rarely obeyed, but because he rarely obeyed so spectacularly. The remainder of Liddell's life presents a steady portrait of decisions based on obedience to Christ.

Eric Liddell's career cannot be separated from his Christianity: If he could not be a Christian runner, then he did not want to be a runner at all, and he never allowed himself the false luxury of saying that his Christianity was a private affair that he need not live out in everything he did.

Anecdotes abound concerning Liddell's Christian compassion and witness during his athletic career. One incident, recounted by a university student, tells of one occasion when a "colored student" was present who was

"He that honours me, I will honour."

spurned by his fellow athletes. But Liddell "went up to him, put his arm in his, and engaged him in a friendly conversation." His good-natured generosity to his racing opponents was also observed:

I had heard a lot about him, and now I had seen him. I came away feeling that I had witnessed a gentleman doing all that a gentleman should do. Afterwards, when I heard he had gone to China [as a missionary], *I realised that I had been watching a Christian in action.*

Unrelenting obedience

Nonetheless, dwelling on the stellar career of Eric Liddell the honored athlete is somehow missing the point of his life. For example, his world record for the 400—blistering speed at the time—has since been surpassed by nearly three seconds. More is revealed of his true stature in the simple legacy he has left: unrelenting obedience to Christ.

He continually asked: "Does this path I tread follow the Lord's will?" While he was still a student, he reached a major turning point. Having already achieved renown as a rugby player and runner, he was asked to join the Glasgow Students' Evangelistic Union, a fellowship of university students dedicated to reaching Scotland for Christ. A campaign for youths was being held in a nearby town, and the students

of G.S.E.U. thought a name like Liddell's might attract people. A young member approached Liddell for help.

In the midst of a very busy schedule, the runner glanced down momentarily. Raising his head, he surrendered himself to God's service for the sake of the lost, a decision he would later identify as a watershed in his life. His willingness to give himself unstintingly to basic urban and rural evangelism in Britain marked the opening of a new life for him. His policy, that as long as an engagement could conceivably fit into his schedule, he would not refuse to speak. Occasionally this translated into a marathon of preaching, as many as five times in a day.

The organizers of the student evangelism campaigns had been right: Liddell's name did bring people into the assembly halls. His words brought many into the fold.

China

Soon after his graduation, however, Liddell's career took a new turn. He traveled to Tientsin, in China, where he had been born of missionary parents, to teach science in the Tientsin Anglo-Chinese College (a combined elementary and high school), for what became twelve years of service. Though he gave classes in the sciences and supervised school athletic activities, the benchmark of his ministry was discipline. The classroom and athletic field were important, but as his biographer writes:

Had that been all, it would not have taken him to China; it would not have kept him on the

staff of the Anglo-Chinese college as long as it did; and it would not have justified the writing of this biography.... He was a completely dedicated disciple of Jesus Christ, and a man who could rest short of nothing but the introduction of those brought under his influence to the Savior and Master who had come to mean so much to him.

Liddell's decision to move to Tientsin to teach (a second turning point) was once again motivated by the chief concern of his life: obedience to the call to serve Christ.

Finally, a third turning point presented itself after more than ten years of teaching in China. He had married his wife, Florence, and they had begun their family of three daughters. Now he faced the decision whether to accept a call to rural evangelism near Siaochang, where the mission was short-handed. For over a year Liddell agonized over the decision. Due to the Japanese invasion, he would have to live apart from his family, in extreme danger. In 1936, he took the assignment as a definite call from the Lord. With all that he possessed, he plunged into the work.

This was no easy assignment. His mission field was located in a war zone, and he practiced the most self-sacrificing kind of compassion when on a number of occasions, Liddell ventured into the countryside to rescue wounded soldiers—whatever their nationality might be—for treatment at the mission hospital. Harboring a Chinese soldier could incur the death penalty from the Japanese. However in February 1938, he traveled by bicycle to an abandoned temple where a Chinese soldier had lain wounded for five days. Even though a Japanese force consisting of a tank and thirty-one truckloads of soldiers was only a mile away, Liddell and a Chinese helper carted this man and another wounded soldier to the hospital, three hours away.

"Be honest and straight"

The night before this incident, whilst wondering how he would react if he was confronted by the Japanese, Liddell recounts that he read Luke 16:10: "Whoever is faithful in very little is faithful also in much; and whoever is dishonest in a very little, is dishonest also in much." Liddell recorded his feelings: "It was as if God had said to me, 'Be honest and straight.'" He persisted in his mission. Armored enemy troops passed nearby, while on the road, a plane circled over Japanese units marching parallel to them a short mile away. He forged a straight course and showed the two wounded men the sort of compassion Jesus commanded for all who would call themselves his disciples.

With the declaration of war between Japan and Britain, the missionaries' risks increased. Florence and the three Liddell daughters fled to the safety of Canada in an exodus of missionaries from China. However, many decided to remain in China, Eric Liddell being one of them. All foreign missionaries were eventually gathered together and interned in a camp in Weihsien by the Japanese. Characteristically, Liddell served others energetically, teaching children and organizing athletic activities for the camp's inmates.

He totally exhausted himself. While Liddell's various labors sapped his body, an undetected brain tumor also depleted his health. As a consequence of the malignancy, he suffered bouts of depression. He interpreted his depression as a sign of faltering faith, not comprehending the physical causes of his condition. Ailing for only a a few weeks, he died in the Weihsien camp on February 21, 1945.

Liddell's consistent obedience in following Christ's leading—from the Paris Olympics to the Weihsien camp—is a wonderful challenge to Christians. Taking every opportunity to show kindness to others, to witness for Christ, or demonstrate faithfulness to God, Eric Liddell offers a compelling model for how we should live, calling himself and others to an honest life and to self-sacrifice:

Let us put ourselves before ourselves and look at ourselves. The bravest moment of a person's life is the moment when he looks at himself objectively without wincing, without complaining. [However] self-examination that does not result in action is dangerous. What am I going to do about what I see? The action called for is surrender—of ourselves to God.

Further Reading

Thomson, D. P. *Eric H. Liddell: Athlete and Missionary.* Crieff, Scotland: Research Unit, 1971.

AN ALL-OR-NOTHING GUY

F ew men have witnessed, let alone experienced, the explosion of professional football in the way that Tom Landry has. His playing career began in 1949 when, fresh out of the University of Texas at Austin, he became a member of the All-American Football Conference New York Yankees. He became a player–coach in the mid-fifties, an assistant coach soon afterwards, and he then became the youngest head coach in the National Football League in 1960 at the age of thirty-five.

Landry was the first and—for twenty-nine seasons—the only head coach of the expansion Dallas Cowboys. He saw pro football grow from being a part-time, half-year diversion to the media giant, multimillion dollar business it is today. Regarded as one of the great, innovative strategists in football history, he is a true gentleman, and a legend. Yet both the beginning and ending to his pro coaching career were most ignominious. His first team was 0–11–1, his last team 3–13, and he was fired unceremoniously when new owners took over the Cowboys.

In 1965, after five straight losing seasons, Landry saw his team break even, and begin its record twenty straight years of winning seasons. During the seventies alone he led the Cowboys to five Super Bowls.

Though Landry had become synonymous with dignity, class, and leadership, when the Cowboys began to struggle and the winning seasons ended, the press and some detractors said the modern game had passed him by. When the team was sold, the new owner brought in his own head coach, and Landry was dismissed.

The outcry from fans—even many who had themselves been negative toward him—resulted in Tom Landry Day in Dallas, April 22, 1989. This huge out-pouring of sentiment only made Landry's legend more epic.

New York Giant

At the end of the 1958 pro foot-ball season, the defensive coach of the New York Giants went back to his home in Dallas. Big-time football was just coming into its own, and most of the players and coaches still held off-season jobs in other walks of life to make ends meet.

Landry was no exception. Having had experience of living through both the Depression and World War II, one of the primary goals of his life was to provide for his wife and three children. He wanted them to have the things he had never had, especially security.

Early in 1959 a friend invited him to a breakfast where men studied the Bible. Landry had no interest, considering himself to be a moral, church-going, principled man. He rarely read the Bible and never studied it, but he was unable to think of a gracious way to decline.

He was a stoic, analytical, quiet man with a well-earned military bearing. He had calmly lived through turmoil, having lost his older brother in World War II and having himself survived thirty bombing missions. He didn't need more religion, he decided, but he still attended the breakfast with his friend.

Turning point

There he found people who took the Bible seriously and literally. He almost didn't go back. His scientific mind didn't allow him to believe everything he read, especially things miraculous and spiritual. But two passages spoke to his soul during that first discussion of the Sermon on the Mount:

Therefore I tell you, do not worry about your life, what you will eat or drink; or about your body, what you will wear. Is not life more important than food, and the body more important than clothes? Look at the birds of the air, they do not sow or reap or store away in barns; and yet your heavenly Father feeds them. Are you not much more valuable than they? Who of you by worrying can add a single hour to his life? ...

Therefore do not worry about tomorrow, for tomorrow will worry about itself. Each day has enough trouble of its own. (Matthew 6:25–27, 34)

Therefore everyone who hears these words of mine and puts

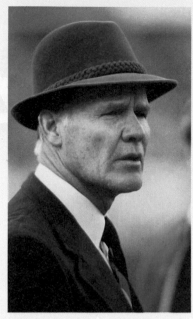

Tom Landry .

them into practice is like a wise man who built his house on the rock. The rain came down and the streams rose, and the winds blew and beat against that house; yet it did not fall, because it had its foundation on the rock. (Matthew 7:24–25)

As many others had before him, Tom Landry had seen his initial excitement over athletic and professional achievements, and even family joy fade, only to be replaced by a sense of restlessness. Because he wanted to excel and achieve, he still continued to pursue his goals, but he found himself becoming less satisfied every time.

The next level

"I wondered if that was all there was to life," he acknowledges. "And I continually asked myself if I had what it took to reach the next level."

And now there were those passages, challenging him, speaking to the very issues he

was dealing with in his life. He kept going back to the breakfasts, eager to know what else the Bible had to say about him. He focused on the key teachings of the New Testament, treating them as he would an opposing team's offense.

In his book *Tom Landry: An Autobiography* (with Gregg Lewis, 1990), he writes what he discovered:

That we've all sinned; none of us can measure up to God's standard; and our failure stands between us and God (Romans 3:23). *That God sent Jesus to take the punishment for our failure* (John 3:16). *That His salvation was a free gift for anyone who accepted it* (Romans 10:13). *That we can't do anything to earn it, we just have to believe* (Romans 5:1). *And once we come to that belief, God wants us to turn our lives over to Him and let Him direct us and provide for all our needs* (Romans 12:1–2).

Tom Landry says he realized that even though he'd been a churchgoer all his life, he had never really understood who Christ was or what He was all about. "I had always figured I was a pretty good person. Now here was the Bible saying I was as much a sinner as anyone in the world."

Landry nearly stopped going to the Bible studies once he had figured out what the Bible was saying about him and about his approach to life. "That was no time to become confused about my goals," he admits, especially now that he was understanding something that he wasn't at all sure he liked. "The Bible was saying that knowledge and good works didn't make the ultimate difference in life. Faith did."

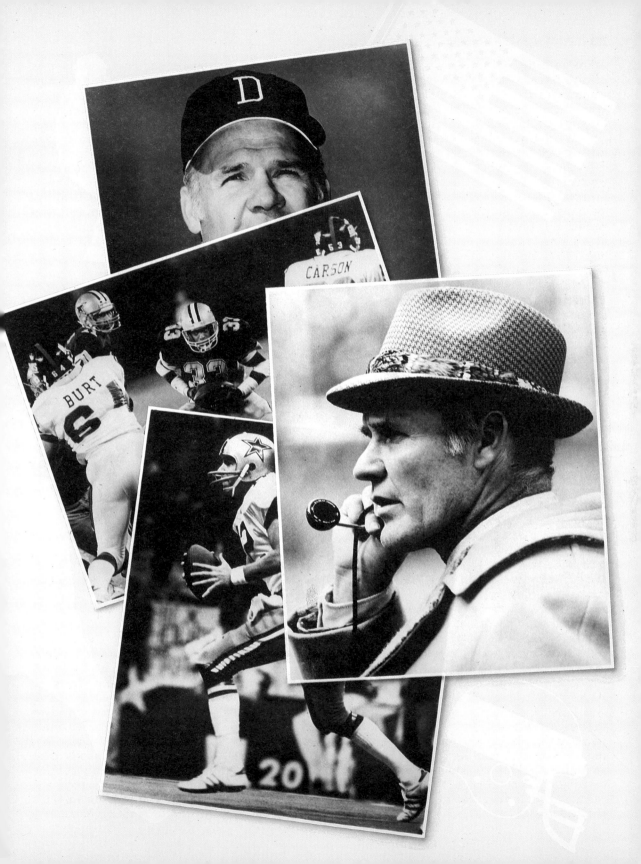

All or nothing

Always having been an all-or-nothing kind of a guy, Landry sensed that the answer to his life's frustration was in Jesus. He was attracted to Christ while stunned at the truth of his own inadequacy and sinfulness. He could neither quit going to the breakfasts, nor could be stop studying the Bible, though he wondered if Christ could really be all He claimed to be. The analytical mind of the pro football coach would not let go of these bedrock doubts.

One day, after several months of study and pursuit of truth, he realized that faith had overcome his doubts. Landry gave his life to Christ and committed himself to live for God. Although he did not notice a dramatic change in his life, and his conversion was not an emotional decision, he recalls an almost instantaneous change in his priorities. Football had been first in his life, the rudder by which he steered his family and his future. Now God came first, then his family, and then football.

With his selection as an NFL coach and the gradual but sure success of the Cowboys' franchise came fame. Landry became a familiar figure, sternly stalking the sidelines on national television, chin thrust out, arms folded, hat in place, seemingly impassive eyes studying, studying.

Colleagues, acquaintances, players and friends all attest that Landry was not as quiet and humorless, and certainly not as emotionless, as he often appeared on the field. But he certainly suffered through tough losses and a reputation as the coach of a team that "couldn't win the big ones."

> *"The Bible was saying that knowledge and good works didn't make the ultimate difference in life. Faith did."*

He had his share of problem players, bridled under the reputation as a dictatorial leader, and despite twenty consecutive seasons with winning records, found himself with three straight losing years as the eighties came to a close.

Ironically, the National Football League itself had contributed to the parity in the game. Its rules for drafting players and scheduling teams against each other are based on performance. The better you finished one year, the later you drafted and the tougher your schedule was the next. That catches up to the super teams eventually; it especially caught up to Dallas.

Out!

Ever the optimist, he followed his second worst season (1989, 3–13) knowing that, with an easier schedule and a higher draft, Dallas could begin the process of rebuilding. But it was not to be. With the sale of the team came a new owner and a new coach, and Landry was out. Just like that.

The replacing of one of football's greatest coaches ever was monumentally mishandled. Before Landry or even his boss had been told anything, the new owner was photographed in a Dallas restaurant, celebrating with the new coach. Before

Landry had even met the new owner to learn his fate, the new coach had started recruiting his assistants from other staffs.

Having been among the last to be informed, Landry was crushed by the news and told the new owner how displeased he was at the way in which it had been handled. His disappointment was personal and deep, but it only scratched the surface of emotions in Dallas when the public came to learn the truth.

No chance had been offered for Landry to step aside or for the owners, new or old, to give some form of recognition to his remarkable contributions to the game. There was no orderly transition, simply notice given and no looking back.

Getting through

Landry was forced to rest in the strength of his faith in Christ and remind himself how he had always dealt with losses. He told Bob St. John, author of *The Landry Legend: Grace Under Pressure* (Word, 1989):

Fortunately, I do recover quickly. My relationship with Christ gives me a source of power I would not have otherwise. What eats you up is fear and anxiety. God does not give us fear, but power and love and self-control. As a Christian, I know my life is in God's hands. He has a plan for me. Therefore, I never worry about tomorrow and try to keep winning and losing and the good and bad things that happen in my life in perspective. The knowledge that my life is in God's hands helps my to keep my composure or regain it in tough situations.

St. John, also a columnist for the *Dallas Morning News*, says that it is "doubtful [Landry] would have gotten through the ordeal ... if his faith had not been so strong."

The Landrys fled Dallas for a few days in California to get out of the media spotlight, but the White House was able to locate them. President Bush called with his condolences and best wishes. When they returned to Dallas there was a mountain of mail wishing them well and protesting the handling of the changing of coaches. Billboards were erected in Landry's honor and several novelty songs featured the controversy. Baylor University announced plans to name a multimillion dollar sports-medicine complex after him. Tens of thousands lined the streets of Dallas for Tom Landry Day in April 1989, thus making Landry among the most celebrated fired men in history.

Further Reading

Landry, Tom, with Gregg Lewis. *Tom Landry: An Autobiography.* New York: Zondervan and Harper Collins, 1990.

St. John, Bob. *The Landry Legend: Grace Under Pressure.* Dallas: Word, 1989.

Bobby Richardson

Yankee Hero

THE LIFE OF

Bobby Richardson

1935	Born in Sumter, South Carolina
1949	Converted
1955	Debuts as a NewYork Yankee, shortly before twentieth birthday
1956	Marries Betsy Dobson
1960	Sets record for RBIs in World Series; named Series MVP
1962	Leads American League with 209 hits
1966	Retires from professional baseball at height of career
1969	Named head baseball coach, University of South Carolina
1975	Coaches South Carolina to 51–6 record and second in the College World Series
1984	Named head baseball coach, Coastal Carolina
1986	Wins Big South Conference and playoff Named conference Coach of the Year Becomes athletic director, Liberty University, Lynchburg, Virginia
1990	Retires

The New York Yankees dominated major league baseball from 1921 through 1964 as no team has ever monopolized a sport. In those forty-four seasons the Yankees won the American League pennant twenty-nine times, including three streaks of three years, two of four years, and two of five years in a row. During that span, they won twenty World Series. During the sixteen seasons from 1949 through 1964, the Yankees won the American League pennant fourteen times.

What made the club so dominant was its reputed farm system where young players were assigned and developed as not only ballplayers, but also as Yankees. The club looked for a certain type, a certain potential, a certain character.

Despite the fact that they had the winningest team in major league history and appeared to be solid at every position, still the Yankees scoured the country for talent. Then in Sumter, South Carolina, they discovered Bobby Richardson, a superstar infielder with the potential to replace their second baseman, Billy Martin.

Martin was not, at that time, ready to hang up his spikes, and Richardson needed seasoning, but the Yankees signed him in June of 1953. In summer 1954, his first full year in professional baseball, he played every inning of every game for the Binghampton, New York, minor league club. It was there he met a teammate who would become a lifelong friend, but more importantly, who would help set him on his course as a professional athlete able to maintain his Christian faith and witness: Bobby Richardson

Converted

Bobby Richardson had grown up in a church-going home and was already a Christian when he became a professional baseball player. When he was fourteen years old his mother had asked Pastor J. H. Simpson of Grace Baptist Church in Sumter, South Carolina, to visit the Richardson home and clarify the issue of salvation for her three children: Bobby and his older and younger sisters.

"We'd all been active in Sunday school and church," he recalls, "but when Pastor Simpson opened the Scriptures with us that Sunday afternoon in 1949, I realized that I knew about Christ but didn't really understand Him or have a personal relationship with Him." That was the day on which Bobby received Christ.

Four years later, when he was on his own for the first time, he found himself in Binghampton, New York, with his sights set on the faraway big leagues. Many careers start and end in the first minor league city because the young players are not ready to make their own life decisions and have little support in staying away from the temptations of life.

But one of the first people Bobby Richardson met was a teammate, a utility infielder named Johnny Hunton. "He was also a Christian, and he took me under his wing, spent time with me, encouraged me to go to church, and discipled me. That really made the difference for me that first year in pro ball."

Denver Bear

On excelling in Binghampton, Richardson was sent to the Denver Bears, where he played and roomed with Tony Kubek, the shortstop who was his roommate for years in the majors. The 1956 Denver Bears are considered by baseball experts to be one of the best minor league teams of the 1950s. Most encouraging was that Kubek was also a believer, who shared with Richardson the desire to avoid partying and carousing.

During the 1956 season Richardson asked club owner Bob Howsam for permission to take a week off so he could go home and marry Betsy Dobson. He was told no, to wait till the end of the season. "So I asked my manager, Ralph Houk. He said, 'Sure, take a week off and get married.'"

Bobby Richardson saw action late in the season with the Yankees in both 1955 (a few days before he turned twenty) and in 1956; the following year he made the big league club for good. For between 1957 to 1964 the Yankees were only to lose the American League pennant only once. Yet not all was rosy for the young second baseman. Despite the fact that he was seven times an all-star and a five-time Golden Glove winner, his first two seasons with the big club were frustrating.

Waiting for the Yankees

He played behind Billy Martin, the starting second baseman, and there were some occasions when Richardson thought that Martin's career would never end. Several of his young teammates were traded, and Bobby Richardson wanted to do the same. He asked the front office

Bobby Richardson, photographed as Coach at Liberty University, Virginia.

to trade him to a team where he could play regularly, rather than in only about half the games. But he was told to be patient, that he fit into the Yankees' plans.

Betsy stuck right with him during that rough time, he says of her. "She had such a wonderful relationship with the Lord. I had a wife who really loved Jesus, not only as her Savior, but also as her Lord. She was such an example to me that it helped me want to become grounded in God's Word."

Most Valuable Player

And his wait for the Yankees was worth it. When he finally became the regular second baseman in 1959, he played in 134 games and hit .301. From then until the year in which he quit the game as a thirty-one-year old in 1966, at the height of his career, he played in virtually every game of every season. In 1960 he became one of the few players in history to be named Most Valuable Player of a World Series while he was playing on the losing team.

That Series is remembered for the dramatic ninth inning homer by Pittsburgh's Bill Mazeroski (ironically the opposing second baseman), which gave the Pirates a 10–9 win in the seventh game. The Yankees had outscored the Pirates 46–17 going into the final game, having lost three close games while winning 16–3, 10–0, and 12–0.

Richardson had the Series of his life with a grand-slam home run, two triples, two doubles, six singles, and a record twelve runs batted in. He had had only one homer in 460 at bats during the regular season. In 1962 he would lead the American League in hits with 209.

Bobby Richardson became well-known for his Christian testimony, for the work that he did with the Fellowship of Christian Athletes, and for his outstanding sportsmanship. Film clips of his final World Series, another four-games-to-three loss (this time at St. Louis), shows a lone Yankee fighting his way through the delirious Cardinal fans at the end of the last game, looking to congratulate his victorious opponents. That Yankee was Bobby Richardson.

When Richardson announced his wish to retire after the 1966 season, the Yankees could hardly believe it.. They offered him a blank contract and told him to fill in his own salary. But as he assured them, his decision was not about money. What he wanted was to spend more time with his family.

He became baseball coach first at the University of South Carolina, and then at Coastal Carolina. Eventually he became athletic director and baseball coach at Liberty University in Lynchburg, Virginia. During all those years his assistant was Johnny Hunton, who, after not making the majors, had become a high school teacher and coach. When Richardson retired from Liberty at age fifty-five in 1990, it was Hunton who replaced him as head coach.

Bobby Richardson credits his wife as having been the major spiritual influence on his life, especially during the difficult years of travel and business as a big leaguer. "Betsy was a tremendous influence on the children, especially when I had to be gone so much." Both of his older boys are now pastors in Sumter, where the Richardsons have returned and where most of their children and nine of their grandchildren also live. As Richardson says, "We have two churches to go to: one in the morning, and one at night."

Cliff Richard

Savior's Day

In British and Commonwealth terms, there is no one else in the music scene who has enjoyed a career that spans five decades. In 1958, an eighteen-year-old British boy, Cliff Richard, reached number two with his very first record "Move It." At the beginning of the 1990s he was topping charts throughout the world with his single, "Savior's Day," and an album, *From a Distance*. In Britain, as 1990 ended and the New Year began, he had run through almost forty successive evenings playing before ten thousand people nightly.

Rightly, he claims a career that can almost be said to have had three top ten hits for each and every one of his thirty-two years in music. He remembers at the end of each year saying to himself that he would be around the next year!

Cliff Richard has survived the onslaught of new artists and critics and done things his way. He has proved that rock 'n' roll is not just about sex and drugs and whatever else. Many megastars have dabbled in areas that he has not touched, and yet he has survived umpteen changes in culture and numerous youth

---

Christian Pop

While many of the early American rock 'n' rollers had a religious background—for instance, Elvis Presley, Jerry Lee Lewis and Little Richard—the same was not true in Britain.

However, American music of all kinds dominated British radio airwaves, early television, and record charts until the Beatles began a British wave of hit solo and group acts in 1963, and spearheaded a "Brit" invasion of the United States a year later. Several British music acts did find success at home without "covering" existing American hit records, and one of these was Cliff Richard.

Naturally, there were artists, mostly American, who sold religious music albums in Britain, and they included the Roger Wagner Chorale, Jo Stafford and Tennessee Ernie Ford. Religious music was also popularized by popular American TV entertainers such as Andy Williams and Perry Como. But religious music rarely featured in the general record scene, apart from the occasional "Christ-centered" Christmas hit.

When Britain's most popular singer Cliff Richard told the nation that he was a Christian, the reaction was one of

Cliff Richard on a Tear Fund trip.

amazement. The British newspaper and magazine world shrieked their surprise.

Relevant faith
Yet Cliff Richard had been searching for a relevant faith since the beginning of the 1960s. Several of his backing group "The Shadows" had joined the Jehovah's Witness faith, as did his mother and one sister. However, some Christians, notably Mrs. Jay Norris, a former schoolteacher of Richard's, Bill Latham, and journalist David Winter, convinced Cliff that he should choose otherwise.

Since 1966, Cliff Richard has told his faith to anyone who will hear, making it clear through countless public appearances, during his pop "live" sets, and on film and record. He has done this worldwide and also in the United States, though the latter has been one of the few areas where he has never achieved major pop stardom.

THE LIFE OF

Cliff Richard

1940	Born in Lucknow, India
1948	Arrives in England on wartime troopship
1958	Forms rock 'n' roll band under proper name Harry Webb
	Takes name Cliff Richard
	His first single reaches number two
	Begins constant hit career
1960	Sings before Queen Elizabeth II at the Royal Variety Performance
1966	Makes public his Christian conversion at a Billy Graham meeting
1968	Appears in Christian film, *Two a Penny*
1978	Helps celebrate tenth anniversary of Christian relief organization, Tear Fund
1988	In Britain, he has number one single, album, video, and book
1990	Hits the chart heights with "Savior's Day," song for Christmas

explosions. And he has trusted his instincts.

He has had a constant music "family," retaining close helpers ever since 1961 to the present day. Often, through the years, people have attempted his musical assassination, especially the music press. However, overall, his positive approach has won many friends and grudging respect from musical areas where cultist elitism does not always lend itself to praise outside of its own narrow parameters.

Yesterday's man?
Quite a few times Cliff Richard has been written off as yesterday's man, but he has kept bouncing back, and the period from the latter part of the 1980s through today has been his most successful period in record sales and concert attendances since his first days of the late 1950s and those pre-Beatles years of the following decade. But it should be said that even when the Beatles were grabbing print and overall media attention, he was still making hit records.

His success has been worldwide. It is only America that has largely remained indifferent, although he has some hit records, especially in the early 1960s and toward the end of the next decade. Richard has hankered after American success since he, as most music-minded people who were in their teens during the 1950s, has always considered the United States the home of popular music.

During the early years of his career he was much featured in the teen journals of his time, and often was asked general questions, such as what were his favorite foods or colors. After he announced that he was a Christian, before a vast array of media observers, he was questioned on his faith. The print world then became just one of the areas in which he could speak of Christ. In a sense he became a curiosity, but he soon proved himself both intelligent and thoughtful.

Christ's witness
To many it was quite amazing that Britain's best-known male pop star could be found Sunday by Sunday in church, and that he would happily go off on Bible and prayer weekends. So, too, he made room for speaking at universities, colleges, and schools about his faith. He may not have been theologically trained, nor an intellectual, but he could witness to Christ in a simple, clear, and cogent way.

Cliff Richard, an ever-popular English performer.

Richard had the strength and verve to run what seemed at times almost two careers. He ran Gospel tours, wrote articles and features, and issued books about the faith in a language and style understandable by younger people. He also lent his support to major British evangelistic campaigns. In more recent times, although he still does some gospel concerts for charity, his general concerts have been marked by definite Christian testimony, and as well as telling of the gospel, he also sings several meaningful and pointed songs.

He has involved himself with Tear Fund, a British-based Christian organization devoted to finding means and ways of alleviating poverty in the Third World. He has made a number of visits overseas on behalf of this charity. On one particular visit to Bangladesh he saw sights that deeply affected him, and this has renewed his efforts to support Tear Fund's work.

Over the years Cliff Richard has probably raised over a million pounds for Tear Fund and other charitable concerns. His various fan clubs also contribute much money to causes that are dear to Cliff.

He has involved himself in, and indeed was co-founder of, the Arts Centre Group, a base for Christians in the Arts, where artists can meet for Bible study, prayer and help, as well as more social affairs, general talks and discussions. The ACG has bases throughout the world. Cliff often throws dinner parties at the ACG or elsewhere, with countless celebrities from the

world of entertainment attending. He has also had a major influence on the lives of many famous British personalities.

A proud moment

Numerous awards have been given Cliff, both for his music, and in recognition of his efforts for charity work, and overall clean living and example. His proudest moment came on July 24, 1980, at 10:10 a.m. when he arrived at Buckingham Palace, London, with his mother, and received the Order of the British Empire. He has often entertained British royalty and is friends with several figures of Britain's Royal Family. In more recent time he was a staunch supporter of the longest-lasting British Prime Minister since World War II, Mrs. Margaret Thatcher.

Richard has been accused of supporting apartheid in South Africa, by visiting and performing in that country. This is something which he vehemently denies. He has also incurred criticism from a number of fringe groups, including the gay movement. To many people he lacks rough edges, for they find him too squeaky clean, but then much of this criticism comes from people whose life philosophy is different from his. Critics expect him to support their causes, but there is always the reply, "Why should he?"

His singleness has given rise to repeated suggestions of his being gay, but this he has consistently denied. Some of these pressures have come from within the Christian community, but mostly from those who cannot see how someone can be a pop star and a Christian. It is unlikely that he could do anything

that would obviate their often hurtful criticism.

His strength, other than that given by God, comes from his self-determination and total professionalism. He belongs with the "old" school, which holds that if you are going to do something, then you do it well. He prepares as avidly for a school concert as a main arena. Undoubtedly he loves music. He adores performing. Apart from music, he is wild about tennis, enjoys swimming, and likes dogs. Also he is a keen traveller when time permits.

Survivor

For twenty-five years Cliff Richard has exercised a unique Christian ministry. Those who carp are not mindful of the fact that countless thousands of younger people would have heard nothing of the faith if they had not heard him sing or speak, or possibly read a number of his Christian teaching books that have been compiled with the help of Bill Latham, who handles his personal and Christian affairs. Again, an innumerable number of people have made Jesus their Lord and Savior because of his ministry. Of that, there can be no doubt.

His close friendship with Dr. Billy Graham, and the respect from him, and the younger Luis Palau is clearly shown in letters from each that are found in the book *Survivor: Tribute to Cliff*. In addition, a number of major British religious figures, including the then Archbishop of Canterbury, Robert Runcie, paid their respects.

For years and years, the British press has waited for something that can smear Richard's seemingly clean

lifestyle, and it is reported that one major tabloid daily given to the more sensational has closed its file on him!

But constant news is Cliff Richard's living faith. This has grown in strength and surety, albeit wider and more aware as the years have progressed.

Further Reading

Jasper, Tony. *Survivor: Tribute to Cliff*. London: Marshall Pickering, 1989.

Jasper, Tony and Patrick Doncaster. *Cliff*. Basingstoke, England: Sidgwick and Jackson, 1981.

Winter, David. *Which One's Cliff?* Revised. London: Hodder and Stoughton, 1990.

Reformers

Abolition:
William Wilberforce   *David Bebbington*

Poor Man's Earl:
Lord Shaftesbury   *John Pollock*

None Turned Away:
Dr. Barnardo   *John Coutts*

God's General:
William Booth   *John Coutts*

Watergate and After:
Chuck Colson   *Ellen Santilli Vaughn*

Abominable Trade

In the late eighteenth century people from Africa were still being shipped across the Atlantic Ocean to be sold as slaves. The human cargoes were usually confined in tiny spaces and often punished mercilessly. It was time for the slave trade to be suppressed.

Resistance

Although a growing number of Europeans wished the trade to cease, there was the problem of resistance from the merchants whose income was threatened. In Britain they could erect political obstacles in the way of abolition. It would take enormous time, energy, and political skill for the trade to be brought to an end.

The champion

Who had the ability to lead a campaign for abolition? William Wilberforce was the man. He was leisured and well connected. He was already a seasoned politician. And he had the dynamic that came from a sense of God's calling. Wilberforce had been converted to vital Christianity in 1785. He threw himself into the moral improvement of Britain, and he soon realized that the slave trade was the worst blot on the nation's record. He became the champion of the slaves.

Opposite: William Wilberforce, 1759–1833.

Abolition
WILLIAM WILBERFORCE AND THE SLAVE TRADE

William Wilberforce, born in 1759, was raised in Hull, Yorkshire, which was then one of the six most flourishing ports in England. His grandfather, also called William, had made a fortune by trading with northern Europe. Because young William's father died when he was only eight, his forceful grandfather exerted a strong influence over the growing lad, who became both high-spirited and ambitious. He attended the local school before going on to St. John's College in the University of Cambridge. There he mixed with young men who afterward could expect to run the affairs of the nation. One of them was William Pitt, who became prime minister in 1784 at the age of twenty-four. Already in that year Wilberforce was a member of parliament alongside him.

William Wilberforce had been sent to the House of Commons to represent Hull in 1780. In 1784 he determined to stand for

The Houses of Parliament, Westminster.

"A man who acts from the principles I profess reflects that he is to give an account of his political conduct at the Judgment seat of Christ."

election as M.P. for the vast county of Yorkshire. Because he gathered so many promises of support, opposition melted. Despite attempts by frustrated political opponents to unseat him, Wilberforce was to remain M.P. for Yorkshire for twenty-eight years. During crises in Britain and abroad, he gave stalwart support to William Pitt. The French Revolution, which began in 1789, served merely to reinforce his loyalty to the government, and, with substantial inherited wealth at his disposal, Wilberforce launched into a successful political career.

Religion in the soul

During his first decade in Parliament, however, there was a sharp turn in the direction of his life. Like nearly all his con-temporaries in high places, he had given formal assent to the doctrines of the Church of England and was more or less regular as a churchgoer. But in 1784–85 he began to examine religious questions more seriously. He traveled the continent with Isaac Milner, a brother of his former schoolmaster and now a clergyman. Milner was one of the relatively few ministers in the Church of England who belonged to the growing evangelical movement. He drew the attention of Wilberforce to the need for personal faith in Jesus Christ. Together they read *The Rise and Progress of Religion in the Soul* by Philip Doddridge. Wilberforce reached the conclusion that "in the true sense of the word I was not a Christian."

He became increasingly aware of the emptiness of the life of the rich. Painfully conscious of his own sins, he gradually submitted his will to Christ's. What he called the "great change" had taken place, and he now longed to escape from the clamor of politics to find spiritual peace in solitude. He sought the advice of John Newton, who had once been a slave trader but was now another evangelical clergyman.

Newton was firm: Wilberforce should remain in public life. His political career must be put at the service of Jesus Christ.

Wilberforce began to see himself as a Christian politician. "A man who acts from the principles I profess," he wrote to a constituent in 1789, "reflects that he is to give an account of his political conduct at the Judgment seat of Christ." Accordingly he set about encouraging higher moral standards in the nation at large, "the reformation of manners." In 1787 he persuaded the king, through William Pitt, to issue a proclamation which would urge magistrates to enforce existing legislation against drunkenness, blasphemy, and similar misdemeanors. Wilberforce then set up a Proclamation Society consisting of members up and down the country who would prod magistrates into action. The effect was undoubtedly to make certain sections of the lower classes think twice about unseemly behavior.

Vital Christianity

Wilberforce, however, cannot justly be criticized for only censuring the poor, for he was at least as concerned to reform the manners of the social elite. In 1797 he published *A Practical View of the Prevailing Religious Systems of Professed Christians*. It was aimed at the "Higher and Middle Classes," the landlords and merchants. The book portrayed the religious attitudes of the normal English gentleman, who, according to Wilberforce, possessed only the veneer of Christian belief, but not its substance. A gentleman excused dueling, gaming, and theatergoing because these activities

Eighteenth-century slave-traders.

threatened. Meanwhile he took a deep interest in other schemes for the welfare of the slaves. He gave generously, for example, to the enterprise whereby freed slaves were transferred to the small community of Sierra Leone on the west coast of Africa.

His concern for oppressed black people was shared with a circle of friends, nearly all of whom were evangelicals, the "Clapham Sect"—so called as most of them lived in the select London suburb of Clapham. One of the friends, a lawyer named James Stephen, was to become Wilberforce's brother-in-law. It was Stephen who devised the strategy that led to the end of the trade. A bill for the partial abolition of the slave trade was dressed up as an emergency measure in the wartime circumstances of 1806. In the following year the precedent made total abolition far easier to achieve. A friendly government also helped the task. Yet the slave trade might have persisted had not Wilberforce and his friends in the Clapham circle persevered in championing the cause for eighteen years.

The struggle against the trade did not end in 1807, however. The effort to ensure that British merchants did not carry on transporting slaves illegally was one of Wilberforce's continuing duties. Another was the task of persuading the other European nations to ban the trade. He was particularly active during 1814 in trying to incorporate abolition of the trade in the peace treaty with Napoleon's France. He also recommended ways in which the conditions of slaves in British territories could be improved. Gradually,

were customary in his circles. No thought was given as to whether they were consistent with the Christian religion. With such nominal Christianity Wilberforce contrasted "vital Christianity," the true faith that he had discovered for himself. The book was immensely successful, selling over seventy-five hundred copies in six months. The upper classes, reeling from the overthrow of their counterparts in revolutionary France, were ready to heed his message. A serious concern for spiritual values began to spread through the aristocracy and gentry.

The political effort for which Wilberforce is most famous is his campaign against the slave trade. British vessels were still carrying cargoes of black slaves from Africa to the West Indies. Much cruelty was involved, but most serious was the reducing of human beings to goods that could be bought and sold. Educated opinion had already turned against the trade, and philosophers had demonstrated

that it conflicted with the goal of human happiness. Gentlemen began to assume that slavery was an unwelcome aspect of life. Those who took part in the trade carried on, however, not wishing to see any decrease in their profits. It was Wilberforce, together with a group of evangelical friends, who recognized that action was essential. To traffic in human beings was quite wrong: "Where the actual commission of guilt is in question," he wrote, "a man who *fears* God is not at liberty." The slave trade had to be put down.

Campaigning commences

Wilberforce began his abolition campaign in 1789 by proposing resolutions against the trade in the House of Commons. The Commons agreed to assemble evidence on the question, only— an effective delaying tactic. For year after year Wilberforce had to press the issue against dogged resistance from the champions of the West India merchants, whose business was

Wilberforce House, Hull, England.

as he considered the state of the slaves in the West Indies, he started to consider taking a step beyond abolishing the trade. He began to wonder if slavery itself could be extinguished. Even as late as 1825 he still did not think such a policy righteous or practicable. That year he finally retired from parliament, having sat for the small borough of Bramber in Sussex since 1812. In his last years Wilberforce gave his total support to the younger generation of politicians who demanded an end to slavery in Britain's colonies. Shortly before he died in 1833, he heard that the House of Commons had passed the law emancipating the slaves, which gave him great satisfaction.

Reform

Wilberforce took part in other political issues. He remained a loyal follower of "the principles of Mr. Pitt" even after the death of the former Prime Minister of 1806. A staunch defender of the established constitution, he made a point of speaking in the House of Commons in favor of every law designed to uphold public order between 1795 and 1819. Yet he was not opposed to well-considered change, believing in moderate parliamentary reform. He favored giving full civil rights to Roman Catholics. He disliked what he called the "barbarous" method of execution by hanging.

Wilberforce was constantly eager to further the interests of the Christian faith through his political influence. He persuaded Pitt to give his friend Isaac Milner promotion in the Church of England. He defended the Methodists from charges that they were political subversives. He led a campaign in 1813 to open British India to Christian missionaries. His role was sometimes difficult. During the wars against France, Parliament discussed fast days when the nation should be summoned to prayer for victory. Ideally Wilberforce would have wished to speak of this as a duty to God, but the secular tone of public life made it impossible to gain a hearing for such spiritual reasons. Like many other Christian politicians before and since, Wilberforce felt a painful tension between his inner convictions and the pressures of circumstance.

Testimonies abound to the warmth of Wilberforce's personality. "Being himself amused and interested by everything," wrote a son of a close friend, "whatever he said became amusing or interesting." He was not married until the age of thirty-eight, and he seemed to exhibit the demeanor of an undisciplined bachelor into his closing years. If this made him popular, it also made for something close to irresponsibility. His unanswered correspondence would pile up. Pitt thought him unfitted for high office because of his carelessness in business. Moreover, Wilberforce's use of opium for medical reasons made him feel indolent and muddle-headed—personal traits against which he had to struggle during his adult life, while at the same time dispensing enormous energies in his reforming activities. And yet, despite all, the tact and charm of his character made him a skillful persuader of potential allies. His buoyancy of spirit, clearly rooted in the Christian quality of joy, was his greatest political resource.

Further Reading

Howse, Ernest M. *Saints in Politics: the "Clapham Sect" and the growth of freedom.* Toronto: U. of Toronto, 1952.

Pollock, John. *Wilberforce.* London: Constable, 1977.

National Conscience

By the early nineteenth century the Industrial Revolution had caused factories, mills, and mines to become a fact of life in many parts of Britain. When employers needed more and more labor they began to use children, whose wages were minimal, until child labor, often in grievous conditions, was taken for granted as necessary for national prosperity.

Then, in 1833, a young aristocrat raised his voice against it. Thereafter, for fifty-two years, as Lord Ashley until his father's death, then as the seventh Earl of Shaftesbury, this sensitive, nervous Christian stood as the conscience of the nation.

He pushed social reform after social reform through Parliament, often in teeth of opposition. It was said of him in his old age: "The myriads of children who from the tenderest age were kept standing for sixteen hours a day in hot factories—the poor half-clad women who, harnessed to cars in coal mines, used to draw them along low, dark passages — the gutter children of London and all great towns—the uncared-for lunatic—the prisoner in the foreign dungeon—the oppressed of every clime —owe him thanks for exemption from misery. And inasmuch as he did it to all these, he did it to the Saviour whom he always loved so well."

Lord Shaftesbury

THE POOR MAN'S EARL

Early in February 1833 two gentlemen called at the London home of a thirty-two-year-old member of Parliament, Lord Ashley, heir to the Earl of Shaftesbury.

They had come to urge him to take up a Bill introduced by an M.P. who had since lost his seat. The Bill would reduce the daily hours worked by children in mills and factories to ten. In most textile mills little children were working impossible hours, often under blows from their overseers. Denied education, many of them died young or were crippled for life, earlier Factory Acts having scarcely touched their plight.

One of the two callers, the Reverend George Bull from Yorkshire, poured out graphic details of the horrors of the factory system. Lord Ashley's heart was touched. He loved children. He was especially upset that countless hundreds should be

The slum buildings of Victorian London.

growing up brutalized, without moral guidance or the help of religion, to the lasting damage of the nation. But to accept the leadership in such a cause as this would bring labor, expense, and pain, and might damage the political career on which he was set. Nor was he eloquent. "I can perfectly recollect," he wrote five years later, "my astonishment, and doubt, and terror at the proposition."

"Go forward to victory!"

He consulted with two fellow members of Parliament. He then interviewed Bull again. He prayed for guidance and sought it from the Bible. Still undecided, he went upstairs to his young wife, Minny, who was pregnant with their second child and laid the whole question before her. She did not hesitate: "It is your duty," she said. "Go forward, and to victory!"

Victorian London was inhabited by thousands of homeless and deprived people.

When Bull returned for his answer, Lord Ashley told him, "I dare not refuse the request you have so earnestly pressed. I believe it is my duty to God and the poor, and I trust He will support me."

At two-thirty in the afternoon of February 5 1833, Lord Ashley announced in the House that he would reintroduce Sadler's Bill. He was loudly cheered, thus receiving no indication that a battle of fifteen years was about to begin. "As to Lord Ashley," wrote Bull, "he is as noble, benevolent, and resolute in mind as he is manly in person." And the poet Southey wrote him, "Thousands of thousands will bless you for taking up the cause of these poor children."

Neglected child

Ashley himself had known a miserable childhood. His aristocratic parents had neglected him and the only grown-up who showed him any affection was the middle-aged housekeeper, Maria Milles, who had earlier been the personal maid of his mother, daughter of the Duke of Marlborough.

Each evening, before a nursemaid came to hurry little Anthony Ashley off for bed, Maria would take him on her knee and tell him stories from the Gospels and teach him how to pray. She told him of Calvary and the empty tomb, and spoke of the Lord Jesus as the risen Redeemer who could be a Friend. A strong, simple faith like hers, which Whitefield and Wesley had preached to thousands in the open fields and in parlors, was rarely found in aristocratic households, above or below the stairs.

When Ashley was ten, and away at school, Maria died in her fifty-first year. He mourned grievously and felt alone in the world. Despite the jeers of other boys he took refuge in the Bible she had taught him to love, and prayed to the Friend they shared. Maria left him her gold watch. He wore it always and would often show it, saying, "This belonged to the best friend I ever had."

A dropped coffin

His father sent him to Harrow, the famous public school, and while there he was shocked to see a pauper's funeral. The coffin was dropped by drunken, swearing men. "Good heavens!" thought young Ashley. "Can this be permitted simply because the man was poor and friendless?"

In the perspective of the years he saw this event as "the origin of my public career.... It brought powerfully before me the scorn and neglect manifested towards the poor and helpless. I was deeply affected, but for many years afterwards I acted only on feeling and sentiment. As I advanced in life, all this grew up to a sense of duty; and I was convinced that God had called me to devote whatever advantages He might have bestowed upon me in the cause of the weak, the helpless, both man and beast, and those who had none to help them."

Dedication to Christ and to the poor was not evident, however, during a brilliant career at Oxford, though Ashley was

THE LIFE OF
Lord Shaftesbury

moral and hardworking, unlike many young aristocrats. He was a delightful character. As one contemporary said, "I have hardly ever known any man with a greater sense of humor than himself, or with a greater appreciation of humor in other persons." And he was a favorite with the girls: "I thought him the handsomest young man I had ever seen," recalled one in old age. "He was very tall, and his countenance radiant with youthful brightness." Underneath, however, he was highly sensitive and a prey to depression, like many descendants of the great Duke of Marlborough, such as Sir Winston Churchill.

In 1824, after an unhappy love affair in Vienna, Ashley rededicated himself to Christ, though the details cannot be known because he tore out the relevant pages of the diary he wrote daily throughout his life. A few years after this he wooed and won Lady Emily Cowper (Minny), a beautiful and intelligent girl whose mother was the wife of dull Earl Cowper, and a close friend of Lord Palmerston, so close, in fact that society gossip hinted that Lord Palmerston was Minny's real father. The Ashleys were deeply in love.

The cry of the children
Elected to Parliament, Lord Ashley's concern for the weak and helpless was fostered when he joined a Select Committee to examine the needs of "pauper lunatics," but his ambitions were political; he aimed to be prime minister one day. Then came the cry of the children.

The fight for the Ten Hours Bill was long and hard: powerful interests maintained that it would ruin the country, and Ashley sometimes felt every hand was against him except that of "the great unwashed." As he complained to his diary: "I am as much fretted by anxiety as worn by labor. I cannot feel by halves, nor only when the evil is present. I take it I suffer very often much more than the people do themselves!"

Within a few years he was engulfed by another crusade, to stop children being worked to death or deformity down in the coal mines. He had pushed Parliament into examining the conditions of child employment and when the Select Committee reported in 1842, the nation was horrified to learn of girls, almost naked and chained to heavy carts, drawing coal up the low, narrow passages far underground; girls working alongside naked men, who sometimes sexually abused them. Children of five or even younger were incarcerated without light, to work trapdoors in the rat-infested mines; children who stood all day ankle deep in water at the pumps, twelve or fourteen hours a day, six days a week.

As soon as he could, Ashley introduced a Bill. "As I stood at the table, and just before I opened my mouth, the words of God came forcibly to my mind, 'Only be strong and of good courage.'" His quiet eloquence won over the Commons, and despite some delay by the Lords, Parliament abolished child "slavery" in the mines.

"My hands are too full"
Wherever he met cruelty or poverty, Lord Ashley attempted to relieve it, either by personal generosity and, where necessary, by putting a Bill before Parliament. He helped the homeless and orphans; and he organized emigration to the colonies for those who had no future in Britain; he attacked the sending of small boys up chimneys, but though he could rescue these child sweeps, it took him thirty-five years to make Parliament outlaw the practice. "My hands," he once lamented in the diary which was his safety valve, "are too full, Jews, Chimney-sweeps, Factory Children, Church Extension, etc., etc., I shall succeed I fear, partially in all, and completely in none. Yet we must persevere; there is hope."

Behind him he had the loving support of his wife Minny and his growing family of sons and daughters. The eldest son was a disappointment, though much loved and probably watched over too zealously. The second son, Francis, had a brilliant mind and a fine physique and, although he was an unashamed Christian, was the most popular boy in the rough and tumble of Harrow School. In the holidays he acted as his father's secretary. In May 1849, however, he fell desperately ill at Harrow. His parents rushed to his bedside. Francis asked them to read from the Bible and they "talked much of the free and full mercy of God in Christ Jesus." To calm any fears, they urged him to remember that God is love: "Human love," said Ashley, "is capable of great things. What then must be the depth and height and intensity of Divine Love. Know nothing, think of nothing but Jesus Christ and Him crucified." He repeatedly kissed his father and blessed his parents for bringing him up to love God.

Francis seemed to get better and asked for prayers of thanksgiving. "I have learned," he said "what a futile thing must be a death-bed repentance! I feel that I have been reconciled to God. But what could I have done, lying on this bed, to make my peace with Him, had I not been brought before to a knowledge of the Truth!"

As the sun set on the last day of May in 1849, Francis had a sudden collapse and died while his parents stood amazed. The whole school followed him to his grave. His parents were in a daze of grief, and yet felt joy, for Francis had taken them to heaven's gate; and they were comforted, as Minny wrote, that he was "enjoying the blessed presence of his Maker and singing the praises of his Lord and Saviour."

Anthony Ashley Cooper, seventh Earl of Shaftesbury.

Seventh Earl

Two years later Ashley's mean, crabbed, old father died, he who had opposed and thwarted him, and even banished him from his ancestral home when he took up the cause of agricultural reform. Lord Ashley (a courtesy title) succeeded as the seventh Earl of Shaftesbury and he therefore vacated his seat in the House of Commons. The M.P. who moved a writ for the bye-election, said in

his eulogy of him that he was "the friend of the friendless. Every form of human suffering he has sought to lighten, and in every way to ameliorate the moral, social, and religious condition of our fellow-subjects. And out of this House his exertions have been such as at first sight might have seemed incompatible with his duties here. But he found time for all; and when absent from his place on these benches he was enjoying no luxurious ease, but was seated in the chair of a Ragged School meeting, of a Scripture-reader's Association, or of a Young Man's Christian Institution."

The new Lord Shaftesbury was now owner of estates in Dorset, but these were encumbered with debt; not only the mansion but the cottages also were in poor condition. He sought to improve the material and spiritual lives of his tenants and employees, but the estate added to his worries. He was never placid about his personal affairs. Minny, when worried by the moral weakness of their eldest, wrote to their excellent third son that she was "more harrassed than I dare own to your Papa, who is also very anxious and takes fire if he feels that others participate in those fears." Lord Shaftesbury marveled at the patience of his wife. "How many times," he once confessed to his diary, "have I, in my excitable spirit, said unjust and cruel things to her! What a placable spirit! What a power to forgive! and what a sublime power to forget!"

By this time Minny's widowed mother had married her lover, Lord Palmerston, and when Palmerston became prime minister in 1854, at the height of the Crimean War, he tried hard to persuade his stepson-in-law to join his Cabinet. Minny and her mother nagged hard but Shaftesbury "could not satisfy myself that to accept office was a divine call; I was satisfied that God had called me to labor among the poor." At last he gave in, but just as he was about to leave for Buckingham Palace to kiss hands, Palmerston found a substitute. Shaftesbury, middle-

"To have changed the whole social condition of England, to have emancipated women and children from a condition almost worse than slavery, to have reclaimed the neglected and regenerated the outcast—these are results which give the aged philanthropist a foremost place among those who have labored for the welfare of England."

aged though he was, danced round the room for joy.

Working bishops

Palmerston was a jolly atheist, a relic of eighteenth-century unbelief in an age which became increasingly Christian. Lord Shaftesbury, although he loved him, was appalled that such a man should have the sole right to appoint archbishops, bishops, and deans: his "appointments will be detestable." However, Palmerston virtually handed the whole church patronage to Shaftesbury, who became, in the nine years of Palmerston's two premierships, largely responsible for the appointment of

five archbishops and twenty bishops. For the first time the despised Evangelicals received due share, though Shaftesbury was scrupulously fair. Rather than choosing dry academics, superannuated headmasters, or men with no claim but lineage, Shaftesbury sought to make bishops of those clergy who had worked hard in parishes, and especially among the poor.

With all his labors for social reform Lord Shaftesbury never ceased to promote the preaching of the gospel. Rock-like in his own faith in the Cross and Resurrection of Christ, and walking daily with Him, he was always looking for new ways to reach those in the slums and backstreets who were scarcely touched by the church.

Theater services

And thus, in 1860, he and his friends shocked the polite world by hiring seven theaters in the roughest parts of London for Sunday evening services. When Shaftesbury visited one of them he found over three thousand of the poorest and wildest present, and a theater manager who was amazed at the quietness of their demeanor. Shaftesbury later shared what he had experienced with the House of Lords: "Think of the rough, uncouth, wild, and half-savage creatures, male and female, who came there, persons of such strange aspect and appearance that many who saw them for the first time, pressing forward on the front benches, could hardly imagine where they came from. Well, there they sat, mute and motionless, with open eyes, drinking in, with grateful hearts, the pure and simple Gospel which was addressed to them."

Although theater services became a feature of mid-Victorian London, they could only touch some of the poor. Shaftesbury exerted a far wider and permanent influence by his support of the Ragged Schools movement, which gave a smattering of education and religion to thousands of boys and girls in cities throughout the land, who otherwise would have had no teaching. When at length, in 1870, the state introduced compulsory education for all, Shaftesbury tried to make sure that clear Christian teaching should be included; but the Churches could not agree on what should be taught, so that in the end the Education Act's religious clause was a "meager, washy, pointless thing," as he complained, and would lead inevitably toward secularization. With an insight which the following century would prove right, Shaftesbury lamented that the Education Act of 1870 would bring "the greatest moral change that England has ever known."

In 1872, when Shaftesbury was entering into old age, his beloved Minny died. Despite the devotion of his children and grandchildren his melancholy increased, even though his sense of humor never left him: "Wherever the ripple of laughter was to be heard, and the most fun going on," wrote his host during a holiday in Scotland, "there Lord Shaftesbury was invariably to be found."

Changing a country

In 1881 Shaftesbury celebrated his eightieth birthday. He had brought in some great reforms, launched great movements, and had made life better for millions in many lesser ways, such as by organizing purer water supplies, better drainage, and more sanitary cemeteries. *The Times* commented that, "It is given to few men to see so completely the fruit of their labors as he has done. To have changed the whole social condition of England, to have emancipated women and children from a condition almost worse than slavery, to have reclaimed the neglected and regenerated the outcast—these are results which give the aged philanthropist a foremost place among those who have labored for the welfare of England."

He could not retire. "If," he once remarked, "I followed my own inclination I would sit in my armchair and take it easy for the rest of my life. But I dare not do it. I must work as long as life lasts." He wrote to a friend, "When I feel old age creeping upon me, and know that I must soon die—I hope it is not wrong to say it—I cannot bear to leave this world with all the misery in it." He prayed daily for Christ's second coming.

He remained active almost until the end. And when he died, on October 1, 1885, a wave of mourning crossed the land. His funeral in Westminster Abbey was unforgettable. Inside the Abbey the representatives of nearly two hundred missions, schools, societies, hospitals, and funds joined a vast congregation from every class and rank in the kingdom, while thousands more waited outside.

"When I saw the crowd which lined the streets," wrote Lord Shaftesbury's youngest son, "as my Father's body was borne to the Abbey—the halt, the blind, the maimed, the poor and the naked standing bare-headed in their rags amidst a pelting rain patiently enduring to show their love and reverence to their departed friend, I thought it the most heart-stirring sight my eyes had ever looked upon and I could only feel how happy was the man to whom it had been given to be thus useful in his life and to be laid at last to his long sleep amidst the sob of a great nation's heart."

Further Reading

Battiscombe, Georgina. *Shaftesbury*. Boston: Houghton Mifflin, 1975.

Finlayson, Geoffrey. *The Seventh Earl of Shaftesbury*. London: Eyre Methuen, 1981.

Pollock, John. *Shaftesbury: The Poor Man's Earl*. Oxford: Lion, 1990.

Dr. Barnardo of Stepney

None Turned Away

Thomas Barnardo was one of the greatest Christian pioneers of the nineteenth century—the age of "empire building." But Barnardo, who sought to apply the teaching of Jesus to the needs of the children of his day, built an empire of compassion.

Barnardo was born in Dublin, in Ireland, in 1845. His family belonged to a Protestant minority in that very Catholic country. They attended the Church of Ireland, and young Thomas was sent to St. Patrick's Cathedral Grammar School. The future friend of children, however, here detested the headmaster: "The most cruel as well as the most mendacious man that I ever met," he recalled. "He seemed to take a savage delight in beating his boys."

In 1859 there was a great spiritual awakening, which swept over Protestant Ireland. Barnardo, it seems, was to find revival meetings much more interesting than school! "I was brought to Christ in the year 1862," he later wrote. "A Dr. Hunt, of Harcourt Street, Dublin, had been the means in God's hands of awakening inquiry in the mind of my brother George. I actually found Christ without any human intervention when alone, some days after a special interview with my brother Fred and Dr. Hunt."

Barnardo's new faith led him from the Church of Ireland, and he was baptized as a believer in the Baptist Church, Abbey Street; and soon afterwards he joined the Plymouth Brethren.

The Plymouth Brethren were attempting to return to the simplicity of the earliest church. They had no separate ordained ministry, accepted the inerrancy of the Bible, and expected the imminent return of the Lord.

Called to London

What was Thomas Barnardo to do with his talent and energy, now dedicated to the service of Christ? Hudson Taylor had founded the international China Inland Mission, which was open to all talents that would accept its simple basis of faith. Was not Barnardo's call to China? Should not he study medicine to fit himself for the task? With the backing of Brethren in Dublin, Barnardo made his way to England and enrolled as a student at the London Hospital. He was to find his mission field not in far-off China, but just a few streets away.

Within only one generation, the population of London had doubled to more than a million.

East End Doctor

The nineteenth century felt the impact of the Industrial Revolution. The cities of Europe and America grew rapidly and engulfed the people who flocked to find work in them. Churches struggled as their ancient structures failed to cope.

Nowhere were the problems greater than in the East End of London. Here were large numbers of homeless men, women, and even children. Charles Dickens, in his classic *Oliver Twist,* showed the fate that lay in store for the unwary or unfortunate child.

The young Thomas Barnardo came to London to train as a doctor. His goal was to work in China as a medical missionary. But he ended up in his mission field just a few streets away

Energetic and hard driving, Barnardo used his talents to tackle problems that governments were still ignoring. He was determined that no child in need should ever be turned away. Attracting followers, arousing opposition, Barnardo fought on to set up the great charity that still bears his name. He prepared the way for much wider progress in child care and law reform. And to the last he remained a preacher, combining social skills with faith in the love of Christ.

In 1868, he rented, with the help of a few friends, a pair of small houses in Hope Place, which became the center of the East London Juvenile Mission. In later folklore, they would become a "converted donkey shed." Here Barnardo worked at the Ragged School; and here, sometime in the winter of 1868–69, he had his famous meeting with Jim Jarvis.

Jim Jarvis's story

Charles Dickens had described in *Oliver Twist* the world of a child adrift in London. He had drawn the unforgettable picture of the "Artful Dodger." Barnardo was inclined to think that young Jarvis was a dishonest "dodger."

It was half past nine in the evening. Jim lingered in the warm room, unwilling to leave. Barnardo simply did not believe that the boy had no mother and nowhere to sleep. But Jim seemed genuine, "He was a quaint little vagabond, and ...

beneath all his external appearances of mirth ... there was a sad undercurrent ... of sorrow ... that brought tears to our eyes."

At last Jim led Barnardo to the roof of a shed. Barnardo was shocked. "With their heads upon the higher part of the roof and their feet somewhat in the gutter ... lay eleven boys huddled together for warmth—no roof or covering of any kind was over them and the clothes they had were in rags."

Barnardo saw this encounter as a call from God. East London, not China was to be his parish. As he later commented, "We were enabled to renounce a life of usefulness in another and more distant land."

Capturing Satan's citadels

He began as an all-round evangelist, concerned to save both soul and body. He captured one of the "citadels of Satan" by taking over the Edinburgh Castle public house and turning it into

Many were crammed into the wretchedness of the East End. Here they were the victims of wretched housing, poor sanitation, temporary employment, and the curse of gin addiction. An epidemic of cholera broke out within only a few weeks of Barnardo's arrival.

The young student soon linked up with a congregation in Sydney Street, Stepney, and began working as an open-air preacher. He also published his first story, concerning a deathbed conversion. The man who was to be "the father of nobody's children" was a born journalist. Without his talent for telling true tales, if at times one-sided, the organization he founded would never have paid its way.

Barnardo's today helps children with mental handicap meet their potential.

build the Girls' Village, at Barkingside in the green fields of Essex. "Of the divine character of our mission," he wrote, "we have no doubt."

Controversy

Others had doubts in plenty. The young Barnardo worked without an overseeing committee. He called himself "Doctor," but had he not dropped out of medical school? And did he not raise money by the use of phony photographs of poor children? A lamentable controversy erupted between him and Frederick Charrington, a rival evangelist who was allied to a local pastor, George Reynolds. The Charity Organization Society, a watchdog body, joined in the battle. It too had grave suspicions about Thomas Barnardo!

But he counterattacked with the greatest vigor. A mysterious "Clerical Junius" wrote articles in the *East London Advertiser*. In a dream sequence Barnardo was hailed as "Dr. Doogood" while Frederick Charrington, who had renounced a fortune in a brewery, was satirized as "Mr. Brewgoose"!

A lengthy arbitration was to follow. It resulted in a qualified victory: Barnardo in the future would work with a committee; and there were to be no more "posed" publicity photographs. But the identity of "Clerical Junius" was never revealed, the author whose writing style was so suspiciously like his own.

Kidnapped

Barnardo was never one for half measures. If no destitute child was to be refused, then handicapped children must be found a place too. "I have at Stepney," he wrote, "a boy with no legs at

Dr. Barnardo himself took many photographs of needy children for publicity.

a mission hall and community center. Sermons were prepared with care, written in purple ink and with key passages underlined in red. Medical studies were left uncompleted. And a tragic encounter with another child caused a further change in the course of his life.

John Somers, known as "Carrots", due to his red hair, was found by Barnardo in one of his night patrols. But the home in Stepney was full! "Carrots" was told he would be admitted later, only to be found dead of

hunger and exposure inside a sugar barrel. The stricken Barnardo felt called upon to adopt a new slogan, one which read: **NO DESTITUTE CHILD EVER REFUSED ADMISSION.**

This was a brave commitment. Trained social workers did not exist. Money had to be raised. Destitute children needed a future as well as a roof over their heads! The charismatic, energetic Barnardo was able to attract large numbers of Christian volunteers to staff his growing organization and to all. The youngster swims like a porpoise." Barnardo stipulated that although some children's homes of that time refused to accept the "illegitimate," the child of unmarried parents could not be rejected. And if the laws of the United Kingdom did not protect the child from the unworthy or vicious parent, then could not "philanthropic kidnapping" be justified?

In his pamphlet *Kidnapped*, he wrote "I could not forget the pressure of the little hot hand, nor could I forget the faces and forms of those little girls standing there in their wet clothing, and scarcely daring to look at the woman for fear of being beaten." Later he seized his chance: "The old woman was not there now.... Why should I not TAKE ALL THREE AT ONCE?" Which he did! The very name "Barnardo" was enough to cause "a loudly expressed murmur of sympathy from the crowd."

But not all were sympathetic, especially as it seemed Thomas Barnardo also wanted to save children from Roman Catholicism! Here his outlook was apparently limited by his Protestant Irish background. Three custody cases—of Henry Gossage, Martha Tye, and John Roddy—were fought through the courts. Were they "Catholic" or "Protestant" children? Once again Barnardo the fighting journalist played a debatable part. He was fined for contempt of court. But some good came out of the bitter battle, for the law was amended to give children greater protection. Henry Gossage, it seems, made good in Canada, but no one knows what became of Martha and John.

Henry's move to Canada was made along the "golden bridge

of emigration," which Barnardo believed was the best way to provide a bright future for his destitute children. Here too he shared the views of his time. It was, after all, the heyday of the British Empire. His own visits to Canada convinced him of the value of the policy. He wrote, "I was greeted by one young fellow, so muscular and robust, he seemed capable of lifting me off the ground.... 'Doctor, don't yer know me.... Don't yer remember the thrashing you gave me ... and the jawing yer gave me afterwards? I've thought of what yer said many a time since.'"

Overdraft

But by the 1890s Barnardo's kingdom fell into deep trouble provoked by the honorable dilemma of the Christian philanthropist. "The bane of the Institution," wrote a member of the committee, "is what Dr. Barnardo most prides himself on: 'No absolutely destitute child ever refused admittance'.... The overdraft at the bank is as big as ever."

Barnardo's response, typically, was to appeal for funds through his magazine *Night and Day*, asking, "Shall I... meet the need of every second destitute child who appeals for aid?"

But a one-man campaign was no longer enough. In 1899 the organization became named "The National Incorporated Association for the Reclamation of Destitute Waif Children." The public, however, went on calling it "Dr. Barnardo's Homes."

In his final years, Barnardo returned to the Church of England and became a Lay Reader. He was patriarch of the large children's charity that was known by his name, but he

scarcely looked the part of the children's friend. One observer made the comment that, "Even his moustache was martial." Appearances were deceptive! At his death Barnardo was "maintaining the largest children's hospital in London.... Of the seven thousand nine hundred and ninety eight children in care, over one thousand three hundred were crippled or disabled.... There was no public money to pay for the continuous care they needed."

In the United Kingdom, and not only in that country, legal reform followed the lead marked out by Barnardo and others like him. His prejudices were those of his age; his insights were forever inspired as they were by the love of the Master whom he served. In his last address given to children about to leave for Canada, he spoke about the four anchors "dropped ... from the stern" of the storm-tossed ship which is described in Acts 27:29. Thomas Barnardo's anchors were (1) The Bible, (2) Prayer, (3) A good conscience, and (4) Christ Himself. Despite his manifest failings, Dr. Thomas Barnardo sought to follow his Lord by ministering to England's forgotten children.

Further Reading

Wagner, Gillian. *Barnardo*. London: Weidenfeld and Nicolson, 1979.

Williams, A.E. *Barnardo of Stepney: The Father of Nobody's Children*. London: George Allen and Unwin, 1966.

God's General
William Booth

Times were hard indeed in nineteenth-century Nottingham. England was in the grip of the Industrial Revolution, and the poor were paying the price. The machinery of this new age was serviced by stocking-weavers who crowded into Nottingham's 8000 back-to-back houses. Conditions of work were horrendous, and cholera a nightmare, for the sanitation of today had not been invented.

Pawnbroker's apprentice
Among the many casualties of these hard times was a small-time builder, Samuel Booth. His economic failure put an end to the schooling of his son, who was thereupon apprenticed to a pawnbroker. Beneath the sign of the three brass balls, the poor would pledge their treasures—rings, watches, snuffboxes—in return for a loan at interest.

The son was William Booth, founder of the Salvation Army. Young Booth detested the pawnbroking trade, but it brought him face-to-face with human need; he looked for an answer to that need in religion. "I was brought up in attendance at the services of the church of England," he wrote, "which at thirteen I exchanged at my own choice for...the more interesting meetings of the Wesleyan Methodists.... There was nothing remarkable in the measures that led to my conversion...when fifteen years of age."

No conversion is unremarkable. Booth's conversion was tied up with his making amends to some of his friends by returning a silver pencil case that should have belonged to them.

"I remember," he said, "as if it were but yesterday ... the rolling away from my heart of the guilty burden ... and the going

Practical Christianity

Methodism was a vibrant force in nineteenth-century England. The revivalist tradition continued as the churches sought to keep in touch with the masses, whose way of life was being altered forever by the Industrial Revolution.

William Booth, founder and first General of The Salvation Army, was born in Nottingham in 1829. His work in the pawnbroker's shop brought him face to face with poverty. His links with Broad Street Chapel led him to personal faith.

Moving to London, he was able to begin work as a full-time preacher. There he met Catherine Mumford, the love of his life. She also would become a famous preacher. Their man-and-wife ministry helped shape the Salvation Army.

Ordained in the Methodist New Connexion, Booth felt that his vocation was to serve as a traveling evangelist. In 1865, the Booths worked with a Revival Society in East London.

In 1878, The Christian Mission, which was growing rapidly throughout Britain and beyond, became The Salvation Army. Booth served as the General. But too soon he lost his beloved Catherine, who died in 1890 after a courageous battle with cancer.

In old age, the once reviled William Booth was an honored figure. The Army he had founded continued to spread around the world with its message and mission of practical Christianity.

A Salvation Army march through the slums of Glasgow, Scotland.

General William Booth at Exeter Hall,
London, 1890.

forth to serve my God and my generation from that hour."

"In this manner," St. John Ervine, in his great biography, wrote, "a saint was born."

More interesting meetings

Young William Booth found that proceedings at Broad Street Wesleyan Chapel could be very interesting indeed. Methodism was moving into the third, even the fourth generation since John Wesley. How could the fire of faith be kept burning brightly? One much disputed answer was revivalism: unscripted worship, centered on passionate preaching, with full emotional participation and response from the people. These indeed had been the tactics of John Wesley himself.

But now the style of revivalism developed in camp meetings on the American frontier were brought back to the Old Country by popular evangelists such as James Caughey, whose mission in Nottingham held young Booth spellbound. He recalled, "an extraordinary preacher, filling his sermons with thrilling anecdotes and vivid illustrations." A roving evangelist who made "striking appeals to the conscience." Booth longed to go and do likewise.

Booth lacked Caughey's broad education. He had renounced "worldly culture," which, for him, consisted chiefly of novels by James Fenimore Cooper and Sir Walter Scott! His literature was the Bible, and his music consisted of the classic English hymns, above all those of the Wesley brothers. Years later, as a very old man, he would salve his loneliness by singing aloud:
Though waves and storms go o'er my head,
Though my heart fail and strength be gone;
Though joys be withered all and dead,
Though every comfort be withdrawn"
On this my steadfast soul relies:
Father, Thy mercy never dies.

This was hymn number 189, in "Wesley's Hymns," John Wesley's translation of a German classic. Booth himself was to write fine gospel songs.

The young revivalist may have been ignorant of secular culture, but he knew a great deal about human misery. With his friend Will Samson, he found a room for "a tatterdemalion old woman"; he brought the sensational wife-beater "Besom Jack" to the Lord. Booth's methods were based on "common sense, the Holy Spirit and the Word of God."

After a miserable year of unemployment, William Booth left Nottingham for London. Pawnbroking was his trade and free-lance preaching was his calling. He did well at the latter, so well that he caught the attention of Mr. Rabbits, the pious owner of a chain of shoe shops. Rabbits gave Booth a double blessing: he offered to back him as a full-time preacher for a full year at a pound a week, and he invited him to a tea party where William Booth met his Catherine.

A marriage of true minds

Like her William, Catherine Mumford was born in 1829. Like him she belonged to the Puritan tradition of English Christianity. Catherine had been made to read the Bible from Genesis to Revelation four times by the time she was twelve. She had no fear of being in a minority. As a child, she walked beside a man who was being dragged to the lock-up. She once jumped on a boy who was beating a donkey with a

A young Salvation Army bandsman.

hammer. She longed to abolish slavery of blacks. At twelve she was afflicted with curvature of the spine. Unable to attend school, she read far more widely than William Booth would ever do. At the age of sixteen, in Brixton, London, she was saved. But saved from what? Catherine explained: "I would place my Bible and hymn book under my pillow praying that I might wake up with the assurance of Salvation. One morning, my eyes fell on the words "My God I am thine: what a comfort divine: What a blessing to know that my Jesus is mine." The words that brought Catherine to living faith were composed by Charles Wesley. Who else?

Catherine Mumford and William Booth were a match. Soon, in St. John Ervine's words, "the young lovers of the Lord were lovers of each other."

But could they get married on Mr. Rabbits' pound a week?

Booth sought the guidance of the Lord by casting a biblical lot. He opened the Scriptures at random and the what he read was a favorable omen: "Join them together into one stick so that they will become one in your hand" (Ezekiel 37:17).

So far so good. Methodism was in turmoil, however. Booth had to leave London and minister to a small circuit at Spalding in Lincolnshire, far from his beloved in that phoneless age. Catherine wrote long and loving letters full of wise counsel. She knew that revival meetings, night after night, left little time for study: "Could you not rise by six every morning and convert your bedroom into a study?" She advised against too much "Bible punching." She gently noted: "Remember Caughey's heavenly carriage.... He did not shout." Booth, however, was dubious about women preachers, "I do not encourage a woman to begin preaching," he wrote, "although I would not stop her." Little did he know that his Catherine would be famous one day, like James Caughey, for her "heavenly carriage" in the pulpit! On strong drink she took a firm stand. "Flee the detestable drink as you would a serpent. Be a teetotaller in principle and practice." Above all she tried to give her man confidence in the Lord. "Spalding will not be your final destination," she told him.

These were prophetic words, fulfilled in the Army to be.

Interrupted study

But surely Booth needed some training? The Congregational ministry seemed to offer the way forward. But the dragon of predestination lay in the path. William Booth was told he must

read and agree with Booth's (no relation) book *Reign of Grace!* This proclaimed the doctrines of John Calvin: Christ did not die for all, but only for the "elect" whom God had predestined to be saved.

But his beloved Methodism taught him Christ died for all. The Calvinist doctrine, as he understood it, seemed to imply that the poor in the public house were damned before they had a chance to repent. He read thirty or forty pages of the other Booth and then flung the book across the room!

In the end Booth got a brief theological education at Dr. Cooke's Methodist seminary in Camberwell, London. But as he observed, "My studies were ... sadly interrupted by the more practical business of saving souls." Dr. Cooke was understanding. William Booth was made a minister in the New Connexion (yet another branch of Methodism) and allowed to marry his Catherine earlier than the rules laid down. The wedding took place on June 16, 1855, and the honeymoon was followed by a revivalist tour of the island of Guernsey.

The world of the Booths was Biblical, Puritan, and evangelical. They lived among people who debated whether Christ had died for all mankind or for the elect. Yet in 1846 novelist Marian Evans—under the pseudonym of George Eliot—translated into English the skeptical *Life of Jesus* by the German, David Strauss. Its readers might wonder whether Christ had lived at all! William Booth wanted a good sermon on the Flood to take to Guernsey, but in 1859 Charles Darwin brought out *The Origin of*

"The Marechale" preaches in a Paris bar.

William Booth recalled, "a great deal of open-air and theater preaching." David Livingstone had gone back to Africa in 1858, but were there not a million "heathen" to be found close at hand, in the East End of London? To try and win them for the gospel, "a large tent had been erected in a disused burial ground belonging to the Society of Friends in Baker's Row, Whitechapel.... Meetings were being held every night, and to conduct them I was invited for a fortnight." "Where," he put it to the hesitant Catherine, "can you go, and find such heathen as these?"

A Salvation Army
The new mission encountered its own "hard times." When the tent was blown down (or were the guy ropes cut?) the Booths moved to a dancing academy. The dancing went on into the small hours of Sunday; thereafter the missioners had to start by clearing up the leftover litter. By 1867 William Booth had begun in the Effingham Theater. The *East London Observer* was damning in its faint praise of him: "The Revd. gentleman's style of preaching, though manifestly an imitation of the great Spurgeon, lacks the fiery energy and eloquence of his style."

The East London Revival Society (under superintendent William Booth) claimed to be unsectarian, but its seven-point creed was in fact Methodist. Basing belief on the inspiration of the Bible, it affirmed belief in God, the Trinity, the divinity and humanity of Christ, the fall of Adam, and the atonement of Christ for the whole world. Repentance, regeneration, and faith were held essential to

Species, which would force millions to re-think their views on the Book of Genesis.

"Such heathen as these!"
The Booths were concerned at "infidelity," but their personal, Biblical faith was hardly challenged. Their calling was to be evangelists. They led campaigns in Hull, Sheffield, Leeds, Halifax. Their eight children arrived and survived. The second son, Ballington, was baptized by James Caughey himself. And in the midst of her duties as wife and mother, Catherine wrote her pamphlet "Female Ministry" in response to an attack on the American evangelist Phoebe Palmer. She affirmed that Paul's ban on women speaking referred to idle chatter and not the preaching of the Word. And in Gatehead, at first timorously, she began to preach herself.

Some in the New Connexion were far from happy at the Booths' fame: they were "taking the cream and leaving the skimmed milk to others ...!" Booth, they said, should be made to work in a circuit like other ministers. A crucial decision was made. In 1861, Booth recalled, "I resigned my position and went out, from home and salary, with a delicate wife and four little children under five years of age."

They found work as freelance missioners among the Cornish Methodists, but the Conference closed the chapel doors against them. In the English Midlands Booth formed the Hallelujah Band, explaining, "We invited a (converted) poacher, a couple of prize-fighters, a ... jailbird .... We had a morning march, wagons in the hollows of a broken field, and meetings all day."

Thus the ideas and ideals that were to make the Salvation Army began to take shape. By 1864 the Booths were back in London. The evangelical awakening that began in Ireland in 1859 had swept on into England. There was, as salvation. There would be the final judgement, with eternal happiness for the righteous and endless punishment for the wicked.

Such was the simple, stark creed of William Booth. These seven points would later be expanded to eleven, in order to include the Wesleyan doctrine of "entire sanctification." Perfect love must be the believer's goal. These points make up the Salvation Army's articles of faith to this day.

Gradually the East London Christian Mission gained ground. Strong personalities were attracted to Booth's banner. There was James Dowdle, the Saved Railway Guard. Once he had played a bass viol in the last Church of England bands. Now he found scope for his Hallelujah fiddle in East London. Booth presided at his marriage. Dowdle and his new wife were placed in charge of a food depot in Shoreditch: "From five in the morning till eleven at night they were selling to the poorest of the poor penniworths ... soup, meat, and coffee."

War in Whitby!
There was George Scott Railton, a crank or a saint—who could tell? He joined up after reading Booth's pamphlet "How to reach the masses with the Gospel" and became the Mission's General Secretary. There was Elijah Cadman, the Fighting Sweep, who put up sensational posters in Whitby (outside East London now!) proclaiming "WAR, WAR, WAR IN WHITBY!" and summoning two thousand men and women to join the Hallelujah Army. He was "Captain Cadman from London" and "Mr. Booth the General"

would soon be coming to "review the troops."

The military images went right back to the Bible, via the writings of John Bunyan. They appealed to the popular imagination. Many a stirring melody from the American Civil War was pressed into the service of the gospel. "Why should the devil have all the best tunes?" If William Booth never said it, he certainly meant it!

The Annual Conference of 1878 was also the first War Congress of The Salvation Army. The printer's proof for the Annual Report declared:

THE CHRISTIAN MISSION IS ... A VOLUNTEER ARMY.

But these "Volunteers" were second-line, part-time troops: and consequently the corrected version announced:

THE CHRISTIAN MISSION IS ... A SALVATION ARMY

The new name soon superseded the old one!

That same conference also put an end to democracy (in the Army) and voted absolute power into the hands of William Booth. He was given power to station evangelists, to act as sole trustee, and to nominate his successor. "Confidence in God and me is indispensable," he had declared a year earlier, "both now and ever afterwards."

The new Christian army soon acquired uniforms, brass bands, and a system of officers' ranks. It spread rapidly in the 1880s, attracting ridicule, admiration, persecution, and contempt. At Sheffield the Booths and their

followers were beaten up by a mob. "Now's the time to get your photograph taken," said Booth to his battered followers. The Quaker statesman John Bright wrote to Catherine from the House of Commons: "The people who mob you would no doubt have mobbed the apostles."

Quaker influence played its part in another controversial decision of the time. Like the Friends of the seventeenth century the Salvation Army ceased to observe the traditional sacraments of baptism and the Lord's Supper. Catherine Booth and George Scott Railton were the prime movers. The latter looked back with admiration to "George Fox and his Salvation Army 220 years ago." William took a more utilitarian line. Would converted drunkards fall foul of fermented communion wine? If the Army was a "Mission" and not a "Church" did it in fact need to celebrate sacraments? Would there be opposition to women preachers, now well established, presiding at the Lord's Supper? On June 2, 1883, the *War Cry* gave the decision: baptism by water and the Lord's Supper would no longer be observed. "Is it now wise for us to postpone any settlement of the question, to leave it to some future day, when we shall have more light? Meanwhile, we do not prohibit our own people from taking the sacraments."

And there the matter has rested, for over a century.

Traveling alone
In middle age William Booth found himself leading a growing army in five continents. He had become an international celebrity, and he stepped forward as a

An open-air meeting conducted by Salvation Army officers at St. Helier, Jersey, the Channel Islands.

social reformer with his sensational book, *In Darkest England and the Way Out*. Written with the help of the journalist W.T. Stead, it called for the establishment of a "Cab Horse Charter": "Every cab-horse in London has a shelter for the night, food for its stomach, and work ... to earn its corn."

The Darkest England Scheme seeded similar plans all round the world: from Cincinnati, U.S.A., where the Slum Post was set on Rat Row, to Japan, where poet Gumpei Yamamuro led an attack on the traditional forms of forced prostitution. Booth was now governor, under God, of a growing international empire of goodwill.

But he ruled alone, for in February 1888, as William Booth prepared for a preaching visit to Holland, Catherine came home. She told him that she had breast cancer and at most two

years to live. He wrote: "I was stunned. I felt as if the whole world were coming to a standstill. Opposite me on the wall was a picture of Christ on the cross. I thought I could understand it as never before. She talked like a heroine, like an angel to me. I could only kneel with her and try to pray."

Catherine preached her last sermon in June 1890, and on October 4, 1890, she died. Her funeral was a great public occasion. Some said it was a stunt. Booth wrote in his diary: "I have ... made an exhibition of myself for my master's sake all my life ... a large party of my company has gone before.... I must travel the journey alone."

General before father

Members of the Booth family were now public figures, and a "cult of personality" grew up around them. Bramwell, who

was the eldest, was the Chief of the Staff and his hold on power grew tighter as his father grew older. Railton opposed the Army's move into ownership of property and Life Insurance. He was left on the sidelines. Far-flung territories did not always take kindly to strict control from London. Ballington Booth resigned in 1896, but Evangeline Booth, a future General, held the line for the international Army. Herbert Booth, a pioneer of the cinema, resigned his commission while he was serving in Australia, calling for a "government in which ... leading spirits throughout the world shall have a voice." Emma, the "Consul," perished in an American train crash. And Catherine Booth-Clibborn, the eldest daughter Kate, left with her husband in 1902. This, for William Booth, was the unkindest cut of all. "I am your general before I am your father," he wrote to her. In his diary he reduced his eldest daughter to a mere "Mrs. Clibborn." No longer should she bear the name of Booth.

Promoted to glory

Just one limit was set to absolute monarchy: a Deed Poll of 1904 provided for the deposition of an "unfit" General. It was to be used later in 1929 to depose Bramwell Booth and substitute election by High Council. Thus, a generation later, Bramwell fell victim to the system his own father had set up. But the old man in his last years cared little for power. Famous, awkward, and received now by kings and presidents, he returned to his calling of traveling evangelist.

Great congregations sang his famous hymn:

O Boundless Salvation—deep ocean of love:
O Fullness of mercy, Christ brought from above—
The whole world redeeming, so rich and so free:
Now flowing for all men, come roll over me!

And hundreds of young people, as officers in the Army he founded, promised: "For Christ's sake, to feed the poor, clothe the naked, love the unlovable and befriend the friendless."

Blind at the end, William Booth gave his last address in the Albert Hall, London, on May 9, 1912. "I am going into dry dock for repairs," he joked. And reviewing his life's work, he said: "I might have chosen ... the housing of the poor ... the material benefit of the working classes ... the interests of the criminal world ... the improvement of the community through politics.... [But] The object I chose ... contained in its heart the remedy for every form of misery and sin to be found upon the earth."

On October 20, 1912, William Booth was "promoted to Glory." The American poet Vachel Lindsay imagined his entry into heaven:

Booth died blind and still by faith he trod,
Eyes still dazzled by the ways of God....
Christ came gently with a robe and crown
For Booth the soldier, while the throng knelt down.
He saw King Jesus. They were face to face,
And he knelt a-weeping in that holy place.

Further Reading

Begbie, Harold. *Life of William Booth, the founder of the Salvation Army*. London: MacMillan and Co., 1920.

Booth, William. *In Darkest England and the Way Out*. New York: Funk and Wagnalls, 1890.

Carpenter, Minnie Lindsay. *William Booth, Founder of the Salvation Army*. London: Epworth, 1944.

Collier, Richard. *The General Next to God, the Story of William Booth and the Salvation Army*. New York: Dutton, 1965.

Chuck Colson and Prison Fellowship
Watergate and After

"Faithfulness, not success," reads the simple wooden plaque on Chuck Colson's desk. The motto sits between two heavy, silver "in" and "out" boxes, mementos of a time when success alone was Chuck Colson's goal.

The silver trays came from Chuck Colson's White House days, when Richard Nixon was his hero; the wooden plaque was a gift from a prisoner. Its credo, which is that of Mother Teresa, captures Colson's commitment to his greatest hero, the Lord Jesus Christ.

Perhaps uniquely among evangelical leaders of the late twentieth century, Colson has lived two lives: one in positions of power in the secular world, the other as leader of a Christian ministry dedicated to the powerless.

What hinged these extremes was a dramatic encounter with Christ, who changed Colson's life forever and compelled him to birth Prison Fellowship, a movement that has introduced countless inmates to new life.

Colson's leadership of Prison Fellowship and his efforts as a speaker and author have, like his efforts in his "first life," enjoyed great success. But Colson has fought not to forget the lessons he learned in failure. Paradoxically, God used not his greatest accomplishments, but his greatest defeat—the fact that he went to prison—to build a significant movement of true evangelical outreach.

"God will use you how He wills," Chuck Colson constantly reminds anyone who will listen. It is not up to you to orchestrate some grand success for His purposes. Are we off the hook, then? No. God calls us to something tougher: obedience. And though Colson has his warts, his Christian life has been a model of such faithfulness.

Two principles

Colson's parents sacrificed much in the Depression years to build a secure life for their only son. His father worked long hoursas a bookkeeper at a meatpacking plant, making his way through law school at night.

As a result, young Chuck did not have much time with his

Chuck Colson, founder of Prison Fellowship.

THE LIFE OF

Chuck Colson

Colson visits with a prison inmate.

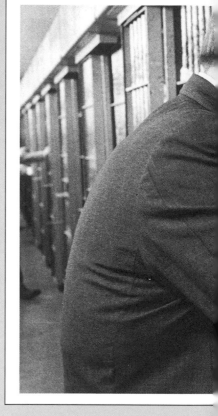

a fervent student. During his military stint, *Semper Fidelis* (always faithful), the Marine motto, became more a creed than a slogan, merging with his father's teachings of truth and excellence to forge a core of loyalty in Chuck Colson that would characterize him for the rest of his life.

After the Marines, Chuck Colson embarked on a career track to the top. He was assistant to the assistant secretary of the Navy in 1955–56; administrative assistant to U.S. Senator Leverett Saltonstall (R–Mass) from 1956 to 1961 (during this time he completed a law school degree); and then senior partner in a law firm in Washington, Gadsby and Hannah, from 1961 to 1969.

Watergate

It was in 1969 that Chuck Colson got the call he had been anticipating all his life: Richard Nixon, president of the United States, needed him.

In the White House circle of senior aides to the president, Colson was part of a group of brilliant men linked by the height of their ambitions and the breadth of their egos. His days were a blur of meetings, memos, briefings, jousting with Democrats, Communists, the press, and his colleagues.

All this brought out the finest of Colson's fighting instincts. A master of manipulation, he kept his father's creed of excellence, although truth was sometimes a casualty of the political cross fire. His reputation as a cold-blooded infighter provided colorful copy for Washington's

dad, but sometimes on Sunday afternoons they would sit together on the back steps of their small Boston home. "Two things," Wendell Colson would tell his son. "First, always tell the truth. And second, whatever you put your mind to—it doesn't matter if it's cleaning toilets—do it with excellence."

As a child, Chuck did not have much specifically Christian instruction; his parents were occasional churchgoers whose large, dusty family Bible was used to record births and deaths. But his father's character-shaping admonitions set the stage for what was to follow.

Semper Fidelis

Colson threw himself into Brown University with gusto: an enthusiastic member of his fraternity, class officer, commandant of his ROTC (Reserve Officer Training Corps) unit, and also, after his second year,

political-gossip pages; Nixon, who knew a man who could get the job done, egged him on.

Colson was later to write:

British novelist C.P. Snow tells the story of a man who chooses not to be king but king-maker, the ultimate achievement power affords. Snow might well have been writing about me.

I entered government believing that public office was a trust, a duty. Gradually, imperceptibly, I began to view it as a holy crusade; the future of the republic, or so I rationalized, depended upon the president's continuation in office. But whether I acknowledged it or not, equally important was the fact that my own power depended on it.

Surely those twin strands— misguided political zeal and the

protection of personal power—were key elements of the intrigue and cover-up that became Watergate. It would lead to the first-ever resignation of a U.S. president, the imprisonment of many of his aides; and it would become a synonym for scandal in the American lexicon.

For Colson, the political crisis merged with his personal spiritual crisis. He had sought to solve his odd sense of emptiness by leaving the White House and returning to law, establishing his own Washington firm, Colson and Shapiro. It was there that Watergate's tentacles reached him in the summer of 1973. And it was there that Colson found he was the object of an even more relentless pursuit by the Hound of Heaven.

Spiritual torpedo

God snared Chuck Colson through the power of the Holy Spirit and two assistants: Tom Phillips and C. S. Lewis. The former, a Colson client, sensed his need, invited him home, and told him bluntly about Jesus Christ. Phillips also read to Colson from *Mere Christianity*, Lewis's cogent work on the essence of faith. Lewis's description of pride—a spiritual cancer that destroys everything else in a person's life and prevents one from knowing God—struck Colson, as he wrote later, like a torpedo that "hit me amidships." He bade his host good night—but a few minutes later, in Phillips's driveway, he found himself pierced to the heart. He sobbed a prayer in a flood of

tears that dissolved the armor around his soul. "Take me," he prayed, over and over.

But if Colson's heart had been pierced, his brain had to be persuaded. So, several weeks later, with *Mere Christianity* in one hand and a yellow legal pad in the other, he outlined the case for Christ. As he did so, and read the Bible, he found that Christ held up to intellectual, moral, and spiritual scrutiny. He determined to follow Him for the rest of his life. He had found the Source and ultimate object of faithfulness.

Most who convert to Christianity do so in relative privacy; Colson's "born again" experience hit the pages of newspapers across the country. He likes to say that he singlehandedly kept a small army of political cartoonists fed and clothed for a year.

Supported by new friends—brothers and sisters in Christ—he made another tough decision, pleading guilty to a Watergate offense for which he had not even been charged: that of passing derogatory information to the press regarding Daniel Ellsburg, the anti-war activist who had stolen the classified military briefing materials which came to be known as the Pentagon Papers.

Jail

That step sent him to prison. As prisoner #23226, the former special counsel to the president was now in charge of Maxwell Federal Prison's washing machine. No White House inner circle here; his colleagues were drug dealers, Mafia kingpins, petty offenders, and lifers. Some were in prison because of laws he had helped legislate.

Colson studied his Bible, met with fellow Christians, and tried to absorb everything. He saw firsthand why American prisons did not rehabilitate offenders. And when released in January 1975, he found that God had planted a seed in his soul while behind bars. He had to go back.

Passing up lucrative business opportunities, Colson caucused with fellow Christians to determine how to bring real hope and inner change to those in prison.

A new vision

One day while shaving he saw a picture in his head: programs by which prisoners could be discipled, then taught how to equip other inmates in the faith. The prisons could be a training ground, not for further crime, but for growth in Jesus Christ! He dashed cold water on his face and ran to the telephone.

With the help of Christian friends, and with royalties from his spiritual autobiography, *Born Again* (a best-seller that has led to the conversion of many, many skeptics), Colson founded Prison Fellowship in 1976. The ministry soon grew like a vine, flowering into programs that introduced prisoners to Christ, discipled them, and equipped them for transition to life outside the walls as contributing members of society. There have been outreaches to inmates' families; seminars on marriage; gifts to prisoners' children at Christmas; criminal justice reform efforts; restoration for victims of crime, and restitution to communities through inmate work projects.

Fifteen years after its inception, Prison Fellowship had grown to a network of forty thousand Christian volunteers from churches across the United States and thousands more in forty countries abroad.

A new mission

For Colson, the ministry God had started through him is not just a far-flung organization, however. Prison Fellowship is something much more organic—a movement, a mission, even a way of thinking about faith and action, which he hopes will galvanize Christians everywhere to leap out of their pews and into the streets and the prisons, wherever they can help people in need.

It is for Colson a vision—not just a picture in his shaving mirror now, but a whole concept of what it means to be a Christian, a challenge to a church grown soft to its biblical mandate and a culture grown hostile to the life and witness of Christianity.

His efforts to communicate his vision have led to an extensive writing and speaking schedule. In addition to his thousands of articles, columns, and speaking engagements, the years after *Born Again* yielded eight books, all written with an urgency of expression that added lines to Colson's face and took years off his editor's life.

Like many who are vision-driven, Colson has been criticized for being too impatient, too negative, painting with too broad a brush, always harping about one issue or another. Sensitive to criticism, he is nonetheless undaunted by those who wish he would just go take a vacation. His passion comes from both tracks of his "two life" experience. The White House shaped him to think in terms of the big sweep of history, of lives lived to the hilt in the service of some great cause. His conversion was to show him what his cause was.

Faithfulness—not success

The Marines taught Colson about *semper fidelis*; Mother Teresa's example of "faithfulness, not success," however, took him further. His father, with his emphasis on excellence, instilled in his son a sense of drive that had no neutral gear. But then Chuck discovered Christian heroes whose drive exceeded his own—believers like the Apostle Paul, who pressed on toward the upward call of Christ, continuing all the way to martyrdom; Augustine, who chronicled not only his own conversion but also outined the right relationship between the political world and the spiritual world; Martin Luther, who turned his whole world upside down; William Wilberforce, the British politician who sacrificed his career and his health to fight for twenty years for the abolition of Britain's slave trade—people who expended themselves for the sake of Christ and His kingdom.

But just when you think Colson is a train that will run over anyone who is not moving at the same speed, he will surprise you. And just when you put him in a box, thinking that he is so fervent in his visions of Christian activism or Christian thinking that he has either overintellectualized or perhaps oversocialized the faith, he will surprise you again. At the heart of Chuck Colson is a deep love for the heart of the gospel, the good news that brings men and women from death unto life.

Speaking the truth in love
Two rather different examples embody that desire to speak the truth in love.

On Christmas Day, 1985, Chuck Colson was preaching at a women's prison in North Carolina. After the service, a prison official asked if he would like to visit Bessie Shipp, a prisoner in solitary confinement. "Of course," Colson responded. "One thing," the man said, "she has AIDS."

At that time much less was known about AIDS and its transmission. Colson struggled to think of an excuse why he could not see this prisoner. Then he remembered seeing Mother Teresa on television the evening before, at an AIDS hospice in New York; and she had said: "They need to know God loves them."

Chuck Colson visited Bessie Shipp in her prison cell. It was Christmas, she was alone, and she was dying. He held her cold hand and gently talked with her about Jesus, then prayed with her as she received Christ as her Savior.

Bessie Shipp died three weeks later. To some, she was only an insignificant life, a prisoner with AIDS at the very bottom rung of society, but for Colson she sparked a renewed sense of mission. "We are not just engaged in some vague philanthropic exercise," he wrote. "We are dealing with life and death. And we had better get on with this business of proclaiming the Gospel!"

Several years later, Colson's speaking schedule included a prayer meeting arranged by Christian leaders in a major city who, for months, had been timidly courting one of the best-known corporate businessmen in America. The meeting was in his office.

It soon became clear to Colson that this corporate leader, while he was cordial to Christianity, had never been confronted with his *need* for a Savior—that is, his own sin. Colson did not deal gently here, as with Bessie Shipp, but let loose with one of his favorite lines, one always guaranteed to get a reaction. "Do you know, Mr. X, that you are more like Adolf Hitler than you are like Jesus Christ?"

A red flush appeared above the man's crisp collar. The Christians blanched. Colson held steady—and, after a startling conversation, the man invited him to a private office.

There he confessed that no one had ever awakened him to the reality of sin, and that yes, he needed Christ and His forgiveness. He prayed to follow Him that day.

Colson's life in government prepared him to deal with people in power; prison enabled him to share the suffering of people without power. During Colson's years as a believer, God has used both experiences for His glory. And for Chuck Colson, whatever God plants in his fertile mind to do, it is clear he will faithfully do it—whether he is successful or not.

Further Reading

Colson, Charles. *Born Again*. Old Tappan, N.J.: Chosen, 1976.

_____. *Life Sentence*. Old Tappan, N.J.: Chosen, 1980.

_____. *Loving God*. Grand Rapids: Zondervan, 1983.

Colson, Charles, with Ellen Santilli Vaughn. *Kingdoms in Conflict*. Grand Rapids: Zondervan/William Morrow, 1987.

_____ *Against the Night*. Ann Arbor, Mich.: Servant, 1989.

_____. *The God of Stones and Spiders*. Westchester, Ill.: Crossway, 1990.

Student Work

Reaching Out

The leading advocate of the worldwide expansion of Christianity in the late nineteenth–early twentieth century, John R. Mott was an energetic speaker, writer, and traveler who headed many committees and boards responsible for missionary and ecumenical ventures. As a youth he had a deep religious experience, and from his mentor D. L. Moody he learned the value of total commitment to Christ and the ideal of working with all Christians regardless of denominational differences to spread the gospel. Neither theologically trained nor ordained, he was employed as an official of the American Young Men's Christian Association (YMCA).

Organization man

Mott founded the Student Volunteer Movement and the World's Student Christian Federation, and was a convener of the 1910 World Missionary Conference at Edinburgh. He chaired its Continuation Committee and was involved in the creation of the International Missionary Council and the meetings leading to the formation of the World Council of Churches. An ecumenically oriented evangelical who emphasized "now" as the time of crises, promise, and action, Mott saw missionary outreach as the way to bring all nations into the body of Christ and to break down every barrier to racial and international understanding.

Opposite: John R. Mott.

John R. Mott: Missions Enthusiast

Evangelizing the World in a Generation

Born at Livingston Manor, Sullivan County, New York, on May 25, 1865, John R. Mott was the son of John Stitt Mott, a lumber merchant, and Elmira Dodge. (According to his biographer Howard Hopkins, he never had a middle name but adopted the initial R. as a teenager.) Four months later the family moved to Postville, Iowa, where the elder Mott prospered in the lumber and hardware business and served as mayor. Raised in a devout home, at age 13, he was led to Christ by an itinerant YMCA evangelist and joined the local Methodist church. Thanks to the influence of the scholarly pastor of his congregation, in 1881 Mott enrolled in Upper Iowa University, a nearby Methodist college, where he began developing his literary and oratorical skills.

Four years later he transferred to Cornell University in New York and at once became involved in student Christian work. In January 1886 he gave his life to Christian service after meeting the popular English athlete C. T. Studd, who was on a YMCA-sponsored American tour. Mott decided to undertake a rigorous program of prayer, meditation, and Bible study, and through this achieved the "higher ground" (as he called it) or the "second blessing," of total consecration to Christ and the commitment of his energies to further the kingdom of God. The young student wrote his father about the change that had occurred: "When I gave up to God in this way, I settled forever the question what I am to do in life. It is to be soul saving."

Mount Hermon Hundred

He planned to study for the ministry, but that summer he attended D. L. Moody's first "College Students' Summer School" at Mount Hermon, Massachusetts. There he caught the vision for foreign missions and was one of the "Mount Hermon Hundred" who volunteered for service. He also learned the importance of Bible study, prayer, and the working of the Holy Spirit and the need to subordinate denominational differences to the compelling thrust toward action. From this humble beginning came personal loyalty to Jesus Christ as Lord and Savior and the ecumenical and biblical sense of urgency, which overshadowed all other considerations which were the hallmarks of his life's ministry.

That fall Mott took charge of the Christian student chapter at Cornell, and after completing a Ph.D. degree in history and

"When I gave up to God in this way, I settled forever the question what I am to do in life. It is to be soul saving."

THE LIFE OF

John R. Mott

1865	Born in Livingston Manor, New York State
1881–85	Studies at Upper Iowa University
1885–88	Studies at Cornell University
1886	Mount Hermon Conference
1888	Founds Student Volunteer Movement
1895	Founds World's Student Christian Federation
1900	Publishes *The Evangelization of the World in This Generation*
1910	Attends World Missionary Conference, Edinburgh
1915	Serves as YMCA General Secretary
1920	Resigns as head of SVM and WSCF
1921	Formation of the International Missionary Council
1926	Serves as Chairman, World Alliance of YMCAs
1928	Retires from American YMCA and WSCF
1946	Receives Nobel Peace Prize
1948	Founding of the World Council of Churches at Amsterdam
1954	Attends Evanston Assembly of World Council of Churches
1955	Dies in Orlando, Florida

political science in 1888 he accepted an appointment as traveling secretary for the inter-collegiate YMCA. He started his career as a lay Christian worker and remained so throughout his life. Although John Mott consistently identified himself as a Methodist, he never obtained a theological education or was ordained. He traveled incessantly, first in North America and then throughout the world (this has been estimated at 1.7 million miles), even though he suffered from motion sickness.

A gifted speaker and writer as well as a creative and energetic organizer, his achievements were prodigious. He authored eighteen books, edited *The Student World*, and his collected addresses and papers fill six volumes. Possessing remarkable powers of judgment and concentration, he could lead meetings, motivate colleagues, and raise funds with great skill. He was a compulsive worker, who seemingly utilized every moment of time in some form of productive labor, and could manage almost any given number of enterprises simultaneously. Moving freely in the highest circles of politics and business, he was the friend of presidents and captains of industry alike.

Moody's influence

The person who probably had the greatest influence on him was Dwight L. Moody. Like Mott, the great evangelist also was unordained, possessed boundless energy, and although

John Mott became a great missionary statesman.

theologically self-educated had a respect for learning. Moody communicated the importance of unswerving devotion to Christ to his protégé, the value of unity in Christian effort, a vision of the inherent linkage between evangelism and social concern, and an understanding of how the releasing and use of money could be a spiritual process. Mott helped organize the summer student conferences that met under Moody's auspices at Northfield, Massachusetts, and in 1893 he was offered the directorship of Moody Bible Institute in Chicago but turned it down.

In the YMCA Mott built on the groundwork laid by Luther D. Wishard, the organization's first world secretary. To channel

the missionary enthusiasm unleashed at Mount Hermon in 1886, Mott and several friends formed the Student Volunteer Movement for Foreign Missions on December 6, 1888, which was linked to the YMCA, and he served as its chairman. The group's vision was summed up in its watchword, "The Evangelization of the World in This Generation," and was coined by A. T. Pierson, the leading spokesman for foreign missions in America at the time. Beginning in 1891 the SVM held large conventions known as "Quadrennials," which challenged students to consider service abroad; it is estimated that as many as twenty thousand missionaries may have gone out as a result of the SVM. John Mott, addressing the Ecumenical Missionary Conference in New York (1900), explained what he believed to be the nature of the Church's duty to spread the Gospel:

It is the obligation of the church to evangelize the world in this generation. It is our duty because all men need Christ. The Scriptures teach that if men are to be saved they must be saved through Christ. The burning question is, Shall hundreds of millions of men now living, who need Christ, and who are capable of receiving help from Him, pass away without having even the opportunity to know Him? To have knowledge of Christ is to incur a responsibility to every man who has not.... What a crime against mankind to keep a knowledge of the mission of Christ from two-thirds of the human race! It is our duty to evangelize the world in this generation because of the missionary command of Christ.

Sadly, after World War I the Student Volunteer Movement declined due to the loss of Mott's original vision and a shift in student concerns.

International Missionary Council meeting at Tambaram, Madras, India, 1938.

Christian cooperation

Perhaps Mott's most enduring achievement was in the realm of Christian cooperation. He had a talent for bringing people together and smoothing over their differences, and he never engaged in destructive polemics against people with whom he differed. Rather, he saw the key to world evangelization as cooperation, and he promoted this vigorously through the World's Student Christian Federation, which he formed in 1895 and led as its general secretary until 1920. A lay movement that also included women in its leadership, the WSCF sought to unite student Christian movements throughout the world by exchanging information, developing leaders, organizing groups, and coordinating their activities. He was among the founders of the Federal Council of Churches but refused an offer

in 1909 to become its executive secretary because he believed that providing leadership to the world missionary movement was a more pressing task.

John Mott was gripped by the vision of foreign missions. In 1893 he helped initiate regular conversations among mission boards that eventually resulted in the formation of the Foreign Missions Conference of North America in 1911. He was intimately involved in the planning of the World Missionary Conference that met in June 1910 at Edinburgh, served as its chair, and headed its Continuation Committee whose goal was fostering unified effort in the proclamation of the gospel.

Mott strongly supported the creation of both national Christian councils in Africa and Asia and cooperative missionary councils in the "sending" countries of the West as a basis for

cooperation. He also worked to build bridges to the Eastern Orthodox churches and thereby draw them into the circle of the growing ecumenical movement. Although the optimistic hope of concerted effort in missionary work was shattered in the fratricidal conflict that engulfed Europe in 1914, ties were gradually reestablished after the return of peace, and in 1921 a genuinely global body, called the International Missionary Council, was formed.

As a close friend of President Woodrow Wilson, Mott was offered the post of ambassador to China in 1913 but turned it down. Afterward, he did agree to serve on the Mexican Border Commission (1916) and the Root Mission of Russia (1917). After the war began, he attempted to maintain the student Christian effort and carry out YMCA work among war prisoners on both sides of the lines, but his relationship with President Wilson led to a growing estrangement with his German counterparts in the missionary movement. The rupture in relations, which occurred after the U.S. entry into the conflict, required several years to heal.

Reconciliation

In 1915 John Mott gave up his position as student and foreign secretary to order to become the general secretary of the American YMCA. In this capacity he was responsible for the administration of, and fundraising for, YMCA programs, and he headed its National War Work council, created in April 1917. At the same time, he kept his missionary lines open, and with with the coming of peace he promoted reconciliation and freedom for mission operations in former German territories. However, recognizing that the times had passed him by, in 1920 he resigned as chairman of the SVM and general secretary of the WSCF, although he stayed on for an additional eight years as chairman of the latter. John Mott retired from the American YMCA leadership in 1928, but he presided over the World Alliance of YMCAs from 1926 to 1947.

His remaining years were devoted to ecumenical efforts. As chair of the conference at Lake Mohonk, New York, in 1921, where the International Missionary Council was formed, he saw the fulfillment of the Edinburgh vision. This was to be an organization of churches, mission societies, and boards that would determine missionary policy but would not deal with ecclesiastical or doctrinal questions. It would be united in the belief that Christians had the duty to bear witness to the gospel of Jesus Christ among peoples of all nations.

As chair of the IMC until 1942, John Mott presided over its meetings at Jerusalem (1928) and Madras (1938). He was also involved with the Life and Work and the Faith and Order movements, and was a prominent figure at both groups' conferences, in both Oxford and Edinburgh, in 1937. He played a key role in the founding of the World Council of Churches in that he was vice-chairman of the provisional committee, which continued working during World War II, and in 1946 was chosen as one of the provisional presidents. At the Amsterdam meeting in August 1948 where the WCC was formally created, he was named honorary president for life. In 1946 he was awarded the Nobel Peace Prize for his participation in so many church and missionary efforts and his devotion to bringing people together.

In 1891 he married Leila Ada White, a schoolteacher, and they had four children. After Leila's death in 1952, John Mott married Agnes Peter, a friend since World War I days. Active until the end, he died at his home in Orlando, Florida, on January 31, 1955. His life's work was summed up quite well in a statement he made at one of his last public appearances, the World Council of Churches Assembly at Evanston, Illinois, in August 1954: "Gentlemen, when John Mott is dead, remember him as an evangelist."

Further Reading

Hopkins, C. Howard. *John R. Mott: A Biography*. Grand Rapids: Eerdmans, 1979.

Mackie, Robert C. *Layman Extraordinary: John R. Mott 1865–1965*. New York: Association Press, 1965.

Mott, John R. *The Evangelization of the World in This Generation*. New York: SVM, 1900.

_____. *The Decisive Hour of Christian Missions*, New York: SVM, 1910.

C. Stacey Woods

For Christ and the University

The name C. Stacey Woods is synonymous with university student ministry. He inaugurated two great university movements. Though born an Australian, he led InterVarsity Christian Fellowship–Canada for nearly two decades. He also helped found, and became the first general secretary of, InterVarsity Christian Fellowship–USA. He remained in that position for another two decades. Meanwhile he helped organize the International Fellowship of Evangelical Students, which encompasses nearly a hundred national university movements around the world, and served as its first general secretary.

Woods was only twenty-five when he took the reins of IVCF–Canada. But his greatest contribution was impressing upon IVCF–USA the principles, policies, and philosophy that would characterize it for decades. In spite of various obstacles, Woods persevered in the vision for worldwide student work that God had given him. For Woods, evangelism was a natural part of being a Christian. His goal in campus work, therefore, was to establish evangelizing fellowships that would be faithful to the Word of God.

C. Stacey Woods firmly believed that each Christian needs a personal, vital, and growing relationship with his Lord. He said, "We seem slow to realize that God can only work his work in our hearts and lives when we give him time. Too often our lives are cluttered with masses of extraneous material, unrelated activities which result in the central core of our being, namely ourselves as individual persons, being lost. But each of us should have a personal and individual relationship with the living God, be taught by him, formed by him and grow up into him to the measure of the fullness of the stature of Christ." Such a Christian was C. Stacey Woods.

IVCF–Canada
Woods was born in Australia and completed his postsecondary education in America. But he had no intention of staying in America or of ministering to American students. His eventual goal was to return to Australia. But God had other plans, as is so often the case with people He uses. After seeking the Lord's will, Woods accepted an invitation in 1934 to become the general secretary of IVCF–Canada, but for only one year—or so he thought. That one year became eighteen.

God gifted Woods to be a pioneer in student ministry. Besides having a great compassion for students, he was an effective fund-raiser and a recruiter of qualified people. Not only did he lead IVCF–Canada for nearly two decades, he was the first general secretary of IVCF in the United States for even longer. He administered two national movements, contacted churches and donors, wrote long letters to staff members, and spoke on campuses. His ability to shoulder all these responsibilities was amazing.

IVCF–USA is the oldest college campus ministry in America, having celebrated its fiftieth anniversary in 1991. It has also ministered to more students on more American campuses than any other organization. C. Stacey Woods was in the vanguard of this movement and indelibly stamped his character on it.

Three ministries
Later Woods became the first general secretary of the International Fellowship of Evangelical

C. Stacey Woods, 1905–83.

THE LIFE OF
C. Stacey Woods

1905	Born in Sydney, Australia
1934	Goes to America to complete education at Wheaton College and Dallas Theological Seminary
1934–52	General Secretary, InterVarsity Christian Fellowship–Canada
1941–60	First General Secretary, InterVarsity Christian Fellowship–USA
1941	Founds *HIS* magazine
1947–71	First General Secretary, International Fellowship of Evangelical Students
1950–52	Editor, *HIS* magazine
1978	Writes *The Growth of a Work of God*
1983	Dies in Lausanne, Switzerland, in April

Stacey Woods at an early IVCF Missionary Convention, Urbana, Illinois.

Students (IFES), an organization that united campus ministries in ten countries and has grown to represent nearly one hundred member countries. In consequence, he was simultaneous leader of three campus ministries. This immense challenge lasted five years. For a total of another fifteen years, he was the leader of two campus ministries (IVCF–Canada and IVCF–USA for seven years; IVCF–USA and IFES for another eight years). Few men could have accomplished such a feat.

Woods did not shrink from monumental tasks and challenges. Rather, as an overcomer, he thrived on them. As writers Keith and Gladys Hunt observe, "Stacey Woods was never one to look at the obstacles and be defeated. He believed that he would find a way if the Lord was in it."

A glorious adventure

During World War II, he had the vision of building a camp on donated land on Fairfield Island, Ontario, to minister to students. The problem was that building materials were strictly regulated because of the war effort. Undeterred, he and his coworkers scoured the countryside for wood, paint and other materials and made trips to America for nails and screws. Slowly the project progressed, but the Canadian government intervened and canceled the building permit. Time after time they appealed against the government's policy, all the while continuing the construction and risking prosecution. When a government official finally came out to the island in person to give them the order to desist, the last nails were being driven in. Campus-in-the-Woods was ready for students. Whenever he retold the story, Woods would say, "It was all a glorious adventure."

Stacey Woods experienced unexpected opposition from the very pastors and churches he thought would be supportive of his work with InterVarsity. Many conservative Christians were convinced that a believing student could not retain his biblical faith at a secular university. Therefore, when a student became a Christian through the work of IVCF, these well-meaning believers would talk him into transferring to a Christian college. For a number of years, this continually undermined Woods' work.

110 percent

He gave 110 percent for the Lord, whether it concerned what he did or what he believed, and

International Christian student hostel, London.

people loved him for it. He upheld a strong commitment to biblical inerrancy and Reformed doctrine. He defined worldliness as "a self-indulgent attitude of the heart and mind toward life—this material universe and all of life's relationships." Worldliness consisted in what a person is, not in what he does. His view of women in leadership was decades ahead of his time. In IVCF–USA, women staff members were given the same assignments as men.

His strong beliefs coupled with his sometimes abrasive or aggressive personality occasionally alienated people. For instance, he was strongly opposed to Bill Bright and Campus Crusade for Christ for many years because of what he felt was insensitivity and uncooperativeness on Campus Crusade's part toward other campus groups. He was also critical of modern evangelism's deemphasizing of the lordship of Christ, the eternal lostness of man, and the necessity of repentance. He stressed that the historic church has always viewed salvation as a process climaxing in commitment to Jesus Christ.

A bribe?

Woods had a tendency to be very direct with people. With him, principle was often more important than preserving relationships. A wealthy potential donor promised to give $100,000 if InverVarsity would change its doctrinal statement. Woods did not mince words:

"What you suggest sounds very much to me like a bribe. The answer is no, we shall not change our basis of faith. We are interdenominational. Good afternoon." Another time he was invited to speak at a missionary conference at a church in Detroit. When he noticed that deacons were posted at the doors to keep black people from entering, he was furious. After the service he told the pastor that he would never enter that church again as long as such a policy was continued. In fact, for several years he refused all invitations to speak in that city.

On the other hand, Woods was fun to be with. In spite of the pressure of directing two national movements he saw the funny side of his own actions. He was a vivid storyteller, and he had a great love for playing pranks and for shocking people. Being in his company was described as a high-energy experience.

Woods allowed the same freedom of character and conviction that he himself practiced. He did not want followers; he wanted people who were leaders. People who felt free to disagree with him. He expressed confidence that God could help his staff do whatever he asked. Such an attitude engendered both love and respect among his colleagues.

Stacey Woods' favorite verse was "I press on toward the goal...." (Philippians 3:14). He was highly motivated and full of energy, continually setting new goals for himself. Even after he retired, he looked for ways to help students establish a witness in the Soviet Union. Howard Larsen, a former IVCF staff member who became secretary and treasurer of the International Legal Center in the United Nations, said, "Stacey was one of the most remarkable men I have ever worked for. He was a dynamic, exciting man who would drive you to exhaustion but make you glad to do it again the next day. I was inspired by Stacey."

Further Reading

C. Stacey Woods. *The Growth of a Work of God.* Downers Grove, Ill.: InterVarsity, 1978.

Keith and Gladys Hunt. *For Christ and the University.* Downers Grove, Ill.: InterVarsity, 1991.

Torrey Johnson

Reaching Youth for Christ

I t was nearly midnight when the phone rang at Doug Fisher's home in Chicago. The high-pitched voice on the line was that of his friend Torrey Johnson, the pastor of Midwest Bible Church.

"Doug, we've got to start holding rallies in Chicago to reach youth for Christ," barked the evangelist–pastor to his musician friend. "I've just come from a prayer meeting here at the National Association of Evangelicals meeting in Columbus [Ohio], and I'm convinced the Lord wants us to do what Bev Shea and Lacy Hall have been urging us to do."

George Beverly Shea, a musician on WMBI, the Moody Bible Institute radio station, and Lacy Hall, a student at the Institute, had been exposed to youth rallies headed by Jack Wyrtzen and Glenn Wagner on the East Coast. They were convinced that similar evangelistic rallies were needed in the heartland of America, and they saw the pastor of a three-hundred-and-fifty-member church located on the northwest side of the city as the key to the effort. The Chapel Hour, Johnson's weekly evangelistic broadcast on WAIT, had already created an audience which drew more people to his church on Sunday evenings than for the worship service in the morning.

Wartime beginnings

The phone call set the stage for twenty-one weeks of Saturday night rallies in Orchestra Hall during the summer of 1944. Broadcast over radio station WCFL, the extravaganzas gave birth to Chicagoland Youth for Christ by capturing the interest of the military personnel who crowded the streets of America's second-largest city, together with a broad cross section of evangelical churches and their young people.

Close to three thousand crowded Orchestra Hall on May 26, 1944, to hear Billy Graham,

Making Things Happen

Torrey Johnson made things happen in the evangelical movement. Not only did he help found Youth for Christ International, but he served as its first president. He had a knack for bringing people and ideas together. Not one to shun high-powered promotions and co-operative efforts, Johnson took his cue from another Chicago evangelist–pastor, Paul Rader, and forged a national coalition to evangelize youth.

Though many people take credit for providing opportunities for Billy Graham, it was Johnson who asked Graham to speak at the first youth rally sponsored by Chicagoland Youth for Christ, employed Graham as the first full-time employee of Youth for Christ International, and later passed the radio program, *Songs in the Night*, along to the younger pastor. Johnson had an excellent eye for spotting gifted people and fitting them into ministry situations.

Innovator

While not an original thinker, Torrey Johnson was quick to insist on the incorporation of innovative ideas into evangelistic strategies. When Christian radio stations were gaining strength, Johnson insisted on placing his broadcasts on secular stations. When Jack Wyrtzen proved successful in doing evangelism through evening cruises on the Hudson River, Johnson did the same thing in the heartland of America.

At the high point of the youth rally movement, the president of Youth for Christ International called for a club program similar to the Chicago based Hi-C (High School Crusade) Clubs, an idea which was not adopted until the year 1950.

THE LIFE OF

Torrey M. Johnson

1909	Born in Chicago, Illinois
1927	First certainty of salvation
1930	Graduates from Wheaton College
	Ordained to ministry
	Marries Evelyn Nilsen
1933–52	Founds and pastors Midwest Bible Church, Chicago
1936	Graduates from Northern Baptist Theological Seminary, Chicago
1936–40	Instructor of New Testament Greek, Northern Baptist Theological Seminary; President of Wheaton College Alumni Association
1941	Begins *Chapel Hour* radio broadcast
1944	Youth for Christ Rallies for 21 weeks in Chicago
1945	Named first President, Youth for Christ International
	Begins *Songs in The Night*
1953–67	Evangelistic ministry
1967–82	Pastors Bibletown Community Church
	President of Bibletown Bible Conference and Concerts, Boca Raton, Florida

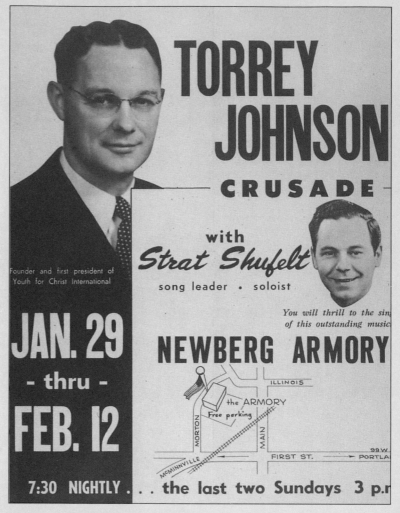

Poster for a Torrey Johnson crusade.

a little-known pastor from suburban Western Springs, preach the gospel. An estimated forty-five inquirers responded to the call for spiritual commitment, and the seed had been sown for Saturday night rallies in Chicago. National media attention was attracted a year later when close to seventy thousand people converged on Chicago's lakefront and Soldier Field to hear Percy Crawford climax the 1945 Memorial Day rally with a youth-oriented message and evangelistic invitation.

Though Torrey Maynard Johnson was an evangelist, the greatest contributions which he made in the resurgence of evangelical Christianity during the middle of the twentieth century were by his ability to bring a broad cross section of Bible-believing people together for the purpose of spreading the gospel. He bridged the generation between such great leaders of the early part of the century as Bob Jones, John Brown, Louis Talbott, and Will Houghton, and young voices like Billy Graham, Bob Pierce, Charles Templeton, Jack Wyrtzen, and Jack Shuler, who came to lead American evangelistic efforts in the latter half of the century.

Torrey Maynard Johnson was born on March 15, 1909, the third of six children of Jacob Martin and Thora Mathilda Evensen Johnson, who were Norwegian immigrants. Appropriately enough the baby was named for R. A. Torrey, the evangelist who worked closely with D. L. Moody and was the President of the Bible Institute of Los Angeles (now BIOLA University).

Torrey Johnson was raised on the northwest side of Chicago, where his father provided for the family by selling coffee and dabbling in real estate. The family settled in a home located only two doors from Salem Evangelical Free Church, which they decided to attend. Torrey's view of the world was shaped by family values, by the pulpit ministry of C. T. Dyrness, and by his Sunday school teacher, Oscar Larson, a concrete contractor. Larson led a class of ten to twenty-five young people who met on a weeknight at his home. Calling themselves the Christian Crusaders Class, the group focused on Bible study and prayer and were serious about their relationship with God. Yet it was not until his freshman year at Wheaton College that Torrey Johnson was to realize an assurance of his salvation.

Mixing youth programs

His father was a great admirer of evangelist–preacher Paul Rader, and by his college years Torrey Johnson had come to share that high regard for the man he saw as a daring pioneer in evangelistic methodology. Rader's vision included radio, great musical programs, a creative mix of testimonies and surprise elements, in evening services climaxing with appealing preaching. These elements, combined with some promotional techniques and youth programs, provided a model that Johnson would later imitate and expand in the very much more receptive climate of the war years.

Torrey Johnson exhibited his entrepreneurial instincts throughout his ministry, and these were as much a product

of his Norwegian work ethic as of the influence of Dyrness, Larson, and Rader. By age ten he worked in a Chinese laundry. Other jobs followed. During his years at Carl Schurz High School he was employed as a tinsmith for a man who touted his belief in the theory of evolution and had no time for God.

Torrey Johnson at the rostrum.

Above: Torrey Johnson;
Right: A selection of youth rally bills.

It was a perfect opportunity for a Christian boy to share the gospel. There was one problem. Torrey Johnson had not yet made a commitment to Christ despite his exposure to some of the best preaching the city of Chicago had to offer. He later would reflect on his high school job and confess that he was too timid to provide a verbal witness about Jesus Christ.

Enterprise
As a businessman, however, Torrey Johnson was not timid. In summertime the Johnsons were to be found at the family cottage in Williams Bay, Wisconsin, where in his college years the athletically inclined young man purchased an ice delivery route and thereby paid his way through college. This willingness to take risks and handle money was to set the stage for evangelistic ventures throughout his life time.

In January 1927 at Wheaton College's Pierce Chapel, Torrey Johnson first gained assurance

of his salvation. The evangelistic message may have seemed a wasted to those leading the meeting, for Johnson was the only person to make a decision for Christ that night. Such was not the case, as time would tell. He had enrolled at the college primarily because his father wanted him to do so; he had wanted to be a dentist and oral surgeon. Soon afterwards his priorities changed.

Upon graduation from Wheaton College in 1930 with a bachelor of science degree, the twenty-one-year-old accepted a call to be pastor at Messiah Church in Chicago, was ordained to the Baptist ministry, and married Evelyn Nilsen, whom he had known since high school. His first pastorate lasted but one year, when his entrepreneurial instincts drew the man whom Billy Graham would later describe as

"an old fashioned Southern Baptist preacher" into full-time evangelistic preaching. For two years Torrey Johnson teamed with a musician friend to travel and hold evangelistic meetings.

In October 1933 the pastor and evangelist accepted the challenge to organize a non-denominational church on Chicago's northwest side. Though he later commented that he was not much enamored with the name Midwest Bible Church, because of the connotations of separatism associated with the Bible church movement, Johnson helped the church grow from twenty-six people in 1933 to nearly seven hundred in evening services ten years later (evening services consistently outdrew morning worship). While active in the ministry the young pastor's desire for biblical knowledge led him to study at Northern Baptist Seminary, from which he graduated in 1936. Two radio broadcasts (*Chapel Hour* begun in 1941 and *Songs in the Night*

formed a corporation to develop housing complexes for people approaching, or in, their retirement years. Abounding in both ideas and energy, the former ice deliveryman, pastor, and evangelist has spent his lifetime ministering to the pre-baby boom generation in the United States.

Three principles

Despite Johnson's enormous organizational and leadership skills, he viewed another issue as essential for the endeavors he undertook. Describing the strategy required to organize a Saturday night rally, he commented, "The first, second, and third thing you do in getting started are, in order of importance: 1. Pray 2. Pray 3. Pray." It was Torrey's conviction that prayer was the one essential ingredient for either a single rally or a lifetime of ministry.

added four years later) were instrumental in expanding the church's ministry from an isolated urban pulpit to an innovative voice of evangelism.

Youth for Christ International
Torrey Johnson's late-night phone call to Doug Fisher well demonstrated his willingness to take risks and to gather other creative people to join him in evangelistic endeavors. Paul Guiness in Brantford, Ontario; Oscar Gillan in Detroit; Jack Wyrtzen in New York; and Roger Malsbary in Indianapolis had already used the "Youth for Christ" slogan prior to the Chicago rallies. Nonetheless, it was the success of Chicagoland YFC that gave the movement national attention and led to the formation of Youth for Christ International in 1945 with Torrey Johnson as president.

In 1948 Johnson resigned the presidency of Youth for Christ to devote his energies to his church. Some in the YFC movement resented his forceful leadership and the notoriety that the Chicago rallies received. Nonetheless, Torrey's brother-in-law and his former associate pastor, Bob Cook, was named the second president of YFC. Johnson's pastorate continued until 1953 when he returned to full-time evangelistic work preaching across the United States, Europe, South America, Africa, and the Far East.

From 1967 through until 1982 Johnson tackled another challenge; he became the pastor of Bibletown Community Church and president of the financially strapped Bibletown Bible Conference and Concerts in Boca Raton, Florida. Business and entrepreneurial abilities again prevailed, and when combined with his preaching skills, shifted the focus of the ministry from entertainment for wealthy evangelicals to a complete church ministry, which included the Bible conference activities.

In his "retirement" years Torrey M. Johnson continues to bring evangelicals together. He

Further Reading

Johnson, Torrey, and Robert Cook. *Reaching Youth for Christ.* Chicago: Moody, 1944.

Larson, Mel. *Young Man on Fire.* Chicago: Youth for Christ International, 1945

_____. *Youth for Christ: Twentieth Century Wonder.* Grand Rapids: Zondervan, 1947.

Dr. Henrietta C. Mears

Dream Big!

THE LIFE OF

Henrietta Mears

1890	Born in Fargo, North Dakota
1897	Conversion
1907	Dedicates herself for Christian service
1913	Graduates from University of Minnesota
	Begins to teach high school chemistry
1928	Becomes Director of Christian Education at First Presbyterian Church, Hollywood, California
1933	Founds Gospel Light Publications
1938	Founds Forest Home Christian Conference Center
1946	Cofounds National Sunday School Association
1949	Receives honorary Doctorate from Bob Jones University
	Sponsors Hollywood Christian Group
1961	Founds Gospel Literature International (GLINT)
1963	Dies of heart attack in her sleep

Henrietta Mears was a woman of vision and excellence, single-mindedly devoted to Jesus Christ. That devotion began when she was a young child. Even then she hungered for God; and at the age of seven, she put her trust in Christ as Savior. Godly parents nurtured her spiritually through their example and teaching. For Henrietta Mears, unquestioning faith was but a natural part of life.

My grace is sufficient

Her faith did not go untested, however. From a young age, Henrietta was extremely nearsighted, a condition that grew worse over the years. Believing that God could heal her, she prayed for good vision. The Lord did not choose to heal, however. Instead, He reminded her of His words to Paul in 2 Corinthians 12:9: "My grace is sufficient for you, for my power is made perfect in weakness." Through this trial, Henrietta learned more about depending on God.

Henrietta's faith in God led to dedicating herself for Christian service when she was a high school senior, thinking God would call her to be a foreign missionary. He did not, a fact that greatly troubled her. But, as usual, she reacted to the situation by praying and focusing on the present—college. The doctors, however, predicted that she would go blind before she

Christian Educator

Dr. Henrietta C. Mears was one of the leading figures in Christian education in this century. As Earl Roe observes, "Few people have forged such strong ties of influence and impact and produced so many enduring monuments— monuments of fruitful lives and influential Christian institutions—as [she] has."

Three years after becoming Director of Christian Education at First Presbyterian Church in Hollywood, California, she had increased Sunday school attendance from 400 to 4,000. As a direct result of her teaching, over 400 young men and women went into full-time Christian service. Among them are Bill Bright, founder of Campus Crusade for Christ; Richard Halverson, Chaplain of the United States Senate; and Dr. Paul Carlson, a missionary martyred in Africa.

She developed a closely graded Sunday school curriculum to provide comprehensive Bible survey for children and teens. From her first mimeographed copies grew Gospel Light Publications, a leading evangelical curriculum publisher.

As a result of requests to translate Gospel Light materials into other languages, Henrietta later started Gospel Literature International. This nonprofit organization assists missionaries in obtaining, translating, and publishing Christian education materials in foreign languages.

Henrietta challenged and encouraged countless Sunday school teachers through frequent speaking engagements and her column in *Teach* magazine. She also started Forest Home Conference Center, which still promotes spiritual growth.

Dr. Henrietta C. Mears.

was thirty and recommended she terminate her studies after high school.

Instead of letting this obstacle defeat her, she determined to keep on growing. She ignored the doctors' advice and enrolled in the University of Minnesota to prepare to teach high school chemistry. God's promise, "My grace is sufficient for thee," again bolstered her.

Before she graduated from college, her mother died.

Henrietta was devastated; she had lost a spiritual guide and friend. But as was her custom when facing a problem or challenge, she prayed. And from her mourning grew surrender to the Lord and complete dependence on Him.

"Commit your way.... "

A couple of years after college, Henrietta dated and grew to love a man who did not share her faith in God. She wanted very much to establish a home, enjoy the companionship of marriage, and have children. But she knew their faith differences would keep them apart. While battling this conflict, she prayed and surrendered these desires to the Lord. Then she broke their engagement.

Henrietta was learning by experience a biblical truth that later became her answer to problems when counseling others: "Commit your way to the Lord; trust in him" (Psalms 37:5).

Henrietta did commit her way to the Lord. And eventually He directed her from teaching high school students to becoming the Director of Christian Education at the First Presbyterian Church in Hollywood, California. There the Lord gave Henrietta what she very much wanted—

The first warehouse for Gospel Light books.

a home, companions, and thousands of children.

"To know Christ.... "

Almost immediately she agreed to teach the college department. Her primary message was the lordship of Christ, a truth she lived daily. As Ruth Bell Graham said, "It isn't Miss Mears herself who impresses you; it's her Lord." In fact, the motto of her department was: "To know Christ and to make Him known." And with her help, thousands of students were able to make that motto a reality in their own lives.

She did more than teach though. She trained leaders who discipled others all around the world. In fact, she reached more people with the gospel through her teaching ministry than she could have as a foreign missionary, as she realized.

I have had the thrill of going around the world many times, and practically every place my plane lands—whether it is in India or Hong Kong or the islands of the sea or Africa—I find a young man or woman who has come up through my
college department and is there preaching the gospel of the Lord Jesus Christ. How I thank God!

Her vision for Hollywood included making Christ known to people in the entertainment industry. Although this goal seemed as if it was impossible, Henrietta approached it with characteristic faith. Claiming the fact that nothing is impossible with God, she began to pray with a group of friends for these people. After discouraging years with no visible results, the Hollywood Christian Group eventually began in her home. And many actors, actresses, and other entertainment professionals became believers and grew as disciples of Jesus Christ.

Give God your best

Whether she was discipling movie stars, college students, or Sunday school teachers, Henrietta emphasized the importance of giving God one's best, a concept she modeled. She refused to settle for *mediocre* or even *good*, but looked for ways to do or make things *better*. For example, she was appalled at the quality of the Sunday school curriculum being used in her church. Since she could not find any that met her standards, she began to write her own. Other people heard about these lessons—and the results they produced in students' lives—and asked for copies. These requests led to the founding of Gospel Light Publications and later, to Gospel Light International, which helps missionaries with their Christian education literature needs.

Part of Henrietta's emphasis on excellence was her "one-time philosophy." She taught people to do their best the first time and to be well prepared even in all the details. She would not tolerate winging a meeting, or failing to prepare a Sunday school lesson, or even distributing poorly done flyers. She realized that often we have only one chance to minister to a person; so all aspects of a program should be excellent every time.

Superwoman?

In spite of her great accomplishments and seemingly endless energy, Henrietta Mears was not Superwoman. She experienced times of exhaustion when she wanted to quit. But instead of feeling sorry for herself, she turned to the Lord and His Word. During one of these times, she read Deuteronomy 33:25: "And your strength will equal your days." Barbara Powers writes: "She realized the great truth that the Lord will never ask you to do one more thing than you are able to do. She learned to tend to the task that the Lord has given for today, trusting Him to give the needed strength, but knowing that if tomorrow's task is heaped upon today's burden, it will be calamity."

Three characteristics probably influenced Henrietta Mears' ministry more than any others. First, she "dared to believe in the greatness of her God." She faced obstacles and trials with prayer and faith that God would work it out. And God honored her faith.

Second, she practiced what she taught. As a coworker with her testified:

The vital quality of Miss Mears' ministry is the fact that she is constantly learning, even as she is constantly teaching. Her secret is that she does not teach with head-knowledge only; she teaches with heart-knowledge, and she must experience the truth first, completely, wholly, wonderingly, and then she is so alive with her message that it gushes forth in streams of living water.

Finally, she instilled her sense of vision in those she taught and trained.

"Dare to look ahead!"

"Have unlimited vision under God, have enthusiasm and faith in what God can do. Without this vision you will become discouraged with the situation at hand; with it you will know that with God all things are possible. Beginning with things as they are and having the vision of what God can do, you will make an unbeatable team."

Further Reading

Baldwin, Ethel May and David V. Benson. *Henrietta Mears and how she did it!* Glendale, Calif.: Regal, 1966.

Doan, Eleanor L. (compiler), *431 Quotes from the Notes of Henrietta C. Mears.* Glendale, Calif.: Regal, 1970.

Powers, Barbara Hudson. *The Henrietta Mears Story.* Old Tappan, N.J.: Fleming H. Revell, 1957.

Roe, Earl O., ed. *Dream Big: The Henrietta Mears Story.* Ventura, Calif.: Regal, 1990.

Bill Bright and Campus Crusade

Finding It!

"HAVE YOU HEARD OF THE FOUR SPIRITUAL LAWS?"

Tens of millions around the world have been introduced to a simple, straightforward explanation of the gospel with a question found on the cover of a little sixteen-page booklet. This evangelistic tract, in a four-step outline, lays out God's love, mankind's sinfulness, Christ's uniqueness, and the need for each individual to make a decision. The question is direct: Is Jesus Christ in your life, or isn't He?

Like the booklet he created, Bill Bright has lived with one simple, straightforward purpose: to present the gospel of Jesus Christ to as many people in the world as possible. Toward that end, Bright, who scribbled the first draft of the "Four Spiritual Laws" in 1965, established what has become one of the largest evangelical parachurch organizations in the world.

In 1951, he and his wife, Vonette, founded Campus Crusade for Christ, an evangelism and discipleship ministry that has grown to include some 30,000 full-time staff and trained volunteers serving in 138 countries around the world. Bright's Four Spiritual Laws, though often ridiculed for its simplicity, nonetheless proved an innovation in church outreach and was soon copied in various forms by many other organizations and churches. In the late seventies, Campus Crusade's Here's Life America "I Found It" campaign teased millions of Americans into hearing the gospel. Additional tens of millions were exposed to the gospel on every continent through "Here's Life World," with many millions more receiving Christ. And through the eighties, multitudes more were evangelized through the "Jesus" film, a biblically faithful account of Christ's life, which by 1991 had been translated into 210 languages and is used by more than 325 mission agencies and denominations.

Behind those projects and many others lies the vision of Bill Bright, who for more than forty years has been driven by one verse of Scripture, Christ's Great Commission of Matthew 28: "Therefore go and make disciples of all nations."

A hitchhiker's invitation

William R. Bright was born in Coweta, Oklahoma, on October 19, 1921. Bright grew up in cattle country with four brothers and two sisters, and distinguished himself in school by

---

THE LIFE OF

Bill Bright

1921	Born in Coweta, Oklahoma
1943	Graduates from Northeastern (Oklahoma) State College
1944	Moves to Southern California to go into business
1947	Pledges "absolute consecration to Christ"
1948	Marries Vonette Zachary
1951	Founds Campus Crusade for Christ
1962	Campus Crusade purchases Arrowhead Springs in San Bernardino, California, as its headquarters
1965	Writes the evangelistic booklet *Have You Heard of the Four Spiritual Laws?*
1972	EXPLO '72 in Dallas draws 80,000 delegates for training
1974	EXPLO '74 in Seoul draws 300,000 delegates for training
1976	"I Found It!" campaign begins
1979	"Jesus" film premieres in English
1985	EXPLO '85 uses video and satellite technology to link delegates on 5 continents
1987	Campus Crusade launches New Life 2000

hard work and ambition. At Northeastern (Oklahoma) State College, he served as editor of the school yearbook and student body president before graduating in 1943. He then began teaching extension students of Oklahoma State University.

In spite of the daily prayer and Bible reading of his mother—whom he still credits as the most influential person in his life—Bright left Oklahoma a firm agnostic. Intent on making his fortune in business, he headed to Southern California. But on Bright's first evening in Los Angeles, he picked up a hitchhiker who was the roommate of Dawson Trotman, founder of the Navigators, another parachurch ministry. He spent the first night on his arrival in California in the homes of the Trotmans and Charles E. Fuller, founder and speaker of the "Old Fashioned Revival Hour." Later, Bright began attending Hollywood's First Presbyterian Church, the home of a popular and vital young adults group. There he met another of the great influences in his life, Henrietta Mears. Mears, Director of Education for the church and leader of the church's young adult group, was an articulate, inspiring woman, and it was she who was to plant and cultivate in Bright's heart the vision for Christian service that would come to characterize his life.

"There is no magic in small plans," Mears said. "When I consider my ministry, I think of the world. Anything less than that would not be worthy of Christ nor of His will for my life."

Absolute consecration

As Bright's business interests—a line of fancy candies called Bright's California Confections—grew and prospered, so too did his commitment to Christ. In 1947, with Mears and several other of "her boys," he pledged himself to "absolute consecration to Christ" in the Fellowship of the Burning Heart.

Ministry increasingly competed with business pursuits for his time and attention. When, after one year at Princeton Seminary, business brought him back to Los Angeles, he enrolled in the fledgling Fuller Theological Seminary where he studied from 1947 through 1951.

In 1948, after a three-year engagement, he married Vonette Zachary, whom he had known

Bill Bright, founder of Campus Crusade for Christ.

back in his Oklahoma hometown. For the Brights, 1951 proved to be the most momentous year of their lives. Together, they once and for all turned their backs on Bill's early dreams of business success, signing a covenant in which they renounced all their material ambitions. Though the decision was significant in itself, it set the stage for something even greater.

In February of that year, while studying for a Greek exam at Fuller, Bright was overwhelmed by what he says could have been "the presence of the Lord." In that moment, Bright says, he was commanded to invest his life to help fulfill the Great Commission by helping to take the gospel the world, beginning with college students. Though only months from graduation, Bright dropped his studies to fulfill that command by founding Campus Crusade for Christ. The name for his organization was given him by Wilbur Smith, one of his favorite professors. His founding board of directors included such noted evangelicals as Henrietta Mears, Dawson Trotman, Billy Graham, Daniel Fuller, J. Edwin Orr, and Richard C. Halverson.

With the backing of a 24-hour prayer chain, Bill and Vonette began evangelizing students at UCLA and training others to do the same. By the end of the first year, the new ministry saw more than 250 students indicate they had received Christ as their personal Savior. The group included the student body president, the editor of the school paper, and a number of top athletes (such as all-American football player Don Moomaw and Rafer Johnson, who later became an Olympic gold medalist in the decathlon). Soon, Campus Crusade had spread to other schools and had added its first six additional staff members.

World vision

To talk about Bill Bright's life from that point on is to talk about Campus Crusade. Devoting himself wholly to the ministry, its high points have been his joys, its low points his struggles. Always his vision, in an echo of Henrietta Mears, was set on nothing less than the world. By 1958, Campus Crusade had begun its first international work, in South Korea. In 1959, the ministry had expanded to nearly forty campuses in fifteen states and moved beyond the campus to offer its evangelism and discipleship training to lay people.

Perhaps no episode demonstrates Bill Bright's capacity for big dreams and limit-stretching faith better than Campus Crusade's acquisition of its international headquarters, Arrowhead Springs.

It is a story Bright recounts often; one that serves for him as a reminder of God's miraculous provision.

As a resort hotel that had catered to some of Hollywood's biggest names for several decades, Arrowhead Springs had, by 1962, been eclipsed by other more glamorous destinations. Closed for several years, it had become something of a white elephant. But when Bright visited this beautiful hotel, with its panoramic view of the San Bernardino valley, he became convinced of its future.

"Though not audibly, God spoke to me as clearly as if there had been a public address system in the room," Bright recalls. The message from God: "I have been saving Arrowhead Springs for Campus Crusade for Christ." Though the young ministry had no money to finance the $2 million deal, Bright committed to buying the property. In fact, Campus Crusade did not even have the $15,000 needed to pay for the option. But in a series of eleventh-hour answers to prayer, all the money came in. The property became the headquarters and conference center for Campus Crusade for the next twenty-nine years. (In need of more office space, the ministry moved its headquarters to Orlando, Florida, in 1991; Arrowhead Springs remains a conference center run by Campus Crusade for Christ.)

For Bright, the equation at work in the Arrowhead Springs acquisition—and in the whole of the Christian life—was simple: God had promised it, and God does not promise what He cannot provide. To believe, and to act upon, anything less is not faith but sin. And sin has no place in the life of a Christian.

A pragmatic theologian

His biographer Richard Quebedeaux, writing in *I Found It! The Story of Bill Bright and Campus Crusade* (Harper & Row, 1979), dubbed Bright the "pragmatic theologian of the Holy Spirit." Indeed, Bright's approach to the Christian life is, after being Bible-based, most thoroughly pragmatic. Whilst emphasizing the supernatural work of the Holy Spirit in the life of the believer, what matters to Bright is what works. As a reflection of Bright's approach, the evangelism and discipleship training offered by Campus Crusade is, for good and bad, formulaic. Written by Bright in the ministry's early days and essentially unchanged since then, its concepts, actions, phrases, and answers have been proven in field action. Some laud the simplicity of such an approach. It works, and it is easily understandable. Indeed, many millions have benefited from it.

At the same time, others fault it as simplistic, failing to touch the complexities of life and Christian truth. With its emphasis on personal piety, this pragmatic approach to the Christian way of living has also been accused of slighting the social aspects of Christ's call to discipleship.

Some of the ministries of Campus Crusade/Agapé.

Highlights

There have been many other highlights in the forty-year ministry of Campus Crusade. In 1967, some 600 staff and students converged on the University of California at Berkeley. Countering campus radicalism with the gospel, the "Berkeley Blitz" saw over 700 students and faculty members indicate they received Christ as Savior during the week.

Conferences had long played a major role in Bright's world-winning strategy. Weekend retreats and summertime institutes offered Campus Crusade's training to scores and hundreds at a time. Beginning in the seventies, however, Bright's penchant for superlatives prompted a series of stadium-filling events. First came EXPLO '72, which drew 80,000

staff, students, and laypeople to the Cotton Bowl in Dallas. The final event in the week of witnessing and training, the Jesus Music Festival, drew 200,000.

Two years later, EXPLO '74 in Seoul drew more than 323,000 delegates. An estimated 1.5 million people attended an evangelistic meeting held on the open fields of an abandoned airfield.

The 1970s also saw the unveiling of another innovative, and often controversial, evangelism program. Beginning in 1976, in 246 cities across America, millions faced billboards and bumper stickers bearing the cryptic message "I Found It!" What had they found? "New life in Jesus Christ," came the answer, delivered by some 300,000 Christians coordinated and trained in the campaign by Campus Crusade.

The Here's Life Korea event in 1980 proved to be the largest in the history of Campus Crusade. Here, two to almost three million participated nightly in a week-long training in evangelism and discipleship.

Christ's life on film
In 1979, Bill Bright saw the fulfillment of a long-held personal dream, that of creating a biblically accurate portrayal of Christ's life on film. In the early days of his ministry, while still closely tied to Hollywood Presbyterian Church, Bright was inspired by Cecil B. DeMille's great classic, "King of Kings," to produce a modern biblical film on the life of Jesus. For years, however, the project had remained little more than a dream, lacking the funds and the professional commitments needed.

Bright eventually connected with Bunker Hunt, who financed the film, and director John Heyman, who had undertaken eventually to put the whole story of the Bible on film. Campus Crusade's production of Christ's life, drawn from the gospel of Luke, was filmed on location in Israel. After its premiere and showing across the United States in 1979, Campus Crusade began to translate the film into every major language of the world. Today, it is the most translated film in history, dubbed into 210 languages and having, in 1991, been viewed by 470 million people. It is one of the most widely used and effective missionary tools ever developed, and itts showings often draw hundreds of people, who walk for miles through the most remote areas to hear Jesus speak in their own language.

The 1980s brought further expansion to Campus Crusade, which by 1991 had grown to count some 30,000 full-time staff and trained volunteers in more than 138 countries, thus representing 97 per cent of the population of the world. Reaching far beyond its campus roots, it expanded to work in high schools, inner cities, prisons, to laymen, government leaders, and executives. Special teams have utilized sports, music, drama, and mass media to present the gospel in virtually every setting imaginable, and almost 2000 Campus Crusade missionaries went out from North America in traditional roles of evangelist and church planters, as well as in vocational work in medicine, education, and other areas.

With each of these ministry milestones, Bright has celebrated the faithfulness of God and expanded his vision to multiply what has been accomplished. And with each accomplishment, each answer to a prayer, the foundation for the next, larger glimpse of vision has been laid. "At first I prayed for ten students, and we saw tens and scores come to Christ," Bill Bright says. "Then God placed it on my heart to pray for hundreds, and we saw Him accomplish that. Then we prayed for thousands, then millions, and I now pray that we will see one billion men and women around the world come to Christ by AD 2000."

Difficulties
But the successes have not come without failures and criticism. One of the most difficult episodes Bill Bright has faced in the life of the ministry came in 1968, when several top-level leaders challenged the founder and president's direction of Campus Crusade. It was a confrontation that ended with their departure. But the incident obviously surprised and deeply troubled Bright. He remains reticent to talk about the event and provide details; he never mentions it publicly and only rarely refers to it even among his current leadership.

When asked about his reluctance to speak about this episode in his life, he responds, "I love the six men who left this ministry. I had discipled them for many years and had given them major responsibilities. When they chose to leave the ministry my heart was saddened, but the Lord never allowed me to be critical of them. I love them still after more than twenty-five years since they left."

In part, it is the unbending optimism of Bill Bright—a direct product of his world-size faith in God—that has helped him achieve what he has in ministry. At the same time, in his charge-ahead vision there is little room for negatives. Critical questions, he believes, indicate a lack of spirituality. So there is little room for self-examination and reflection on the lessons of failure. Today the ministry of Campus Crusade for Christ encircles the globe with more than forty different ministries including the college campus, athletic ministry, executive and family ministries, prison and inner city. Most of the leadership in the 138 countries is made up of trained nationals. Still, the vision of Campus Crusade's president has sometimes far outdistanced the ability of the organization to bring it to fruition.

At no time in Campus Crusade's history was that more evident than in the early 1980s, when another long-held dream of Bill Bright's, the establishment of a world-class Christian university, rose quickly and fell hard. Bright's vision, one shared by other great Christian leaders, was of a university that could match the academic reputation of the nation's greatest schools, yet with a distinctively Christian worldview. A first step toward that institution was taken in 1978, when Campus Crusade established the International School of Theology at its headquarters in Arrowhead Springs. Though enrollment has remained small, plans grew rapidly for the creation of a graduate university.

Property was purchased for a new campus near San Diego. But after years of struggle to meet payments, settle with developers, and change zoning restrictions, the project quietly faded. Though the ministry still holds an interest in some valuable Southern California land, but the frustrated plans caused serious financial strains for the ministry and left many staff members disillusioned. Since that time three additional schools have been established—one in Nairobi, Kenya, another in Singapore, and the third in Manila.

Integrity

Though critics may find fault with Bright's methods or management, none have ever questioned his personal moral integrity. Long before the televangelist scandals of the eighties, the Brights made public their personal finances (most recently showing a total personal income of less than $25,000 for the year). "I pray that God would take my life before he would allow me to disgrace Him in any way," Bright has said. His total devotion to Campus Crusade has led him for years through a grueling schedule, one that wears out assistants half his age in a matter of months. It leaves no time for hobbies (though he occasionally finds time to enjoy horseback riding, a favorite activity from his younger days in Oklahoma), personal vacations, or socializing.

After nearly forty years of ministry, Bright's vision for the world has remained unaltered, except to grow in its size and clarity. His faith stands on the same foundation—God will enable Christians to do what He commands—that it did when he began, yet that foundation has grown stronger and able to support far more. Working under a plan called New Life 2000, Bright's goal for the decade ahead is to see Campus Crusade, working in cooperation with other ministries, reach the world's 6 billion people with the gospel by the year 2000.

Those closest to Bill Bright believe God has granted him true humility in his accomplishments, virtually blinding him to his own part in Campus Crusade's success. What he sees, he has written, is simply God's view of the world. And the plans Bill Bright has made are simply the obedient response to that vision, no more, and no less.

Further Reading

Bright, Bill. *The Holy Spirit: Key to Supernatural Living*. San Bernardino, Calif.: Here's Life, 1980.

_____. *The Secret: How to Live with Power and Purpose*. San Bernardino, Calif.: Here's Life, 1989.

_____. *Witnessing Without Fear*. San Bernardino, Calif.: Here's Life, 1985.

Bright, Bill, and Vonette Bright. *Managing Stress in Marriage: Help for Couples on the Fast Track*. San Bernardino, Calif.: Here's Life, 1990.

Quebedeaux, Richard. *I Found It! The Story of Bill Bright and Campus Crusade*. San Francisco: Harper & Row, 1979.

Brother Roger of Taizé;
Ecumenical Leader
YEAST FOR THE CHURCH

Taizé is a sleepy village nestling in the hills of Burgandy, France, and is so small that most road maps fail to show it. Its buildings and grounds are not much to look at: a few barrack-like structures, a large kitchen, many tents, an ungrandiose church made of concrete and wood. The heart of Taizé, however, is not buildings, but a community of brothers, joined by a common pledge to live together for the sake of Christ and the Gospel. They display an intense commitment to a life without pretense, following the precepts of Jesus' Sermon on the Mount. They try to unite a love for God with a love for God's people, especially the poor and unfortunate. Some of them spend years living in places of poverty and division across the earth. And their lives have become a ringing witness to many tired, secular visitors— the majority of them young— who have lost their way in life and have come seeking what it means to be fully human and fully alive.

Dust of despair
As with so many Christian monastic movements throughout history, Taizé owes its existence to one person, Brother

Against the Odds

"Often through the centuries, against seemingly hopeless odds, a small number of women and men spread across the earth, and change the course of history. Through Christ and the Gospel, they reinvent the world. What before had seemed doomed to disintegration entered instead into the current of a new dynamism." So wrote Brother Roger, founder of the ecumenical monastic community in Taizé, France, and tireless spokesman and worker for unity among divided Christians. His own life is probably the best illustration of these words.

When Brother Roger came to Taizé in 1940, the world was at war. The north of France was occupied by Hitler's armies, and Jews and others were being mercilessly persecuted. Nations and churches were divided; economic poverty was rife. The temptation to resignation and despair was great. Yet one man, because of his faith in Christ, stood firm and determined to risk his own safety to help others. Leaving security in his native Switzerland, he settled in the rundown village near the demarcation line that cut France in two and began to hide Jewish refugees and help them across the border to safety.

Today, because one man risked his life for Christ fifty years ago, the small village of Taizé is a centre of Christian renewal that welcomes tens of thousands of people each year, most of them between the ages of eighteen and thirty, from every corner of the earth. It is the home of a community of ninety brothers from a variety of Christian traditions and some twenty different nations, whose daily life together is marked by worship, work and hospitality. Their life has become a powerful magnet and source of inspiration for others searching for meaning in their lives and trying to discover what it means to be a disciple of Jesus in today's world.

Above: Taizé from the air. Below: Brother Roger with children.

Roger. With World War II breaking out around him, he left his native Switzerland and traveled to France to find a house for sale. He visited Cluny, a region rich in monastic history, and heard of a house for sale in nearby Taizé. As he rode to the village by bicycle, he was aware of the thick dust of despair which had settled all around: crop failures had turned the hills into a wasteland, many villagers had already packed up and left, and the few who had remained seemed old and tired. Hope was in very short supply.

The elderly peasant woman who showed Brother Roger the house pleaded with him. "Buy the house and stay with us here. We are so alone." And he did.

A generous spirit

The founder and eventual prior of the Taizé community, Roger Schutz, was born in Provence, on May 12, 1915, in a small village near Neuchâtel, Switzerland. The youngest of nine children, Brother Roger quickly learned from his parents a charitable tolerance for diverse Christian traditions. His father, who was a pastor of the Reformed church, and his mother both taught him to have a generous ecumenical spirit, and were open, charitable and broad-minded. Reflecting on his training, Brother Roger could say later in his life: "I owe my

Roger of Taizé

1915	Born in village of Provence, Switzerland
1928	Leaves home to attend secondary school
1939	Becomes president of Student Christian Federation
1940	Dreams of a community dedicated to helping those in need
	Buys house in Taizé, France
	Hides Jewish refugees fleeing the Nazis
1942	Returns to Switzerland when the Gestapo discover his work
1944	Returns to Taizé to work with children and prisoners of war
1949	With six others, commits himself to celibacy and a life of material and spiritual sharing
1952	Writes *Rule of Taizé*
1962	Church of Reconciliation dedicated at Taizé
1960s	Youth flock to Taizé
1974	40,000 attend first Council of Youth
1980	Travels worldwide
1990	Taizé's meeting in Prague, Czechoslovakia, brings together 80,000 young adults

Brother Roger travels widely in the Third World.

ecumenical vocation to the generosity of my parents."

During his teenage years, the growth of Roger's faith was anything but smooth. Leaving home at thirteen to attend secondary school in a larger town, he boarded with a desperately poor Catholic widow and her family, whose generosity too shaped his later ecumenical vision. At school, however, he bumped into a natural history teacher whose Darwinian explanation of the universe shook his faith in God to the very roots. He discussed with his Catholic landlady how it is possible to believe. Her faith held him fast: "She left an indelible mark on me; she was the living expression of the Gospel's sovereign freedom," he later commented.

It was during those years that young Roger Schutz, ever the inquiring and pensive student, became deeply fascinated with the monastic tradition. He read Blaise Pascal, who himself had known what doubt was, but who, amid the struggle, chose to take the risk of faith and encouraged others to do the same. Schutz became interested too in the history of Port-Royal, where the reform of a small monastic community of women had untold repercussions on the Catholic Church in seventeenth-century France.

Inner peace

Neither the study of Pascal nor Port-Royal were by themselves enough, however, to return the searching young teenager to trust in God. It took an encounter with serious lung disease for Roger eventually to declare again his dependence on God and to find inner peace.

With his teenage years behind him, he considered settling into a combined career of writing and farming. When a publisher suggested a number of changes in his first manuscript, however, Schutz refused—and then abruptly switched careers, taking up the study of theology, first at Lausanne and then later at Strasbourg.

In 1939 Roger Schutz was elected to be President of the Student Christian Federation in Lausanne, a group whose meetings he had never attended, and about which he knew very little. But he accepted the post—and his experience leading the group, quite to his surprise, set the entire course for the rest of his life. For out of it evolved the *Grande Communauté*, a group of twenty students who dedicated themselves to prayer and work and to helping other students find meaning and purpose in life. The *Communauté* organized discussion groups and planned spiritual retreats dedicated to deep introspection and honest confrontation with God.

Worship is at the centre of the Taizé Community.

The village church, Taizé.

The *Grande Communauté* was the precursor to Taizé, for through it Brother Roger came to see how crucial an authentic spirituality and a monastic-type discipline are to living a fully Christian life. To practice the precepts of the Gospel himself, and to help others discover and practice them too, became his driving passion—and eventually his life's work.

A living parable
At the same time, in those years Brother Roger became more and more convinced that, if people were to be touched by the Gospel message, then concrete, visible signs incarnated in human lives were much more urgently needed than words. And for him the clearest such sign was that of a community, of people visibly praying together and living as one body out of faithfulness to Jesus Christ. And so, although it was not a part of his background, with surprising openness he turned to the monastic tradition in search of inspiration.

What motivated this simple and self-effacing man of God to establish this community of brothers? In his own words:

"I never wanted to be part of a process of 'restoration' of the monastic life. I have never believed in such a process. Nor did I simply want to integrate monastic life into the Churches of the Reformation.... What I am passionately seeking, I believe, is something very concrete: a parable of communion incarnate in the lives of a few men, for words have no credibility until they are lived out. I was haunted by the idea: why not put into the dough of the divided churches, indeed all the churches, a leaven of communion?"

Taizé's calling is to be a sign of reconciliation for Christians tragically and bitterly divided. The community today is as international as it is ecumenical; the brothers come from some twenty countries around the world and from a variety of Christian backgrounds: Protestant, Anglican and Catholic. "Our common prayer," states the *Rule of Taizé*, "is set within the communion of saints, but for this communion with the believers of every age to become a reality, we have to give ourselves to fervent intercession for mankind and the Church."

Council of Youth
Starting in the late 1950s and spurred by the events of the 1960s, young adults searching for meaning, for God, for a deeper faith, began coming to Taizé. At first unsure of how to respond, the brothers gradually organized what are now known as the intercontinental meetings of young adults, a week of prayer Bible study, work and sharing between people from all over the world. Since 1966 an international community of women begun in Belgium, the Sisters of Saint Andrew, has been collaborating with the brothers in the work of welcoming the many visitors to Taizé. The Taizé community was not interested in starting a movement centred on itself, but rather in helping young visitors

to return home with renewed hope and faith and a deeper will to get involved in their own local situations.

In 1970, Brother Roger proposed the idea of a "Council of Youth." "For months past," he admits, "one thing has been pre-occupying me: with the present discord in the Church, what act could give peace to those who are shaken and strength to those who are committed? I sense that such an act should be a gathering of an exacting nature, regularly repeated for the years to come ... a council of youth." After four years of preparation, it opened in 1974 when 40,000 young people came to Taizé. At a time when the young were falling prey to discouragement and deserting the churches, this was an attempt "to build a world of justice and to place Christ at the center of our lives," as one participant put it. In its *Letter to the People of God*, the Council urged Christians the world over to be "a contemplative people, thirsting for God; a people of justice, living the struggle of the exploited; a people of communion, where the non-believer also finds a creative place."

Pilgrimage of trust
The Council of Youth gradually evolved into the "pilgrimage of trust on earth" announced by Brother Roger during a visit to Lebanon in 1982. The "pilgrimage of trust" is a means to encourage each person to live out, in their own situation, the search for God in prayer and silence, as well as to be bearers of reconciliation to those around them. Regularly, larger meetings are held outside Taizé as "stations" on this pilgrimage. As

each year ends, a European meeting brings together tens of thousands of young adults for a period of six days. For this meeting Brother Roger writes an open letter, often from a place of poverty where he has gone to spend time with those leading difficult lives. Letters have come from such places as Calcutta, Ethiopia, Warsaw, Haiti, and Madras. In 1990, 80,000 young adults came to Prague for the European meeting that was held there. Similar gatherings have taken place in India, the Philippines and the United States.

Since 1962, Taizé has been present in the lands of Eastern Europe, at first through discreet visits to Christians in perilous situations. In the 1980s, youth meetings became possible, similar to those in the West, in East Germany, Yugoslavia and Hungary. On the one thousandth anniversary of the arrival of Christianity in Russia, in 1988, Brother Roger was present and Taizé collected enough money to despatch one million copies of the New Testament to that country.

Brother Roger and the community are likewise concerned that human rights be respected. He makes discreet interventions from time to time, as well as public gestures for peace in the name of the young. He has twice visited the Secretary General of the United Nations, Mr Perez de Cuellar, in the company of children from every continent, eliciting this response: "The pilgrimage of trust on earth organized by Taizé with young people is bringing us closer to the ideal of peace to which we all aspire." Church leaders, including several Archbishops of

Canterbury, have come to Taizé to show their support for the community's work. And on October 5, 1986, Pope John Paul II made a short visit to the community, saying: "One passes through Taizé as one passes close to a wellspring."

So what started as one man's dream, and one man's risk, has today become world renowned. Brother Roger has won awards, including the coveted Templeton Prize (in 1974), the UNESCO Prize for Peace Education (in 1988) and the international "Karlspreis" for his contribution to the reconstruction of Europe (in 1989). But it is not a thirst for fame or honors that drives him. "We may achieve marvels," he has written, "but only those will really count which result from Christ's merciful love alive within us. In the evening of life, we shall be judged on love, the love we allow gradually to grow and spread into merciful kindness towards every person alive, in the Church and throughout the world."

Further Reading

Brother Roger, *No Greater Love: Sources of Taizé.* Liturgical Press, Collegeville, MN.

————. *His Love is a Fire.* Liturgical Press.

————. *The Taizé Experience.* Liturgical Press.

J. L. Gonzalez Balade, *The Story of Taizé.* Liturgical Press, 3rd ed. 1988.

Thinkers

Sir William Ramsay: Archaeologist

RE-TRACING
ACTS

At the end of the nineteenth century, European biblical scholarship was almost completely dominated by the radical German scholarship associated with the Tübingen school of F. C. Baur. This form of scholarship largely denied that Paul had written most of the letters attributed to him, and it also contended that many of the writings of the New Testament were actually not composed until the second century. Among the writings that these scholars held in such disrepute was the Acts of the Apostles, considered by many to have been written late in the second century AD and to have been largely an imaginative and idealized account of the origins of the church.

Alongside this German scholarship, in England there existed a coterie of scholars who were more conservative, but who at times came under the influence of German scholarship. Notable amongst these British scholars were B. F. Westcott, F. J. A. Hort, and J. B. Lightfoot. These three scholars were committed to a full-scale examination, based on the original texts, of the results of the Tübingen school. Although their plan was never fully executed (Westcott published important commentaries on Hebrews and the Johannine writings; and Hort wrote incomplete commentaries on Mark, Romans, Ephesians, James, 1 Peter, and Revelation), J. B. Lightfoot perhaps came closest. He published significant commentaries on Galatians, Philippians, Colossians, and Philemon, along with pioneering studies in early patristic writings. His works were so incisive that they are still in print today. The goal of this "Cambridge triumvirate," as they are sometimes called, was to interpret the entire New Testament in the light of its historical and social context and so demonstrate to Europe that the Tübingen model was inadequate.

It can be said that, although their personal designs were never fully met, their ultimate goal was reached; by the early part of the twentieth century the Tübingen school had become largely passé. To be sure, the erosion of the Tübingen school was not accomplished by these Cambridge scholars alone. Another decisive blow against radical criticism was in fact dealt by an Aberdeen graduate whose purpose was simply to study the meeting of Greek culture with Eastern culture, through the medium of archaeology as found in Asia Minor. For William Ramsay the decision to study archaeology led to an encounter with the author of the Acts of the Apostles that changed, not only his life, but the history of critical scholarship on Paul.

William Mitchell Ramsay is one of the greatest examples in the history of the church of how, as a result of an honest open-mindedness that is willing to change on the basis of archaeology and historical evidence, a scholar's entire orientation toward the Bible may be reversed. He was a determined individualist who developed a distaste for established viewpoints in either history or theology unless those views were firmly based on evidence. His willingness to distance himself from traditions, contemporary fads and currents in scholarship brought him to the field of archaeology and to brilliant, independent insights. In Ramsay, we find the life of a solitary, single-minded historian.

Student's resolve

The moment when he decided to be a scholar was preserved by William Ramsay, fortunately for our sake, when he later reflected upon the course of his career. He states, "In March 1868, at the end of my second year at the University of Aberdeen, I was feeling every day that college work had been an unalloyed happiness, and every moment spent in class-work or in preparation a delight." This absolute delight, felt so it seems by every great scholar, made him wonder about the course his academic work might follow.

When, at the end of that year, the results and prizes of his class were announced, he was deemed the best student; he made a decision, stating, "In that room my life was determined: I formed the resolve to be a scholar, and to make everything else subservient to that purpose and career." And so he did; and those who have interpreted Acts, Galatians, and the Revelation have benefited greatly from that resolve.

One suspects that it was personal determination that propelled him onwards, in spite of setbacks, illnesses, and discouraging responses to his writings. Early in his career Ramsay lost a complete manuscript of a work on archaeology that had taken him approximately a decade to research and write. Without a trace of the manuscript he rewrote the entire book, and added a second part. It was published in 1890 as *The Historical Geography of Asia Minor*. It forms the foundation of modern-day scholarship on the archaeology of Asia Minor.

In the life of most scholars there are one or two teachers who make lasting impacts upon their student, which endure a lifetime. A scholar who made a significant impact on Ramsay's life was Theodor Benfey, who taught Ramsay Sanskrit at the University of Göttingen. From Benfey Ramsay learned that real scholarship is not simply the learning of another scholar's view in the history of interpretation; rather, it is fresh discovery and interpretation of facts based upon hard evidence.

At Aberdeen Ramsay's interest in Greek thought had been spoiled temporarily by a cynical professor. Then he discovered that Greek thought could be useful. This new insight was prompted notably by the lectures at Oxford of a certain Mr. Bidder. Ramsay prepared himself well for his future work; he mastered Latin and Greek and studied carefully the cultural worlds of both Romans and Greeks. This learning permitted Ramsay to make quick and penetrating observations, whether at an archaeological site or in his study.

Sir William Mitchell Ramsay, 1851–1929.

Change of judgment

The most important insight that Ramsay made he called "the first change of judgment." It refers to his conversion to the belief that the author of Acts was a highly informed historian. In view of the fact that the insight determined Ramsey's future, its origin deserves to be described in some detail. When Ramsay arrived in Asia Minor in the late nineteenth century, there were no trustworthy maps of the country. Consequently, he was obliged to make his own. This forced him to read the original sources and some of these happened to be Christian inscrip-

tions. What was for him at that time, by his own confession, a waste of time, became his greatest delight. Included in his "must-reading" list was the Acts of the Apostles. He says, "I began to [read Acts] without expecting any information of value regarding the condition of Asia Minor at the time when Paul was living." Ramsay's thinking on Acts was still dominated by the Tübingen approach: that Acts is both historically and geographically useless. And so he says, "I began then to study the Acts in search of geographical and antiquarian evidence, hardly expecting to find any."

His change of judgment occurred when he became curious about Acts 14:6. In the history of the church probably only William Ramsay came to faith on the basis of this verse. The verse reads: "But [Paul and Barnabas] found out about it and fled to the Lycaonian cities of Lystra and Derbe and to the surrounding country." Here we

THE LIFE OF

Sir William Ramsay

1851	Born in Glasgow, Scotland, on March 15
1866–71	Studies at University of Aberdeen
1872–76	Studies at Oxford University
1885	Professor of Classical Art and Archaeology, Oxford
1886–11	Regius Professor of Humanity, Aberdeen
1890	*The Historical Geography of Asia Minor*
1895	*St. Paul the Traveller and Roman Citizen*
1899	*A Historical Commentary on St. Paul's Epistle to the Galatians*
1904	*Letters to the Seven Churches of Asia*
1906	Knighted
1907	*The Cities of St. Paul: Their Influence on His Life and Thought*
1908	*Luke the Physician and Other Studies in the History of Religion*
1913	Lectures in U.S.A.
1915	*The Bearing of Recent Discovery on the Trustworthiness of the New Testament*
1939	Dies

are led to believe that, when Paul and Barnabas left Iconium, they entered into another district, namely, Lycaonia, which contained Lystra and Derbe. The archaeologist Ramsay had grown accustomed to think that Iconium was also a part of Lycaonia; the author of the Acts was simply mistaken. Thus, it appeared to him that Luke was saying the equivalent of the description: Paul and Barnabas left Chicago and fled to Illinois. This could only be an error.

Luke the historian

However, what Ramsay discovered was that Luke was in fact amazingly accurate here. One hundred years earlier Luke would have been inaccurate but in the first century Luke had it right. For at that time, Iconium was in Phrygia, was populated by people of a different race, and its inhabitants spoke a different language (see Acts 14:11). That Luke was geographically precise here impressed Ramsay, and it was this discovery that led Ramsay, eventually, to alter his stance regarding Acts—from skeptic to apologist. He states, "I set out to look for truth on the borderland where Greece and Asia meet, and found it there. You may press the words of Luke in a degree beyond any other historian's and

they stand the keenest scrutiny and the hardest treatment, provided always that the critic knows the subject and does not go beyond the limits of science and justice."

Eventually, Ramsay charted the entire life of Paul and wrote a magnificent work that chronicled his travels (*St. Paul the Traveller and Roman Citizen*, 1895). Read by young and old alike, the book continues to be reprinted due to its lucidity and insight. Here the real Paul seems to grab the reader and takes the reader with him throughout his journeys, illustrating how he was Roman, Greek, and Hebrew at the same time.

W. F. Howard has said this about Ramsay's Paul: "Many who have devoted their lives to New Testament studies would say that their first eager interest in the Pauline writings was aroused by Lightfoot's *Galatians*, but their enthusiasm for Paul the man was kindled by this never-to-be-forgotten book of Ramsay's." In *The Traveller and Roman Citizen*, Ramsay becomes the reader's guide through Paul's journeys across the Roman Empire. In it, he points out some geographical nicety and then reveals some hidden name or custom at a given location, which illuminates the setting for the reader. We can say that Ramsay comes as close as any at providing for us a substitute trip for not having actually traveled with the great apostle.

Which Galatians?

Nonetheless, even after careful study, he was not entirely convinced of the trustworthiness of the Acts of the Apostles. In particular, the rock of offense to him was squaring the data of Acts with the data of Galatians. Ramsay proposed an interpretation which confronted major opponents: German scholarship and J. B. Lightfoot. Against these two traditions Ramsay contended that Paul wrote Galatians not to the northern districts of ethnic Galatia but to the southern districts of provincial Galatia.

Guided by the evidence, Ramsay demonstrated that the northern districts were not the kind of city areas that Paul normally visited, that the evidence for Christianity in the northern areas is much later, that the southern districts more naturally would be called "Galatia," that it would have been unlikely for Paul to convalesce in northern Galatia (Galatians 4:13), and that, when compared with all the evidence in Acts

(9:22–25; 11:27–29; 14:26; 15:2; 18:1,18; 20:2–3) Galatians and Acts can be harmonized neatly, accurately, and fairly. In particular, Ramsay made the case that Galatians 2:1–10 is the same as Acts 11:27–29 (not Acts 15, which might make Acts appear unreliable). And it has been observed that, without exception, all archaeologists who have examined this question agree with Ramsay that Galatians was written to South Galatia.

A fundamental rule to ensure accuracy in interpretation is the need to interpret a text in its historical context. While Ramsay may have had his faults, such as being either overly optimistic about his own archaeological research or too dogmatic in his apologetics, he can never be faulted for failing to ask what a given text meant in its historical context. Perhaps his finest example of this is his careful study on the seven churches of Revelation 2–3 (*The Letters to the Seven Churches*). Put simply, Ramsay's work on these churches was pioneering: he was the first to examine both archaeological data on the churches and to apply that material to the text of Revelation.

Although great progress has been made since his work, no one doubts that it was William Ramsay who charted the map to our present knowledge. Furthermore, over and over Ramsay offered fresh insights that have gone down as secure knowledge. Patient readers of Ramsay's study will avoid fantastic interpretations as they come into contact with the actual terrain of those churches.

Independent spirit

It is perhaps Ramsay's independent spirit that has given readers some doubt about his ideas. As alluded to above, he was severely criticized (and his writings frequently ignored) for his overt, aggressive, apologetic style. This applies to his writings after the turn of the century. Frequently in these later writings one gets the impression that Ramsay's zeal for his particular view outstrips the evidence that he cites (and sometimes does not cite).

More significantly, Ramsay simply was not willing to express his views of New Testament theology in the terms of traditional theology. Perhaps it was his temperament and approach to knowledge that creates this impression; Ramsay was stubbornly independent, suspicious

of traditions, and always in need of finding hard (usually archaeological) evidence for every view he espoused.

For a scholar who was as fiercely opposed to prevailing winds in scholarly circles as Ramsay, it is as ironic as it is surprising how often his views on the nature of Christ and on the nature of Pauline theology are reflections of the contemporary intellectual scene in Europe. In particular, his view of Christ often sounds like classical liberalism, where Jesus is the world's greatest embodiment of God's Spirit; and his view of Pauline theology occasionally smacks of social evolutionism, in that Paul's essential teachings are explained as aspects of world evolution and spiritual growth. Our indebtedness to Ramsay's careful historical and archaeological work leads us to wish that he had been more careful when he donned the mantle of theologian, a field in which he had no educational training.

Reflecting upon his life-changing career, Ramsay observed that it "was marked out by the judgment and will of others. In each step I had no thought of the succeeding step, but drifted without plan as fate chose." He continues, "Nature and the world were wise and kind, and always guided where I was erring and ignorant: or dare one venture to use a more personal form of the idea, and speak of Providence?" In retrospect, today we see the hand of God guiding Ramsay's mind, both in preparation and execution, to lead him to examine the New Testament, especially the travels of Paul, and to throw fresh light on the meaning of Paul from those surviving fragments of archaeology Ramsay found strewn across Asia Minor.

Further Reading

Gasque, W. W. *Sir William M. Ramsay: Archaeologist and New Testament Scholar*. Grand Rapids: Baker, 1966.

Ramsay, Sir W. M. *The Bearing of Recent Discovery on the Trustworthiness of the New Testament*. 1915. Reprint. Grand Rapids: Baker, 1979 [esp. pp. 3–52].

_____. *St. Paul the Traveller and Roman Citizen*. Grand Rapids: Baker, 1949.

GEORGE WASHINGTON CARVER

"MR. CREATOR—WHY THE PEANUT?"

Moses Carver and his wife, Susan, were shaken from sleep by the frightening sound of galloping night riders. The masked horsemen, who during the Civil War besieged helpless families by stealing and reselling their slaves, were already on Carvers' land. Mary, a young slave girl, and her sickly infant were still asleep in their hut, some distance from the Carver home. Moses bounded from bed to guard his property, and in self-defense, Mary screamed. Moses was too late. The slave traders rode off with Mary and her baby boy, George.

In a sketch of his life, George Washington Carver later wrote, "I was born in Diamond Grove, Missouri, about the close of the great Civil War, in a little one-roomed log shanty on the home of Mr. Moses Carver .... the owner of my mother." He told how the Ku Klux Klan abducted him and his mother, selling her to new owners. Moses hired a friend who ransomed George for a race horse valued at $300 and returned the boy to be raised among the Carvers, never to see his mother again.

A simple conversion

George's utterly helpless condition and turbulent beginning proved to be his greatest asset. As a defenseless orphan, he trusted in God and became a Christian. Many years later, Carter described his childhood faith: "I was just a mere boy when converted, hardly ten years old.... God just came into my heart one afternoon while I was alone in the loft of our big barn." George recalls kneeling down by a barrel of corn and praying to God as best he could. Reflectively, as a man in his late sixties, he wrote, "That was my simple conversion, and I have tried to keep the faith."

From his boyhood through his senior years, George possessed an insatiable desire to learn the secrets of nature and to apply them to benefit all mankind. This driving force pressed him in an unrelenting pursuit of formal education, beginning with his attempt as a boy to learn his letters in a raw, one-room cabin school in Locust Grove, Missouri. This first ambition was frustrated when the white instructor refused to teach George because he was black.

However, with renewed determination at fourteen, George left the Carver farm to attend the Lincoln School for Colored Children in Neosho, Missouri. Upon receiving a diploma after one year of study, he traveled to Fort Scott, Kansas. There Carver worked at odd jobs and

George Washington Carver.

THE LIFE OF
George Washington Carver

1861(?)	Born in Diamond Grove, Missouri
1891	Enrolls in Simpson College to study piano and art
1894	Receives B.S. degree from Iowa Agricultural College
1896	Receives Master of Agriculture degree from Iowa State College
	Joins faculty of Tuskegee Institute
1921	Appears before U.S. House of Representatives Committee on Ways and Means regarding tariff on peanuts
1923	Receives Springarn Medal for Distinguished Service to Science
1939	Receives Roosevelt Medal for Outstanding Contribution to Southern Agriculture
1943	Dies at Tuskegee Institute, Alabama

went to school irregularly for about a year before moving west to further, with indomitable persistence, his education.

Barred!

After he had gained a high school education, which he had paid for mostly by washing and cooking for whites, George was accepted, by mail, to Highland College in Kansas. When he arrived, however, he was rejected by the administration because he was black. In spite of this—one of the most disheartening setbacks of his life—George drew strength from adversity. He went on to study at Simpson College in Iowa and later at Iowa Agricultural College, where he graduaed in 1896 with a master's degree in botany.

Around this time, Booker T. Washington, a former slave, hoped to expand Tuskegee Institute, a trade school he had founded in 1881. His dream was to equip blacks to survive in America by teaching them occupations that were indispensable. Impressed with Carver's genius as a botanist, Washington shared his vision with Carver and invited him to join the Tuskegee faculty in 1896. His acceptance of this position was a turning point in his life. Responding to Washington's offer, he wrote, "To this end, I have been preparing myself for these many years, feeling as I do that this line of education is the key to unlock the golden door of freedom to our people." Carver, while on faculty at Tuskegee for

Carver at work among the plant trays.

Carver in his botanical laboratory.

forty-seven years, shaped the lives of innumerable students; he also dramatically influenced both farming in the South and the economy of America.

Carver received the Roosevelt Medal for Outstanding Contribution to Southern Agriculture in 1939 mainly because of his research on the peanut and the sweet potato and their contribution to Southern farming. Because Southern farmers had planted cotton for hundreds of years without crop rotation, he realized, the soil had worn out and the farmers were going into interminable debt. To restore the soil Carver advised the planting of peanuts and sweet potatoes instead of cotton. After much persuasion, planters gradually increased their peanut and sweet potato acreage, until these became number-one crops in the South. However, was no substantial market for peanuts and sweet potatoes! Forced to let the produce rot in the fields, the farmers ended up losing more money than before.

Under this disaster's crushing weight, Carver beseeched God, "Mr. Creator, why did You make the peanut?" Many years later, he shared that God led him back to his laboratory and worked with him to discover some 300 marketable products from the peanut, including lard, mayonnaise, cheese, shampoo, instant coffee, flour, soap, face powder, plastics, adhesives, axle grease, and pickles. Likewise, from the sweet potato he made more than 100 discoveries, among them starch, library paste, vinegar, shoe blacking,

George Washington Carver.

ink, and molasses. These new products created a demand for peanuts and sweet potatoes. Economists and agriculturalists agree that Carver contributed more than any other individual to rejuvenate the Southern economy.

Being helpful to the world

In 1921 Southern farmers were pleading with Congress for a tariff which would place an import duty on peanuts produced abroad with cheap labor. Fearing the devastation of their $200 million-a-year industry in peanuts, businessmen asked George Washington Carver to argue their case before the House Ways and Means Committee. His presentation was so overwhelmingly impressive that Congress asked him to speak for one hour and forty-five minutes, rather than the customary ten, and they wrote the tariff into the bill. (Yet elsewhere, in Washington D.C., for example, he was scorned and forced to ride in freight elevators because he was black.)

Carver died in 1943 and was buried with the epitaph, "He could have added fortune to fame, but caring for neither, he found happiness and honor in being helpful to the world."

Through Carver's trust in God, he overcame poverty and racial prejudice to earn the admiration of his contemporaries and the grateful recognition of later generations.

Further Reading

Elliott, Lawrence. *George Washington Carver: The Man Who Overcame.* Englewood Cliffs, N.J.: Prentice-Hall, 1966.

Kitchens, J. W. and L. B. Kitchens, eds. *Guide to the Microfilm Edition of the George Washington Carver Papers at Tuskegee Institute.* National Historical Publications and Records Commission, 1975.

Kremer, Gary R. *George Washington Carver in His Own Words.* Columbia, Mo.: University of Missouri, 1987.

McMurry, Linda O. *George Washington Carver: Scientist and Symbol.* New York: Oxford University, 1981.

J. Gresham Machen and Orthodoxy

CHRISTIANITY *v.* LIBERALISM

In 1923, a relatively obscure professor of New Testament at Princeton Seminary, a man named J. Gresham Machen, entered the public spotlight with the publication of *Christianity and Liberalism*. Machen's sudden notoriety was all the more odd because his book defended fundamentalism, a cause that was not popular.

Professor J. Gresham Machen.

Even so, Machen drew praise from the political pundit Walter Lippmann and the irreverent journalist H. L. Mencken, and in fact, the book was to become what Yale historian Sydney Ahlstrom called "the chief theological ornament of American fundamentalism."

It was indeed remarkable that Machen should identify with fundamentalism. The scion of an elite Baltimore family and a graduate of highly respected universities, Machen was not personally or socially predisposed to join a movement thought by many to represent rural Protestants from the South who opposed higher learning. Yet he believed that the issues of the fundamentalist controversy concerned the essence of the gospel.

But Machen's opposition to liberalism eventually ran afoul of Presbyterian church leaders when he founded Westminster Seminary in 1929 and a rival Presbyterian mission board in 1933. Forced out of the denomination, he founded the Orthodox Presbyterian Church in 1936. Although they were smaller than their mainline counterparts, these institutions carried forward Gresham Machen's twin commitment to academic excellence and theological orthodoxy, and were important for training a new generation of evangelical leaders.

Intellectual dishonesty
Fresh from seminary and still uncertain about a career, J. Gresham Machen at the young age of twenty-four embarked on a trip to Germany in 1905 to study with some of the leading lights of Protestant liberalism

years. As Machen himself years later described the trouble, he had to face in Germany the problem of "holding on with the heart to something that one has rejected with the head." He was particularly concerned about critical views of the Bible, a challenge which required "moral and intellectual decisiveness." His caring and protective mother tried to console him with a Christian faith which "though not contrary to reason, [transcended] reason." However, Gresham Machen would have none of his mother's appeal to religious emotion. If he did not address the central problem of Christianity's historical truthfulness, he said, he would be guilty of "intellectual dishonesty."

Gresham Machen's doubts were not to be resolved during his stay in Germany, but his studies there were crucial to his emergence during the 1920s as an outspoken opponent of Protestant liberalism. With some misgivings, in 1906 he returned to Princeton Seminary to teach New Testament and threw himself into research that resulted in two important books, both of which made strong cases that the Bible was trustworthy.

Jesus and Paul

The first was *The Origin of Paul's Religion*, published in 1921. The study of the apostle Paul was especially important for Machen's personal development. He countered the efforts of biblical scholars who tried to separate the teachings of Jesus from the theology of Paul. Paul was not only a contemporary of Jesus' disciples and received their blessing, but, according to Machen, a close reading of the

> *"Liberalism appeals to man's will, while Christianity announces, first, a gracious act of God."*

New Testament showed overwhelming agreement between the apostle and the Savior he worshiped. Put simply, "Paul was a true follower of Jesus if Jesus was a divine Redeemer, come from heaven to die for the sins of men."

Machen's study of the apostle made the historical veracity of the New Testament central. "Everywhere in the Epistles," he wrote, "Paul stakes all his life upon the truth of what he says about the death and resurrection of Jesus." The gospel Paul preached was not a system of philosophy or a set of rules for life; it was "an account of something that had happened." Machen concluded that the rise and spread of Christianity could not be explained apart from the epoch-making death and resurrection of Jesus. Either Paul's account of Jesus was true, or the church was based upon an "inexplicable error."

To be sure, Machen, by posing this alternative had not demonstrated that the Bible was true. That kind of certainty, as he admitted, could only come through the witness of the Holy Spirit. But the plain message of the New Testament did mean that mainline Protestant churches could not continue to hold Jesus in high esteem while hedging on

and biblical criticism. Machen was not unaccustomed to the rigors of advanced learning, having studied as an undergraduate at Johns Hopkins University, the first American institution which was dedicated to specialized research. Then he had pursued a master's degree in philosophy at Princeton University at the same time as completing the course of study for prospective ministers at Princeton Seminary.

Still, Machen's work in Germany would be more difficult because it brought to a head a crisis of faith, which had been intensifying for several the miraculous events which permeated His life. Either the Bible was correct about Jesus, or it was a book of fables, which had to be rejected.

Controversy

Machen's biblical research, far from being an ivory tower affair, had direct implications for the life of the church. The same sort of intellectual honesty that Machen required of himself he began to demand of the leaders of Protestant denominations of America. This tactic involved Machen directly in the fundamentalist controversy that was emerging during the early 1920s. Believing that clergy and church officials had embraced Protestant liberalism, Machen wrote his most popular and important book, *Christianity and Liberalism*, published in 1923 by Macmillan, a major New York publisher.

The thrust of this work was that liberalism was not a variety of Christianity but was an entirely different religion. From insights gleaned from his study of Paul, Machen argued that Christianity had always been rooted in the saving historical acts of Christ's death and resurrection. The term "gospel" itself implied the historical character of Christianity. It meant "good news," a "report of something new," which established an entirely different relationship between God and sinners. Liberal Protestantism, in contrast, reduced Christianity to a set of general religious principles about being good and following the moral teaching of Jesus. Historic Christianity and liberalism, were thus at odds. "Liberalism appeals to man's will, while Christianity announces,

Portrait of J. Gresham Machen, from Westminster Seminary.

first, a gracious act of God." By focusing on the redemptive character of Christianity, Machen's book clarified the issues which separated conservative and liberal Protestants.

Christianity and Liberalism also proposed a remedy for the controversy within American churches. Because Christianity and liberalism were two religions, Machen argued, conservatives and liberals should part company. The simple virtue of honesty demanded that liberals leave existing denominations. The evangelical churches were bound by their constitutions to proclaim a certain view of Christ's death and resurrection, and for that reason liberals should not preach in these churches. They could, of course, form their own churches and preach their own religion. But until the founding documents of the Protestant denominations were altered, Machen argued, liberals should be banned.

Expelled!

This stance led to what was to be the most difficult period of Machen's life. He became embroiled in a series of conflicts within in his own denomination, the Northern Presbyterian Church. In 1929, when conservatives lost control of Princeton Theological Seminary, Machen provided both able leadership and financial resources for the foundation of Westminster Seminary in Philadelphia. Concerned about liberalism within Presbyterian missionary endeavors, Machen next helped to form a rival missions board, in 1933. This effort, however, was more than Presbyterian leaders could endure. Machen was brought to trial for insubordination and formally expelled from the church in 1936. At that time, he and 100 other ministers founded the Orthodox Presbyterian Church.

Despite numerous efforts on behalf of the conservative

Presbyterian cause, he could not shake his interest in the New Testament and 1930 he published his second scholarly monograph, *The Virgin Birth of Christ*. In many respects this book was the capstone of his scholarship, as well as a culmination of his critique of liberal Protestantism. In it he defended the miraculous birth of Christ against liberal scholars who tried to explain it away either by natural causes or the cultural conditioning of the apostles. Nevertheless, the book went beyond an apology for the Bible's truthfulness to assert that God's supernatural intervention into human history was at the heart of Christianity. According to Machen, the virgin birth raised "the question of all questions ... What shall we think of Jesus Christ?" Though many had tried to make the virgin birth a secondary issue or merely a historical detail, Machen did not think that it could be isolated from the overarching message of Scripture. Viewed "in the light of God and against the dark background of sin," the virgin birth ultimately led to the conviction that "because [Jesus] loved us, he came into this world to die for our sins upon the cross."

A grand faith

Although his critics on occasion accused him of not evincing a spirit of love, Machen won the intense devotion of many of his students at both Princeton and Westminster. Not only did they admire his mental acumen and defense of orthodoxy, they often viewed him as a personal friend. They knew him to be one who walked closely with the Lord.

In December, 1936, Machen decided to honor a series of speaking commitments in North Dakota despite suggestions from family members that he cancel the engagements because he was suffering from a cold. The weather in North Dakota was freezing—twenty degrees below zero. Machen preached on several occasions, while trying to cover up the fact that he was desperately ill. But the raging effects of pneumonia began wearing him down. Finally, he became bed-ridden. When Pastor Samuel Allen visited Machen in the hospital on New Year's Eve, Machen related that he had had a vision of heaven. He said, "Sam, it was glorious, it was glorious." Then he added later, "Sam, isn't the Reformed Faith grand?" On New Year's Day, 1937, at around 7.30 p.m., J. Gresham Machen went to be with his Lord.

Further Reading

Machen, J. Gresham. *What is Christianity?* Edited by Ned B. Stonehouse. Grand Rapids, 1951.

Stonehouse, Ned Bernard. J. *Gresham Machen: A Biographical Memoir.* Grand Rapids, 1954.

J. I. Packer

Surprised by Grace

Theology is a contentious word to many people—even Christians. Doctrine is thought of as divisive. And theologians? Monkish men surrounded by dusty tomes, who involve themselves in obtuse and hair-splitting argumentation. They are totally irrelevant in the minds of contemporary Christians, who have a pragmatic and experiential orientation.

Imagine walking onto this scene a white-haired man with Coke-bottle eyeglasses and conservative clothing. A Britisher trained at erudite Oxford University. A man so scholarly that even in his youth his peers in the Inter-Varsity Christian Fellowship at school gave him the job of librarian. Outward appearances blended with the inner characteristics of an academician and a shy deportment. A perfect candidate for a monk. A real theologian.

Latter-day Puritan

Although James Innell Packer fits this description, he has broken our mold of a theologian. Despite a nearly fatal accident in his youth, the bugaboo of a shy spirit, and the current aversion to theologians, God has used this man to reestablish the place of the mind in the Christian life. Incredibly, there are other surprising things about him that might threaten to sink any extensive ministry. He is a Calvinist (a nickname, he insists, for historic Christianity). And as if this were not enough to insure the consignment of James I. Packer to the library for eternity, we find he is a Puritan pusher! Nevertheless, he carries on a world-wide ministry via lectures, consultations, and books, which help keep the evangelical church on the track of truth. A latter-day Puritan (without their loquaciousness), his words enthrall both mind and spirit while occasionally tickling our funny bone.

Dr J. I. Packer.

J. I. Packer: pastor, churchman, lecturer, and author. Theologian *par excellence*. A man who makes righteousness readable and grooves on hobbies as varied as steam trains and early jazz musicians. Who is this surprising man?

Instead of a bike

"Surprised by grace" encapsulates J. I. Packer's life and ministry. On his eleventh birthday Jim Packer was hoping to be surprised with his first real bicycle. While searching the room for his long-awaited gift, his eyes fell instead on a typewriter. Through the providence of God and the perceptiveness of his parents, Jim was being moved inexorably toward a career of communication by writing and lecturing. It was at the age of seven, while coming onto the street one day, that Jim was seriously injured by a truck. He nearly died due to a head wound that left a one-inch hole in his skull bone. He had to wea an aluminum protective patch strapped to his forehead until the age of fifteen, and had been cautioned to not ride bicycles.

Growing up near Gloucester, the birthplace of the great Puritan evangelist George Whitefield, Jim Packer did not realize how the shadow of this man and many other English Puritans would fall across his path. It was not until he entered the University at Oxford in 1944 that he had his first encounter with biblical Christianity.

Tracked down

At the age of eighteen Packer was visited by a student from the Oxford Inter-Collegiate Christian Union, a local branch of InterVarsity Christian Fellowship. Although he believed mentally in Christ and had even argued with a friend in defense of the Trinity, he now realized this was not sufficient. "I saw myself standing outside a house looking in on a tremendous party with laughter and joy. The Lord tracked me down and found me. I was surprised by grace. I became an avid Bible reader and my initial doubts soon evaporated in the atmosphere of solid Bible exposition at the Christian Union."

During these formative years God led Jim Packer into contact with his first volume of Puritan wisdom—John Owen's treatises on *Indwelling Sin, Manifestation of Sin,* and *Temptation.* He could find nothing in modern Christian writers to compare with its insight. This began a lifelong love affair with the Puritans. Meanwhile his scholarly skills were being honed. After graduation he was asked to teach for one year. "It was then that I found I not only could teach, but I loved it. I knew what my calling was." He returned to Oxford for a second B.A. (Theology) and stayed on for a Ph.D. Meanwhile he was carrying on a courtship with a young woman, Kit Mullett, whom he married in 1954 shortly after finishing his degree. God was to grace the marriage with three children: Ruth, Martin, and Naomi.

From the time of his conversion, Jim Packer saw the importance of the church. After working through some initial resentment toward the Church of England for covering up the gospel, he gave himself wholeheartedly toward that church and a recovery of the gospel as embodied in the doctrines of grace. "I stuck with these Anglican folk because I truly believe they

THE LIFE OF

J. I. Packer

1926	Born in Twyning, England, on July 22
1933	Hit by a truck and nearly dies
1944	Enters Oxford University
	Conversion to Christ
1948	Graduates from Oxford with a degree in Classics and Philosophy.
1950	Receives Theology degree from Oxford University
1952	Church of England (Anglican) ordination
1954	Receives Ph.D. from Oxford University
1958	Publishes *"Fundamentalism" and the Word of God*
1961	Becomes librarian at Latimer House, Oxford
1970	Becomes principal at Tyndale House
1979	Begins teaching at Regent College, Vancouver, British Columbia, Canada

are among the richest and wisest of the various traditions within Christendom."

The writing ability of J. I. Packer was not hidden for long. In 1957 he was co-translator of Martin Luther's famous book, *The Bondage of the Will.* His first book appeared in 1958, *"Fundamentalism" and the Word of God.* It played a key role in evangelical apologetics by giving a scholarly response to attacks on the veracity of Scripture. Academic evangelicalism had a spokesman. Few realized it at the time, but this man was to help toward a reassertion of theology even as C. S. Lewis was moving people to a reassertion of faith. At the same time these men were influencing the British scene and beyond, there were other forces at work within the Anglican Church. Feeling increasingly stymied by these and by the burden of administrative duties, Jim Packer began to wonder what God's next surprise might be.

A square peg

In God's timing an invitation arrived from Regent College in Canada to take a position that would free him to lecture worldwide and to write. Hesitating for quite a while (it meant leaving his beloved England), he finally capitulated in 1979 and now says his Canadian years have been his happiest. He comments, "God had prepared a square hole for a square peg. Packer is my name and packing became my game" (speaking of his frequent lecture trips).

Packer carries on an extensive ministry as a writer. In 1973 *Knowing God* ("As clowns yearn to play Hamlet, so I have wanted to write a treatise on God") became his most popular book. Always a cheerleader for others, Packer has perhaps written more recommendations for the books of fellow Christians than anyone else. The introduction he wrote to one book became more famous than the book itself (*Death of Death in the Death of Christ*). Potential embarrassment was avoided because the book was a reprint, and the author, John Owen, the prince of Puritan theologians, was long dead. "For me, being an author is comparable to a woman giving birth—great pain during delivery yet great satisfaction afterwards. I can only write because I'm driven to it. And I sweat away. God has laid the task of communication on me."

Freaky bookworm?

How does Jim Packer himself summarize his life so far? "I could brood and regret that I had not done better at all I put my hand to (and it's true it should have been done better), but I will not. I am a shy, freaky, bookworm type person whom God has taken and set upon a rock. My stability comes from an ever fresh realization that God is my Father and I am His child. Adopted. Assured. Therefore I'm living in a less nervy, more relaxed way. My prayer was answered. Although I wanted a bike and other lesser things, God had something better constantly in mind. His strength is perfected in my weakness."

J. I. Packer has ability to present doctrinal truth with clarity and pungency. You cannot get far in his writings without meeting up with his dry wit. If you are to hear him in a question-and-answer session, get ready to be treated to a quick mind. And if you need a person to write a report overnight summarizing the deliberations of an important consultation, who do you call? J. I. Packer. The marriage of doctrine (theology) and devotion (piety) is something that God has joined together, and Jim Packer will not let any person rend it asunder. In particular he is a leading advocate for reformed theology, which he considers best exemplified among the much maligned Puritans. In his book *Quest for Godliness*, we are exposed to the Puritan vision for the Christian life. Just as we found that theologians were not so bad after all, we see the Puritans are strong in the very areas the Western church is weakest. Packer has drunk deeply from the Puritans and invites us to do the same. "He lives in another era," say some. He contends that by sitting on the shoulders of the Puritans he can see today's world better.

Jim Packer teaches the whole counsel of God. Never one to avoid controversy (he has taken a stand for Biblical inerrancy, evil consequences of liberal theology, moderation and balance among charismatics, equality yet diversity of function for male and female roles), people attest to his catholic and irenic spirit. Instead of trying to get everyone to use the right labels, his desire is for them to think biblically and turn all theology into doxology. If criticized for being too precise, he responds with the words of a Puritan: "Well, sir, I serve a precise God!"

"Think of theologians as the church's sewage specialists. Their role is to detect and eliminate intellectual pollution, and to ensure, so far as man can, that God's life giving truth flows pure and unpoisoned into Christian hearts" (J. I. Packer, *Hot Tub Religion*).

Further Reading

Catherwood, Christopher. *Five Evangelical Leaders.* Wheaton: Shaw, 1985.

Packer, J. I. *"Fundamentalism" and the Word of God.* Grand Rapids: Eerdmans, 1958.

Packer, J. I. *Evangelism and the Sovereignty of God.* Downers Grove: InterVarsity, 1961.

Packer, J. I. *Knowing God.* Downers Grove: InterVarsity, 1973.

Packer, J. I. *Keep in Step with the Spirit.* Old Tappan: Revell, 1984.

Packer, J. I. *Hot Tub Religion.* Wheaton: Tyndale, 1987.

Packer, J. I. *Quest for Godliness.* Wheaton: Crossway 1990.

Byang H. Kato

AFRICAN PROPHET

A personal account by Harold Fuller

The staggering news crackled over the mission radio: "Byang Kato drowned off Mombasa." I was traveling on the edge of the Sahara in West Africa. Mombasa was three thousand miles away, on the east coast. It was incomprehensible that Dr. Byang H. Kato, voice for evangelicals all over Africa, was dead!

I was stunned. I was angry with God. All of the expatriate missionaries were dispensable—but Byang Kato? We needed him. The church of Jesus Christ in Africa and around the world needed him. He was just beginning to be heard as a strong evangelical voice in the face of the onslaught by forces that would like to wipe out gospel witness on the continent. In two weeks' time he was to have started on an extensive, strategic tour of the continent.

Although Byang Kato's name was not a household word on other continents, evangelical leaders worldwide were well aware of the strategic ministry of the thirty-nine-year-old Nigerian. They sent their condolences. Typical was the reaction of Dr. Francis Shaeffer, evangelical philosopher and theologian in Switzerland: "I literally wept. The loss for Africa and the Lord's work seemed so great."

Those who knew Byang were affected like this because of the life and vision of this dynamic black theologian. And his vision continues to make an impact on the continent of Africa.

Fetish priests

Byang Kato was born into the family line of fetish priests of Sabzuro, a village in the heart of Nigeria, West Africa. His father proudly ded-

---

THE LIFE OF
Byang Kato

1936	Born in Nigeria
1946	Tribal initiation
1948	Conversion
1957	Graduates from Bible school
1958	Begins teaching, counseling ministries
1966	Graduates from London University/London Bible College, B.D
1967	Appointed General Secretary ECWA, Nigeria
1971	Graduates from Dallas Theological Seminary, S.T.M.
1973	Elected General Secretary, AEAM Graduates from Dallas Theological Seminary, Th.D.
1974	Appointed Secretary of the World Evangelical Fellowship Executive Committee
1975	Dies in drowning accident

---

icated him to become a fetish priest. At the age of ten, Byang and other boys his age went through the traditional secret initiation rites of his Jaba tribe.

A year later Byang heard the gospel for the first time, from an itinerant missionary. At the age of twelve he enrolled in a Sudan Interior Mission school, where a teacher showed him how he could have eternal life.

I first met Byang when he was twenty-three. He had quickly made up for his late academic start, completing Bible college, teaching at an Sudan Interior Mission Bible school, and was married with two children. He arrived at the office of *African Challenge*, of which I was editor, to be a counselor for readers who wrote in.

A man of 23 is considered a youth in most African cultures, but I was impressed with Byang Kato's maturity, wisdom, intelligence, spirituality, and vision for Africa. That was the beginning of a close friendship.

Eager to sharpen his sword spiritually and intellectually, he went on to further studies in Nigeria, England, and America, assisted by SIM scholarships. He passed courses and earned degrees, right up to the Th.D., in record time and with outstanding honors.

Evangelicals in his own continent and around the world soon noticed this disciplined, clear-thinking theologian. His church, the Evangelical Churches of West Africa (ECWA), elected him General Secretary. The Association of Evangelicals of Africa and Madagasacar

Above: Dr. Byang Kato with other Christian leaders. Below: Dr. Kato.

(AEAM) appointed him as General Secretary and the World Evangelical Fellowship made him vice president, and chairman of WEF's Theological Commission. Dr. Kato gave two papers at the 1974 Lausanne Congress and was in demand at other international conferences, such as InterVarsity's Urbana.

Anemia

Dr. Kato's AEAM appointment in 1973 not only recognized his leadership qualities but also emphasized the predicament Africa's evangelicals found themselves in at the time. Many people had turned to Christ, but they laced teaching with other things. At the same time, the World Council of Churches had been pouring money into the training of African leadership in liberal theology. They bolstered their teaching with appeals to "African authenticity" and nationalistic emotions. If evangelical missionaries objected were accused of cultural imperialism. Most

evangelical pastors did not have the academic stature to make themselves heard. The fruit of dedicated evangelism by both black and white missionaries over the past century was in danger of being lost.

This was the scene that God brought Byang Kato into. In 1973 he blew the whistle at the third general assembly of the AEAM with his paper on "Theological Anemia in Africa," when he declared:

"Biblical Christianity in Africa is being threatened by syncretism, universalism, and Christ-paganism. The spiritual battle for Africa during this decade will be fought, therefore, largely on theological grounds."

Kato then outlined his vision for developing theological leadership. The response of the AEAM delegates was to ask Kato to be General Secretary of the Association. They knew that

SIM and ECWA were depending on him to be principal of their seminary in Nigeria. "Giving up Dr. Kato will be a sacrifice for you," they told me, "but none of our churches or missions has anyone at his level."

They were right. This was the evangelical dilemma in Africa. And this was one reason Byang's death just two years later hit me so hard. The church of Jesus Christ in Africa needed a whole army of Katos.

However, Dr. Kato's vision was so strong and his efforts so tireless, that in those two brief years he was able to set in motion programs that have given evangelicals today a strong voice. He courageously faced criticism from the WCC-related All Africa Council of Churches. One prominent liberal theologian threatened to sue him for defamation. A liberal newspaper attacked him.

An African religion?

Byang's own background of traditional African religion gave him credibility in opposing the nationalistic call for "an African religion"—in effect, syncretism. He forcefully argued that Christianity was not "the white man's religion." He declared that "the Bible must be the final judge of every culture."

Several of Dr. Byang Kato's papers have been published and to this day continue to be a voice on such topics as salvation, contextualization, syncretism, and Biblical inerrancy.

In spite of his international recognition and intellectual debates, Kato lived a humble and disciplined life. His travels took him to far-off places such as South Africa and Alaska, but it was always his joy to return home to sit with his mother in her mud hut, or to go on a picnic with his wife and three chidren. Always ready to point someone to Christ, he was overjoyed when his elderly father, once having dedicated him to Satan, turned to the living God and found eternal salvation.

Today's AEAM commissions on society, youth, women, missions, theology, ethics, and justice reflect its wide impact on the continent. Other projects now include an evangelical theological society, a theological journal, a continent-wide theological accreditation organization, and two graduate seminaries—all of which are projects which Kato envisaged.

AEAM's current General Secretary, Dr. Adeyemo Tokunboh, was personally challenged, while a student, by hearing Byang Kato share his vision for Africa.

"Kato was a prophet," says Dr. Tokunboh, who is also chairman of the International Executive of the World Evangelical Fellowship. "Evangelicals throughout Africa today are grateful to God for the vision of leadership training given to Kato."

The shock of Byang Kato's death is still with me, but so are precious memories of my closest African colleague. And the shock has been tempered with thankfulness that Kato's vision is being fulfilled in the lives of Africa's new generation of evangelical leaders.

Further Reading

de la Haye, Sophie. *Byang Kato: Ambassador for Christ*. Achimota, Ghana: Africa Christian Press, 1986.

Kato, B.H. *African Cultural Revolution and the Christian Faith*. Jos, Nigeria: Challenge Press (SIM), 1975.

_____. *Theological Pitfalls in Africa*. Kisumu, Kenya: Evangel Publishing House, 1975.

_____. *Biblical Christianity in Africa*. Achimota, Ghana: Africa Christian Press, 1985.

Henry F. Schaefer III

Computer Chemist

Put away the Bunsen burners and beakers. A lot of chemistry is going onto the computer!

That's not the only thing unconventional about Dr. Henry Schaefer III and his work. Each fall, the Nobel nominee sets aside his cutting-edge research to teach freshmen. Instead of advancing agnostic views, he lectures on the faith of famous scientists, the resurrection—and how God helped him through a personal tragedy.

When someone mentions the three times he has been nominated for the Nobel Prize in Chemistry, he jokes about a teasing putdown from his teenage daughter.

Dr. Schaefer performs his experiments with software instead of glassware. This is such an innovative idea that he has been nominated three times for the Nobel Prize in Chemistry.

And the point of computerizing chemistry? A monitor screen does not explode in your face, or consume costly chemicals. Therefore, it is being implemented first in places where experiments are difficult, expensive, or dangerous.

A computer chemist can also do a lot of "what if"—to see what would happen if he combined several substances, and what properties the new compounds would have. Schaefer says, "We can study molecules that, as far as laboratory people are concerned, don't exist"—to determine whether or not they *can be made* to exist. By 2010, he expects as many people will be doing chemical research by computer as by laboratory methods.

Yet Schaefer spends the fall quarter teaching freshman chemistry: "Our university places a high value on teaching. I enjoy getting students before they're brainwashed into believing chemistry is hard and boring. It can actually be quite exciting and fulfilling."

Easy as Psi

Quantum chemistry is the study of molecules through mathematical equations that describe the way that subatomic particles move and behave. "The fundamental equation in quantum

Dr. Henry F. Schaefer III.

mechanics is something called Schrödinger's Equation"—the chemical "theory of everything." In 1926 Austrian scientist Erwin Schrödinger developed the equation that could answer all chemical questions based on the "wave function" psi.

Schrödinger received the 1933 Nobel Prize in Physics. But until recently his equation was too complicated to solve for anything but the simplest molecules. With supercomputers Schaefer is "beginning to be able to solve this horrific equation reliably for more and more systems." Ten programs, totalling a million lines of computer code, instruct his computers how to solve Schrödinger's Equation.

Most important discovery
What Dr. Schaefer calls "certainly the most important discovery of my life" did not occur in a laboratory, however: "During my fourth year at Berkeley, I received Jesus Christ into my life."

The eight-year trail began while he was visiting his fiancée Kären in 1965. "She was a religion minor," Schaefer recalls, "and one of her professors ... asked how Jesus Christ gained so many followers throughout the world." After the crucifixion, the disciples cowered in a locked room—"apparently not able to do anything except be terrified of the authorities." Several weeks later they were running around telling everyone the wonderful things they had seen and heard. "This professor had no particular belief of his own, but he asked the students how this radical change could have taken place in Christ's followers." He gave several possibilities, including: "Maybe Jesus Christ really had physically risen from the dead."

When Kären recounted that lecture, Schaefer replied, "Now that's an interesting thought!" It incubated three years until an Easter service near Stanford. The minister said that all of Christianity is a sham—*unless Jesus really rose from the dead!* After the service, Schaefer asked, "So you really think it's all true?" He replied, "Yes, I do." That statement catalyzed with the input from three years earlier.

Schaefer avidly read various views on the matter: *The Passover Plot* claimed that Jesus did not die. From half-dead dehydration and blood loss, he revived and came back with great

THE LIFE OF
Henry F. Schaefer III

1944	Born in Grand Rapids, Michigan
1966	Graduates from M.I.T.
	Marries Kären Regine Rasmussen
1969	Receives Ph.D. from Stanford University
	Appointed to faculty of University of California, Berkeley
1973	Conversion
1977	Elected Fellow, American Physical Society
1979	Adoption and death of son Pierre
	Receives American Chemical Society Award in Pure Chemistry
1983	Given American Chemical Society Leo Hendrik Baekeland Award
1984	Cochairman of "Nobel Laureate Symposium on Applied Quantum Chemistry," Honolulu
1986	First nominated for Nobel Prize
1987	Becomes director, Center for Computational Quantum Chemistry, University of Georgia
1988	Elected: Fellow, American Institute of Chemists and Fellow, American Scientific Affiliation
1990	Annual Medal, World Association of Theoretical Organic Chemists
1991	Publishes 500th professional paper

energy a few days later. "I reacted to that book.... If you believe that, you'll believe anything! It is probably as good as any of the [anti-resurrection] theories—and it's horrible! In terms of any kind of probalistic analysis, it's very poor."

Making much more sense were Frank Morison's *Who Moved the Stone?* and works by F. F. Bruce and Josh McDowell (see Further Reading). "I became convinced that, as a historical fact, it was just overwhelmingly probable that Jesus had risen from the dead."

About a year later, not yet a believer, Schaefer was leading a Bible study. He was struck by 1 John 5:13, "I write these things to you ... so that you may know that you have eternal life.". When he asked the study group what they thought of this, one man said that if you trust in Christ, you can know for sure that you have eternal life.

Schaefer recalls, "Within about 24 hours ... I knew Jesus had risen from the dead—and that there was a strong historical proof that He was and is Almighty God. I was convinced that He had died to forgive my sins, and that based on what He had done and my belief in Him, I was going to heaven."

Free speech rights

While teaching freshman chemistry at the University of California, Berkeley (UCB), Dr. Schaefer casually mentioned having attended church the previous Sunday. After class, many students remained and asked him if this were unusual for a scientist.

He began a series of noncredit, extracurricular lectures. In the "anything goes" atmosphere of Berkeley, "I certainly had a lot of people who didn't agree with me, and they didn't hesitate to say so. But nobody challenged my constitutional right to present my opinions in public."

Ironically, the challenge began when he moved to the Bible Belt. At the University of Georgia, "Some people genuinely seemed to think that what I was doing was illegal." Complaints percolated up to the president of the university, who consulted the vice president for legal affairs. "She discovered what I had known all along. Free speech with respect to spiritual things is every bit as protected as free speech for a person who wants to explain why he's a communist." There were usually about three hundred students attending the lectures.

After a full day's teaching and research, no one can doubt that his religious expression is "on his own time." His secretary even schedules interviews regarding religious matters after 5:00 p.m.

The fall quarter topic is "Science and the Christian Faith"—stressing that virtually all of modern physics and chemistry was developed by committed Christians. Pioneer scientists like Kepler, Faraday, and Maxwell wrote about God and their relationship to Christ.

Other lectures are "A Physical Scientist Looks at Creation and Evolution," plus one about his personal experiences as a Christian. In April 1991, he traveled to Leningrad to lecture on his quantum chemistry specialty, and on "Modern Science and the Christian Faith."

Is a Christian chemist different? "I don't know that I do science very differently. Certainly my wonder at scientific discoveries is greatly enhanced—to make a discovery and say, 'So that's the way God laid out [that part] of the universe!' There is joy in thinking God's thoughts after Him."

The stress of success

"I have a problem with pride and arrogance," Henry Schaefer admits. "Often people tell me how wonderful I am, and that's not an easy thing to cope with. I might be stupid enough to believe them."

Dr. Schaefer has published more than five hundred professional papers. In a 1990 survey, he was a "citation superstar"—one whose publications had been quoted an exceptional number of times by other scientists. He was nineteenth among chemists worldwide, with virtually all those ahead of him being much older.

> *"So that's the way God laid out ... the universe!"*

What antidotes for pride does God provide? "There's never a year that goes by when one of my papers doesn't get rejected by some journal." Even amid forty accepted papers in a typical year, one rejection bothers him—especially when the referees "say rude things" about the author.

Pride-jolting put-downs also come from their teenage daughter, Charlotte. Bringing home a copy of *The Atlanta Constitution* in 1987, she announced, "Dad, look at this! It says you've been nominated for the Nobel Prize!"

Suspecting that his daughter thought he had leaked confidential information, Dr. Schaefer responded, "Charlotte, it's not my fault, I didn't give them that."

Charlotte answered, "Dad, it's okay! You're not going to get it!"

When Schaefer asked what made her so sure, she answered, "It's simple, Dad. You're just not smart enough!"

After Pierre

Even a life this successful has not been exempt from tragedy. In 1979, Dr. Schaefer had been spending several months researching at the University of Texas—alternating two weeks there, then several weeks at home. During one absence, Kären awoke to find their five-month-old son not breathing.

On Sunday December 9, Schaefer had just returned from church when a friend phoned him in Texas to tell him that Pierre had died. "My wife was even more distressed because she didn't know what had *caused* Pierre's death." She feared that somehow it might have been her fault.

The coroner determined the problem was Sudden Infant Death Syndrome (SIDS), or "crib death." "That was an enormous relief to know it was a natural cause, not one we could have prevented 'if only.'"

All their children are adopted. After waiting five years for Pierre, "Monday morning I had to call the agency from which we got Pierre and tell them." An agency employee assured them they understood the circumstances; after the grieving period, Schaefers would be number one on the list to adopt a baby boy.

More than a decade later, Schaefer still chronicles life as "before Pierre" or "after Pierre." "It's really a watershed in my life."

It was also a growth experience: "Never have I been so overwhelmed with the certainty of the love of my heavenly Father. When I got home from the airport, there was a large group of Christian friends waiting with my wife. We sat down and prayed together that in some way that we couldn't understand, God would be glorified in this situation."

Through Pierre's death, God mellowed the Schaefers. Having been "pretty free of any kind of trauma," they had not learned how to be sympathetic to someone suffering. About a year after Pierre, Kären could comfort a mother whose son died of a respiratory problem while she was driving him to the hospital. "Kären ... was able to comfort this woman who became a Christian within a few weeks. We're different people than we were before Pierre with respect to understanding people's problems."

Summons to Stockholm?

After having been nominated several times, will Henry Schaefer be awarded the Nobel Prize in Chemistry in some future year? What might he say in his acceptance speech if he is summoned to Stockholm in order to receive this ultimate accolade?

"I certainly would want to say something about Jesus." However, "if it was too heavy-handed, it wouldn't be effective, and if it was too wimpy, it wouldn't be effective either." If and when the Nobel committee invites him to their platform, he will rely on God to help him say something convincing but not caustic—a provocative comment to demonstrate that a world-class intellect can love the Lord with all his mind.

Further Reading

Bruce, F. F. *The New Testament Documents: Are They Reliable?* Revised. Grand Rapids: Eerdmans, 1960.

McDowell, Josh. *Evidence That Demands a Verdict.* San Bernardino, Calif.: Campus Crusade for Christ, 1972.

Morison, Frank. *Who Moved the Stone?* Grand Rapids: Zondervan, 1958.

Ross, Hugh. *The Fingerprint of God.* Pasadena, Calif.: Reasons to Believe, 1989.

Industry & Commerce

Cyrus McCormick

Bringing in the Sheaves

Cyrus Hall McCormick, 1809–84.

A McCormick reaper at work.

Before Cyrus McCormick invented the mechanical reaper, the harvesting of grain was a grueling and slow process. Using a sickle, a person could at best harvest an acre a day. Even with a cradle, no more than three acres of grain could be cut in that amount of time. Farm hands rebelled against sweating in the fields for twelve to fourteen hours each day for only about five cents an hour. It was hardly surprising, then, that many farmers found it difficult, if not impossible, to hire enough workers for the short period of time in which wheat and other cereal crops could be gathered.

Cyrus McCormick's American reaping machine.

Many people had previously tried to create a mechanical reaper. But it was not until McCormick had reworked his father's defective model that a successful one was invented.

Feeding a nation

As a result, farmers can now harvest more acres in an hour than a farm hand could cut by hand in a whole day. The production of food has increased enormously, making the industrialization of the West possible. When Cyrus McCormick was elected to the French Academy of Science, one of the speakers said he had done "more for the course of agriculture than any other living man." And one of his biographers also added, "He fed his country as truly as Washington created it and Lincoln preserved it."

McCormick's invention of the reaper was one of the most revolutionary in all of history. This is well known. What is less well known is that McCormick was a convinced evangelical Christian who, among other things, helped Moody Bible Institute get started.

"That boy is beyond me!"

If a lot of formal education is what it takes to make a person destined to enjoy success, Cyrus Hall McCormick would not qualify. He attended the rural Old Field School near his home, "Walnut Grove," in Virginia. His desk was a slab bench and his

school texts included an arithmetic book, a spelling book, a grammar, the Shorter Catechism of the Presbyterian Church, and the Bible.

But one incident when he was aged fifteen perhaps reveals his future genius. On a winter morning in 1824 he brought to school an elaborate map he had drawn in ink on paper, then mounted on linen and hung from two rollers. The teacher was most impressed. "That boy," she said, "is beyond me!"

But like most sons of farmers in his day he was soon at work for his father, a relatively well-to-do farmer and inventor who owned about eighteen hundred acres of land and a number of auxiliary businesses, which included a small farm implement shop, distillery, and grist mill. Robert McCormick had invented a Clover huller, blacksmith's bellows, a hemp brake, and a hydraulic-power machine, but he could not make a reaper that would work.

Walk out

The McCormicks were deeply religious. Coming from a Scotch-Irish Presbyterian background like the rest of the family, Cyrus McCormick's maternal grandfather, Patrick Hall, was such a strict Covenanter that when a new preacher selected a hymn by Isaac Watts instead of a psalm, his grandfather picked up his hat and walked out, rather than suffer such frivolity in church. Cyrus himself attended church services on Sunday and Wednesday evening all through his life, and generously supported seminary education as well as Christian publishing. Although this is undoubtedly an exaggeration, one biographer says, "His chief relaxation was to discuss theological questions with Presbyterian clergymen"!

When Cyrus was twenty-two old he worked for six weeks on the invention of a reaper, and, by changing the assumptions his father had made, he created one that worked! In July 1831 he gave a demonstration to his parents and his siblings. The blades cut the wheat, which fell on a platform and was raked off, just as it was supposed to do. After some further adjustments he gave the first public demonstrations of his noisy machine. One farmer complained, "Stop! You're rattling the heads off my wheat!" But another farmer, who was later to be the governor of Virginia, volunteered his crop for the experiment, and before sunset the reaper had cut down six acres of wheat.

Slowly but surely his new machine attracted attention, and even a few sales. After a number of setbacks, including bankruptcy following the bank panic of 1837, McCormick realized that the Midwest would be the future center of wheat production. In 1844 he headed to western New York, Ohio, Michigan, Illinois, and Missouri. He chose a small, insignificant port town called Chicago as the site for a factory that would supply reapers to farmers throughout the Midwest. From the first single sale in 1840 to Abraham Smith, he gradually rose to eight hundred in 1847.

Lawsuits

In 1848, however, the patent he had taken out in 1834 ran out. Competitors multiplied like maggots and pressured the U.S. Patent Office and even Congress not to renew his patent. With a sense of righteousness instilled in him by his Christian forebears McCormick fought these greedy vultures in court until his dying day.

So strong was his sense of justice that even in small matters he would institute a lawsuit if someone tried to cheat him. In 1862, for example, a railroad clerk in Philadelphia overcharged him $8.70 for one of his wife's suitcases. Though many people have criticized him for the twenty-three years of litigation that resulted from this, he refused to let anyone get away with the smallest injustice and ultimately won the case.

McCormick turned the administration of his Chicago factory over to his two brothers so that he could go to Washington and New York and devote his full time to promoting reaper sales and putting out of business those people who tried to steal his patent rights.

Prizes

McCormick was not only a brilliant inventor but an unusually gifted salesman. He decided to expand his market by trying to sell his machine to European farmers, so in 1851 he gave a demonstration to skeptical viewers at the first world's fair, the London Exhibition, and was awarded the grand prize, the Council Medal. Similarly, in 1855 he traveled to the Paris International Exhibition and won the Grand Medal of Honor. A long series of further honors compensated for the lack of recognition and praise from his American compatriots, and by 1856 he was not only a millionaire, he was also a world figure, his factory producing more than four thousand reapers a year.

In 1858, when he was forty-nine, he married twenty-three-year-old Nancy Maria ("Nettie") Fowler, a devout Christian girl whom he met when she left her upstate New York home to visit a friend in Chicago. During the 1857–60 depression, McCormick bought large tracts of Chicago real estate to add to his wealth.

McCormick's stand during the Civil War is not one of which to be proud. As a conservative Democrat he was vehemently opposed to Abraham Lincoln's presidential candidacy and tried to keep the North and South together by getting the North to give up its stand on slavery, which he was convinced was biblically acceptable. Ironically, it was McCormick's reaper that had produced the crops and wealth which did so much to enable the North to win the war.

Though he was actively involved in Democratic politics and ran not only for governor of Illinois, Congressman, but even for vice president of the United States, he never won an office. He was so unpopular in antislavery, Republican, pro-Lincoln Chicago that he deemed it wise to leave the country and head to Europe from 1862 to 1864.

However in religious matters McCormick was a staunch supporter of traditional evangelical Presbyterianism. To support those views he persuaded the Theological Seminary of the Northwest (later renamed in his honor) to move from Albany, Indiana, to Chicago in 1859 and endowed its four professorships, one of whom, Dr. Nathan L. Rice, he had earlier brought to Chicago to be his pastor.

Chicago fire

His devotion to evangelical causes led him to give $10,000 to Dwight L. Moody for the building of the Chicago YMCA in 1869. But when that building burned to the ground in the great Chicago fire of 1871, Moody prevailed on McCormick to make a similar contribution, though McCormick had lost his huge factory to the fire.

McCormick was already more than sixty and wealthy enough to retire, but at his wife's encouragement he promptly rebuilt on real estate on Blue Island Avenue which he had purchased earlier. After receiving several other awards France in 1879 elected him to the French Academy of Sciences.

Before he died in 1884 his many involvements included silver, gold, and copper mines in South America, the directorate of the Union Pacific Railroad,

the Nicaragua canal project, the crusade for the annexation of Santo Domingo (Haiti and the Dominican Republic), promoting free trade with Great Britain (the Mississippi Valley Society), and making contributions to many colleges and seminaries. In 1886, for example, his ties with Moody led to a $100,000 gift to get Moody Bible Institute started. His son, Cyrus Jr., was to become the first chairman of the school's board.

McCormick may have been a product of his times, but he was also a devoted Christian and a great inventor who was able to pass his faith on to his oldest son and successor, Cyrus Hall McCormick, Jr., who, with the financial support of J. Pierpont Morgan, was to become the first president of a combined reaper firm, the famed International Harvester Corporation.

Further Reading

Casson, Herbert N. *Cyrus Hall McCormick: His Life and Work.* Chicago: A. C. McClurg, 1909.

Hutchinson, William T. *Cyrus Hall Mccormick.* 2 vols. New York and London: The Century Go., 1930, 1935.

McCormick, Cyrus. *The Century of the Reaper.* Boston and New York: Houghton Mifflin, 1931.

Roderick, Stella Virginia. *Nettie Fowler McCormick.* Rindge, N.H.: Richard R. Smith, 1956.

John Wanamaker

Sunday School Times

February 21, 1858, was not a promising day on which to hold a Sunday school. It was the middle of winter in Philadelphia, and it snow was falling. But cold weather or no, the young superintendent—John Wanamaker—and his two teachers—his sister, Mary, with her friend and his future wife, Mary Brown—hoped that more children would attend this second week of their school in spite of the weather. Their hopes were rewarded, fifty-two "scholars" arrived, nearly doubling the numbers of the previous week. But this hopeful beginning was not without problems, however: John Wanamaker and his colleagues met resistance from Catholic residents who resented the intrusion of this Protestant institution into their neighborhood; and street gangs harassed them.

Dramatic expansion

By summer, John Wanamaker had a different problem to contend with. The school had grown too big for its premises, and somewhere larger was needed to house the numbers wanting to attend. No other building in the neighborhood was suitable, so at the start of summer he decided to conduct the school in a tent on an empty lot, beginning in July, 1858.

Over 300 children attended the first tent session, and as interest in the school continued to grow, plans were made to construct a building for the school. Dedicated in January 1859, it held twenty-seven teachers and 274 scholars.

The school continued to prosper during the Civil War, and in September 1865 Wanamaker's plans to organize a church bore fruit. The church then had only 100 members, the school over 900. But within ten years, Bethany Presbyterian Church and Sabbath School had grown to over 800 church members and over 2300 pupils. Both church and school continued their explosive growth. From 1875 to 1905, with church membership and Sunday school enrollment combined, Bethany became almost the largest Presbyterian church in the United States.

Much of this growth was due to the energy and commitment of one man who, despite daunting obstacles, wanted to make the Sunday school an important part of the religious and social life of his community. Born in Philadelphia in 1838, the grandson of a Methodist preacher, Wanamaker grew up in a pious home. Following his conversion at age eighteen, he became a Sunday school teacher, and soon

A New Frontier

Sunday schools are so much a part of church life for American evangelicals that it is hard to believe how recently they began. Although developed in England during the late eighteenth century, to give both basic education and religious instruction to working-class children, in the U.S.A. it was not until the nineteenth century that Sunday schools became an important part of evangelical efforts to build a "benevolent empire" and transform American society.

In part, the leaders of the movement intended the religious training in Sunday schools to supplement the secular education given in public schools; but their greatest hope was that the schools would be an effective way of establishing churches among the pioneers on the western frontier.

Over the course of the nineteenth century, a new frontier developed as the growth of industries and arrival of immigrants transformed American cities. Could Sunday schools be similarly employed to build evangelical churches in urban areas? The story of John Wanamaker of Philadelphia, and the Sunday school he founded and led for over fifty years, show that not only could Sunday schools help evangelize the people of the cities, but also that they could be the means of delivering services that addressed the social needs of the growing urban population.

Wanamaker's store Philadelphia. Inset: John Wanamaker, of Philadelphia, retailer and Christian philanthropist.

THE LIFE OF

John Wanamaker

1838	Born in Philadelphia
1856	Converted
1858	Begins Bethany Sabbath School
1858	Employed as secretary for the Philadelphia YMCA
1860	Marries Mary Brown
1861	Starts career as clothing retailer
1865	Founds Bethany Presbyterian Church
1868	Dedication of building for church and Sunday school
1871	Purchases *The Sunday School Times*
1876	Opens the Grand Depot, forerunner of his department store
1881	Bethany College begins holding classes in the Sunday school building
1888	Organizes the First Penny Savings Bank in basement of Sunday school
1897	Sunday school enrollment peaks at 6,097
1922	Dies at home in Philadelphia

afterwards became involved in the Young Men's Christian Association (YMCA), which in 1854 had opened a chapter in Philadelphia. In 1858, John Wanamaker was hired by its leaders as the organization's secretary, his duties including supervision of the daily operation of its building, recruiting members, and raising money for the support of the YMCA.

Retail revolution

It was during these years that Wanamaker had to choose between continuing in Christian service or pursuing a career in business. Although his mother hoped that her son would become a minister, Wanamaker chose a career in retailing. In 1861 he resigned his secretaryship of the YMCA and began his famous mercantile business in a Philadelphia clothing store for men and boys.

Though they never expanded beyond two, the Wanamaker stores grew into an huge commercial enterprise. A pioneer in the development of department stores, Wanamaker initiated many of the retailing practices adopted by large retail outlets today: marking each piece of stock with a price; guaranteeing the quality of the merchandise; setting the same price for the same items; and offering to exchange goods. A master of both advertising and promotion, he timed the opening of his Grand Depot to coincide with the Centennial Exhibition in 1876.

John Wanamaker, 1838–1922.

A conservative both by nature and in politics, Wanamaker was active in the Republican party, and lived by strict Sabbatarian and temperance principles. He was instrumental in supporting the Philadelphia revivals of D. L. Moody and Billy Sunday, loaning his mammoth Grand Depot for Moody's use in 1875. Nor did he lessen his involvement with the YMCA or the Sunday school. Though he was to resign as secretary, he was elected president of the YMCA from 1870 to 1887. But Bethany Sunday school remained foremost in Wanamaker's Christian life, and, in establishing it as a model of the virtues of efficient organization, he demonstrated how Sunday schools can help in the work of evangelizing city residents and of church growth. Beginning punctually at 2:30 in the afternoon with elaborate opening exercises, which were led by the superintendent, the school had classes for all ages. Wanamaker divided the two to three thousand scholars who usually attended into several departments, which were subdivided by age and gender into classes of eight to twelve pupils. The central auditorium, which was as large as many churches' sanctuaries, held classes for those of fourteen and older. Several hundred adults attended the Bible Union in a smaller hall, where lectures were the means of instruction. Classes of the four children's departments met in rooms surrounding the main hall.

The teachers profited from the sessions which were held each Friday evening, when Bethany's ministers helped them prepare their lessons for the following Sunday. And in fact, while A. T. Pierson pastored Bethany, his Teachers' Meetings occasionally had over 1000 in attendance, and attracted not only adult members of Bethany who did not teach at Sunday school but also ministers and teachers from other churches. All of the students studied the same Bible text, and instruction on Sunday afternoon sought to apply the text in the daily lives of the pupils. The teachers of children in particular sought to bring their pupils to a saving knowledge of Christ.

Bethany Church benefited as a steady stream of scholars joined on confession of faith. According to an 1891 note in Wanamaker's record book, on one Sunday alone, the elders at Bethany admitted 206 converts from the Sunday school to church membership. Moreover, as Bethany's members moved into other Philadelphia neighborhoods, they were responsible for starting five new churches, several of which had begun as mission Sunday schools.

Bethany's example

Meeting the spiritual needs of the scholars through instruction did not exhaust the programs Wanamaker developed in Bethany Sabbath School. He oversaw the development of projects designed to make his Sunday school a vital institution in its community by providing needed services for its residents. He established a savings bank in the school, which accepted deposits as small as one penny, to teach its scholars the virtues of saving and "laying by against a rainy day." He encouraged the women of the church to manage a dispensary, which provided free medical care to members of the school, their families, and other residents of Bethany's neighborhood. He helped shape the curriculum and served as President of Bethany College, an evening school that provided the opportunity for Sunday school pupils to learn vocational skills. In Wanamaker's less than unbiased judgement, these programs transformed "this entire section of the city [into] what it is today" and made it "a desirable place for residences."

Although few churches had the money or the manpower to sustain these kinds of activities on this scale, Bethany's example of community involvement and its influence on the development of the church, vindicated hopes that Sunday schools could be an effective means to reach those living in the urban frontiers. In 1922, the year he died, John Wanamaker reflected on the significance of his involvement in Sunday schools: "When I look back over my life, I feel that I have never done half the good for the Sabbath School that it has done for me." Millions today can testify to the "good" that Sunday school has done for them because of the dedication of John Wanamaker.

Further Reading

Boylan, Anne M. *Sunday School: The Formation of an American Institution, 1790–1880*. New Haven, Conn.: Yale, 1988.

Gibbons, Herbert Adams. *John Wanamaker*. 2 vols. New York: Harper and Bros., 1926.

Lynn, Robert W. and Wright, Elliott. *The Little Big School: Two Hundred Years of the Sunday School*. 2nd edn. Birmingham, Alabama: Religious Education Press, 1980.

Jeremiah Lanphier and Revival

"What Wilt Thou Have Me To Do?"

In a small darkened room, in the back of one of New York City's lesser churches, a man prayed alone. His request of God was simple but earth-shattering: "Lord, what wilt thou have me to do?"

It was the summer of 1857, and Jeremiah Lanphier found himself approaching mid-life without a wife or family, or very much in the way of upward mobility. His work was among New York's most forgotten citizens, the poor of the city's lower wards. Each day their numbers, and their misery, multiplied, and every day they seemed more unreachable.

Certainly Jeremiah Lanphier had rejected the "success syndrome" that drove the city's businessmen and bankers—but was it too much to ask for some sign of progress?

God's answer, like Lanphier's request, was simple but earth-shattering: the people should pray. God's enabling threw Lanphier directly into the middle of a gathering revival which was soon to turn New York's commercial empire on its head.

The first of Lanphier's midday businessmen's prayer meetings convened in the Old Dutch Church on Fulton Street on September 23, 1857. The six who met followed a simple program of Scripture reading and prayer. By October 7, the crowd of praying businessmen had overflowed into a neighboring church; within a few months twenty noonday meetings convened daily throughout the city, including huge gatherings in Burton's Theater and the Music Hall. Both the *New York Tribune* and its rival, the *New York Herald*, issued streams of revival news and editorials. In April 1858 the *Herald* released a "revival edition" to report what had become the city's biggest news.

The prayer-meeting revival Lanphier helped to spark was in fact a national conflagration. By spring 1858, two thousand met daily in Chicago's Metropolitan Theater and in Philadelphia the meetings mushroomed into a four-month-long tent meeting. In

Nineteenth-century Wall Street, New York City.

large cities and small towns, in Baltimore and Washington, Cincinnati and Chicago, New Orleans and Mobile, thousands met to pray.

Annus Mirabilis, the year of national revival, had begun.

Summer 1857 was a time of discouragement and promise for evangelical Protestants in the North. National attention had finally focused on the evils of slavery, but at rising human cost. In the wake of a violent state election in "bleeding Kansas," Northern politicians postured and Southern "fire-eaters" demanded secession; the nation seemed to be stumbling inexorably toward civil war.

Every day urban Christians encountered the moral ambiguities of mid-nineteenth-century life on city streets. In the commercial districts of New York wealthy bankers and real estate speculators congratulated God for their success. But the dark slums of Hell's Kitchen and the Five Points were walled in by poverty. Irish immigrants crowded into airless tenements, forced back by signs that read "No Irish Need Apply."

Twenty years had passed since the financial panic of 1837 had cooled the spectacular revival fires of the Second Great Awakening. Although churches had grown, yet the unreached masses multiplied even faster. "Dear Christian brethren," pleaded the Presbyterian *New York Observer*, "we must have *revivals* ... or we are undone."

Lay missionary

Few New Yorkers experienced this frustration as directly as Jeremiah Lanphier. A former businessman, he signed on in the summer of 1857 as a lay missionary for the Old Dutch Church on Fulton Street, one of the city's poorest sections.

Nearly forty years old, Lanphier was tall and energetic, affable and intelligent. With twenty years experience as a businessman, he accepted the new challenge of lay ministry with confidence. His diary entry for July 1 recorded his faith in Paul's declaration, "I can do all things through Christ, which strengthens me."

But Lanphier's sponsors at the Old Dutch Church had given him little guidance. Striking out expectantly, he employed what were then the evangelistic techniques. Doggedly he handed out tracts, preached, and visited door-to-door. Months passed without the results he expected. The daily trips through New York's poorest neighborhoods only heightened his awareness of personal helplessness. To reach the perishing thousands, he concluded, he would need a thousand selves.

Honest prayer

Lanphier's frustration led him to the upper room on Fulton Street. The tried-and-true methods had failed. It seemed clear that even his personal energy and piety were simply not sufficient to challenge the pain and indifference of urban life. At that point Lanphier prayed the most honest prayer that any one can utter, without excuses and without complaint: "Lord, what wilt thou have me to do?"

The answer came to Lanphier not in his prayer room, but on his daily rounds of the Fulton Street neighborhood, when it appeared as a passing thought that grew and took hold: God wanted the people to pray. Lanphier's idea was to hold a prayer meeting in the middle of the business day, during the noon lunch hour. The program would be simple and flexible, adapted to the needs of the schedule-driven businessmen. It would include singing, prayer, and exhortation: any speaker who passed a five-minute time allotment would be interrupted by the quiet ringing of a bell.

The idea found few immediate supporters. Even Lanphier's friends passed it over without enthusiasm. On September 23, the day appointed for the first meeting, he sat alone for the first half hour. The first six who prayed with Lanphier in late September had become a crowd of forty by October 7. Weekly meetings turned into daily ones, each with new participants. Soon they would be overflowing Fulton Street's meeting rooms into neighboring churches.

New York was soon to have reason indeed to turn to God. On October 14 a financial panic paralyzed the city. It quickly swept over the entire Northeast, collapsing an overextended economy into a brief but severe depression. Real estate prices fell precipitously; farm produce rotted on empty wharves; in the South, cotton planters, largely untouched by the economic depression, exploited the disaster to tout the advantages of slavery. More and more businessmen turned to God.

Foxhole piety?

The precipitous growth of the businessmen's prayer meetings after the October stock market crash might suggest that "foxhole piety" was the reason for their success. Certainly prayer did become a refuge for many men facing economic ruin. But the revival, which was actually underway in the weeks before the crash, extended far beyond the corridors of Wall Street. Prayer meetings dotted prosperous Southern cities as well as the economically depressed Northern ones, in the rural towns and villages as well as in the metropolitan centers.

The power of the revival was in the laymen and laywomen who prayed, called by some the "Flying Artillery of Heaven." Observers commented approvingly that clergymen formed a minority in attendance and professional revivalists were few in number. "The great revival in the times of Wesley, Whitefield, Edwards, and the Tennants was marked by powerful preaching," one commentator enthused. "The present by believing, earnest praying."

The revival was also unique as a religious movement led and supported by men. Protestants of the nineteenth century were already used to women praying and urging revival; in fact, some cynics disparaged religion as an occupation restricted to the "women's sphere." But for the ordinary person the spectacle of praying businessmen, a group long considered the least prone to any form of evangelical fervor, was an unusual one.

The outpouring in 1857–58 gave new life to revivalism. The "union prayer meetings" of sometime rival Presbyterians, Baptists, and Methodists anticipated the citywide revivals of D. L. Moody and Billy Graham. Lanphier himself issued one of the first revival press releases, thus alerting the editors of New York's rival papers to the sudden religious fervor sweeping the city's commercial districts. New technology, the telegraph and teletype, spread revival news across the country.

Reverberations

The awakening also renewed evangelical Protestant social compassion. Observers reported that the prayer meetings were bringing together black and white Christians; prominent businessmen sat alongside workingmen trailing dust and dirt. The Young Men's Christian Association became an institutional channel for revival energies, offering both physical shelter and spiritual direction to urban newcomers.

Lanphier, like many other Christians, probably wondered about the providence of God during the national bloodbath that followed the revival. The faithful prayer of thousands in 1858 did not avert war in 1861. But they did, however, prepare thousands of Christians to offer humanitarian service. Agents of the United States Christian Commission, an organization of evangelical Protestants, wrote letters, changed bandages, prayed, and preached to the homesick Union soldiers on countless Civil War battlefields. Meanwhile, behind the lines, godly women nursed the wounded troops, rolled bandages, and raised millions of dollars for army supplies.

Revival enthusiasm spread through both armies. One estimate listed 150,000 Southern converts in a wave of religious interest following Confederate victories at Fredericksburg and Chancellorsville.

The Great Revival was to call Christians away from the daily striving for success on Wall Street, and into the company of others who prayed for national righteousness. Their prayers were answered, in ways they could not believe or dare.

Further Reading

Conant, William C. *Narratives of Remarkable Conversions and Revival Incidents*. New York, 1858.

Prime, Samuel I. *The Power of Prayer Illustrated in Wonderful Displays of Divine Grace, at the Fulton Street and Other Meetings in New York and Elsewhere in 1857–58*. New York, 1858.

Smith, Timothy L. *Revivalism and Social Reform: American Protestantism on the Eve of the Cold War*. Gloucester, Mass.: Peter Smith, 1976 [1957].

J. C. Penney

Living by the Golden Rule

The J.C. Penney depart-ment store chain is an American institution. Some fourteen hundred stores spread across every state of the union and Puerto Rico, and in 1990 sales totaled $18 billion. The company employs nearly a fifth of a million people. Penney employees are sometimes called "associates," because for more than eighty years all have shared in the company profits. Today nearly one-quarter of the stock is employee owned.

The man who started it all, James Cash Penney, built his business on bedrock Christian ethics—and even named his first outlet in Kemmerer, Wyoming, "The Golden Rule Store." Nevertheless, it might be said that both his career and his sense of business ethics started in a pigpen.

When Penney's father, a Primitive Baptist preacher, in-formed his eight-year-old son that he would have to start buy-ing his own clothing, the boy acted quickly. He ran errands and he sold junk, and he then invested his meager savings in a pig. When the business soon exploded into a dozen pigs, neighbors began to complain about disturbing sounds and smells, and his father called a halt to the enterprise.

Don't take advantage

"We can't take advantage of our neighbors," his father explained. Young Penney picked up the message: never take advantage of others. It became a lifelong part of his business philosophy.

After high school Penney clerked in a dry goods store for $2.27 a month, then moved west for health reasons, and opened a butcher shop in Longmont, Colorado. When Penney refused to provide the chef of the local hotel a bottle of bourbon every week, what amounted to a bribe to keep his best client, the hotel withdrew its business. Related accounts pulled out and the meat shop failed.

The owner of a small dry goods in Wyoming gave Penney his next chance. The man soon saw Penney's potential and helped him open his own store in the nearby mining town of Kemmerer. Penney furnished it with makeshift counters and shelves made from packing crates. The Penneys lived in the attic over the store.

Shrewd merchants and bankers laughed at Penney's Golden Rule ethics, predicting his prompt failure, especially since Penney insisted on cash-and-carry. His chief competitor was the mining company store, which offered credit.

THE LIFE OF

J. C. Penney

1875	Born September 16 in Hamilton, Missouri
1902	Opens first store in Kemmerer, Wyoming
1907	Launches "The Golden Rule" chain; introduces profit sharing
1910	First wife dies
1913	Incorporates as the J.C. Penney Co.
1914	Moves corporate head quarters from Salt Lake City to New York
1917	Resigns as president Becomes Chairman of the Board
1923	Second wife dies
1929	J. C. Penney worth $40M
1931	J. C. Penney broke after stock market collapses Rebuilds following spiritual renewal
1951	Corporate sales surpass $1 bilion
1962	Penney company's foremost goodwill ambassador
1971	J. C. Penney dies at 95

Penney's sales soon passed up the company store. By 1907 he owned three stores in Wyoming and envisioned a chain of stores covering the Rockies.

Rapid growth

Two years later Penney established headquarters in Salt Lake City. By 1912 he owned thirty-four stores with sales over $2 million. It was said that Penney had the uncanny knack of choosing the right man for the right job. In 1913 the chain incorporated as the J.C. Penney Company, and the next year Penney moved the headquarters to New York City. In 1917 he resigned as president and became Chairman of the Board.

The company grew most in the West, although in 1916 the first stores opened east of the Mississippi in Watertown and Wausau, Wisconsin. From 1917 to 1929 the business exploded— growing to nearly 1,400 stores nationwide.

Penney's business success was not without its personal trials. In 1923, after giving birth to a son, Kimball, his second wife died. He remarried in 1926.

Economic disaster struck also. The 1929 stock market crash sent J.C. Penney stock plunging from 120 points to only 13. Penney himself lost $40 million! By 1932 he had to sell out to satisfy his creditors. This left him virtually broke. Penney had to drop many of his Christian philanthropies, among them *Christian Herald* magazine. (For many years he wrote a popular column for this magazine called "Lines of a Layman.")

Crushed in spirit from his loss and his health suddenly failing, Penney wound up in a Battle Creek, Michigan sanitorium. One morning he heard the distant singing of employees who had gathered to start the day with God:

Be not dismayed, whate'er betide
God will take care of you....

Penney followed the music to its source and slipped into a back row. He left a short time later a changed man, his health and spirit renewed, and ready to start the long climb back at age fifty-six.

Renewal

"Most men of middle age," wrote *The New York Times*, "would have been crushed by the blow." But Penney started anew with money borrowed on his life insurance, regained a foothold in

the company, and was soon back as Chairman of the Board.

The company's employee force had grown to 50,000. Each shared in the company profits. But "associates" also had to stay sober. For many years, anyone who used tobacco or liquor was discharged.

Penney, a teetotaler, once put aside a rum-laced dessert at a dinner and suspiciously asked a colleague, "That was liquor of some kind, wasn't it?"

"Yes," replied the other man.

"I'm glad I didn't have any," Penney said. "It doesn't do the soul any good."

"My doctor tells me," the other man persisted, "that a little spot of whiskey is good for you, especially before a meal."

"Time to change doctors, I think," Penney advised.

Resisting alcohol

Penney's resistance to alcohol was not automatic, especially in the period after the sudden death of his first wife in 1910. As he was later to admit, "I was assailed by an intense desire to drink—perhaps with the unconscious thought of drowning my sorrow. The desire was persistent and terrible, lasting not only through weeks and months, but even years. Many a night I walked the streets battling with this temptation and the darkness that had settled upon me."

Following his 1932 recovery Penney threw himself back into the business arena with enthusiasm, renewed his interest in the breeding of purebred cattle, and reorganized his charities. As a tribute to his parents, he had earlier founded the Memorial Home Community in Penney Farms, Florida—for those retired men and women

J. C. Penney celebrates a birthday in his nineties.

delight, for wherever he went Mr. Penney was news.

Though anticipating that he would reach 100, Penney died in 1971 at the age of 95, following a fall during the Christmas holidays. Fifteen hundred people attended his memorial service in New York City, among them many of the nation's most prominent people in business and government. President Nixon sent a telegram.

J. C. Penney's Golden Rule credo of humane conduct toward both employees and customers, said *The New York Times* at the time of his death, "aroused ... skepticism in a mercenary age." But the success of his department store chain, "put the lie to the cynics."

who had spent their lives in church and mission work. He gave this property in 1946 to the Christian Herald Association. He gave his 705-acre purebred Guernsey dairy farm to the University of Missouri in 1952.

By 1951 there was a J.C. Penney store in every state, and for the first time sales surpassed $1 billion a year. The company did not introduce credit until 1958, but the ironic link with Penney's middle name—Cash—was only coincidental. Rumors once surfaced that Penney had manufactured his middle name to attract attention to his cash-and-carry stores. But most knew better. Explained Penney, "The full name of my father, a Baptist preacher who ironically never got any cash at all for preaching, was James Cash Penney."

In the 1950s, in order to to keep pace with trends in consumer buying, the J. C. Penney Company broadened its merchandise lines to include major appliances, home electronics, furniture, and sporting goods. In 1962 it ventured into catalog sales—with great success. The company added J. C. Penney Financial Services in 1967, and purchased the Thrift Drug Company in 1969.

Ambassador—for Christ

Though Penney had stepped out of the company's direct management years earlier, he remained a director and continued to be the company's premier goodwill ambassador. He enjoyed waiting on customers in his stores and always wore Penney clothes—usually a dark-blue suit and a bow tie. Even when aged eighty-four, he attended 51 store openings in 24 states, participated in 27 programs on television and radio, gave 105 major addresses, and traveled 62,000 miles throughout the Penney chain. This gentle man, who retained a twinkle in his eyes even when age had began to dim them, was the public relation department's

Further Reading

Beasley, Norman. *Main Street Merchant.* New York: McGraw Hill, 1948.

Penney, James Cash. *Fifty Years with the Golden Rule: A Spiritual Autobiography.* New York: Harper and Brothers, 1950.

Penney, James Cash. *Lines of a Layman.* Grand Rapids: William B. Eerdmans, 1956.

Penney, James Cash. *My Experience with the Golden Rule.* Kansas City, Mo.: Frank Glen, 1949.

Penney, James Cash. *View from the Ninth Decade.* New York: Thomas Nelson and Sons, 1961.

Scull, Penrose. *From Peddlers to Merchant Princes.* New York: Follett, 1967.

R. G. LeTourneau

Moving Heaven and Earth

If R. G. LeTourneau were alive today, as a keen and well-intentioned youngster trying to find his way through life's maze, he might be given as a case study of all the reasons someone should *not* succeed as a businessman—let alone as a Christian businessman.

The fourth of eight children, he was plagued throughout his school days by a chronically short attention span (today we might call such a problem an

R. G. LeTourneau beside one of the giant tires used widely on his machines.

A Humble Start

In our success-oriented culture, biographies recounting the marvelous success and prosperity of those who are celebrities as well as Christians can be terribly discouraging for the "common man." While we hold high the demigod of accomplishment and wealth, in reality few of us will ever attain the stature or status of so many who are virtually indistinguishable from the world's elite (except for their Christian testimonies).

For all his ultimate success and fame, however, industrialist/inventor R. G. LeTourneau was most assuredly not one of the "beautiful people" who found wealth first and Jesus Christ second. For LeTourneau, all of life was nothing more—nor less—than an extension of a frank, humble, heartfelt commitment made to Jesus Christ at one of the lowest points of his life.

Encouragement
Though he went on to invent the biggest, most powerful, most productive machines of this century, LeTourneau's journey with God began when he was an uneducated, discouraged, broke, and broken young man. And though it is not popular to admit such a lowly position today, that is where hundreds of thousands of Christians are right now.

For that reason, the story of R. G. LeTourneau may be just what you need to read—and what will encourage you most—right now.

THE LIFE OF
R. G. LeTourneau

"attention deficiency disorder" and place him in a special program). Almost unbelievably strong-willed, though not with malice or brutality, he seemed obsessed with pulling apart his boyhood toys simply to see how they worked.

He ran away from home at the age of thirteen, though he was later reconciled with his parents and returned for a time. His formal education ended in the eighth grade, when he abandoned his studies in favor of manual labor in an iron foundry. Then, as a twenty-eight-year-old, sporadically employed mechanic, he married, eloping with a mere sixteen-year-old as his bride, against the wishes of her parents and to the distress of his own.

If they were taken together on a one-page résumé today, the early credentials of Robert Gilmour LeTourneau would certainly not mark him for success. But as inventor and businessman, builder and engineer, a lay missionary and a Christian benefactor, R. G. LeTourneau must be counted high on the list of those who literally shaped North America throughout the mid-1900s.

Monstrous machines

To put R. G. LeTourneau's contributions to engineering into perspective, all that is needed is a short drive past a major construction project. Look across the job site, and if you see a monstrous piece of machinery, one that does the work of a hundred men or more, or one that can move scores of yards of dirt on a single pass, or one that combines seven operations into one, or one that carves huge jobs down to size—chances are R. G. LeTourneau had something to do with its invention or original design.

Or if you happen to visit your local museum and see there an antique tractor with a cumbersome steam engine, massive gears, and obstinate steel "tires" and wonder who first conceived the idea of transforming that into the agile, rubber-footed wonders of today, the answer is R. G. LeTourneau.

And—whether you love them or hate them—if you ever cast your eyes on the offshore oil rigs that probe under the ocean for inexpensive crude in order to keep our machines running, and our standard of living among the highest in the world, again you can credit the incessant inventiveness of LeTourneau.

In our high-tech age today, machines—really *big* machines that push and pull, lift and move, scrape and dig—are not too popular anymore. They have become the symbolic monsters of "development," the bogeyman that so many of us like to malign and benefit from at the same time.

However, without the kinds of machines that R. G. LeTourneau dreamed of, conceived, designed, and built, the technological age we now live in might never have happened at all. We might still be driving on twisting, two-lane roads instead of on sprawling super highways. Lumber for the construction of our homes and other necessities might still be rare and expensive. The cost of housing, office space, and commercial centers might be many times higher because of the man-hours and effort required to build them.

Or, if the invention of those machines that revolutionized development in this country had been forestalled, we might be many decades behind the stage we have reached today.

Growing pains

When LeTourneau was in his twenties, simultaneously trying to provide for his little family and forge a stable career for himself, North America was still very much in its "wonder years." It possessed an unlimited potential for growth and seemingly unlimited resources. But the country was uncoordinated, disjointed, slow to make progress.

R. G. LeTourneau.

And LeTourneau himself was not much different.

When he left the classroom in 1902, for the cavernous environs of a steel foundry, LeTourneau knew he was trading in his childhood for the life of an adult—something his 6'0", 160-pound frame seemed ready for. He was ready to get busy, to work hard, to make his own way. The only thing for which he was not ready (in spite of the Christian example and nurture provided for him by his godly parents, Caleb and Elizabeth

LeTourneau) was the task of finding meaning, purpose, and fulfillment as the end result of his unrelenting personal drive.

That same person who might well qualify as "least likely to succeed" by today's standards likewise was spiritually dead. Though there was a distinct spiritual heritage stored away in his head, not much had made its way to his heart by the time he turned himself loose on the world. Like so many young men, R. G. LeTourneau's emerging independence as a gainfully em-

ployed teenager camouflaged his spiritual needs as a human being. He recounted it this way:

"Hardest hit during the two years before my 16th birthday was my spiritual life. I went to church with the family on Sunday, sleeping through the sermons, so I knew some form of spiritual life was there. But to say the best for it, it was dormant. Nor was I worried about myself."

Wrong road

He once told a writer concerning this period in his life, "I was raised in a Christian home by a father and mother who loved Jesus and served Him with all their hearts. We had a family altar where we worshiped God. Father prayed and asked God to make his children useful in His kingdom. In spite of that, at the age of sixteen I found myself on the wrong road going the wrong way. I knew the right way, but I'd forgotten about it."

Even so, God was working on young LeTourneau, and with maturing teenhood came the awareness that all was not well in his life.

"About the time I was sixteen," he once recalled, "I began to realize that something was wrong in my life. I tried to turn over a new leaf many times, but each time I failed and each time I got worse. It wasn't that I didn't know the Bible or the way of salvation. The trouble was I knew it too well. In our home we had to memorize Scripture, and I had memorized a great deal of Scripture. But I recited it in a parrot-like way. I knew the words, but they had no meaning for me. Revival meetings would come to town, and I would go and get all worked up;

but after the revival I'd go back to my old kind of life."

In many ways, LeTourneau was not unlike many of today's offspring of the "Jesus generation"—saturated with Scripture, but unconvicted, unconvinced, and unsaved. What happened next, however, not only drew LeTourneau into a right relationship with God, it formed a seedbed for the ways in which God would use him later in his life to see that multiplied thousands around the world would be reached with the gospel.

In simple terms, young Bob LeTourneau had attended four revival meetings at his church—then stayed home on the fifth night to mull things over. That is when a conviction of sin and lostness came over him. But even after he returned on the last night of the campaign and went forward during the altar call, salvation was not real to him. It was just something he had heard over and over again at home.

It was not until LeTourneau returned home from that final meeting, considered his accountability before God, and cried out, "Lord, save me or I perish!" that he knew he possessed the full reality of salvation. It was a relationship that would change him, change the course of his life, and ultimately change many people's perception of Christian businessmen.

Through the fire
R. G. LeTourneau's relationship with Christ made an immediate difference in the way in which he approached life's challenges. Rather than fighting nose to nose with the obstacles and hardships he encountered, he instead began to look for divine purpose in each suffering or setback—and there were plenty. Shortly after his conversion, for example, the foundry where he worked burned to the ground, throwing him out of work and threatening his apprenticeship.

When he moved to San Francisco to seek work there, he found himself awakened in the middle of the famous 1906 earthquake. (Though at first he thought it was judgment day, he survived by leaving his second-floor apartment as it reached ground level!) After he finished his apprenticeship, he moved on to Stockton, California, where he began honing his skills as a mechanic and subsequently built a successful automobile dealership.

But even that period of his life was not without suffering. From having endured a broken neck in a stock-car crash (thereafter his head had a permanent list to starboard), he had survived a gasoline-doused flash fire in his repair shop, he had alienated his father-in-law for seven years by "kidnapping" young Evelyn and marrying her, he nearly died of Spanish influenza, lost his firstborn son at less than four months of age, and was then plunged into bankruptcy by an inept business partner.

These hardships, more than any other factor in his development as a Christian, forged LeTourneau's spiritual priorities and submission to God. When the death of his son in 1919 brought him to the lowest point of his life, LeTourneau did not try to blame God for his misfortunes. Instead, he opened his heart, asking candidly, "Where have I gone wrong?"

It was then he believes God said to him, "My child, you have been working hard, but for the wrong things. You have been working for material things when you should have been working for spiritual things."

Reviewing the past
In LeTourneau's own account of that time in his life, he recalls:

The words were few, but the meaning ran deep. All that long night I reviewed my past, and saw where I had been paying only token tribute to God, going through the motions of acting like a Christian, but really serving myself and my conscience instead of serving Him. Instead of being a humble servant, I was taking pride in the way I was working to pay my material debts at the garage, while doing scarcely a thing to pay my spiritual debt to God.

For my lesson that night I can now say that when a man realizes that spiritual things are worth more—and certainly they will last when material things are gone—he will work harder for spiritual things. I discovered then that God loves us so much that He wants us to love Him in return. He wants us to cooperate with His program.

Alluding to Matthew 6:33 he added,

That I had not been doing. I had been seeking first my own way of life, and I firmly believe God had to send those difficulties into our lives to get us to look up into His face and call upon Him for His help and guidance.

God first
Though their difficulties did not disappear overnight—and the pain of losing their firstborn was with them for a lifetime—spiritually Bob and Evelyn

LeTourneau beside a giant earthmoving machine at his Longview factory.

LeTourneau were never the same. Within a short period of time, they were deeply involved in the evangelistic efforts of the Christian and Missionary Alliance Church, and it was not long before Bob took to heart a missionary's personal challenge to make himself available to God as His servant first, and a businessman second. It was a decision from which LeTourneau never wavered.

LeTourneau never ceased to view obstacles in the light of their being divine opportunities, and beginning in 1919 he began applying that outlook—as well as his expertise in mechanics, metals, and welding—to various requiremnets for earth-moving machinery. Starting with the design of a better, more efficient scraper (a machine used to level the San Joaquin Valley's fertile bottomland), LeTourneau then developed one innovation after another, ranging from massive front-end loaders to bulldozers, based on his philosophy that

"There are no big jobs, just small machines."

In the same way LeTourneau faced hardships and setbacks (and there were plenty throughout his entire lifetime) with the outlook that a bigger challenge required greater trust in God, he faced big challenges—really big challenges, like cutting a road grade through solid rock, or salvaging an "impossible" job that someone else had botched and abandoned—with the belief that a bigger machine, better built to work more efficiently, could get the job done. And getting the job done was always foremost in his mind.

Revolutionary machines

So it is that LeTourneau can be credited with inventing or perfecting nearly every piece of heavy earth-moving equipment in use today. He is the one who first conceived of and built logging machines that revolutionized the industry, machines that could lift and clear damaged

bombers and unusable landing craft, and some 70 percent of the earth-moving equipment used during World War II, the "Panama tow" for pulling ships through canal locks, and dozens of other machines, including all those that utilize the massive, self-propelled, electric-motor-driven wheel.

LeTourneau brought dozens of innovations to the industry he helped to create, ranging from more efficient manufacturing methods, to the use of personal aircraft in order tor maintain far-flung interests in the most effective way possible.

Priorities for life

Interestingly, however, it is not LeTourneau's inventions, or even his success as a business-man, that keeps his name alive in Christian circles. Instead, it is his lifelong commitment to re-main true to the discovery which he made at the death of his firstborn son—that spiritual priorities are the only correct priorities, and that it is incum-bent on all Christians to "seek first the kingdom of God and His righteousness."

For those millions of us who will never amass a fortune like the one LeTourneau eventually enjoyed, such priorities might appear easy to confess and even easier to keep—once a person has found success. The remark-able thing about LeTourneau is. that those priorities predated his success by many years, and were maintained no matter what external circumstances seemed to demand.

They drove him to maintain his sacrificial missionary giving in spite of financial reversals, to the point that by the end of his life, LeTourneau was giving on an inverted 10-percent basis—10 percent of the profits for himself, and 90 percent for the Lord's work!

"The question," LeTourneau said, "is not how much of my money I give to God, but rather how much of God's money I keep for myself."

His spiritual priorities have motivated him to travel many hundreds of thousands of miles for evangelistic speaking, to maintain a chapel program in order to evangelize and disciple his hundreds of employees, to start a college (LeTourneau College in Texas) to integrate Christian education into the lives of young people; to help hundreds of young believers in a multitude of ways; and always to seek to conduct his business and family life according to the clear principles of God's Word.

To his credit, LeTourneau would be the first to admit that he failed as often as he succeeded. He confessed to having a short fuse, to sometimes acting too fast, to sometimes insisting on his own way too stridently, even to laughing too hard at his own jokes!

Working man

In other words, although his machines were always bigger than the jobs they were built to perform, LeTourneau was never bigger than life—or even too big for his own good. He was—and in memory remains—the "working man's success story." He was a man who simply allowed God to use all that he was, all that he did, all that he had, and all that he became.

Because of his desire to please God in all things, he discovered the divine purpose in even the most mundane, most aggravat-

ing, and most common of life's obstacles and interruptions. He accepted himself the way God had made him, and then trusted God to use those idiosyncracies and quirks in whatever way He deemed best.

Concerning service for the Lord, LeTourneau was blunt, but sincere: "If you're not serving the Lord," he once said, "it proves you don't love Him; if you don't love Him, it proves you don't know Him. Because to *know* Him is to *love* Him, and to *love* Him is to *serve* Him."

In one talk, he summed it up this way: "I think the secret of a real out-and-out Christian life is to fall in love with the Lord.... I'm not trying to tell you how good I am. The Lord knows I'm not perfect; my wife knows it too. But they're both working on me yet. Let's just ask God to do a new thing in our lives and help us come to know Him, and love Him, and worship Him."

Further Reading

Ackland, Donald F. *Moving Heaven and Earth*. New York: Iversen-Ford, 1949.

LeTourneau, R. G. *Mover of Men and Mountains*. Chicago: Moody, 1972.

Lorimer, Albert W. *God Runs My Business: The Story of R. G. LeTourneau*. New York: Fleming H. Revell, 1941.

Stjernstrom, Nels E. *The Joy of Accomplishment*. Longview, Texas: LeTourneau U., 1989.

Robert Laidlaw

The Reason Why

Dunedin, in the deep south of New Zealand, was largely settled by immigrants from Scotland. One such was Robert Laidlaw, who in 1886 came with his wife and their firstborn son, Robert Junior. The Laidlaws, both earnest Christians, brought up their six children in the knowledge and love of God. So when young Robert left school at the age of sixteen and commenced his business career as a junior clerk in the firm Laidlaw and Gray, Hardware Merchants, he already had a good many Bible texts stored up in his mind, but no heart commitment to Christ. It was a year later, in the Torrey Alexander Mission, that he opened his heart to the Lord.

It was no emotional flash in the pan for Robert Laidlaw. It was a deliberate choice, which set the course for the rest of his life. Two years later, after the rest of the family had moved to Auckland, nineteen-year-old Robert took the position of senior wholesale traveler, covering the provinces of Otago and Southland. He did so with some trepidation. Those were hard-drinking days, and commercial travelers were expected to scout clients in local pubs.

In later life, Laidlaw never tired of relating the story of his first meeting with one client, a blacksmith by the name Nat Bates. When he arrived, Bates was shoeing a Clydesdale draught stallion which was kicking violently. Perspiration was running off the smithy's face, and the air was sulphurous with his oaths. Presently he remarked, "I don't hear you swearing, young fellow." "No, Mr. Bates," Robert replied, "I don't swear. I get along fairly well with the King's English." A bit later, "Don't you smoke, young fellow?" "No, Mr. Bates, I don't smoke either. And in a minute you will ask me if I drink, and I will say, 'No, Mr. Bates,

I don't drink.'" With tongs in his left hand the blacksmith was holding the red-hot shoe on the horn of the anvil, and his right hand raised his hammer. He stopped as though petrified, then he put down the hammer on the anvil, and placing his big, dirty, sweaty hand on Robert's shoulder, said, "Stick to it, laddie. Stick to it."

Catalogue No. 1

During his travels, Robert came across a Montgomery Ward mail-order catalogue, which gave him the idea of starting a mail-order business in New Zealand. His opportunity came in 1909, after he had rejoined his family in Auckland. For several months he worked arduously, preparing what he hopefully called "Laidlaw Leeds Catalogue No. 1" of 125 pages, and then opened up for business in a rented room, twenty by thirty feet. The catalogue claimed to supply everything in the wide world, underwear to groceries, cosmetics to farm equipment, and all at bargain-basement prices. The response to something completely new to largely agricultural New Zealand was electric. Orders poured in. The rented room was soon too small. Three times within seventeen months Laidlaw Leeds had to move to larger premises.

By 1913 accommodation was critical. A large site was purchased, and Auckland's largest commercial building was erected. It had five stories and a basement, total floor space of over seven and a half acres. The firm opened in the new premises in April 1914, three months before World War I broke out. It was four and a half years since the first order from Catalogue No. 1 had been received. In 1918 it was merged with the Farmers' Union Trading Company, with Robert Laidlaw as General Manager, a post which he held for over fifty years.

Robert Laidlaw. A successful businessman. But that was not the most important thing to Robert. He was called to be a businessman *for God*. In his youth, soon after his conversion, he made an entry in his diary, promising to give ten percent of all he earned to God's work, and to increase that proportion on a graduated scale if his income increased. And later, when the Laidlaw Leeds business was starting to boom, he duly made a fresh entry in his diary: "September 1919, age twenty-five. I have decided to change my earlier graduated scale, and start now giving half (fifty percent) of all my earnings."

This he maintained for the remaining sixty years of his life, setting up the Bethesda Charitable Trust, which through the years dispersed countless thousands of dollars to all sorts of missionary outreach and evangelism.

Why I am a Christian

Evangelism was always close to Robert's heart. In 1913, when Charles Alexander conducted a mission in Auckland Town Hall, Laidlaw asked his associate missioner, Wilbur Chapman, to address a special noon-day meeting for his staff, now numbering about two hundred. When introducing Dr. Chapman, Laidlaw told his staff about his own conversion, and said, "I cannot speak to each of you individually about your relationship to Jesus Christ, so I promise to write in detail the reason why I am a Christian." To keep that promise he wrote *The Reason Why*, which is perhaps the most effective evangelistic tract ever written. Translated into thirty languages, with more than twenty million copies sold or given away, this little book has been instrumental in helping many hundreds of thousands of people "clinch the deal" with Jesus Christ.

The Reason Why is not the typical four-page leaflet tract. It is a forty-six-page booklet, a thoughtful, reasoned presentation, seeking to answer a series of basic questions about life and faith. Each question is answered carefully, with

Robert Laidlaw.

London, and offered his services to the Soldiers' and Airmen's Association. He traveled all over Britain, organizing workers in various camps and canteens, and speaking in evangelistic meetings. D-Day came, and the Allied troops crossed the English Channel to liberate France. Seven weeks later, Robert Laidlaw, with ten others, crossed to the continent to work among the soldiers of the Allies.

In Caen, a High Church padre asked Laidlaw to speak to a church service. There were eighty or ninety men filling the small church, men who Laidlaw thought might well be hearing the message of God's saving grace for the very last time. He presented that message as clearly and persuasively as he could, and invited those who wanted to respond, to leave their seats and come to the front. He had brought twenty-five copies of *The Reason Why* to give to any who made decisions. But thirty-three men stood, came forward, and received Christ as Savior and Lord. As they knelt before the cross, and the padre said a prayer of dedication committing them into the care of God, Robert Laidlaw shed a few silent tears as he thanked God for the privilege of using his life to win men and women to Jesus Christ.

quotations from Scripture, and the whole book is peppered with telling illustrations, apt for each point. Towards the end is a page headed "My Decision," which a person may sign and date and keep. This is followed by a few final pages of advice for new Christians.

Robert Laidlaw was always eager to speak for Christ. As Oswald Sanders recalls, "He was the only New Zealander I knew in those days who could go into an evangelistic rally in any Town Hall in New Zealand and pack it out. And every time he spoke there were those who stood to their feet in response to the invitation to accept Christ as Savior."

D-Day and after

But for Laidlaw, the time he looked back to as the happiest and most fruitful in his life was during World War II. When war broke out in 1939, his family was in London. He booked the family home on the first available steamer in a convoy, saw them off at Liverpool, returned to

Further Reading

Laidlaw, R. A. *The Reason Why*. Various publishers. Available from S.U. Wholesale, P.O. Box 760, Wellington, New Zealand.

_____. *The Story of the Reason Why*. Auckland: G. W. Moore.

EPILOGUE

A Teenage Triumph

A personal account by John D. Woodbridge

"3 YOUNG PEOPLE KILLED, 3 HURT IN 3-CAR CRASH." Palm Springs, June 6. Three young people were killed and three others injured in a three-car head-on collision on Highway 111 at the northern edge of this desert resort town this afternoon. The dead were

Karen Ruth Johnson.

Robert Joseleyn ... his passenger Karen Ruth Johnson, 17...."

With these words a correspondent for the *Los Angeles Times* broke the front-page news in cold print to the sprawling city of Los Angeles that a horrible tragedy had just taken place in nearby Palm Springs. Three

young people had been cut off in the bloom of their lives, and a fourth soon died from injuries in the accident.

What the correspondent could not have known was that the family of Karen Johnson would publish a brochure in which they described this indubitable tragedy from a human point of view as "A Teenage Triumph." Perhaps as many as 1,000,000 copies of this brochure, in twelve different languages, have since been distributed.

Triumph?

How could a grieving family possibly view the sudden death of one of their dear members as a "triumph"? The answer to this question lies in the fact of Karen and her family's belief that not even death itself can separate us from the love of God. In her "Philosophy of Life," which she wrote just days before the accident, Karen quoted Philippians 1:21: "For to me, to live is Christ and to die is gain".

Dedicated

Like so many other Christian parents, Edward and Joyce Johnson decided to dedicate their first-born daughter to the Lord. One Sunday morning they went to Moody Memorial Church in Chicago where, in a dedication service, Pastor Harry Ironside prayed that the Lord would bless their small child. For the Johnsons this was no mere ceremony. They believed that the Lord had given Karen Ruth to them as a gift; Karen belonged to Him, not to them. To be certain that Karen would later know that she had been dedicated to the Lord, Ed Johnson made a recording of the service. Years later Karen

"3 YOUNG PEOPLE KILLED, 3 HURT IN 3-CAR CRASH." Palm Springs, June 6. Three young people were killed and three others injured in a three-car head-on collision on Highway 111 at the northern edge of this desert resort town this afternoon. The dead were Robert Joseleyn ... his passenger Karen Ruth Johnson, 17..."

THE LIFE OF
Karen Ruth Johnson

1942	Born in Chicago, Illinois on March 31
1953	Johnson family moves to San Marino, California
1959	Dies in Palm Springs, California on June 6
1959	High school diploma awarded posthumously

would be able to hear in an audio recording what had transpired that Sunday morning.

As a small child, Karen was full of life. She loved to play. She also loved to listen to Bible stories which her mother and father read to her. One evening when she was five, she said to her mom: "I want to give my life to the Lord." She got down on her knees and asked Jesus to come into her heart.

Three homes
Not much time later, as the family was driving near the Johnsons' summer home at Bethany Beach, Michigan, with Karen sitting in the back seat of the car, she suddenly piped up with: "Daddy, you know we have three homes." One of her startled parents turned to the five-year-old in the back seat and asked: "What do you mean, Karen?" She responded, "We

have one home in Illinois, one home in Michigan, and one home in heaven." Her father was to remember this incident very clearly later in his life.

The Johnson family moved to San Marino, California, in 1953, and decided to attend Lake Avenue Congregational Church in neighboring Pasadena. It was there I met Karen for the first time. We were in the same youth group at Lake Avenue in junior high and high school.

Karen Johnson was a very special person. Both the fellows and the girls in her youth group found her both kind and outgoing. They held a surprise birthday party for her when she was a senior in high school. Her class-mates at San Marino High School were so impressed by her personal warmth and charm that they described her as a "precious pearl" in her senior yearbook.

But what made her so special? What made her so attractive to literally hundreds of people? It was probably only after Karen's death that some of us began to realize how deep her love for her Savior had been. For she knew Jesus in a way that transformed her relationships with her teenage friends.

On Thursday June 4, 1959, Karen finished a school assignment at San Marino High School. On Friday, June 5, 1959, she gave it to her teacher. On Saturday June 6, the very next day, Karen's earthly life ceased in the split-second trauma of a head-on automobile accident.

It was only after the accident that a next-door neighbor girl reminded the Johnsons that Karen had written the school assignment. The San Marino high school principal looked for it and gave it to the parents. The Johnsons had never read it before. Karen had written it as her last senior paper for her high school teacher. The paper revealed her deep love for the Lord Jesus.

Her teacher commented, "A beautiful philosophy! Not many students, at this age, feel free to write in such a personal way."

When the automobile accident took place on June 6, 1959,

Karen's family was out at the family cabin in Hesperia, near Palm Springs. As a friend and several others came toward the cabin, Ed Johnson sensed that something was wrong. He left the cabin to meet them and asked, "Is it Karen?" The friend sorrowfully explained what had happened and asked

---

June 5, 1959

My Philosophy of Life

by Karen Ruth Johnson

My philosophy of life is based on the Holy Bible and the God that wrote it. I know that he has a plan for my life and through daily prayer and reading of His Word I will be able to see it. As far as my life work or life partner I am leaving it in His hands and am willing to do anything He says.

I feel that this philosophy is very practical and can be applied to everyday life. Every decision can be taken to the Lord in prayer and the peace that comes from knowing Jesus Christ as my personal Savior is something many cannot understand. Many search for a purpose and reason for life. I know that I am on this earth to have fellowship with God and to win others to the saving knowledge of His Son, Jesus Christ. I know that after death I will go to be with Him forever.

Jesus Christ teaches love and respect for everyone through the New Testament and we are not to judge anyone because He will on the judgment day. In God's sight no one person is worth any more than another.

Knowing and loving Jesus Christ personally makes me want to please Him and accomplish things for His Glory. Paul says in the New Testament, "Whatsoever ye do, do it all to the glory of God" and "For me, to live is Christ, to die is gain".

This philosophy contains all of the seven points given in your lecture of April 20th. As I stated in the beginning, it is very

1. practical to have someone to turn to for any decision or problem, small or large. What could be more

2. optimistic than knowing that God has a purpose and plan for one's life and is willing to keep in constant fellowship with anyone who will. To know I have accepted Jesus Christ's gift of Salvation and will have eternal life in Heaven is a most wonderful thing and brings peace to my heart. God has the best for us and if we let Him He will improve our lives and solve our problems.

3. God in His Holy Word teaches us to have love and a burden for every person as Jesus Christ Himself.

4. One of my main purposes in life is to share this experience I have had with Christ and to show them the peace and happiness that it brings.

5. This is an important goal in itself, but more completely, my aim in life is to accomplish what the Lord has for me do, which is certainly the most worthwhile goal in life.

6. The closer I grow to Him the more happiness I find and the busier I am. He has things for me that the world could never offer and I learn to appreciate more and more how fortunate I am.

7. God's standards are higher than anything attainable, and present a great challenge and make me realize how futile it would be for me to do the best I could, because I, being human, could never reach God's standards, and therefore never be worthy of entering Heaven. God has given me contact with the best; in His world, in my born again friends, and in my fellowship with Jesus Christ. It is well known that the highest beauty, truth, justice, and goodness is found in God's Word.

if he could help Ed by telling the family. Ed Johnson thanked him and said that this would not be necessary. He walked back into the cabin and gathered the family around him. Even in this dire situation, the Lord met Ed Johnson's needs as a grieving father. Ed introduced the family members to the tragedy with these words: "Before we ask God why He took Karen home, let us thank Him for the seventeen years we had with her."

One of the police officers who had first come upon the scene of the accident took Ed Johnson aside at the inquest, saying to him: "You are a Christian, aren't you?"

"Yes," replied Ed Johnson.

Then the officer told him, "I will never forget the smile on her face."

Memorial service

Most of Karen's graduating class from San Marino High School came to the funeral at Lake Avenue Congregational Church. There they heard the gospel. Irwin Moon prayed that the Lord would turn Karen's death into a "teenage triumph." Youth for Christ for Greater Los Angeles held a memorial service at the Church of the Open Door for Karen and another victim of the crash, a Youth for Christ staff member. Hundreds of young people from southern California filled the church.

Ed Johnson was asked why Karen turned out to be the wonderful Christian teenager she was. He responded that he and his wife, Joyce, had taught Karen and the other children that they could have a direct and personal loving relationship with Christ, not dependent upon the faith of their parents. The children were responsible to Christ for whatever they did. If everyone in the family walked in fellowship with the Lord, then family members would live in harmony with each other. And if one family member was out of fellowship with the Lord, then the whole family would be affected accordingly. Karen had understood very well what her parents had taught her as a youngster. As her "Philosophy of Life" reveals, she knew the joys of a personal relationship with the Lord Jesus.

Throughout the years the Johnsons have received boxes of letters from people who had read Karen's "Philosophy of Life." Many have noted that they had decided to follow Christ after reading this "Philosophy," and some young men decided to go into the Christian ministry as a result of it. Perhaps the Johnsons were right after all. This was indeed a "Teenage Triumph." Their daughter Karen was at her third home—with the Lord she so dearly loved.

INDEX

Photograph Acknowledgments

Agapé, Birmingham: pp. 293, 295
American Red Cross: p. 47
Ateliers et Presses de Taizé: p. 299
Ms. Sue Andrews, Romford: p. 237
Baker Book House: p. 305
The Banner of Truth Trust: p. 207
Barnados: pp. 253–5
Dr. Eljee Bentley: pp. 58–9
Bible Study Fellowship: p. 83
Billy Graham Center Museum, Wheaton
    III: pp. 155, 283–7
The Billy Graham Evangelistic
    Association: pp. 174, 176, 179, 180
Brown Brothers, New York: pp. 28–9,
    152, 154, 273, 309, 311, 334
The Church of Scotland: pp. 63, 66, 67,
    68
Dallas Cowboys Football Club: pp. 228,
    229
The Dohnavur Fellowship: pp. 69, 70
Mrs. Elisabeth Dole: p. 45
Dr. Tim Towley: pp. 8, 9
Foreign Mission Board, SBC: p. 57
Mr. David Frith: p. 220
Mr. W. Harold Fuller: p. 321
Fuller Theological Seminary, Pasadena,
    CA: pp. 160, 162, 163
Gospel Light Publications: p. 290
Mrs. Elisabeth Gren: pp. 73, 77
Dr. E. V. Hill: p. 212
The Historical Society of Pennsylvania:
    p. 333
The Hulton-Deutsch Collection: pp. 17,
    34–5, 115, 118, 222
Illustrated London News: p. 24
Interfoto, Munich: pp. 39, 40
InterVarsity Press: p. 281
IFES: p. 279
Mr. Edward L. Johnson: pp. 353, 355
Mr. Lincoln Laidlaw: p. 352
Mr. Richard H. LeTourneau: pp. 344,
    346, 348
Liberty University, Virginia: p. 233
Luis Paulau Evangelistic Association:
    pp. 183, 184, 185
The Mansell Collection: pp. 14–15, 23,
    30, 36, 102, 103, 113, 195, 198, 199,
    249, 336
Mary Evans Picture Library: pp. 101,
    329
Moodyana Collection, Moody Bible
    Institute of Chicago : p. 141
National Portrait Gallery, London: pp.
    122, 241
The National Portrait Gallery,
    Smithsonian Institution, Washington
    DC: pp. 17, 27, 33, 312
The Navigators: pp. 165, 166
Sabine Nitzschke: pp. 299, 301
Open Doors, Netherlands: pp. 94, 95,
    97, 98
Operation Mobilisation: pp. 90, 91

Overseas Missionary
Fellowship: pp. 51, 52, 53 (photography
    by Jack Hollingsworth, Grayson &
    Hollingsworth Communications, Inc.),
    54, 79, 156, 157, 159
Dr. J. I. Packer: p. 317
J. C. Penney Archives: pp. 341, 343
Prison Fellowship: pp. 265, 266
The Salvation Army International
    Heritage Centre, London: pp. 258,
    259,
261, 263
Dr. Henry F. Schaefer III: p. 323
Mr. Clifford Shirley: p. 260
Society for Cultural Relations with the
    USSR: p. 105
Tear Fund: p. 235
Corrie ten Boom House, Netherlands:
    pp. 85, 86
Ms. Ruth Thornhill/Women's Missionary
    Union, SBC: p. 58
Tyndale House Publishers: pp. 134–5,
    137, 138
Virginia Baptist Historical Society,
    Richmond, Virginia: pp. 56, 61,
WCC: pp. 43, 274, 276
WEC International: pp. 216, 221
Westminster Theological Seminary,
    Philadelphia: pp. 313, 315
Dr. Paul White: p. 127
Wilberforce House, Hull City Museums
    & Art Galleries: pp. 243, 244
Mr. Peter Wyart: Title page, pp. 50, 102,
    121, 123, 125, 196, 197, 209, 240,
    281
Mr. Jack Wyrtzen: pp. 171, 173

Illustrations:

Shirley Bellwood: pp. 149, 289
Donald Harley: pp. 74–5, 78
Peter Jones: pp. 225, 310–1
Alan Parry: p. 119
Mark Peppé: pp. 87, 142–3, 208
Barry Wilkinson: p. 65–6